Short Trips
in the
PACIFIC NORTHWEST

The Northwest

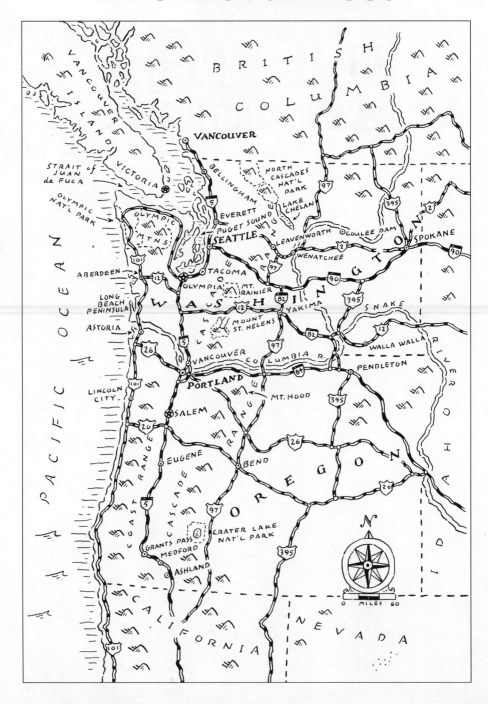

Short Trips in the PACIFIC NORTHWEST

52 Weekend Destinations from Seattle and Portland

BARRY AND HILDA ANDERSON

Clarkson Potter/Publishers
New York

The publisher gratefully acknowledges permission to reprint from *Sunset Magazine* and from John Owen's column of September 5, 1989, in the *Seattle Post-Intelligencer*.

Published by Clarkson N. Potter, Inc., 201 East 50th Street, New York, New York 10022. Member of the Crown Publishing Group.

CLARKSON N. POTTER, POTTER, and colophon are trademarks of Clarkson N. Potter, Inc.

Manufactured in the United States of America

Design by Renato Stanisic

Map drawings by Eric Hanson

Library of Congress Cataloging-in-Publication Data

Anderson, Barry C., 1934–
    Short trips in the Pacific Northwest : weekend destinations from
Seattle and Portland / Barry and Hilda Anderson.—1st ed.
    Includes index.
    1. Northwest, Pacific—Description and travel—1981– —Guide
-books. I. Anderson, Hilda. II. Title.
F852.3.A526   1992
917.9504′43—dc20
                                                                    91-41451
                                                                         CIP

ISBN 0-517-57542-6

10 9 8 7 6 5 4 3 2

*For Laura and David, who have
shared the Northwest adventure with us for
the past two decades*

Contents

Weekend Trips from Portland 143

Introduction

The Pacific Northwest has just about everything you could want for a weekend getaway, from mountains to climb and rivers to raft to back roads and cosmopolitan cities to explore. In the space of a weekend you can follow in the footsteps of Lewis and Clark, go to a rodeo, watch Shakespeare performed on an Elizabethan stage, or just cozy up beside a fire in a bed-and-breakfast inn.

The region is particularly well suited to weekend excursions, with most destinations within a few hours' drive of the major population centers of Puget Sound and the Willamette Valley and a good network of all-weather roads to get you there. We've selected 52 of our favorite weekend trips for inclusion in this book.

Seasons don't mean much to us in the Northwest as far as travel is concerned. Winter weather is seldom severe enough to deter us from driving to a destination, and most hotels, motels, and attractions are open year-round. With the exception of certain trips that include seasonal activities such as salmon fishing or whale watching, or viewing fall foliage or spring blossoms, we've not specified a "best" season for most of the destinations; they're good just about any time of the year.

In the nearly 30 years we've been writing about travel in the Northwest, we've developed a deep and abiding love for this corner of the country and its people. We've also developed an understanding of its shortcomings. Our weekend suggestions represent a distillation of hundreds of visits over the years, selected to have the broadest appeal to the most travelers.

Unless we suggest otherwise, each weekend is suitable for a typical two-day getaway, with arrival at your destination by Friday night and departure for home late Sunday afternoon. With a few exceptions—the Palouse, Hells Canyon, and the Rogue River Valley, for example—all are no more than 250 miles from either Seattle or Portland. If a drive of four or five hours each way cuts seriously into the time you have available, consider taking one of the regional air carriers and renting a car. Air service to regional destinations is frequent and efficient, and the time you save—flying from Seattle to a Shakespearean performance in Ashland, for example—may well make up for the additional amount it costs you.

If you're an experienced world traveler, you may find the Northwest pretty unsophisticated once you get beyond the big cities. Some of the destinations we recommend have meager accommodations and the term "rustic" is a kindness. Many of the restaurants in the smaller towns serve hearty portions, but of strictly meat-and-potatoes fare. We feel that the very lack of sophistication of much of the Northwest is part of its charm. Often, where we've recommended off-the-beaten-track destinations, it's because their virtues—scenery, wildlife, historical sightseeing, or other attractions—outweigh their shortcomings when it comes to ambience.

One other caveat: The nature of tourism is changing rapidly in the Northwest. In many ways we're just coming into our own with new and better resorts springing up every year, better restaurants, more sightseeing opportunities, and more transportation options, especially for water travel. But the increase in available lodgings has not yet kept pace with the demand generated by the boom in tourism. Whereas, as recently as five years ago, you seldom needed to make reservations except on holiday or midsummer weekends, these days reservations are a must. Telephone before you go.

With both lodging and restaurants we've tried to suggest a range of possibilities to suit various tastes and budgets. Prices were accurate when this book went to press, but given the inevitable increases, some of them are bound to be out-of-date by the time you read this. The quality of a restaurant is so dependent on the management and the cooking staff that changes in personnel can make a big difference in quality. If you find any of our recommendations vastly different from your experience, we'd like to hear about it so we can make corrections in subsequent editions.

The $ symbols we use for lodging and dining in the following lists indicate price ranges.

LODGING:

$ = under $50
$$ = $50 to $75
$$$ = $75 to $100
$$$$ = over $100

DINING:

$ = most entrées under $10 per person
$$ = most entrées between $10 and $15
$$$ = most entrées between $15 and $25
$$$$ = most entrées over $25

In some instances, these additional symbols may be used:

AP (American Plan—all meals included)
MAP (Modified American Plan—only breakfast and dinner included)
CP (Continental Plan—no meals included)

Note: Unless preceded by a "C," all prices given in the British Columbia section of this book are in American dollars.

Other sources of information:

Oregon Tourism Division
775 Summer Street Northeast
Salem, OR 97310
(800) 547-7842 (outside OR)
(800) 543-8838 (in OR)

Tourism Development Division
101 General Administration
   Building
Olympia, WA 98504
(206) 586-2102, 586-2088

Oregon Bed and Breakfast Directory
230 Red Spur Drive
Grants Pass, OR 97527
(503) 476-2932

**Northwest Bed and Breakfast
   Reservation Service**
610 Southwest Broadway Street
Portland, OR 97205
(503) 243-7616

Oregon Department of Fish & Wildlife
506 Southwest Mill Street
Portland, OR 97208
(503) 229-5551

Oregon Guides and Packers Association
P.O. Box 10841
Eugene, OR 97440
(503) 683-9552

**Oregon State Parks & Recreation
   Division**
525 Trade Street Southeast
Salem, OR 97310
(503) 378-6305

U.S. Forest Service
319 Southwest Pine Street
Portland, OR 97208
(503) 221-2877

**National Forest Service/National Parks
   Service**
1018 First Avenue
Seattle, WA 98104
(206) 442-0170, 442-0181

**Washington Outfitters & Guides
   Association**
P.O. Box 95229
Seattle, WA 98145

**Washington Resorts and Private Parks
   Association**
22910 Fifteenth Avenue Southeast,
   Suite C
Bothell, WA 98021
(206) 352-7388

Washington State Department of
Fisheries
115 General Administration
 Building
Olympia, WA 98504
(206) 753-6600

Washington State Department of
Wildlife
600 North Capitol Way
Olympia, WA 98504
(206) 753-5700

Washington State Ferries
Colman Dock
Seattle, WA 98104
(800) 542-7052 (outside WA)
(800) 542-0810 (in WA)

Washington State Parks and Recreation
Commission
7150 Cleanwater Lane
Olympia, WA 98504
(800) 562-0990 (summer only)
(206) 753-2027

Weekend Trips
from
SEATTLE

West of the Cascades

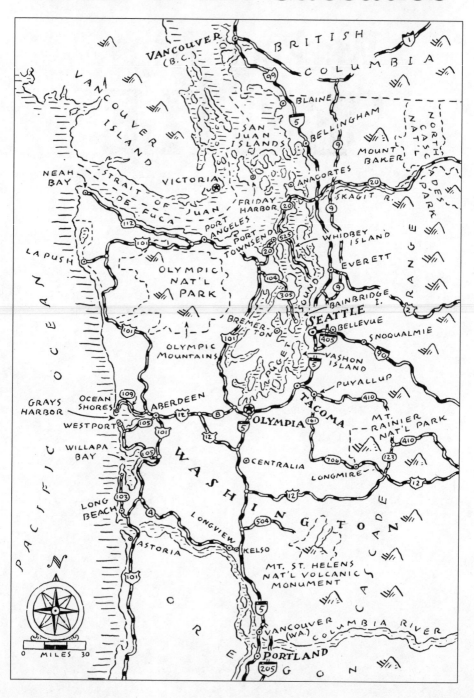

America's Longest Island

Whidbey Island, just 20 miles north of Seattle, gained a measure of notoriety a few years back when the Supreme Court ruled that New York's Long Island is actually a peninsula. Thus, Whidbey could now lay claim to being the longest island in the United States—45 miles from one end to the other.

Whidbey has long been a favorite destination for Seattleites owing to its proximity and the allure of its old frozen-in-time farmsteads, quiet beaches and historic small towns, and leisurely pace. Scarcity of accommodations was once a problem, but in recent years several excellent bed-and-breakfast inns and a luxury inn have opened on the southern end of the island, and new motels have been constructed at Coupeville and Oak Harbor. Anytime is a good time to go, but especially early May and June, when the native rhododendrons and azaleas burst into great showers of blossoms ranging in color from purple to orange and yellow.

The 20-minute ferry crossing from Mukilteo carries you to Clinton, where you pick up Washington 525, follow it for three miles, then detour to the little waterside community of Langley. Neat, trim houses, a white-steepled church, and a main street (officially, First Street) lined with false-fronted shops perch on a bluff overlooking Saratoga Passage. The new upscale Inn at Langley at the north end of First Street combines Oriental and Northwest motifs and offers fine views from its waterside location. Langley is just dandy for browsing on foot; the single main street is only about three blocks long and there's little traffic. Some two dozen shops sell everything from fine art by local artists to kitchen utensils, sportswear, and handmade children's toys.

Continue north on 525 and 20 about 22 miles to Fort Casey State Park, adjacent to the Keystone–Port Townsend ferry landing. Built at the turn of the century to protect Puget Sound from "dreadnaughts" that never came, Fort Casey is one of three coast artillery forts that flank Admiralty Inlet (the others are at Port Townsend). If you're a military history buff, you'll find the old casemates and magazines fascinating. The huge "disappearing" ten-inch coastal rifles are not the originals but were retrieved from similar forts in the Philippines several years ago. The old lighthouse contains a small museum describing the fort.

If you've brought a picnic lunch, Fort Casey's broad lawn provides plenty of space to spread your blanket. It's also a good place to view deep-water ships moving up and down Puget Sound. A nearly constant breeze blowing off the Sound makes the old parade ground an ideal place for kite flying.

Between Freeland and Greenbank turn right off 525 onto Resort Road, where you'll find Meerkerk Rhododendron Gardens, 53 acres planted with more than 2,000 varieties of the state flower, both specie and hybrid. If you're a gardener, this is the place to get some expert advice on raising rhododendrons. Rhododendron State Park, 5½ miles north on 525, features a 1½-mile loop road that leads through magnificent stands of wild rhododendrons, many of them ten or more feet tall.

Coupeville, one of the oldest towns in Washington and the seat of Island County, nestles along the water on the east side of the island and boasts many original buildings dating from the second half of the nineteenth century. Most of them bear plaques giving the name of the original owners and the year of construction. For ten cents you can get a walking tour map at one of the shops along Front Street or at the Island County Historical Museum on Alexander and Front streets. The museum displays collections of historic photos and artifacts and Indian basketry.

Across the street is Alexander's Blockhouse, built in 1855 as protection against the Indians. It's one of four remaining on the island, the best preserved being at Crockett Lake near Fort Casey. At least one settler (Colonel Isaac Ebey) was decapitated when Indians raiding from the north by canoe attacked his homestead and blockhouse several miles away on the west shore of the island. The long dugout canoes on display here are Indian craft that have been used in intertribal races.

Whether or not you plan to overnight at the Captain Whidbey Inn (just north of Coupeville), at least make a stop there for lunch or dinner. This comfortable old log cabin lodge is perched on a rise above Penn Cove and features a handsome stone fireplace in the lobby and small guest rooms furnished with antiques. The inn has been a favorite destination for Seattleites since the early 1900s, when guests arrived by steamer. Penn Cove itself is famous regionally for its succulent mussels; you'll find them on many restaurant menus in western Washington.

Oak Harbor is a navy town with little to offer in the way of sightseeing, but you may want to stop to photograph the curious blue-and-white onion-domed house at the edge of town or the Dutch windmill in the beach park, a reminder of the Hollanders who settled here.

Whidbey has four good waterside state parks for camping or picnicking—South Whidbey, Fort Casey, Fort Ebey, and Deception Pass. Deception Pass is an awesome place. A narrow passageway between Whidbey and Fidalgo islands, it funnels water from Skagit Bay into Rosario Strait and vice versa with each change of tide. If you arrive on the bluffs above the passage at full flood or ebb tide, you'll look down on a maelstrom of churning water trying to force its way through too small an opening. Only experienced sailors are willing to venture here in a small boat, and sometimes you can see them picking their way through with great care.

To return to Seattle you can retrace your route back down the island or continue north on Fidalgo Island to the intersection of Washington 525 and 20, turn east on 20, and rejoin I-5 at Mount Vernon.

Round trip is 152 miles plus ferry.

Area Code: 206

DRIVING DIRECTIONS Drive north from Seattle on I-5 to the Mukilteo exit (189), then follow Washington 526 and 525 down to the ferry landing at Mukilteo. Approximate distance round-trip from Seattle, returning via Fidalgo Island, is 152 miles.

FERRIES *Washington State Ferries,* Mukilteo to Clinton, crossing time 20 minutes, weekend frequency every half-hour from 8 A.M. to 11 P.M., first ferry 6 A.M., last ferry 2 A.M.; car and driver $4.50, passenger $2.15. Keystone to Port Townsend, crossing time 30 minutes, weekend frequency approximately every hour and a half from 7 A.M. to 9:30 P.M. If you've just missed an early morning departure and need a spot of breakfast, there are several good cafés within a block or two of the landing. Fares: car and driver $6.65, passenger $1.65. Schedule and fare information for all routes: (800) 542-7052, (800) 542-0810 (in-state toll-free), 464-6400.

SIGHTSEEING *Meerkerk Rhododendron Gardens,* 15½ miles north on 525 to Resort Road, 321-6682. Hours: Wednesday to Sunday 9 A.M. to 6 P.M. $1. *Rhododendron State Park,* 20 miles north off Washington 525, an unattended drive-through park. Open 24 hours. Free. *Fort Casey State Park,* 3 miles south of Coupeville on Admiralty Inlet, 678-4519. Open 24 hours. Admiralty Head Lighthouse Interpretive Center hours: May through Labor Day, Wednesday to Sunday 10 A.M. to 6 P.M., free. *Island County Historical Museum,* Alexander and Front streets, Coupeville, 678-3310. Hours: May through October, daily 11 A.M. to 4:00 P.M.; April, Saturday and Sunday only; free.

EVENTS *Mystery Weekend,* Langley, 321-6765, mid-February. 2-day event in which visitors participate in solving a crime. *Arts and Crafts Festival,* Coupeville, 678-4606, mid-August. Regional artists and craftspersons exhibit their works, demonstrations. *Island County Fair,* Langley, 321-4677, mid-August. Traditional county fair with agricultural and crafts exhibits, entertainment, amusements, and food concessions.

LODGING *Home by the Sea* (bed and breakfast), 2388 East Sunlight Beach Road, Clinton, 221-2964. Several separate cottages in woods, on beach, and at lakeside; full breakfasts; $$$. *Inn at Langley,* 400 First Street, 221-3033. Elegant new 24-room cedar-shingled inn overlooks Saratoga Passage; complimentary breakfast, dinner available; $$$$. *Cliff House* (bed and breakfast), 5440 South Grigware Road, Freeland, 321-1566. AIA-award-winning home, water, mountain views, full breakfast, $$$$. *Coupeville Inn,* 200 Northwest Coveland Street, 678-

6668. 24-room motel overlooking Penn Cove, balconies, Continental breakfast, $$–$$$. *Captain Whidbey Inn,* 2072 West Captain Whidbey Inn Road, Coupeville, 678-4097. 1907 madrona log inn overlooking Penn Cove, restaurant, $$–$$$. *Log Castle* (bed and breakfast), 3273 East Saratoga Road, Langley, 321-5483. Comfortable 4-bedroom lodging, overlooking Mount Baker and the Cascades; 3-course breakfast; $$–$$$.

CAMPING State Parks: *South Whidbey,* 54 sites; *Fort Casey,* 35 sites; *Fort Ebey,* 50 sites; *Deception Pass,* 246 sites; no hookups, $8 per-night fee. Information on all state parks 753-2027. *City Beach Park,* Oak Harbor, 679-5551. 55 sites, water-electricity, $10.

DINING *Star Bistro,* 201½ First Street, Langley, 221-2627. Lunch weekdays, dinner daily, brunch weekends; light meals; $$. *Dog House Backdoor Restaurant,* 230 First Street, Langley, 321-9996. Lunch and dinner daily; funky, barny old place on bluff overlooking water; fancy burgers, sandwiches, an eclectic vegetarian soup called "Gvetch"; $. *Captain Whidbey Inn* (see "Lodging"). 3 meals daily; fresh seafood including famous shellfish from Penn Cove, lavish desserts; $$–$$$. *Christopher's,* 23 Front Street, Coupeville, 678-5480. Lunch and dinner Wednesday through Sunday, $$. *Garibyan Brothers' Cafe Langley,* 113 First Street, Langley, 221-3090. Lunch and dinner daily; Greek menu includes Souvlaki, Falafel, Moussaka, and Baba Ganoush, $–$$.

FOR MORE INFORMATION Langley Chamber of Commerce, P.O. Box 403, Langley 98260, 321-6765. Central Whidbey Chamber of Commerce, P.O. Box 152, Coupeville 98239, 678-5434.

In the Footsteps of Vikings and Indians

Each weekday morning and evening big green-and-white Washington State automobile ferries carry thousands of commuters from Bainbridge Island and the Kitsap Peninsula to and from jobs in Seattle. On the weekends, these ferries serve as water highways to exploration on the islands and peninsulas to the west.

You can complete the loop we suggest here in a single day or stretch it into a leisurely weekend. One caution: On good-weather weekends the ferries departing Seattle on Friday evening and returning Sunday afternoon are jammed, which can mean you'll wait for an hour or more at the dock at either end. Better to leave early Saturday morning and return either by noon or late evening on

Sunday. If you're looking for a terrific skyline photo of Seattle, you can shoot it from the stern of one of the upper ferry decks as you depart.

From the Winslow ferry dock Washington 305 leads uphill to cross Bainbridge Island. A left turn at the first signal light will bring you into tiny Winslow, the island's only town and easy to explore on foot. From midspring through fall, there's a weekly Saturday farmer's market in Winslow Green, on the corner of Madison and Winslow Way. It's the place to buy a rabbit, a kitten, local handicrafts, island-grown produce, or dried flowers; have your knives sharpened; or get free advice on gardening and plant problems from a master gardener.

Don't miss the Bainbridge Bakery, also in the Green, whose specialties include pesto bread (spinach, basil, pine nuts, olive oil, and garlic rolled into sourdough French bread), a confection called "Chocolate Chestnut Decadence," and chocolate cherry hazelnut torte. For a delightful meal beside the water, try the Saltwater Cafe at the foot of Madison.

Return to Highway 305, turn left, and continue west for about half a mile. On your right is the small Bainbridge Island Winery, just five acres, where 6,000 gallons of chardonnays and rieslings are produced. Except for a handful of local restaurants, the winery salesroom is the only place these wines are available anywhere.

On the west side of Bainbridge Island is Bloedel Reserve. Once a family estate, the 150 acres of woodlands, gardens, ponds, and meadows are now open to the public. Trails lead through the grounds, where you can stroll past exotic plantings brought here from all over the world. Just beyond, Highway 305 soars across Agate Pass on a high bridge linking Bainbridge Island with the Kitsap Peninsula. You can often see flotillas of pleasure cruisers passing beneath; this is a favorite nautical route around the island.

Beyond the bridge turn left onto Sandy Hook Road, which leads through tall firs and hemlocks to the Suquamish Museum, a small gem that presents the history of Puget Sound's Salish Indians from the Indians' point of view. In addition to the usual exhibits of basketry, dugout canoes, fishing implements, jewelry, and weaving, a series of photographs and displays traces the story of Chief Sealth, his contemporaries, and the life of the tribe in the late nineteenth century.

Historians believe Chief Sealth (for whom Seattle was named) was born on the west shore of Agate Pass in 1786. Old Man House State Park commemorates the site of the tribe's great communal longhouse, which is believed to have been from 500 to 900 feet long and 60 feet wide. To reach the park, take the marked turnoff to the right just past the Agate Pass bridge to the village of Suquamish. In about one mile turn right on Division Street and descend to waterside. A few blocks inland, next to Saint Peter's Catholic Mission Church, is the old cemetery where the chief is buried. The grave is marked by a dramatic pair of long canoes mounted on poles.

Return to 305 and continue west four miles to Poulsbo, known locally as "Little Norway." This community has long been a Scandinavian enclave, although rapid growth in recent years has begun to obscure its Viking character. A strip development of malls, fast-food outlets, and motels flanks the highway, but if you detour at the first left you'll be afforded a spectacular view of Liberty Bay and the Olympic Mountains (a popular calendar shot for photographers). It's easy to understand why the Norwegians who came here in the late 1800s decided to stay—it looked like home. In the 1930s, 90 percent of the area's residents were Norwegian. Streets have names like Jensen Way, King Olaf Vei, Peterson, Iverson, Anderson, and Eliason.

Park along Anderson Way and walk out onto the piers to look at the dozens of fishing boats that call this home port. Stroll along the boardwalk that runs between the bluff and the water. Pick up sandwiches and soup-to-go at one of the nearby delis and picnic in Liberty Bay Park (one block west of Front, the main street), with its backdrop of the snow-capped Olympics.

The shops along Front Street include famous (at least in western Washington) Sluys Bakery, which makes a wide variety of sweets and breads including dark, multigrain Poulsbo bread and a Norwegian specialty called "lefse," a flatbread made from potatoes. They also offer free coffee. Several shops sell Scandinavian clothes, toys, wood carvings, and other imports as well as local crafts.

Just outside of town (turn right off 305 at Bond Road) is the Thomas Kemper Brewery, one of the several microbreweries that have made the Northwest a beer drinker's delight. They sell their products at the brewery and feature free live acoustical music on Saturday afternoons from April through October.

Head north on Washington 3 now for seven miles to Port Gamble. Your first impression of this historic lumber mill town is one of New England; it's not surprising, the natives of Maine who settled here in 1853 reproduced many of the architectural styles of their former home. The little town has been preserved as a historic monument commemorating many other such waterside mill towns that once dotted the shores of Puget Sound and shipped their lumber by schooner to California.

Be sure to see the handsome gray-and-white Saint Paul's Episcopal Church (circa 1870) standing beside Highway 104 at the west end of town. It's a replica of one located in East Machias, Maine. At the top of the hill to the south, the old graveyard contains the remains of the first Caucasian killed in Washington, an American gunboat sailor who encountered a raiding party of Indians from British Columbia.

To complete the loop, head east on Washington 104 and board the ferry at Kingston for Edmonds. A short drive beyond the ferry dock, Highway 104 joins Interstate 5 for your return to Seattle.

Area Code: 206

DRIVING DIRECTIONS Board the ferry to Winslow at Seattle's Colman Dock (Pier 52). Debarking on Bainbridge Island, follow Highway 305 to Poulsbo, Highway 3 to Port Gamble, and Highway 104 to return to Seattle via the Kingston–Edmonds ferry. Round trip is approximately 43 miles by car, plus 2 ferry crossings.

FERRIES *Washington State Ferries,* Seattle to Winslow, crossing time 35 minutes, weekend frequency about every 50 minutes from 7:50 A.M. to 11:50 P.M., first ferry 6:20 A.M., last ferry 2:40 A.M.; car and driver $6.65, passenger (round-trip) $3.30. Kingston to Edmonds, crossing time 30 minutes, similar frequency, same fares. Information: (800) 542-7052 and (800) 542-0810 (in WA), 464-6400.

SIGHTSEEING *Bainbridge Island Winery,* 682 Highway 305, 842-9463. Hours: Wednesday to Sunday noon to 5 P.M. Free. *Bloedel Reserve,* Highway 305 at Agate Pass, 842-7631. Hours: Wednesday to Sunday 10 A.M. to 4 P.M., reservations required. Admission $4, $2 for ages 6–13 and 64 and over. *Suquamish Museum,* 15838 Sandy Hook Road, 598-3311. Hours: Daily 10 A.M. to 5 P.M., closed Monday in winter. Admission $2.50, $2 for seniors, $1 for children under 12. *Poulsbo Sea Kayaking Co.,* 17791 Fjord Drive Northeast, Poulsbo, 697-2464. Offers kayaking tours of nearby waters. *Thomas Kemper Brewery,* 22381 Foss Road Northeast, Poulsbo, 697-1446. Hours: Monday to Thursday 11 A.M. to 6 P.M., Friday and Saturday 11 A.M. to 9 P.M., Sunday 11 A.M. to 8 P.M., free.

EVENTS *Viking Fest,* Poulsbo, 779-4848, mid-May. Norwegian independence celebration with a parade, arts and crafts show, folk dancing, and lutefisk-eating contest. *Strawberry Festival,* Poulsbo, 779-4848, mid-June. Strawberry harvest is marked by food fair featuring fresh berries, shortcake. *Chief Seattle Days,* Suquamish, 598-3311, August. Traditional Indian dancing, games, canoe races, story telling, salmon bake.

LODGING *The Captain's House* (bed and breakfast), 234 Parfitt Way, Winslow, 842-3557. Vintage home near ferry dock, $. *Bombay House* (bed and breakfast), 8490 Beck Road Northeast, Bainbridge Island, 842-3926. Turn-of-the-century landscaped home at south end of the island, $$. *Beach Cottage,* 5831 Ward Avenue, Winslow, 842-6081. Cottages on Eagle Harbor, outskirts of Winslow, fine views, you cook your own breakfast from ingredients supplied, $. *Cypress Inn,* 19801 7th Avenue Northeast, Poulsbo, (800) 752-9981 (in WA), (800) 752-9991 (outside WA), $–$$. *Manor Farm Inn,* 26069 Big Valley Road, Poulsbo, 779-4628.

Elegant accommodations on a working farm with 8 guest rooms, 1 cottage, hot tub, full breakfast. Dinner available. No children, pets, or smoking, $$–$$$. *Silverdale on the Bay,* 3073 Bucklin Hill Road, Silverdale, (800) 528-1234. Resort hotel with beach, fishing, tennis courts, and indoor pool. $$–$$$.

CAMPING *Fay Bainbridge State Park,* on beach, north end of Bainbridge Island. 26 sites with water hookups, $8. *Kitsap Memorial State Park.* 43 sites on Hood Canal, no hookups, $8. Information: 753-2027.

DINING *Saltwater Cafe,* foot of Madison Avenue, Winslow, 842-8339. Lunch and dinner daily; seafood specialties, outdoor dining; $–$$. Overlooks Eagle Harbor. *Streamliner Diner,* Winslow Way and Bejune Street, Winslow, 842-8595. Breakfast daily, lunch Monday to Friday; omelettes, quiche, and specialty egg dishes; $. *San Carlos,* 279 Madison Street, Winslow, 842-1999. Lunch Tuesday to Friday, dinner daily; Mexican cuisine; $. *The Viking House,* on the wharf in Poulsbo, 779-9882. Breakfast, lunch, and dinner daily; $–$$. *Henry's,* 18887 Highway 305, Poulsbo, 779-4685. Breakfast, lunch, and dinner daily; Swedish pancakes on breakfast menu; $.

FOR MORE INFORMATION Bainbridge Island Chamber of Commerce, 153 Madrone Lane North, Bainbridge Island 98110, 842-3700. Greater Poulsbo Chamber of Commerce, P.O. Box 1063, Poulsbo 98370, 779-4848.

Bremerton, Hood Canal, and Olympia

Ever since the battleship U.S.S. *Missouri* left for a new home port in San Francisco several years ago, Bremerton has dropped from most lists of western Washington's top sightseeing destinations. But the navy's leading port in the Northwest still has plenty of fascinating sights and, according to *Money* magazine (August 1990), Bremerton is the best place in the United States to live. Combined with the scenic route along Hood Canal to Olympia, Bremerton makes a lovely weekend drive. For a three-day weekend, you could combine the Bainbridge Island–Poulsbo–Port Gamble loop (page 9) with this trip.

Board the ferry to Bremerton at Seattle's Colman Dock (Pier 52). With the exception of the San Juan Islands route, this crossing has always been the most scenic in the Puget Sound. You pass the working waterfront at Harbor Island with its drydocks, container facilities, and barge-towing tugs. On hazy summer and autumn days the Sound and island scenery has the quality of an Oriental painting—soft and gauzy. You thread your way through Rich Passage, passing

Blake Island, Clam Bay, and Point Clover. Dark green cedars, firs, hemlocks, and stately red-barked madronas grow right to the water's edge.

In Bremerton, stop at the Bremerton Naval Shipyard Museum. It's a gem. Among the dozens of ship models, charts, photographs, and other naval memorabilia, you'll find two large wooden blocks salvaged from the original U.S.S. *Constitution* ("Old Ironsides") when she was reconstructed in 1929, and the desk, couch, and chair from Admiral Dewey's office aboard the flagship U.S.S. *Olympia* at the Battle of Manila Bay.

As this is written, the Bremerton Historic Ships Association is completing plans to display the Vietnam War–era destroyer, U.S.S. *Turner Joy,* as a walk-on visitor attraction along the Bremerton waterfront.

Head west and south on Washington 304 and 3 as it hugs the shore of Sinclair Inlet. To your left is the Puget Sound Naval Shipyard, a major repair facility for the navy. One of the big aircraft carriers is usually in port for refurbishing and several mothballed warships are moored at the docks. Several side streets provide a closer look, and the passenger-only ferry to Port Orchard (from Bremerton's ferry dock) provides waterside views of submarines and smaller vessels.

At the head of Sinclair Inlet detour west four miles to Port Orchard. You can also return to Seattle this way via Washington 160 and the Southworth–Vashon Island ferry.

Port Orchard is a good place to browse for local arts, crafts, collectibles, and nautical knickknacks; covered sidewalks along Bay Street keep you dry if it's raining. The 1902 Central Hotel houses 70 separate antiques shops. You'll find glass fishing floats, brass lanterns, dolls in the shape of geoducks (the geoduck is Washington's giant clam and a subject of local humor), quilts, and books on local history. There's an outdoor farmer's market on Frederick Street along the waterfront where you can purchase local produce on Saturday mornings from April to October.

At Gorst, return to Highway 3 and follow it nine miles south, then turn onto Highway 106 and continue southwest along the shores of Hood Canal. Shaped like a fishhook, the canal is actually an 80-mile-long tidal channel that separates the Kitsap and Olympic peninsulas. The British explorer Captain George Vancouver named the canal in 1792 for a British admiral.

For a dozen or more miles you pass vacation homes and year-round residences clustered along the water. You'll see everything from modest cabins to grand retreats, and you'll chuckle over the cutesy nautical name signs—Windward, Hi-Tide, Far-Sea, and Pebble Cove.

The speed limit here is a comfortable 40 miles per hour, restricting you to a leisurely pace so you can enjoy the view. There's also a marked shoulder for bicycles. If it's a clear day, you can see the snow-capped Olympics across the water. This is also a great route for spotting waterfowl, including scooters, gold-eneyes, coots, mergansers, widgeons, and grebes.

Hood Canal is noted for its fine oysters and Dungeness crabs. You'll find them on most local restaurant menus. Fishing for salmon, shrimp, sea-run cutthroat, and bottom fish is also excellent at the lower end of the canal. You can rent boats in Union at the Alderbrook Inn and at Hood Canal Marine (a marine supply company). Inquire locally about public beaches where you can harvest clams and oysters; property owners get a bit upset at trespassing oyster gatherers. You can also buy freshly harvested seafood at roadside stands and country stores in this area.

From the junction with U.S. 101, detour north five miles to Hoodsport and the Hoodsport Winery. The Island Belle wine made and sold only here comes from Lambrusca grapes grown in the first vineyard in the state, established in the 1880s.

U.S. 101 runs south through Shelton, a lumber mill town also noted for its Christmas tree industry. You'll pass Christmas tree farms all along the way and can come and cut your own on one of the U-cut farms in December. As it turns east to join Interstate 5, the highway passes several tidewater inlets—Big Skookum, Little Skookum, Oyster and Mud bays—used by fish farms to raise commercial seafood, chiefly oysters. It is here that the tiny, delicate Olympia oyster, so prized by gourmands, is grown.

Olympia, Washington's capital, perches at the end of Budd Inlet, the extreme southern tip of Puget Sound. Though the lovely capitol campus is a good place for a walk or picnic any time of the year, it's especially beautiful in April when the cherry trees are in bloom. Unfortunately, many of the government buildings are closed on Saturday and Sunday. Be sure to view the capitol rotunda, with its massive Tiffany chandelier. The State Library, designed by famed architect Paul Thiry, exhibits murals, sculpture, and mosaics by Northwest artists James Fitz-Gerald, Mark Tobey, and Kenneth Callahan, and has a Northwest Authors' collection of published works. The capitol greenhouse (on the north side) has a stunning array of blossoming garden plants, and the greenhouse keeper is happy to offer advice to home gardeners. The State Capitol Museum, housed in the lovely 1920 Spanish-style mansion of banker and Olympia mayor Clarence J. Lord, has collections of old logging photos, ships' models, and Indian basketry plus an intact old pharmacy and some curious equipment once used in the oyster industry.

Follow Capitol Way south to the Tumwater Historic District and the trim white Nathaniel Crosby House, built by Bing's great-uncle in 1858. A block away, Henderson House (circa 1905) is another modest home typical of nineteenth-century western Washington dwellings. If you've brought along a picnic lunch, Tumwater Falls Park (adjacent to the Olympia brewery) is a good place to stop.

Green lawns slope down to the Deschutes River. A mile-long trail leads past two waterfalls, good places to watch migrating salmon in late summer and fall.

From Olympia, it's about an hour's drive back to Seattle via I-5.

Area Code: 206

DRIVING DIRECTIONS Board the ferry for Bremerton at Seattle's Colman Dock (Pier 52). From Bremerton follow State Highways 3 and 106 to a junction with U.S. 101, then south to Olympia and a junction with I-5. Approximate round-trip mileage is 118, plus 1 ferry crossing.

FERRIES *Washington State Ferries,* Seattle to Bremerton, crossing time 60 minutes, weekend departures about every 70 minutes from 7:40 A.M. to 7:15 P.M., last ferry from Seattle 2:40 A.M. Car and driver $6.65, each passenger $3.30 round-trip. Information: (800) 542-0810, (800) 542-7052 (in WA), 464-6400. *Horluck Transportation Co.,* Bremerton to Port Orchard (passengers only), crossing time 10 minutes, 70 cents. Information: 876-2300.

SIGHTSEEING *Naval Shipyard Museum,* 151 1st Street (ferry terminal), Bremerton, 479-3588. Hours: Wednesday to Sunday noon to 4 P.M. Free. *Hoodsport Winery,* North 23501 U.S. 101, Hoodsport, 877-9894, 877-9508. Hours: Daily 10 A.M. to 6 P.M. Free. *Ellison Oyster Co.,* 2620 Madrona Beach Road, Olympia, 866-7551. Primary grower of rare Olympia oysters, tours by appointment only. Free. *Capitol Campus,* information 586-8687, 586-3460; visitor center has maps of campus. Hours: Monday to Friday 8 A.M. to 5 P.M. *Legislative Building,* guided tours Monday to Friday 9 A.M. to 4:30 P.M., Saturday and Sunday 10 A.M. to 4 P.M. Free. *Governor's Mansion,* 586-8687 for tour reservations. Hours: Wednesday 1 to 2:30 P.M. Free. *State Library,* 753-5590. Hours: Monday to Friday 8 A.M. to 5 P.M. *Greenhouse Conservatory,* Memorial Day–Labor Day daily 8 A.M. to 4:30 P.M., rest of year Monday through Friday. *State Capitol Museum,* 211 West 21st Avenue, 753-2580. Hours: Tuesday to Friday 10 A.M. to 4 P.M., Saturday and Sunday noon to 4 P.M. Free. *Olympia Brewing Co.,* Custer Way and Schmidt Place, Exit 103, Tumwater, 754-5128. Brewery offers 45-minute tours and tastings daily 8 A.M. to 4:30 P.M. Free. *Henderson House,* 602 Deschutes Way, Tumwater. Hours: May through October daily 9 A.M. to 5 P.M., other months Monday through Friday only. Donation. *Crosby House,* Grant and Deschutes Way, Tumwater, 753-8583. Hours: Thursday 2 to 4 P.M., Sunday 1 to 4 P.M. Donation.

EVENTS *Armed Forces Day Parade,* Bremerton, 479-3588, third Saturday in May. Locals claim this is the nation's largest Armed Forces Day celebration; colorful military parade. *Mountaineers' Forest Theater,* Seabeck Highway, May and

June. Information and tickets: 300 3rd Avenue West, Seattle 98119, 284-6310. Outdoor performances in rustic, forested amphitheater. *Kitsap County Fair and Rodeo,* Bremerton, 692-3655, late August. Features circus, rodeo, entertainment, agricultural exhibits. *Mason County Forest Festival,* Shelton, 426-2021, June. Paul Bunyan parade, carnival, music, loggers' competitions. *West Coast Oyster Shucking Championship and Seafood Festival,* Shelton, 426-2021, early October. Lively weekend of oyster speed shucking contests, wine tasting, seafood cookoffs, music, and entertainment. *Lakefair,* Olympia, 357-3362, second weekend in July. Capital's biggest annual celebration features flower and art shows, parade, boat races.

LODGING *Oyster Bay Inn,* 4412 Kitsap Way, Bremerton, 479-2132. $. *Quality Inn Bayview,* 5640 Kitsap Way, Bremerton, 373-7349. $–$$. *Wilcox House,* (bed and breakfast), 2390 Teiku Road, Bremerton, 840-4492. Elegant former mansion overlooking Hood Canal and the Olympics (8 miles south of Seabeck), $$–$$$. *Summer Song* (bed and breakfast), P.O. Box 82, Seabeck, 830-5089. Cozy cottage on Hood Canal, good secluded getaway, fireplace, adults preferred, $$. *The Walton House* (bed and breakfast), 12340 Seabeck Highway Northwest, Seabeck, 830-4498. 1904 country home on Hood Canal; no children, pets, or smoking; open Thursday through Sunday nights, $$. *Alderbrook Inn,* East 7101 Highway 106, Union, 898-2200. Full-service waterside resort on Hood Canal, cottages and motel units, tennis, golf, $$–$$$. *Harbinger Inn* (bed and breakfast), 1136 East Bay Drive, Olympia, 754-0389. No pets or children, $$. *Westwater Inn,* 2300 Evergreen Park Drive, Olympia, 943-4000. Beautifully sited with view of capitol dome and Capitol Lake, $$. *Tyee Hotel,* 500 Tyee Drive (Exit 102), Tumwater, 352-0511. $–$$.

CAMPING *Belfair State Park,* 3 miles west of Belfair, Highway 300, 133 tent sites, 47 hookups; *Illahee State Park,* 3 miles northeast of Bremerton, Highway 306, 25 tent sites. *Twanoh State Park,* 8 miles west of Belfair, Highway 106, 30 tent sites, 9 hookups; *Potlatch State Park,* 12 miles north of Shelton, U.S. 101, 17 tent sites, 18 hookups. State park fees: $12 with hookups, $8 without. *Glen Ayr RV Park,* North 25381 U.S. 101, Hoodsport, 877-9522. 54 hookups, $14. *American Heritage KOA,* 9610 Kimmie Street Southwest, Olympia, 943-8778. 105 sites, 24 full hookups, 50 water-electricity, $14–$18. *Deep Lake Resort,* 12405 Tilley Road, Olympia, 352-7833. 48 sites, 13 full hookups, 30 water-electricity, mid-April to September, $8–$11.

DINING *Hearthstone,* 4312 Kitsap Way, Bremerton, 377-5531. Lunch and dinner Monday to Friday, dinner Saturday, closed Sunday, $$. *Alderbrook Inn* (see "Lodging"). Breakfast, lunch, and dinner daily, $$. *Bellagamba's,* Lakeland Golf and Country Club, Allyn, 275-2871. Lunch and dinner Tuesday to Sunday, known for its preparation of fresh local seafood, $$. *Carnegie's,* 302 East Seventh Avenue, Olympia, 357-5550. Lunch and dinner Monday to Saturday; in Olympia's former Carnegie Library; steak, seafood, cajun dishes, $-$$. *Budd Bay Cafe,* 525 North Columbia Street, Olympia 357-6963. Lunch Monday to Saturday, dinner daily, brunch Sunday; casual outdoor dining on deck overlooking Budd Inlet; steaks, salads, sandwiches; $$. *La Petite Maison,* 2005 Ascension Avenue, Olympia, 943-8812. Lunch Monday to Friday, dinner Tuesday to Saturday; creative menu using local foods, emphasizes seafood and Northwest wines, $$. *The Urban Onion,* 116 Legion Avenue, Olympia, 943-9242, breakfast, lunch, and dinner daily; eclectic menu includes salads, soups, sandwiches, pasta, and Mexican offerings; $-$$.

FOR MORE INFORMATION Bremerton/Kitsap County Visitor and Convention Bureau, 120 Washington Avenue, #101, Bremerton 98310, 479-3588. Greater Olympia Visitor and Convention Bureau, 316 Schmidt Drive, Olympia 98507, 357-3370.

Vashon: An Island Retreat

It's hard to believe an island such as Vashon could remain an untrammeled, rural retreat in the midst of a metropolitan area of more than 2.6 million people. Yet there it is, just a 15-minute ferry ride from Fauntleroy in West Seattle. Humpbacked and bracketed with beaches, the island is dotted with scores of small farmsteads tucked away among the trees.

Named in 1792 by Captain George Vancouver for his friend, English navy captain James Vashon, the island was homesteaded in 1877 and became one of the leading berry-, fruit-, and poultry-producing areas on Puget Sound.

Viewing Vashon today, it's easy to imagine the way it must have been for those first nineteenth-century settlers who cleared the land, planted their crops, raised barns and houses, and harvested the fish and shellfish from surrounding salt waters. Over the years, the island has remained relatively unspoiled.

There isn't much to do on Vashon. The reason you go is to escape the urban pace, to unwind, to get in touch with the outdoors and with yourself. Though accommodations are limited, staying in one of the island's bed-and-breakfast inns provides the appropriate low-key environment conducive to strolling its beaches and walking or driving its country roads at leisure. The 12-mile-long island is also a good destination for bicycling.

From the ferry dock on Vashon you make a stiff climb of about a mile before the road levels out. Stop and pick up a free map at one of several real estate offices along the way.

A few miles along the main island road, 99th Avenue Southwest, you come to

Vashon, the commercial center. Stop at the Malt Shop (in the Vashon Plaza on 100th Avenue Southwest) to pick up a bag of their big, crunchy homemade potato chips, one of Vashon's treasures.

Potato chips are not the only thing made on Vashon. The little island is the home of several companies whose products are well known in the Northwest and beyond. You can visit them and, with a little planning, tour their facilities.

Island Spring makes tofu and other soybean-based foods that you may have seen at your own local market.

In the skiing world, the name K-2 is a biggie. The skis for which the company is famous are made on the island in a two-story olive-green building on the island highway south of Vashon.

In the last couple of years, the Pacific Northwest's love affair with coffee has attracted national attention. Magazines and newspapers (including the *New York Times*) have reported on the ubiquitous coffee bars in Seattle and the boom in sales of gourmet coffees.

Even before you come to it, you can smell the rich aroma of freshly roasted coffee at the SBC (formerly known as Stewart Brothers Coffee) Roasterie at the corner of the Vashon Island Highway and Southwest 196th Street. Look for the burlap sacks of coffee piled high on the front porch of the white clapboard building with red-and-gray trim. On weekdays, you can watch the roastmaster work his magic on the red drum roaster in the basement of the building, sample fresh-brewed coffee, and purchase the roasted beans to take home.

As soon as you step inside the Maury Island Farm Company gift shop, located at the corner of Southwest 204th at Valley Center, you can smell the jams and jellies made here from Washington-grown fruits. Crammed into the little building, which appears to have been a gas station in its previous life, are production facilities and a retail outlet. Jane Davies, shop manager, says they ship their products and will make up custom boxes. Pick up a copy of their catalog or call (800) 356-5880 to receive one.

Wax Orchards, which has been in business since 1920, makes juices, syrups, fruit butters, chutneys, conserves, and other fruit products at their production facility (including retail sales) on 131st Avenue Southwest, south of Southwest 220th Street. Look for the sign on the east side of the road.

But one of the best ways to sample island food products is to dine at the Sound Food Restaurant. It's a pleasant place with about two dozen tables brightened by fresh flowers and windows that overlook a grassy backyard. Food is simple and delicious. The lunch menu includes soups such as clam chowder and onion gratiné plus a soup of the day, ten different kinds of sandwiches, and a good variety of salads. Make sure you try their homemade breads, especially the chewy whole wheat. Vegetarians will also find lots of choices. Among the nine homemade desserts served daily are mousse and cream and fruit pies.

The Country Store and Farm, on Island Highway south of the town of Vashon, is another good place to pick up island products. An old-fashioned country store, it sells natural-fiber clothing, dried herbs, various foods, and gardening supplies.

Vashon offers plenty of good photographic possibilities. Robinson Point Light Station, at the eastern tip of Maury Island (actually a peninsula connected by a narrow sand spit) off the southeast corner of the island, is one of the best. From here you get fine views across the Sound to Des Moines. If you're lucky, you may see a freighter plying the main channel from Tacoma.

Drive back on Vashon through the tiny community of Burton. The 1908 Harbor Mercantile sells groceries, marine supplies, and hardware. South of Burton, the madrona-lined road skirts Quartermaster Harbor, then scoots inland and ends abruptly at Tahlequah. From here you can catch a ferry for Point Defiance in Tacoma or retrace your route north for the trip home.

Area Code: 206

DRIVING DIRECTIONS Take the ferry from the Fauntleroy terminal in southwest Seattle. Round trip is approximately 24 miles, plus detours and ferry crossing.

FERRIES *Fauntleroy–Vashon,* crossing time 15 minutes, departures about every 45 minutes; first ferry at 5:40 A.M., last ferry at 2 A.M.; route continues on to Southworth. Car and driver $7.50 round trip, each passenger $2.15. *Tahlequah–Point Defiance,* crossing time 15 minutes, departures about every hour beginning at 6:20 A.M., 7:40 A.M. on Sundays and holidays, and ending at 10:10 P.M. Information: (800) 542-0810, (800) 542-7052 (in WA), 464-6400.

SIGHTSEEING *Island Spring, Inc.,* Southwest 188th Street, 463-9848. Watch tofu being made Monday, Tuesday, or Thursday mornings; call 922-6448 for reservations. Free. *K-2 Skis,* Island Highway, 463-3631. 1-hour tours Tuesday and Thursday at 10 A.M., extension 415 for reservations. Free. *SBC Roasterie (formerly Stewart Brothers Coffee),* Island Highway and 196th Street, 463-3932. Hours: Monday to Friday 8 A.M. to 5 P.M. Free. *Maury Island Farms,* Island Highway at 204th Street, 463-9659. Hours: Monday to Saturday 9 A.M. to 5 P.M., Sunday noon to 5 P.M. Free. *Wax Orchards,* 131st Avenue Southwest south of Southwest 220th Street, 463-9735. Hours: Monday to Friday 8 A.M. to 5 P.M., Saturday 10 A.M. to 5 P.M. Free.

EVENTS *Strawberry Festival,* 463-2543, mid-July. Parades, arts and crafts, music, and lots of strawberries.

L O D G I N G *Rock Ranch Inn Bed and Breakfast,* Route 2, Box 570, 463-2116. Separate apartment in home on 10 acres, $$. *The Shepherd's Loft,* Route 3, Box 289, 463-2544. Guest cottage on Maury Island sheep farm, complete kitchen, $$. *The Swallows Nest,* Route 3, Box 221, 463-2646. 4 individual cottages and Victorian house, cooking facilities, $–$$$. *The Smyth House,* Route 5, Box 211, 567-4049. 1920s beach home has 2 bedrooms, kitchen and laundry, deck, sleeps 6, $$$$.

D I N I N G *Sound Food,* Island Highway at Southwest 204th Street, 463-3565. Breakfast Monday to Friday, lunch and dinner daily, brunch Saturday and Sunday; homemade soups, salads, baked goods; $. *Casa del Sol,* north end ferry dock, 567-5249. Lunch and dinner daily, Mexican cuisine, $.

FOR MORE INFORMATION Vashon Business Association, P.O. Box 1035, Vashon 98070, 463-3591.

Tacoma: City of Hidden Charms

Tacoma, Washington's second largest city, is a bit deceptive for the casual visitor. From Interstate 5, the view is of heavy industry, a bustling port, and the blue wooden cap of the Tacoma Dome; most of downtown and the city's prettiest residential neighborhoods are out of sight. The industrious, no-nonsense impression is real. The city is devoted to the lumber, pulp and paper, and shipping industries and doesn't pay much attention to tourists or visitor attractions.

On the other hand, Tacoma has one of the finest urban parks in the Pacific Northwest, historical and art museums, and two jewels of small towns tucked away on its flanks.

Take Exit 133 from I-5 (just past the Tacoma Dome) and follow Pacific Avenue into downtown. The city is a treasure trove of historic architecture, the first example of which is the classic old Union Station on your right at 17th Street. Recently restored, the copper-roofed Neo-Baroque–style structure was begun in 1901 and not completed until 1911. A couple of blocks uphill to the left is the elegant 1918 Pantages Theater, now restored and serving as a performing arts center.

Take some time to poke about downtown. The area around South 7th Street and Pacific Avenue was once the heart of downtown, and the splendid old City Hall (circa 1893) with its Italian Renaissance tower still dominates that end of town. Continue up the hill on Pacific until you come to Stadium Way and Tacoma's most unusual building, Stadium High School. Resembling something out of Camelot, the turreted structure originally was the grand Tacoma Land Company Hotel, built in 1891. All of the streets at this end of town were designed by the nation's most prominent nineteenth-century landscape architect, Frederick Law Olmsted, who also designed New York's Central Park.

Next door to Stadium High is the Washington State Historical Society Museum (which seems to logically belong in the state capital). Plans are to move the museum downtown in a new building next to the handsome old Union Station in 1995. Until then, the present museum will have limited exhibits, including a video history of Washington state.

Work your way around the waterfront to Ruston Way, a good road for viewing ship traffic in Commencement Bay and for dining spots with a waterside view; some of the city's better restaurants are located here.

Big 638-acre Point Defiance Park is a treat just about any time you choose to visit. In spring clouds of rhododendron, azalea, and fruit tree blossoms envelop the hillsides, while in summer and early fall the rose gardens and annual flower beds show off their colors everywhere.

Tacoma's excellent zoo and aquarium are located here on a compact site. The zoo has the usual exotic species as well as a fine polar bear enclosure and pool, a rocky shoreline habitat, a marine mammals exhibit, and a children's zoo featuring farm animals. The aquarium's displays focus on the marine life of Puget Sound.

Point Defiance Park is also ideal for bicycling, featuring a five-mile, one-way road that meanders through dense forest and skirts the peninsula. A thick canopy of trees overhead, massive rhododendrons lining the route, and frequent twists and turns in the road give each glade a remote, hidden-deep-in-the-forest feel. Along the way there are several overlooks with picnic tables and fine views of Puget Sound to the north and west. Trails for hikers branch off the main road; one side road leads down to Floyd Owen Beach, where you'll find a public bathhouse, a snack bar, boat rentals, picnic tables, a shelter with fireplace, piles of driftwood logs, and sweeping views of the sound.

As you near the end of the road, you encounter the log palisades and bastions of Fort Nisqually, commanding a splendid cliff-top view of the Tacoma Narrows to the south. This is a nifty stop if you have small children along; it's easy for them to imagine themselves as Davy Crockett or some such legendary hero defending this fort. Inside the palisades, the 1843 granary is the state's oldest building. A bit farther along this park loop road is Camp Six, a mostly static outdoor museum of logging with a collection of equipment and living facilities. Steam locomotive excursions run in summer.

Gig Harbor, five miles northwest of Tacoma, is one of the prettiest little towns in the Northwest. To reach it from Point Defiance, drive south on Pearl Street to Washington 16, then turn right and cross the Tacoma Narrows Bridge. This soaring suspension span is a replacement for the infamous "Galloping Gertie" that collapsed in a windstorm in 1940.

Built on hills sloping down to the water, Gig Harbor takes its name from a captain's "gig," the kind of rowboat used by an American naval expedition that sought shelter here from a storm during their exploration of Puget Sound in 1841. Today, fishing boats and pleasure craft tie up in these protected waters. On a clear day, big, snow-capped Mount Rainier looms just beyond the harbor's mouth.

Gig Harbor is a town for strolling and browsing. A number of fine specialty shops and boutiques line Harborview Drive, and local restaurants, most of them on or near the water, offer everything from fresh seafood to paella and artichoke quiche.

Tacoma's other fascinating neighbor is Steilacoom, the oldest town in the state (head south on I-5; take Exit 128). It's remarkably well preserved and nearly traffic-free—another good place for walking or bicycling. Simple but handsome old homes cluster along parallel streets that form terraces down the hillside to the shore of the Sound.

Stop first at Bair Drug and Hardware Co., built in 1895, at the corner of Wilkes and Lafayette. Here you're likely to find the locals sitting around a big potbellied stove just as they have done for several generations. The store is a living museum, with display cases filled with long-out-of-date perfumes and cosmetics, movie magazines from the 1940s, old-time medicines, and other memorabilia. The store boasts a working 1906 soda fountain where you can get a Green River soda (lemon-lime flavoring with soda water), a sarsaparilla, a phosphate, a float, an ice cream soda, or a sundae. This is also the place to pick up a free copy of "A Guide to Historic Steilacoom," which details the dozens of historic buildings in town.

Area Code: 206

DRIVING DIRECTIONS Head south from Seattle on I-5 to Tacoma. With detours to Gig Harbor (10 miles) and Steilacoom (8 miles), the round trip is approximately 100 miles.

SIGHTSEEING *Tacoma Art Museum,* 12th and Pacific avenues, 272-4258. Hours: Tuesday to Saturday 10 A.M. to 5 P.M., Sunday noon to 5 P.M. Modest collection of contemporary works, Renoir, Degas, Pissarro, good children's gallery, fine glass collection. Adults $2, over 64 and students $1. Tuesdays free. *Pantages Theater,* 901 Broadway, 591-5894. Call for schedule of performances. *Tacoma Dome,* Exit 133 from I-5, 272-DOME, 24-hour event line 591-5318. World's largest wooden dome, 1-hour guided tours Monday to Friday, twice daily. Adults $2, $1 for children and seniors. *Washington State Historical Society Museum,* 315 North Stadium Way, 593-2830. Hours: Monday to Saturday 10 A.M. to 5 P.M., closed Sunday. Adults $2, seniors $1.50, children 6–18 $1. Free on

Tuesdays. *Point Defiance Park,* 5400 North Pearl Street, 591-5335 (recorded information), 591-5337. Zoo and aquarium hours: April to September daily 10 A.M. to 7 P.M., other months 10 A.M. to 5 P.M. Adults $3.50, over 62 and 13–17 $2.25, 5–12 $1.75, 3–4 50 cents. Fort Nisqually hours: July through Labor Day daily 11 A.M. to 7 P.M., other months Wednesday to Sunday, noon to 5 P.M. Free. *Fort Lewis Military Museum,* 16 miles south off I-5 Exit 120, Fort Lewis, 967-7206. Hours: Wednesday to Sunday noon to 4 P.M. Military history of the Northwest including uniforms, artillery, tanks, firearms. Free. *Bair Drug and Hardware,* 1617 Lafayette Street, Steilacoom, 588-9668. Hours: Daily 9 A.M. to 6 P.M. *Nathaniel Orr Home and Pioneer Orchard,* 1811 Rainier Street, Steilacoom, 568-8155. Hours: Sunday 1 to 4 P.M. Admission $1. *Steilacoom Historical Museum,* 1717 Lafayette Street, Steilacoom, 584-8623. Hours: February through November Tuesday, Thursday, and Saturday, 1 to 4 P.M. Free.

EVENTS *Daffodil Festival,* Tacoma and Puyallup, 627-6176, first Saturday in April. Celebrates spring with grand floral parade. *Taste of Tacoma* and *Art à la Carte,* Point Defiance Park, 627-2836, July. Major food and art fairs. *Apple Squeeze,* Bair Drug and Hardware, Steilacoom, 588-9668, October. Celebrates harvest with old-fashioned cider-making party. *Lighted Boat Parade,* Gig Harbor, 858-7595, early December. Illuminated boats cruise the harbor in evening Christmas display, caroling.

LODGING *Sheraton Tacoma Hotel,* 1320 Broadway Plaza, 572-3200. $$$–$$$$. *Quality Hotel–Tacoma Dome,* 2611 East E. Street, 572-7272. $$$–$$$$. *Best Western Tacoma Inn,* 8726 South Hosmer Street, 535-2880. $$–$$$$. *The Pillars* (bed and breakfast), 6606 Soundview Drive, Gig Harbor, 851-6644. 3 guest rooms, fine views of Colvos Passage and Mount Rainier, no smoking or pets, $$$. *No Cabbages* (bed and breakfast), 7712 Goodman Drive, Gig Harbor, 858-7797. Waterside, views, $. *Krestine,* P.O. Box 31, Gig Harbor, 858-9395. Nicely furnished cabins aboard a 1903 sailing vessel, $–$$.

CAMPING *Dash Point State Park,* Highway 509, 5 miles northeast of Tacoma, 593-2206. 138 sites, 28 with hookups, $8 and $12. *Kopachuck State Park,* 12 miles northwest of Tacoma off Highway 16. 41 sites, no hookups, $8.

DINING *C. I. Shenanigan's,* 3017 Ruston Way, 752-8811. Lunch and dinner daily, Sunday brunch; waterfront, deck for outdoor dining; $$. *Lessie's Southern Kitchen,* 1416 Sixth Avenue, 627-4282. Monday to Saturday breakfast, lunch, and dinner; down-home Southern cooking; $. *Pacific Rim,* 100 South Ninth Street, 627-1009. Lunch Monday to Friday, dinner daily except Sunday; highly acclaimed, wide-ranging menu covers Pacific Northwest and Continental cuisine;

reservations a must; $$$. *Harbor Lights,* 2761 Ruston Way, 752-8600. Lunch and dinner daily; specializes in seafood; waterfront; $$. *Rose Room,* Sheraton Tacoma Hotel (see "Lodging"). Lunch and dinner daily, brunch Saturday and Sunday; elegant dining with rooftop view of Mount Rainier; $$$. *Cliff House,* 6300 Marine View Drive, 927-0400. Lunch and dinner daily, Sunday brunch; perches on cliff with spectacular views; $$$. *Tides Tavern,* 2925 Harborview Drive, Gig Harbor, 858-3982. Lunch and dinner daily; waterfront hangout popular with locals; hamburgers, pizza, and beer; $. *E. R. Rogers,* 1702 Commercial Street, Steilacoom, 582-0280. Dinner daily, Sunday brunch; upscale restaurant in restored Victorian mansion; great Sound views; $$–$$$.

FOR MORE INFORMATION Tacoma/Pierce County Visitor and Convention Bureau, 950 Pacific Avenue, Suite 450, Tacoma 98401, 627-2836, (800) 272-2662.

Sampling the Past in Port Townsend

For the officers and men of the Third Artillery Corps, duty at Fort Worden on the northeastern tip of the Olympic Peninsula must have been pretty dreary. Stuck at Port Townsend—the end of their turn-of-the-century world—engaged in endless parades and practice drills for an enemy that never came, most of them probably longed for the bright lights of the big city.

Escape from the big city is what brings most visitors to the old fort now. They come to fly model airplanes and kites on the broad parade ground, to park RVs overlooking the Strait of Juan de Fuca and Point Wilson lighthouse, to attend jazz and chamber music performances at McCurdy Pavilion or seminars and workshops in the old barracks buildings.

Fort Worden (now a state park) and adjacent Port Townsend make an ideal weekend getaway, especially in the off-season, when crowds of summer visitors have gone home. Plan to snuggle into a bed-and-breakfast inn for the weekend or in one of the refurbished officer's quarters at Fort Worden (*An Officer and a Gentleman* was filmed here). It's the kind of slow-paced town where you'll feel perfectly comfortable settling down beside a cozy fire with a good book or spending a leisurely couple of days exploring the historic old town on foot.

Often described as the finest collection of Victorian architecture north of San Francisco and the bed-and-breakfast capital of the Northwest, Port Townsend in fall and winter is a town full of ghosts. When morning fog off Puget Sound blankets the ornate brick and sandstone facades along Water Street and draws a gauzy veil over the improbable hilltop turret of the Jefferson County Courthouse, the town seems to evoke a past that might have been.

Back in 1890 Port Townsend dubbed itself "the inevitable New York." Larger and busier than emerging Seattle, Port Townsend counted more ship arrivals than any harbor outside of New York. Three transcontinental railroads (Northern Pacific, Great Northern, and Union Pacific) were promising to make this their western terminus. Substantial commercial buildings and lavish mansions were popping up almost daily. Local boosters were heard to say, "We're as big as New York, only the town ain't finished yet."

Port Townsend never was finished.

The railroads never arrived. The boom went bust, and 2,000 souls were left to rattle around in a town built for ten times that many.

Fortunately, the developers never arrived either and there was no incentive to tear down the old and replace it with the new. What's left is the legacy of a museum town.

Fall, winter, and spring mornings in Port Townsend are a delight. If the dawn is not rainy, the morning is likely to be crisp and crystal clear, affording a view of snow-capped Mount Baker and the Cascades framing the waters of Puget Sound to the east. Morning here is also a good time for photographers, with the pale slanty rays of sunlight throwing the rugged old buildings along Water Street into bold relief, etching every crack and cranny.

If the fog is down tight on the town, damp sidewalks seem to echo the toots, whistles, and the mournful moans of foghorns warning vessels offshore. An early arriving ferry from Whidbey Island breaks the silence with the *thump-clank* of cars driving off its ramp. Several small downtown cafés are filled with locals deep in discussions of local politics, the fishing season, or the economy.

Port Townsend sightseeing is on two levels. At water level is the downtown business district, a compact half a dozen blocks long and two blocks wide and easy to explore on foot. The main thoroughfare is Water Street. Local guides lead walking tours that depart from the historical museum at Water and Madison streets several times daily. On weekends horse-drawn carriages provide tours of downtown and the hilltop residential area. In addition to the usual souvenir and knickknack shops, Port Townsend has several excellent galleries selling everything from intricate ship models, metal sculpture, and custom jewelry to designer pottery, fine art photography, and the paintings of local artists.

Quite remarkably, the town has at least seven bookstores, all of which invite browsing. Local selections are quite wide-ranging, from volumes on Northwest mushroom collecting to an excellent history of Fort Worden, *Keepers at the Gate* by V. J. Gregory. You'll also find several excellent guides to local hiking, nature walking, and beachcombing.

Residential Port Townsend, known as "Uptown," is perched on a hill (really a bluff) immediately west of downtown. Its focal point is the red-brick Jefferson County Courthouse, an exuberant version of a medieval château designed by

W. A. Ritchie and built in 1892. It stands on Walker Street (two blocks west of Water), between Jefferson and Cass, and is such a prominent landmark you can use it to get your bearings from nearly any place in town. Scattered over a dozen surrounding blocks, Port Townsend's Victorian homes range in style from Queen Anne and Italianate to Renaissance, Romanesque, and gingerbread Gothic. The Rothschild House at Franklin and Taylor streets and the Commanding Officer's House at Fort Worden welcome visitors and have scheduled daily tours (see "Sightseeing"). You can pick up brochures identifying historic structures at the Fort Worden office and the Chamber of Commerce.

There are more than a dozen bed-and-breakfast inns in Port Townsend, some located in the best of the Victorians. Much-photographed Starrett House, on the corner of Clay and Adams streets, built by a leading lumber mill owner, is dominated by a distinctive octagonal tower and features ceiling frescoes over a spiral staircase. Massive Manressa Castle, at Sheridan and 7th streets, reflects the Prussian heritage of its builder, Port Townsend's first mayor. Downtown on Water Street, the Palace Hotel, a former bordello, is a restored 1889 building with Victorian furnishings.

Area Code: 206

DRIVING DIRECTIONS To reach Port Townsend from Seattle take the Winslow ferry (from Pier 52), follow Washington 305 across Bainbridge Island and Washington 3 north from Poulsbo, or take the Kingston ferry (from Edmonds) and follow Washington 104 westbound. In either case, cross the Hood Canal floating bridge and follow Highways 104, U.S. 101, and 20 west and north. Approximate round-trip mileage from Seattle is 102, plus 2 ferry crossings.

SIGHTSEEING *Jefferson County Historical Society Museum,* 210 Madison Street, 385-1003. Hours: Monday to Saturday 11 A.M. to 4 P.M., Sunday 1 to 4 P.M. Donation. *Rothschild House,* Jefferson and Taylor streets, 385-2722. Hours: Open daily April to October, 10 A.M. to 5 P.M. Weekends rest of year 11 A.M. to 4 P.M. $1. *Fort Worden State Park.* North end of Redwood Street, 385-4730. Hours: Daily 6:30 A.M. to dusk. Free. Includes *Coast Artillery Museum* (May to November Saturday and Sunday 1 to 5 P.M. $1), *Marine Science Center* (interpretive exhibits, walks, workshops; 385-5582 for schedule), and *Commanding Officer's House* (April to October daily 10 A.M. to 5 P.M. $2). *Guided Historical Sidewalk Tours,* 385-1967. 1-hour, 8-block walking tour departs from museum (Water and Madison streets). Hours: Daily 10 A.M. and 2 P.M. Daily May through October. Tours on request rest of year. Adults $4, seniors $3.50, children $2, families $10. *Coast to Coast,* 1102 Water Street, 385-5900. Rents bicycles for touring, $3/hour, $15/day. *Sport Townsend,* 215 Taylor, 385-6470. Rents bicycles for $5/hour, $20/day. *Calm Sea*

Charters, Point Hudson Marina, 385-5288. Has sunset cruises. Operates May to September. Adults $7.50, children $5.50. Fishing charters year-round, 6 hours $55. All-day cruise to San Juan Island from May through September. Adults $22.50, children $18.50. *Port Townsend Bay Co.,* 1042 Water Street, 385-0667. Rents kayaks for exploring nearby waters. $35/day, $110/week. *Old Fort Townsend State Park,* 4 miles south off Highway 20, 385-4730. Commanding views of Admiralty Inlet and Port Townsend Bay from 150-foot cliff top, military history walk. Free. *Fort Flagler State Park,* 20 miles southeast on Marrowstone Island, 385-1259. Coastal defense fort features historical displays, marine views. Free.

EVENTS *Historic Homes Tours,* 385-2722, first weekend in May, third weekend in September. 10 A.M. to 5 P.M. Self-guided tour of privately owned Victorian homes, teahouse refreshments. Adults $10, children $5. *Rhododendron Festival,* 385-2722, third week in May. Week-long event features parades, antiques, art and flower shows, carnival, and fine displays of native rhododendrons in bloom along area roads. Most events are free. *Centrum Foundation,* P.O. Box 1158, Port Townsend 98368, 385-3102. Hosts 8 major cultural events from May through August including a writer's conference, theater, jazz festival, fiddlers' festival, dance workshops, and others. Off-season events include a chamber music festival in January and a hot jazz festival in February. *Olympic Music Festival,* 527-8839. The Philadelphia String Quartet performs 9 weekends of chamber music in a barn near Quilcene from late June through mid-August. *Wooden Boat Festival,* 385-3628, first weekend in September. Lectures and demonstrations on the anachronistic art of wooden boat building.

LODGING Port Townsend has 13 Victorian bed-and-breakfast inns and at least two dozen Victorian hotels, conventional motels, apartments, and historic lodgings. For a complete list contact the Chamber of Commerce (see "For More Information"). *Fort Worden State Park,* P.O. Box 574, 385-4730. Accommodations in 24 former officer's quarters beside parade ground; fireplaces, kitchens, good choice for families or large groups; $$. *Starrett House* (bed and breakfast), 744 Clay Street, 385-3205. Classic turreted Victorian is most photographed home in Port Townsend, spiral staircase, ceiling frescoes, lavish breakfasts, $$ CP. *Palace Hotel,* 1004 Water Street, 385-0773, (800) 962-0741. Former bordello, downtown location, antique furnishings, $$. *Manresa Castle,* Seventh and Sheridan streets, 385-5750. Imposing 1892 mansion perched on hill south of town, 39 rooms, $$. *Tides Inn,* 1807 Water Street, 385-0595. Locally famous as the location of the steamy Debra Winger–Richard Gere bedroom scene in *An Officer and a Gentleman,* waterside location. *The Resort at Port Ludlow,* 9483 Oak Bay Road, Port Ludlow, 437-2222. Full-service waterside resort features condominium-style rooms, fireplaces, marina, 7 tennis courts, hiking and cycling trails, restaurant (see "Dining"), and lounge. Its golf course is rated among the toughest in the Northwest; *Esquire* magazine ranked it in the company of Scotland's Saint Andrews and California's Pebble Beach; $$$–$$$$.

CAMPING *Fort Worden State Park* (see "Lodging"). 50 full-hookup waterfront sites, $12. *Old Fort Townsend State Park* (see "Sightseeing"). 40 wooded sites, no hookups, $8. *Port Ludlow RV Park,* 60A Paradise Bay Road, 437-9110. 40 full-hookup sites adjacent to resort (see "Lodging"), $12.50, $75/week.

DINING *Salal Cafe,* 634 Water Street, 385-6532. Breakfast daily, lunch Monday to Saturday, dinner Friday to Saturday; probably the best spot in town for breakfast, memorable omelets, rub elbows with the locals; $. *The Landfall,* 412 Water Street, 385-5814. Breakfast and lunch daily, dinner Wednesday to Sunday; waterside location; burgers, seafood, fish and chips; $. *Fountain Cafe,* 920 Washington Street, 385-1364. Small, funky place; lunch and dinner daily; known for its oysters and pasta-and-shellfish dishes; $$. *Harbormaster,* Resort at Port Ludlow (see "Lodging"). Breakfast, lunch, and dinner daily; upscale dining overlooking the water; $$$.

FOR MORE INFORMATION Chamber of Commerce, 2437 Sims Way, Port Townsend, WA 98368, 385-2722.

The Olympic Peninsula:
The Northwest Corner

There is a mystique about the Olympic Peninsula that manages to sum up all of the romanticized views of the Pacific Northwest. Sticking up like a giant thumb between the Pacific Ocean and Puget Sound, the peninsula is a place of misty mountains, dripping rain forests, wild ocean beaches, and more roadless backcountry than just about anyplace else in the United States outside Alaska.

Olympic National Park—some 1,420 square miles—occupies most of the peninsula. No roads cross it and just one highway, U.S. 101, skirts its perimeter.

Seeing the entire Olympic Peninsula (it's larger than the entire state of Rhode Island!) in just a single two-day weekend would call for a driving marathon that would leave you little time to do anything else. We recommend you schedule at least three days for two separate itineraries. (We cover the peninsula in two separate sections: this one assumes you will travel as far as Port Angeles with a side trip to Neah Bay; the following one takes you from Port Angeles around the remainder of the peninsula to the rain forest and wilderness beaches.) If your budget will allow, consider flying to Port Angeles, the peninsula's principal town, and renting a car.

Follow the driving directions to Port Townsend (page 24), continuing on U.S. 101 to Port Angeles. First-class accommodations are almost nonexistent west of Port Angeles, so plan to make your overnight stay there, or at Lake Crescent or Sol Duc Hot Springs.

Port Angeles is a brawny, rain-washed town with its face to the Strait of Juan de Fuca and its back to the Olympic Mountains. Big oceangoing freighters anchor just offshore waiting to take on loads of logs for Japan, and on weekdays, trucks heavily laden with logs rumble through Port Angeles streets.

On your first day, stop at Olympic National Park headquarters (follow Race Street south off U.S. 101) to pick up literature on the park, watch the audiovisual presentation explaining the unusual geography and ecology of the park, and inquire about current conditions of roads and trails.

Then head south for the 17-mile drive to Hurricane Ridge. The two-lane road climbs about 5,000 feet and provides dramatic views of the strait and Vancouver Island to the north. On some days clouds clinging to these mountains will make for a foggy drive nearly to the top, when you suddenly break out into brilliant sunshine and look down on the cottony tops of the clouds.

The views from Hurricane Ridge are absolutely stunning. You look into the rugged heart of the park, to glacier-clad Mount Carrie (6,995 feet) and Mount Olympus (7,965 feet). Far below, the lush, green-carpeted valley of the Elwha River slices into the mountains. Park naturalists schedule interpretive programs in the summer.

Although snow often lingers at Hurricane Ridge until late May, during the winter months only are there ranger-led snowshoe hikes and downhill and cross-country skiing. Skis can be rented at the Hurricane Ridge Lodge, which also serves light meals. When spring finally comes, in late June or early July, splendid displays of high-altitude wildflowers carpet the surrounding alpine meadows. Park rangers can suggest any of several easy day hikes from here; a 1½-mile nature trail climbs 500 feet to 5,757-foot Hurricane Hill.

Returning to Port Angeles, you can spend the remainder of the day poking about town. The Feiro Marine Laboratory, on the city pier at the foot of Lincoln Street, displays local marine specimens in open tanks and you can reach in and touch them. The two handsome bronze cormorants next to the building were created by local artist Duncan Yves McKiernan. He is also the director of the Port Angeles Fine Art Center, a small but excellent gallery featuring other local artists. Immediately north of downtown, drive out on Ediz Hook, a mile-long natural sand spit that protects the harbor. At the end of the spit there's a Coast

Guard air station (for rescue work) and a pilot station used by the Puget Sound pilots assigned to each ship coming in through the strait. Neither is open to the public, but you can observe from the roadway.

Charter boats from Port Angeles, and the ports of Sekiu and Neah Bay to the west, offer some of the best salmon fishing in the Northwest in the Strait of Juan de Fuca. The season runs from late May through October, with the big—some in the 60-pound range—Chinook running first, followed by the smaller, but feisty, Coho beginning in about mid-August. An eight-hour fishing trip typically costs about $75 per person and includes license, tackle, and bait; you're expected to tip the bait boy for cleaning your catch. Depending on the tide, charter boats often leave the dock before dawn to be on the fishing grounds by first light. You can usually depend on an early afternoon return if it's important to schedule the rest of your trip activities. A list of charter operators is available from the Chamber of Commerce.

West of Port Angeles, U.S. 101 crosses over a low divide, then descends to hug the southern shore of Lake Crescent. Steep, evergreen-clad mountains, their summits often hidden in clouds, plunge almost straight down into deep, still waters giving the lake the brooding beauty of a Scottish loch. Venerable Lake Crescent Lodge has been a fixture on the lakeshore since 1915 and makes a good stop for lunch or dinner even if you aren't staying there. President Franklin D. Roosevelt and his party stayed here on September 30 and October 1, 1937, a year prior to the passage of the bill creating Olympic National Park. Henry Ford, Frank Sinatra, and the late Supreme Court Justice William O. Douglas also once bedded down at the lodge.

Two one-of-a-kind trout inhabit the lake. The theory is that the Beardslee and Crescenti trout evolved as unique varieties when ancient landslides closed their migration route to the sea, trapping them in the lake. You can fish for them from a boat rented at the lodge for $5.39 an hour or $8.62 for a half-day). Hiking trails lead to the top of nearby Storm King Mountain and along the Elwha River; a ¾-mile hike from the lodge will take you over a signed nature trail to 90-foot Marymere Falls.

If you have the time, consider two additional detours. The Elwha River Road detours south from U.S. 101 nine miles west of Port Angeles. For several miles you thread your way through dense evergreen forest to emerge at Lake Mills and the end of the road. The Elwha is legendary among fly anglers and at least one company schedules raft trips down the river (see "Sightseeing").

At Fairholm, at the west end of Lake Crescent, a paved road detours south up the valley of the Sol Duc River to Sol Duc Hot Springs, a historic spa recently refurbished. You can soak in any of several hot (90 to 106 degrees Fahrenheit) mineral pools or rent a four-person private indoor hot tub fed by the springs.

Save the greater part of a day for the trip to Neah Bay and the Makah Indian

Reservation, 70 miles west of Port Angeles over Washington 112. You wind through dense forest and hug the shoreline of the Strait of Juan de Fuca for most of the way, skirting small coves and beaches ideal for a bit of beachcombing or a picnic.

The crown jewel of Neah Bay is the splendid Makah Museum. A large cedar building with a vaulted ceiling, the museum traces the history of the "People of the Cape" who have lived here more than 2,000 years. You'll see many of the nearby artifacts recovered from the archaeological excavations at the Ozette site, including a group of 500-year-old homes that had been perfectly preserved in an ancient mudslide.

From Neah Bay, good gravel roads lead to several hiking trails (pick up a brochure at the museum), and an 18-mile loop leads around Cape Flattery, northwesternmost point in the contiguous United States.

Area Code: 206

DRIVING DIRECTIONS From Seattle follow directions to Port Townsend (see page 24), but continue on U.S. 101 to Port Angeles from the junction with Washington 20 instead of detouring to Port Townsend. Round trip to Port Angeles is approximately 154 miles, plus 2 ferry crossings.

AIR TRANSPORTATION *Horizon Air* has frequent propeller airplane service from Seattle's Sea-Tac Airport to Port Angeles. Round-trip fares from $108.

FERRY M. V. *Coho* departs Port Angeles for Victoria 4 times daily in summer, twice daily other seasons; crossing takes 1½ hours. Car and driver $24, passengers $6, children 5–11 $3. Schedules and information: Black Ball Transport, 106 Surrey Building, Bellevue, WA 98004, 622-2222; in Port Angeles, 457-4491. *Victoria Rapid Transit* operates a passengers-only ferry between Port Angeles and Victoria in spring, summer, and fall. Crossing takes 1 hour. Round-trip fare is $20, children 5–11 $10. Schedules and information: P.O. Box 1928, Port Angeles, WA 98362, 452-8088 or (800) 633-1589.

SIGHTSEEING *Olympic National Park Entry Permit,* $3 per vehicle for 7 days mid-May to September, free other months. *Pioneer Memorial Museum and National Park Visitor Center,* 3002 Mount Angeles Road, 452-0330. Hours: July through Labor Day daily 8:30 A.M. to 6 P.M., rest of year daily 9 A.M. to 4 P.M. Free. *Hurricane Ridge Lodge,* 452-9235. July through Labor Day, naturalist programs daily; December to April, Saturday and Sunday only. Winter facilities include 2 rope tows, poma lift, cross-country ski trails, snowshoe programs, rentals. *Olympic Raft and Guide Service,* 464 U.S. 101 West, 457-7011. Offers 2½-hour guided raft trips on the Elwha River. Adults $25, children 14 and under $15. *Sol Duc Hot Springs*, 327-3583. Hours: Mid-May through Labor Day daily 8 A.M. to 9 P.M., through mid-October 9 A.M. to 7 P.M. Pool admission $3, private hot tub $3.25 per person per half-hour. *Arthur D. Feiro Marine Laboratory*, city pier foot of Lincoln Street, 452-9277. Hours: Mid-June through Labor Day daily 10 A.M. to 8 P.M., rest of year Saturday and Sunday noon to 4 P.M. Adults $1, children 50 cents. *Port Angeles Fine Art Center*, 1203 East 8th Street, 457-3532. Hours: Thursday to Saturday 11 A.M. to 5 P.M. Free. *Clallam County Historical Society Museum*, East Fourth and Lincoln streets, 542-7831. Hours: June through August Monday to Saturday 10 A.M. to 4 P.M., rest of year Monday to Friday. Free. *Makah Museum*, Neah Bay, 645-2711. Hours: Memorial Day through Labor Day daily 10 A.M. to 5 P.M., rest of year closed Monday and Tuesday. Adults $3; seniors, military, students $2.

LODGING *Red Lion Bayshore Inn*, 221 North Lincoln Street, 452-9215. Waterfront location, $$. *The Tudor Inn* (bed and breakfast), 1108 South Oak Street, 452-3138. Named for the architectural style of this handsome 1910 home; fine views of strait and Olympics; $$. *Lake Crescent Lodge*, HC 62, Box 11, Port Angeles, 928-3211. Closed mid-November to April, $. *Log Cabin Resort*, 6540 East Beach Road, 928-3325. Rustic resort on north shore of Lake Crescent, $$. *Sol Duc Hot Springs Resort*, P.O. Box 2169, Port Angeles, 327-3583. Open mid-May to mid-October; refurbished 1910 family resort, 32 cabins, some with kitchens; $$.

CAMPING *Olympic National Park* campsites are without hookups, trailers limited to 21 feet, fee $5. They are: *Heart of the Hills*, 5.4 miles south of Port Angeles on Race Street, 452-2713. 105 sites. *Elwha*, 9 miles west of Port Angeles, 3 miles on Elwha River Road, 452-9191. 23 sites. *Altaire*, 4 miles on Elwha Road, 452-9191. 23 sites. *Fairholm*, west end of Lake Crescent. 90 sites. *Sol Duc*, 12 miles south on Sol Duc Road, 327-3534. 80 sites. Private campgrounds include *Al's RV Park*, east end of Port Angeles on Lee's Creek Road, 457-9844. 31 sites with full hookups, adults only, $12. *KOA Port Angeles/Sequim*, O'Brien Road, 5½ miles east of Port Angeles off U.S. 101, 457-5916. 90 sites, 18 full hookups, 55 water-electricity, $12 to $17. *Log Cabin Resort* (see "Lodging"). 40 full hookups, $10.

DINING *C'est Si Bon*, 2300 U.S. 101 East, 452-8888. Dinner Tuesday to Sunday; in an area of the Northwest not noted for its fine cuisine, locals drive dozens of miles to dine on the excellent French cooking at this restaurant; $$$. *The Greenery*, 117-B East First Street, 457-4112. Lunch and dinner daily, closed Sunday in winter; homemade soups, salads, and entrées using local seafood; $$. *It's All Greek to Me*, 1506 East First Street, 452-5964. Lunch and dinner daily, Greek fast food, $. *First Street Haven*, 107 East First Street, 457-0352. Breakfast and lunch

Monday to Saturday, Sunday brunch; menu features soups, salads, and sandwiches; $.

FOR MORE INFORMATION Superintendent, Olympic National Park, 600 East Park Avenue, Port Angeles 98362, 452-4501. North Olympic Peninsula Tourism Information, P.O. Box 670, Port Angeles 98362, (800) 942-4042. Port Angeles Chamber of Commerce, 1217 East First Street, Port Angeles 98362, 452-2362. Ask for the free directory and map published by the Olympic Peninsula Travel Association.

The Olympic Rain Forest and Wilderness Coast

The west side of the Olympic Peninsula is one of the most wildly beautiful sections of country in the United States. More than 100 inches of rain a year nurture a primeval forest of giants—firs, hemlocks, cedars, spruces. Here and there stub roads penetrate the river valleys to a dead end where the mountains begin. The coast is as rugged as it gets—massive headlands, rocky promontories, and offshore sea stacks (huge rock formations) pounded by huge waves, interspersed by empty beaches where only the tracks of animals break the smooth sand. For more than 50 miles no roads even come near this coast, a favorite destination for backpackers who brave the rain and wind to savor the solitude.

Heading west from Port Angeles on U.S. 101 can be an emotional experience. Beyond Lake Crescent you share the road with aggressive loggers' trucks and transit mile after mile of logging clearcuts where every single tree has been cut down and piles of shorn branches and other debris mar the landscape. You'll see for yourself what the controversy between conservationists and loggers is all about. Tracts of utter devastation alternate with patches of pristine green forest, a graphic comparison of what was and what is.

It's 62 miles from Port Angeles to Forks, the only real town on this side of the peninsula. A logging community, it has a timber museum displaying tools, equipment, artifacts used in the industry, and historical photos. Adjacent to the museum is a ¼-mile nature trail. With a population of less than 3,000, Forks is commercial headquarters for the surrounding countryside. It's a good place to schedule a lunch stop. Better check your gas gauge here, too; service stations are scarce for the next 60 miles or so.

About a mile north of Forks, a two-lane paved road leads west to La Push, an Indian village on the Quillayute Reservation and the only place where you can reach this part of the coast by car. Six miles before you reach La Push, a branch of the road leads off north a couple of miles to Mora campground and Rialto Beach, center of national park activities on the park's coastal strip. Three wild and rocky beaches, appropriately named First, Second, and Third Beach, are easily accessible from La Push. First Beach starts at the town itself; you can reach the other two by easy trails. These beaches are suitable for stimulating hikes, but the water is much too cold and rough for swimming. Get maps and directions from the park ranger at Mora.

There are several rain forest corridors along the westward-flowing Bogachiel, Hoh, and Queets rivers, but the most accessible and most developed, in terms of visitor facilities, is the Hoh Rain Forest. Drive 13 miles south on U.S. 101 from Forks to the Hoh River Road, then 19 miles east to the visitor center.

Discard the tried-and-true wisdom that says the best time to travel is in fair weather. The best time to visit a rain forest is when it's raining. Scheduling a visit to the Hoh shouldn't be too difficult, since it rains here most days from October through June.

The light filtering through the trees is actually green. Your feet squish into the thick carpet of moss underfoot. Except for the chatter of a few birds, the sounds you hear are rainy. *Drip, drip.* A sudden staccato of drops as they fall from an overloaded bough. The chuckly sound of a streamlet making its way around massive fallen logs.

The place is magnificent. Huge 600-year-old Sitka spruce trees tower 200 feet or more and dwarf even the flanking Douglas firs and western hemlocks. Great hunks of club moss trail off the overhanging branches, giving the illusion of a huge green cathedral draped with spiderwebs.

This is the only wholly coniferous rain forest in the contiguous United States. An average of 142 inches of rainfall a year (Seattle averages 34 inches) creates a rich soup on which plants thrive and in which, on dying, they quickly decompose to feed new life.

There's not a square inch of bare soil anywhere. Ferns, huckleberry bushes, moss, oxalis, and a hundred other species compete for space. There are animals, too, and if you're lucky you may spot some. The largest remaining herds of Roosevelt elk are here, and deer, otter, muskrat, and raccoon are fairly common.

Three signed nature trails lead from the visitor center. The ¾-mile Hall of Mosses Trail takes about an hour to explore adequately, and the 1¼-mile Spruce Trail takes about 1½ hours. A ¼-mile mini-trail is ideal for visitors in wheelchairs or who are otherwise infirm.

From the junction of the Hoh River Road and U.S. 101, it's just about a toss-up which route back to Seattle is quicker. Retrace your steps via Port Angeles and it's about 151 miles; continue south via Aberdeen and it's about 178 miles.

About 13 miles south, U.S. 101 swings west and hugs the cliff tops above the surf for a dozen or so miles. Ruby Beach offers good hiking trails, a fine beach, picnic tables, and splendid views of the rugged coastline. If you want to spend a night communing with wind and sea, Kalaloch is the place. The lodge here offers individual cabins perched atop the cliff and featuring fireplaces.

The next stop on this loop is Quinault, where you can overnight at the venerable, rustic Lake Quinault Lodge. There is also a network of hiking trails here, and regular interpretive programs are offered at the national park visitor center.

Return to Seattle via Aberdeen (see page 36) and Olympia.

Area Code: 206

DRIVING DIRECTIONS From Port Angeles (see page 29) continue around the Olympic Peninsula on U.S. 101. Circling the Olympic Peninsula from Seattle on the route described in these 2 sections is approximately 329 miles.

SIGHTSEEING *Olympic National Park.* Entry fee $3 per vehicle mid-May through September, free rest of year. *Mora Ranger Station.* Beach, tide pool, and forest walks daily in summer, weekends rest of year. *Hoh Visitor Center.* Summer months daily 7 A.M. to 7 P.M., weekends rest of year. Guided rain forest walks. *Kalaloch.* Summer months, tide pool and beach walks. *Quinault Ranger Station.* Summer 9 A.M. to 5 P.M., weekends rest of year. *Forks Timber Museum.* Highway 101 south, across from airport, 374-9663. Hours: Tuesday to Saturday 10 A.M. to 6 P.M., Sunday 1 to 5 P.M. Free.

LODGING *La Push Ocean Park Resort,* P.O. Box 67, 374-5267. Ocean view, fireplaces, $$. *Miller Tree Inn* (bed and breakfast), P.O. Box 953, 374-6806. $. *Manitou Lodge* (bed and breakfast), P.O. Box 600, 374-6295. Secluded log lodge in woods, $. *Forks Motel,* Route 1, Box 1500, 374-6243. $. *Kalaloch Lodge,* HC-80, Box 1100, Forks 98331, 962-2271. Very popular in summer and on winter weekends; make reservations well in advance; $$. *Lake Quinault Lodge,* P.O. Box 7, Quinault 98575, 288-2571. $$–$$$.

CAMPING *Olympic National Park* campsites are without hookups, trailers limited to 21 feet, fee $5. They are: *Hoh,* at Hoh Rainforest Visitor Center, 374-6925, 89 sites; *Kalaloch,* 962-2283, 179 sites; *Mora,* 374-5460, 94 sites. *Bogachiel State Park,* 6 miles south of Forks on U.S. 101, 374-6356. 41 sites, no hookups, May to September, $7. *Hoh River Resort & RV Park,* 15 miles south of Forks on U.S. 101, 374-5566. 31 sites, 25 full hookups, 6 water-electricity, $11.

DINING *Smokehouse Restaurant,* La Push Road and U.S. 101, 374-6258. Lunch and dinner, $. *Kalaloch Lodge* (see "Lodging"). Breakfast, lunch, and dinner; $$.

Quinault Lodge (see "Lodging"). Breakfast, lunch, and dinner; $$–$$$. Both Kalaloch and Quinault offer traditional dining with emphasis on seafood.

FOR MORE INFORMATION Superintendent, Olympic National Park, 600 East Park Avenue, Port Angeles 98362, 452-4501.

Grays Harbor: Salmon, Whales, and Beaches

Look at a map of southwest Washington and you'll find Grays Harbor, one of the Northwest's major deep-water ports and the closest ocean resort area to Seattle. Two long spits of land, one from the north, the other from the south, nearly enclose the harbor mouth and offer very different coastal experiences. Ocean Shores is located on the north spit, Westport on the south spit, and the twin cities of Aberdeen and Hoquiam are at the apex where highways divide.

Ocean Shores is a resort town. Condominiums and motels face surf-pounded beaches that stretch for miles in either direction and are so flat and firmly packed that vacationers drive on portions of them. Low dunes back of the beach give way to flat sandy woodlands and inland marshes.

You can drive to Ocean Shores in under three hours via Olympia and Aberdeen. The variety of accommodations and restaurants at the beach, plus those along Route 109 to the north, makes this a good choice for a weekend base to explore the area. The beach is ideal for kite flying. You can rent mopeds or bicycles for exploring, and if you visit during one of the very low tides of spring, you'll want to join the thousands who come to dig clams.

Depending on the season, schedule one day of your weekend for salmon fishing or whale watching. Salmon usually run from early June through October; the northbound whale migration takes place from late February to May.

The town of Westport, on the south side of Grays Harbor, is totally devoted to sport and commercial fishing and whale watching. You can reach Westport from Ocean Shores in about an hour (46 miles) by driving around the harbor through Aberdeen. A passenger ferry operates between the two cities daily from June through August and on weekends only in May and September.

Dozens of charter boats operate from the Westport marina; motels, restaurants, and other visitor facilities are geared to the angler. Motels and restaurants, for instance, understand that guests will be checking out before dawn and will need a hearty breakfast, as they are open and ready to serve in the wee hours of the morning. A place on a sportfishing charter typically costs between $65 and $85 and includes tackle, bait, and a tip for the bait boy for cleaning your fish. You supply your own lunch, but most of the restaurants and cafés in Westport will make up a box lunch for you and fill your Thermos with coffee. When the salmon season is closed, many of these same charter boats will take you out for tuna or bottom fishing for halibut, cod, or flounder.

Whale watching can be an inspiring experience. The California gray whales that cruise just off the coast range up to 45 feet in length and weigh up to 45 tons. They're gentle creatures and will sometimes come up and nuzzle your charter boat so closely you can reach down and touch their sandpaperlike hide. During the spring the sea can be rough owing to high swells and rainy and windy weather; plan to wear warm, weatherproof clothing and bring binoculars and a camera with a telephoto lens. Whale watching trips start at 10 A.M. or later and cost about $25. Some area motels sell packages that include lodging and the trip for a single price. On weekends, marine biologists give whale seminars at the Westport Museum Meeting Hall.

Another awesome natural spectacle that takes place the same time as the whale migration is the return of shorebirds to Bowerman Basin, just west of Hoquiam off Route 109. Between mid-April and the first week in May, hundreds of thousands of shorebirds descend to feed on 500 acres of tide flats here. The best viewing (bring binoculars) is about an hour before high tide, and tide tables are available at almost every grocery store and gas station in this area. The Seattle and Tahoma Audubon societies schedule field trips. For information, phone 523-4483 or 759-0997.

Grays Harbor is named for Captain Robert Gray, an American fur-trading skipper who discovered the Columbia River and the harbor while exploring this Pacific Northwest coast in 1787 through 1790. His voyages and discoveries were the basis for the American claim to the Oregon country, including Washington. As a state centennial project in 1989, Washington shipwrights built a replica of Gray's ship, *Lady Washington,* at a shipyard in Aberdeen. You can view the ship and ride on it at Grays Harbor Historical Seaport.

If you have the time, drive the 27 miles of Route 109 north along the coast from Ocean Shores to road's end at the Quinault River. You pass through small oceanfront towns—Ocean City, Copalis Beach, Pacific Beach, Moclips—where weather-beaten buildings seem to huddle against the ubiquitous storms and wind-sculptured evergreens have the quality of Japanese bonsai. These are terrific beaches for solitary walking and beachcombing, and stunning seascapes are visible from roadside. The highway ends on the Quinault Indian Reservation. The beaches here are closed to the public but you may see Indian fishermen putting out to sea in their traditional long, slender dugout canoes.

Area Code: 206

DRIVING DIRECTIONS From Seattle follow I-5 south to Olympia, then U.S. 101, Washington 8, and U.S. 12 west to Aberdeen. Here you have a choice of following Washington 109 and 115 along the north side of the harbor to Ocean Shores or Washington 105 around the south end to Westport. Approximate mileage round-trip from Seattle to Ocean Shores is 212.

SIGHTSEEING _Hoquiam's Castle,_ 515 Chenault Avenue, 533-2005. 20-room Victorian mansion. Hours: Mid-June through Labor Day daily 11 A.M. to 5 P.M., rest of year Saturday and Sunday. Adults $3, seniors $2, children 6–15 $1. _Grays Harbor Historical Seaport,_ 813 Heron Street, Aberdeen, 532-8611. Hours: Monday to Saturday 8 A.M. to 5 P.M., Sunday noon to 5 P.M. Adults $1, children 50 cents. _Polson Park and Museum,_ 1611 Riverside Avenue, Hoquiam, 533-5862. Hours: Mid-June to mid-September Wednesday to Sunday 11 A.M. to 4 P.M., rest of year Saturday and Sunday noon to 4 P.M. 26-room mansion and logging museum. Donation. _Aberdeen Museum of History,_ 111 East 3rd Street, 533-1976. Hours: June to mid-September Wednesday to Sunday 11 A.M. to 4 P.M., rest of year Saturday and Sunday noon to 4 P.M. Donation. _Historical Maritime Museum,_ 2201 Westhaven Drive, Westport, 268-9692. Hours: June to September Wednesday to Sunday noon to 5 P.M.; April and May weekends noon to 4 P.M. $1. _Westport Aquarium,_ 321 Harbor Street, 268-0471. Hours: April to December daily 9 A.M. to 5 P.M. Adults $2.

CHARTERS Prices and services vary. Check when you call for reservations. Toll-free numbers are usually good only in-state and operate only during the fishing season. _Westport_ (800) 562-0157; _Ocean_ (800) 562-0105, 268-9144; _Gull_ (800) 562-0175, 268-9186; _Neptune_ (800) 422-0425, 268-0124; _Deep Sea_ (800) 562-0151; _Cachalot_ 268-0323; _Sea Horse_ (800) 562-0171, 268-9100; _Islander_ (800) 562-0147, 268-9166; _Salmon_ (800) 562-0145, 268-9150; _Travis_ 268-9140.

EVENTS _Blessing of the Fleet,_ Westport, (800) 345-6223, last week in May. Memorial service for those lost at sea, Coast Guard air-sea rescue demonstrations. _Saltwater Festival,_ Westport, (800) 345-6223, late June. Parade, fireworks, kite-flying contests. _Sand Sculpture Contest,_ Ocean Shores, 289-2451, July. _Slug Festival, Grays Harbor County Fair,_ Elma, 482-2651, mid-August. _Logger's Playday,_ Hoquiam, 532-0905, second weekend in September. Contests and demonstrations of traditional logging skills.

LODGING _Gray Gull,_ P.O. Box 1417, Ocean Shores, 289-3381. Multistory condominium on beach, $$$–$$$$. _The Polynesian,_ P.O. Box 998, Ocean Shores,

289-3361. Condo on beach, $$–$$$. *The Canterbury Inn,* P.O. Box 310, Ocean Shores, 289-3317. $$–$$$. *Iron Springs Resort,* P.O. Box 207, Copalis Beach, 276-4230. Beachside cabins with fireplaces, $$. *Sandpiper,* P.O. Box A, Pacific Beach, 276-4580. $$. *Ocean Crest Resort,* Moclips, 276-4465. $$. *Chateau Westport,* P.O. Box 349, Westport, 268-9101. $$. Overlooking ocean. *Glenacres Inn* (bed and breakfast), 222 North Montesano Street, Westport, 268-9391. $$. *Lytle House* (bed and breakfast), 509 Chenault Avenue, Hoquiam, 533-2320. $$–$$$. Turn-of-the-century home.

CAMPING State parks charge $8 per night, $12 with hookups. *Ocean City State Park,* Ocean Shores, 289-3553. 178 sites, 29 with hookups. *Pacific Beach State Park,* Pacific Beach. 138 sites, 20 with hookups. *Twin Harbors State Park,* Westport, 268-9565. 272 sites, 49 with hookups. *Ocean Park Resort,* Ocean Park, 665-4585. 100 sites with hookups, $11. *Islander RV Park,* Westport, 268-9166. 68 sites with hookups, $12.50. *Kila Hana Camperland,* Westport, 268-9528. 151 sites, $12.50.

DINING *Home Port,* Point Brown Avenue, Ocean Shores, 289-2600. Breakfast, lunch, and dinner daily; $. *Ocean Shores Inn,* Ocean Shores Boulevard, 289-2407. Breakfast, lunch, and dinner daily; $–$$. *Ocean Crest Resort,* Moclips (see "Lodging"); 3 meals daily, ocean view, $$. *Parma,* 116 West Heron Street, Aberdeen, 533-3166. Lunch Monday to Friday, dinner Monday to Saturday, northern Italian cuisine, $–$$. *Levee Street Restaurant,* 709 Levee Street, Hoquiam, 532-1959. Dinner Tuesday to Saturday, traditional and Northwest cuisine, specializing in fresh seafood, $–$$. *Arthur's,* 2681 Westhaven Drive, Westport, 268-9292. Lunch and dinner Tuesday to Sunday, $$. *Constantin's,* 320 East Dock Street, Westport, 268-0550. Dinner Wednesday to Monday, Greek cuisine, $$.

FOR MORE INFORMATION Ocean Shores Reservations and Convention Bureau, Ocean Shores 98569, (800) 562-8612. Gray Harbor Chamber of Commerce, 2704 Sumner Avenue, Aberdeen 98520, 532-1924. Westport–Grayland Chamber of Commerce, 1200 North Montesano Street, Westport 98595, 268-9422.

The Skagit Valley:
A Bloomin' Good Show

One of the most spectacular shows in the Northwest takes place in April in the Skagit Valley, an hour's drive north of Seattle. Field upon field of tulips, daffodils, irises, and lilies splash the rural landscapes with brilliant combinations of red, yellow, purple, orange, and white.

First to bloom are the daffodils, which are picked at the end of March and the beginning of April. Tulips follow, then irises and lilies, which last into late May. The Skagit Valley bulb industry is big business, with fields covering more than 1,500 acres. Although the flowers are shipped to markets all over the United States, they are grown for the bulbs, which are exported to Holland and other countries around the world.

Perhaps because it's the first big spring event after a typically rainy Northwest winter, the Skagit Valley bloom draws thousands of sightseers and requires a few well-thought-out strategies for maximum enjoyment. First, reservations for overnight accommodations are a must. Try to base yourself in La Conner, because it's the town with the most atmosphere, although Mount Vernon and Anacortes also have good accommodations. We advise you to try to make this trip midweek if possible since weekends at the height of the bloom draw the largest crowds and the narrow roads through the fields are packed with traffic. You might want to park your car in Anacortes or Mount Vernon and take a bus tour of the fields. Be sure to pick up a free Tulip Map from one of the information vans parked in the area (or write ahead to Box 1007, Mount Vernon 98273, and send $1). Plan to visit the fields before 11 A.M. or in late afternoon (when the light is best for taking photographs). There's only one restaurant in the fields so it's a good idea to bring a picnic lunch.

Bring binoculars to view the migratory birds coming north on the Pacific Flyway. If you're lucky—and patient—you may even see the marvelous snow geese and trumpeter swans that visit the Skagit Flats this time of year. Best viewing is at Skagit Wildlife Area, reached by turning south off Fir Island Road onto Mann Road.

Even if you're not a gardener, chances are you'll want to put a few bulbs in the ground at home after visiting these splendid fields. Several growers have display gardens where you can get ideas for your own garden and order bulbs for the fall planting season. The gardens are also a good place to buy cut flowers. They may or may not be cheaper than what you can get at home, but they are fresher and will last longer.

The bulb fields lie west of I-5 between Exits 221 (Fir Island Road) and 230 (Route 20). A network of roads running north-south and east-west crosses the flat farmland and borders the fields; you can see for miles and it's fairly easy to reach that choice spot you can see in the distance by intersecting roads.

Make your first stop La Conner Flats Display Garden at 1588 Best Road (Exit 226 and west on McLean Road to Best). Owners Bob and Margie Hart journeyed to Britain to research the English-style garden. Paths lead through 11 acres with separate areas for perennials, rhododendrons, vegetables, alpine plants, a cutting garden, an orchard, Jackson and Perkins roses, azaleas, and a sunken garden. Everything is labeled. Admission is $2.50, $2 for seniors.

You'll easily spot Roozengarde Display Garden and Retail Center (1587 Beaver March Road; Exit 226 from I-5) by the big windmill and beds of crocuses and tulips reminiscent of a Dutch landscape.

West Shore Acres Display Garden on Downey Road at Swinomish Channel (Exit 226 and west on McLean, which becomes Downey) specializes in daffodils. They've planted dozens of varieties around a lovely, old, white Victorian farmhouse. Bark paths meander past clumps of yellow daffodils and purple crocus border bright green lawns.

Spring is the most spectacular season, but anytime is a good time to explore this rich agricultural valley whose sights include a cheese factory where you can watch the cheese-making process and sample the final product, and produce stands selling local fruits and vegetables. Big old barns make wonderful backdrops for photographs, and on a clear day you can even get a shot of snow-capped Mount Baker on the horizon. One of the best vantage points for a panoramic photo of the valley is from the deck of the Skagit County Historical Museum in La Conner.

Picturesque little La Conner has been "discovered" by the trendy and is an increasingly popular getaway destination. Nestled beside Swinomish Channel with fine views of 10,778-foot Mount Baker and the Cascades, the little town has become a showcase for Northwest artists and is a nifty spot for browsing. It's worth a visit whether or not you stay overnight at one of the delightful bed-and-breakfast inns.

Be sure to visit the restored 1891 Gaches Mansion, which also houses the collections of the Valley Museum of Northwest Art. The Tillinghast Seed Company, in a white clapboard building on the north edge of town, is the oldest seed company (1885) in the Northwest. Both on the site and by mail order, they sell a huge collection of seeds for both common and unusual varieties of vegetables and flowers, some of which are grown in the Skagit Valley. Housed in a tiny 1884 building, Go Outside, at 111 Morris Street, has just about everything a gardener could want, from handsome wooden birdhouses (including a model with a patio and table and chairs) to boot scrapers.

You'll find some interesting shops on South First Street. If you like cats, or know someone who does, Cat Attic, at number 705, has cat-theme posters, paintings, figurines, teapots, you name it. The Wood Merchant, at 707, specializes in wooden craft items—cutting boards, pictures, bowls, and photograph albums. At number 713, Earthenworks Gallery specializes in American crafts such as Indian silver jewelry, local pottery, and hand-knit mohair hats and stoles. Janet Huston Gallery, 413 Morris Street, features the works of Northwest artists.

You get the picture. La Conner's main street is an easy stroll with literally dozens of shops like these.

For a different route on your return to Seattle, follow Washington 530 south through farmlands, past big dairy barns, along the saltwater shore, and through the woodlands of the Tulalip Indian Reservation. You rejoin I-5 at Marysville.

Area Code: 206

DRIVING DIRECTIONS To reach the Skagit Valley drive north from Seattle on I-5 to Exits 221, 226, and 230. Approximate distance round-trip from Seattle is 120 miles.

SIGHTSEEING *Bus tours of the Skagit bulb fields* (call for dates and reservations), Seattle departures: *Don/Diane Funtours,* 282-3508, $36; *Gray Line of Seattle,* 624-5813, $32. Local bus tours run from Mount Vernon, Sedro Woolley, and Anacortes, $3; contact Mount Vernon Chamber of Commerce, 428-8547, for dates, times, and reservations. *Washington Cheese Company,* 900 East College Way, Mount Vernon, 424-3520. Hours: Monday to Saturday 9 A.M. to 5:30 P.M. Free tour plus retail shop. *Gaches Mansion* (Valley Museum of Northwest Art), 602 South Second Street, La Conner, 466-4288. Hours: Friday to Sunday 1 to 4 P.M. $1. *Skagit County Historical Museum,* 501 South Fourth Street, La Conner, 466-3365. Hours: Wednesday to Sunday 1 to 5 P.M. $1, 5 to 12 50 cents. *Rainbow Rentals,* 329 North First Street, La Conner, 466-4054. Rents 12-foot outboard boats, $10 per hour, $50 per day, and bicycles, $3 per hour, $15 per day. *La Conner Boat Rentals,* 539 North Third Street, 466-3300. Rents a 16-foot fishing boat for $100 per day.

EVENTS *Skagit Valley Tulip Festival,* 428-8547, first week in April. 10 days of festivities in Mount Vernon, La Conner, and Anacortes including parades, flower tours, food fairs, boat show, salmon barbecue, concerts. For schedule of events write P.O. Box 1007, Mount Vernon 98273. From late March through the festival a 24-hour hot line provides the latest information on the bloom and festival events; call 976-INFO (50 cents per minute charged to your telephone bill). *Skagit County Fair,* Blackburn Road, Mount Vernon, 336-2332, second week in August. *Christmas Boat Parade,* 466-4778, second Saturday in December. Illuminated boats cruise Swinomish Channel.

LODGING Reserve rooms for the tulip festival well in advance; a year ahead is not too early for the popular B & Bs around La Conner. *Best Western Motor Inn,* 300 West College Way, Mount Vernon, 424-4287. $–$$. *Town and Country Motor Inn,* 2009 Riverside Drive, Mount Vernon, 424-4141. $. *White Swan Guest House* (bed and breakfast), 1388 Moore Road, Mount Vernon, 445-6805. 1898 Victorian farmhouse and separate cottage in countryside 6 miles outside La Conner, $$. *The Downey House* (bed and breakfast), 1880 Chilberg Road, La Conner, 466-3207. Farmhouse overlooking tulips, $$. *Hotel Planter,* 713 South First Street, La Conner, 466-4710. $$. *La Conner Country Inn,* 107 Second Street, 466-3101. $$. *The Heron,* 117 Maple Street, La Conner, 466-4626. $$–$$$. *Channel House* (bed and breakfast), 2902 Oakes Avenue, Anacortes, 293-9382. $$.

CAMPING *Bayview State Park,* 7 miles west of Burlington off Route 20, 757-0227. 90 sites, 9 with full hookups, $8 and $12. *Burlington–Cascade KOA,* Exit 232 and 3½ miles north on Old Highway 99N, 724-5511. 138 sites with hookups, $12.50. *The Potlatch,* 420 Pearl Jansen Road, La Conner, 466-4468. 68 sites with hookups, $14.88.

DINING *The Longfellow Cafe,* 120-B First Street, Mount Vernon, 336-3684. Lunch and dinner Tuesday to Saturday, $$. *Calico Cupboard,* 720 South First Street, La Conner, 466-4451. Breakfast and lunch daily, home-baked goods a specialty, $. *The Black Swan,* 505 South First Street, La Conner, 466-3040. Dinner Thursday to Tuesday, locally famous for its Northwest cuisine, $. *The Longhouse,* across slough on Swinomish Indian Reservation, cross via Rainbow Bridge or summer-only ferry, 466-4444. Lunch and dinner daily, Sunday brunch, $–$$$. *Barkley's of La Conner,* 205 Washington Street, 446-4261. Lunch daily except Sunday, dinner daily, Sunday brunch, $$. *La Petite,* 3401 Commercial Avenue, Anacortes, 293-4644. Breakfast daily, dinner Tuesday to Sunday, French and Dutch-style cuisine, $$.

FOR MORE INFORMATION Mount Vernon Chamber of Commerce, 325 East College Way, Mount Vernon 98273, 428-8547. La Conner Chamber of Commerce, P.O. Box 644, La Conner 98257, 466-4778. Anacortes Chamber of Commerce, 1319 Commercial Avenue, Anacortes 98221, 293-3832.

Whatcom County:
From Shoreline to Snowline

Driving north from Seattle on Interstate 5, you can pass through Bellingham and be well beyond almost before you realize it's there. The freeway threads its way through a narrow gap between steep conifer-clad hills, past the dark waters of Lake Samish. You then swing around a series of curves, each one revealing a cluster of gas stations, fast-food outlets, and motels, around a freeway exit that quickly disappears in your rearview mirror as you enter the next curve.

That's Bellingham from the freeway. It's often easier just to keep going than to select the right exit.

Take a closer look and you'll find that Bellingham and surrounding Whatcom County have plenty to offer for a rewarding weekend, including one of the state's best resorts, island cruising, historical sites, a spectacularly scenic mountain highway, and a steam excursion train.

Your best plan of action is to select a base and make excursions from there. The Inn at Semiahmoo, Washington's newest full-service resort, perches on a peninsula just to the west of Blaine, 19 miles north of Bellingham and within sight of the Canadian border. Constructed from the remains of a historic salmon cannery, the resort enjoys stunning views of the San Juan Islands and miles of beaches at the mouth of Drayton Harbor. Sudden Valley, a condominium-style resort on Lake Whatcom, six miles east of Bellingham, is another good choice. Both have 18-hole golf courses and are about a two-hour drive north of Seattle, an easy Friday after-work jaunt.

If you're making the trip anytime from May through mid-October, you can spend four hours of one of your weekend days aboard the *Star of Semiahmoo,* a big diesel-powered excursion boat, cruising through the San Juan Islands. The route wanders through the narrow waterways between forested Sucia, San Juan, and Orcas islands, sometimes encountering pods of orcas (killer whales), before docking for a brief stop at Friday Harbor on San Juan Island. You return to Semiahmoo by midafternoon.

Another good day-long alternative is to drive the Mount Baker Highway, then poke about the back roads of Whatcom County. Begin by heading south on I-5 from Blaine to Exit 262 (Axton Road) at Ferndale, then drive west to the railroad underpass and turn left (south) on Neilson Road. Follow the signs to Hovander Homestead and the big red barn that marks this pioneer farm, now a county park. You can tour the old farmhouse and barn and walk the nature trails of adjacent Tennant Lake Park. Returning north on Neilson Road, turn left on Main Street and south two blocks on First Avenue to reach Pioneer Park, another interesting stop.

Your next objective is the Mount Baker Highway (Route 542), a magnificent mountain road. From Ferndale drive directly east on Smith Road; it's about 11 miles until you join 542. If you're coming from Bellingham, take I-5, Exit 252.

Crossing the Nooksack River, you skirt the foot of Sumas Mountain and pass through the little community of Nugent's Corner. If you've made an early start, the bakery here is a good place to pick up bran muffins, apple fritters, crullers, and other breakfast pastries.

This drive is lovely any time of the year, but in October it's absolutely spectacular with fall color, among the best in Washington. Huge big-leaf maples, their leaves orange and gold, form a canopy over the road in places. As you drive east, morning sunlight backlights these trees and the smaller, brilliant red vine maples. The road meanders through small rural valleys where farmers till a few acres of cleared land, then it plunges into dark corridors between stands of tall evergreens. You follow close beside the white water Nooksack River most of the way; from May through summer this is a popular rafting river.

Two miles beyond Nugent's Corner, stop for a tour and tasting at Mount Baker Vineyards; the crushing of the grapes takes place here from late September through October. From time to time, the road opens up to provide views of snow-capped 10,778-foot Mount Baker in the distance as you pass through Deming, Kendall, Maple Falls, and Glacier. Schedule your lunch stop for Graham's in Glacier; it's a funky old place where you cook your own hamburgers and swap conversation with the locals.

From Glacier, the highway begins to climb as it narrows and twists in and out around the mountain; the 24 miles between Glacier and Artist Point has been designated a national forest scenic byway, the first such designation in the Northwest. Seven miles beyond Glacier, a short side road to the right leads down to Nooksack Falls. Thirteen more miles and you reach Heather Meadows, with spectacular views of 9,127-foot Mount Shuksan to the east. Mount Baker Lodge is a day-use facility; a road winds from the lodge to 4,700-foot Austin Pass for fine views of Mount Baker. Several good hiking trails also begin at the lodge.

From November through mid-May, Mount Baker provides one of the longest skiing seasons in the Northwest, with an average annual snowfall of 750 inches. Day-use facilities include six double chair lifts—one operating as a sightseeing lift in summer—three rope tows on 1,500 vertical feet of slopes, a ski school, rentals, cross-country skiing, and a restaurant. For information, call 734-6771; for a recorded ski report, call 671-0211 or 634-0200 (from Seattle).

Retrace your route down the mountain as far as the junction of Routes 542 and 9 just east of Deming. Turn south on 9 as it crosses the Nooksack River past Christmas tree farms and herds of dairy cattle. At Van Zandt stop for a "Nickle Pickle" at Everybody's Store. In addition to a delicious dill pickle for five cents, the little crossroads store is jam-packed with local produce (much of it organically grown); locally made jams, jellies, beef jerky and cured meats, grains, herbs, and spices; and craft items that range from knitted caps to wood carvings.

At Wickersham you can ride behind a vintage Northern Pacific steam locomotive on the Lake Whatcom Railway Tuesdays and Saturdays, June through August. Turn west at Wickersham on Park Road, which becomes South Bay Drive, then Lake Whatcom Boulevard as it skirts the south shore of long, slender Lake Whatcom. Midway along the lake you pass Sudden Valley Resort; continue another four miles to I-5 at Exit 253.

On your return to Seattle on Sunday, plan to include at least a couple of hours of sightseeing along the way. Tops on the list should be Fairhaven, the handsome old historic district of Bellingham (I-5 to Exit 250, then west on Old Fairhaven Parkway). A boom in Fairhaven in the 1880s, fueled by a speculation that the town would become a major railroad terminal, resulted in its almost overnight growth from a rural community around Bellingham Bay to a thriving city that boasted 35 hotels. The terminal never materialized and the old district today houses restaurants, boutiques, and specialty shops. You can pick up a self-guiding walking tour brochure at the information stand at the corner of 12th and Harris or at the convention and visitors bureau office. The route leads you past ten of the most significant buildings and sites. Fairhaven may yet enjoy a boomlet of sorts as the southern terminal of the Alaska Ferry System, relocated here from Seattle in late 1989.

From Fairhaven follow 12th Street south as it becomes Chuckanut Drive (Route 11). For the next ten miles the highway winds around high bluffs above Bellingham and Samish bays with splendid views of the San Juan Islands and Rosario Strait to the west. Frequent pullouts allow you to stop to take pictures or just to enjoy the view. You can reach the shore and explore some easily accessible tide pools at 1,884-acre Larrabee State Park. At its southern end, Chuckanut Drive emerges from the hills to make a straight run of about ten miles across cultivated farmlands and rejoin I-5. From here it's about 65 miles back to Seattle. Before you reach the Interstate, stop at the Rhododendron Cafe in Bow for their locally famous Sunday brunch. The offerings range from omelets to baked goods, all imaginatively prepared.

Area Code: 206

DRIVING DIRECTIONS From Seattle follow I-5 north to Bellingham and Blaine. The round trip to Semiahmoo is approximately 218 miles. Add another 144 miles if you opt to take the Mount Baker side trip we describe here.

AIR TRANSPORTATION *Alaska Airlines, Horizon Air,* and *United Express* serve Bellingham from Seattle with frequently scheduled departures. Round-trip fares begin at about $118.

SIGHTSEEING *Tennant Lake Natural History Interpretive Center,* end of Neilson Road, Ferndale, 384-3444. Riverside farmstead includes ½ mile of nature trails, boardwalks through marsh, bird-watching tower, and fragrance garden. Mid-June to Labor Day Thursday to Sunday noon to 6 P.M. Free. *Pioneer Park,* end of First Avenue, Ferndale, 384-6461. Tours of 7 pioneer log buildings. May through September Tuesday to Sunday, noon to 6 P.M. Free. *Hovander Homestead,* Hovander and River Lea roads, 384-3444. Renovated 1903 farmhouse, barn, equipment displays, children's farm zoo, trails. June to Labor Day Thursday to Sunday noon to 4:30 P.M.; May weekends noon to 4:30 P.M. Free. *Western Washington University,* visitor center at South College Drive and College Way, 676-3440. Lovely 180-acre campus has great views of waterways and islands to the west, extensive outdoor sculpture garden, Western Gallery of Art (676-3963; Monday to Friday 10 A.M. to 4 P.M., Saturday noon to 4 P.M.; free). Guided tours of sculpture garden Wednesday at noon. Free. *Whatcom Museum of History and Art,* 121 Prospect Street, 676-6981. Tuesday to Sunday noon to 5 P.M. Free. Housed in turreted former City Hall (circa 1892), museum is one of the best regional museums in the Northwest, with changing exhibits of Northwest art, birds of prey, Indian masks and bentwood boxes, Victorian room displays, and logging memorabilia. Gift shop is good place to pick up Northwest food, books. *Lake Whatcom Railway,* P.O. Box 91, Acme 98220, 595-2218. Trains leave Wickersham Junction (Route 9), June to August Saturday and Tuesday 11 A.M. and 1 P.M. Adults $10, under 18 $5. *Cascade Flight,* 2052 Airport Way, Bellingham 98226, 733-3727. Sightseeing flights of Mount Baker and the North Cascades, San Juan Island, and Victoria (call for prices, times). *Mount Baker Vineyards,* 4298 Mount Baker Highway, Everson 98247, 592-2300. Tasting and sales Wednesday to Sunday 11 A.M. to 5 P.M., January to March weekends only. *Northwest Adventures,* 7616 79th Avenue Southeast, Mercer Island 98040, 232-1490. Hot-air balloon flights in the area between Bellingham and the Canadian border. $125 per person Monday to Friday, $150 on weekends, half fare for children under 12. *Captain Bill's Charters,* P.O. Box 581, Ferndale 98248, 384-6945. Sailing cruises from Bellingham to the San Juans. All-day, $50 per person including lunch ($30 off-season); half-day, including lunch, $25 per person; also sunset and guitar cruises. *Gray Line Water Sightseeing,* 9600 Semiahmoo Parkway, Blaine 98230, 371-5222. Offers 7½-hour narrated San Juan Islands cruise aboard the *Star of Semiahmoo;* May to October, adults $39, 6–18 $39. Sportfishing trips for bottom fishing; adults $80, 6–18 $50. *Maritime Heritage Center,* 121 Prospect Street,

Bellingham 98226, 734-8866. Has Bellingham Harbor and San Juan Islands cruises, May to September. Call for schedule and prices.

EVENTS *Ski-to-Sea Festival,* 734-1332, Memorial Day weekend. Celebration features relay race from Mount Baker to Marine Park in Bellingham involving skiing, running, cycling, canoeing, and sailing. *Lummi Stommish Water Festival,* 734-8180, mid-June. Indian festival held on Lummi Reservation includes dramatic war canoe races, arts and crafts exhibition, traditional dancing, salmon bake. *Christmas Boat Parade,* 733-7390, mid-December. Illuminated pleasure craft cruise Bellingham Bay.

LODGING *Inn at Semiahmoo,* 9565 Semiahmoo Parkway, Blaine 98230, 371-2000. Full-service resort with restaurants, golf course, water activities, $$$$. *The Resort at Sudden Valley,* 2145 Lake Whatcom Boulevard, Bellingham 98226, 734-6430. Full-service resort with golf course, $$–$$$$. *Best Western Heritage Inn,* 151 East McLeod Road, Bellingham 98226, 647-1912, (800) 528-1234. $$. *Best Western Lakeway Inn,* 714 Lake Way Drive, Bellingham 98226, 671-1011, (800) 528-1234. $$. *North Garden Inn* (bed and breakfast), 1014 North Garden Street, Bellingham 98225, 671-7828, (800) 922-6414. $. *Schnauzer Crossing* (bed and breakfast), 4421 Lakeway Drive, Bellingham 98226, 733-0055, 734-2808. No smoking, $$$. *The Castle* (bed and breakfast), 1103 15th Street, Bellingham 98225, 676-0974. No smoking, pets, or children under 12; $$. *The Hill Top* (bed and breakfast), 5832 Church Road, Ferndale 98248, 384-3619. No smoking, $. *Yodeler Inn* (bed and breakfast), 7485 Mount Baker Highway, Maple Falls 98266, 599-2156, (800) 642-7334. $. *Snowline Inn,* 10429 Mount Baker Highway, Glacier 98244, 599-2788. Condos, $–$$. *The Logs at Canyon Creek,* 9002 Mount Baker Highway, Deming 98244, 599-2711. Log cabins, $$.

CAMPING *Birch Bay State Park,* 5105 Helwig Road, Blaine, 371-2800. 167 sites, 20 water-electricity, $8 to $12. *Larrabee State Park,* on Chuckanut Drive (Route 11) 7 miles south of Bellingham, 676-2093. 79 sites, 26 water-electricity, $8 to $12. *Diamond S RV Park,* 5330 Guide Meridian, Bellingham 98226, 671-2443. 50 sites with full hookups, $12 to $14. *The Resort at Sudden Valley* (see "Lodging"). 89 sites, $10 with full hookup, $8 without. *Silver Lake County Park,* 9006 Silver Lake Road, Maple Falls 98266, 599-2776. 50 sites, some with electricity, $7.50 to $9. *Mount Baker National Forest Ranger District*—3 campgrounds (no hookups) on Mount Baker Highway (Route 542): Douglas Fir, 2 miles east of Glacier (30 sites); Nooksack, 2½ miles east (18 sites); and Silver Fir, 13 miles east (21 sites)

DINING *Rhododendron Cafe,* 553 Chuckanut Drive, Bow, 766-6667. Lunch Friday and Saturday, dinner Wednesday to Sunday, Sunday brunch; imaginative menu using local seasonal ingredients; $–$$. *The Oyster Bar,* 240 Chuckanut Drive, Bow, 766-6185. Dinner daily; known to generations of Northwesterners, this unpretentious restaurant has a reputation for outstanding seafood; $$$. *Pacific Cafe,* 100 North Commercial Street, Bellingham, 647-0800. Lunch, dinner, and Sunday brunch; Northwest cuisine with an Oriental touch; $$–$$$. *Blue Water Bistro,* 1215½ Cornwall Avenue, Bellingham, 733-6762. Breakfast, lunch, and dinner daily. Sunday brunch with jazz. Imaginative menu includes interesting preparations of pasta, seafood, and other seasonal foods: $–$$. *Il Fiasco,* 1309 Commercial Street, Bellingham, 676-9136. Lunch Monday to Friday, dinner daily; upscale Northern Italian cuisine; $$. *Pepper Sisters,* 1222A Garden Street, Bellingham, 671-3414. Dinner Tuesday to Saturday, New Mexican fare, $. *Mannino's,* 130 East Champion Street, Bellingham, 671-7955. Lunch Monday to Friday, dinner daily; traditional home-style Italian food; $$$. *Stars Restaurant,* Inn at Semiahmoo (see "Lodging"). Breakfast, lunch, dinner daily; $$$. *Graham's,* 4989 Mount Baker Highway, Glacier, 599-2833. Breakfast, lunch, dinner daily; $. *Innisfree,* 9383 Mount Baker Highway, 599-2373. Summer: dinner Thursday to Monday; call for winter hours; $$.

FOR MORE INFORMATION Whatcom Visitor and Convention Bureau, 904 Potter Street (1-5 Exit 253), Bellingham 98225, 671-3990. Mount Baker District, Mount Baker–Snoqualmie National Forest, P.O. Box 232, Sedro Woolley 98284, 856-5700.

The Serendipitous San Juans: Lopez and Orcas

The late Jim Faber, one of the Northwest's most distinguished travel writers, told of the time several years ago when a panel of environmentalists named Washington's San Juan Islands as one of the nation's seven most desirable places to live. According to Faber, the reaction of one islander was typical. "It's like having your daughter selected as a *Playboy* centerfold. Who needs that kind of attention? We're already messed up with too many people."

Today, the reaction of residents to any more visitors probably would be even stronger. For, like Yosemite, the San Juans are in danger of being loved to death, especially in the summertime. Paradise has been discovered, and once you've been there, you too will readily understand why everyone wants to go.

The San Juan archipelago consists of 172 islands—about 450 at low tide—that lie scattered over 179 square miles at the eastern end of the Strait of Juan de Fuca and within sight of Canada. (This is not, as some mistakenly call it, Puget Sound;

the Sound extends southward from the southern end of Whidbey Island.) Many of the islands are so small they are really just rocks sticking out of the water at high tide, but more than a dozen are inhabited, and four of the largest—Lopez, Shaw, Orcas, and San Juan—are connected to the mainland and Vancouver Island by automobile-carrying ferries.

The San Juans are truly islands in time: a world apart from the mainland. Set in placid waters that team with fish, shellfish, whales, and other marine mammals, they're tranquil places with only a couple of spots that are big enough to be called towns. Inland, fields of waving, waist-high grass alternate with small farmsteads and patches of woods studded with evergreens, madrona, and alder. Though shorelines are mostly rocky, they're punctuated at intervals with coves and isolated, driftwood-strewn beaches, vacation retreats and retirement cottages. The quiet country roads are almost devoid of traffic and ideal for bicycling except when a ferry docks and disgorges scores of cars to clog the roads all at once. Weather, for the most part, is mild and sunnier than in Seattle, since these islands lie in the "rain shadow" of the Olympic Mountains to the west.

The San Juans may remind you of parts of New England—small fishing fleets in snug harbors, subsistence farms carved from evergreen forest, and quiet settlements studded with clapboard and shingle-sided buildings. The slow pace provides an ideal retreat for urbanites. You can go hiking, beachcombing, bicycling, whale watching, fishing, or just curl up with a good book in a cozy bed-and-breakfast inn.

Making a trip to the San Juans requires a bit of planning and strategy. In the interest of preserving these fragile places, as well as to avoid summertime crowds, consider going off-season. September and October are delightfully uncrowded and warm; winter brings a misty solitude; in spring you can watch flights of waterfowl heading north. And, because island accommodations are limited, off-season you have a much better chance of staying at that special bed-and-breakfast or country inn.

Whenever you go, make lodging reservations well in advance. Don't even consider going without reservations or you may wind up sleeping in your car. On weekends, arrive at the Anacortes ferry dock as early on Friday afternoon as possible and plan to board a return ferry from the islands before noon on Sunday. Or stay over and return Monday morning. Ferries are loaded to capacity westbound Friday evenings and Saturday mornings, eastbound Sunday afternoons. If you must make the trip on a busy summer weekend, consider leaving your car at the secured parking lot at the Anacortes ferry terminal and going as a pedestrian. It's cheaper, and most island lodgings will gladly pick you up at the ferry dock if you request it in advance.

The ferry trip through the islands is a destination in itself. Many out-of-state visitors, who don't have the time to stay in the islands, sample the San Juans by taking the all-day (about nine hours) round trip on the international run that stops at all the islands before going on to a landing at Sidney, British Columbia, on Vancouver Island. Big picture windows on the ferries make for easy viewing, and a lunch counter serves hot meals as well as snacks.

The ferries wind in and out through narrow passages between the islands, coming so close to madrona-fringed bluffs you can almost reach out and touch the tree branches. Brave the wind and stand on the forward deck to watch the passing parade of fishing boats, pleasure cruisers, kayakers, sailboats, diminutive tugs towing long rafts of logs, and, if you're fortunate, a playful pod of the big black-and-white orcas (killer whales). At island stops you can stand on the wing of the forward deck to watch bread trucks, grocery vans, automobiles, trailers, and all manner of island vehicles *clank-clank* over the steel apron and drive up the narrow pier. Watch with admiration as skilled deck officers squeeze the last boarding car into an impossibly small space, saving the driver from a two- or three-hour wait for the next ferry.

First stop, 45 minutes after leaving Anacortes, is Lopez Island. Nearly flat, Lopez is a favorite of bicyclists. Quiet country roads crisscross the long, narrow island past flocks of sheep grazing in the high, lush grass. Spur roads lead to bays and beaches ideal for strolling or spreading a picnic lunch. From Shark Reef Preserve, an unspoiled forested point on the southwest corner of the island, you can watch seals sunning themselves and may even spot some orcas. The island has only a small village, no real town.

The Islander Lopez, overlooking Fisherman's Bay, is the only full-service hotel on Lopez, but there are several B&Bs.

The next ferry stop is Shaw Island, and though you can debark, there are no accommodations on this residential island. One hour and twenty minutes after leaving Anacortes, you pull in to the dock at Orcas. Shaped like a horseshoe, and at 57 square miles the largest of the San Juans, Orcas is heavily forested and hilly, with some summits reaching to 2,000 feet or more. Biking is more challenging here. Rental bicycles are available. You can also rent mopeds from a firm in the town of Eastsound for leisurely exploring for about $10 an hour. Secluded coves, gravel beaches, and forested bluffs line 125 miles of shoreline, where low tides expose tide pools teeming with marine life.

Eastsound, ten miles from the ferry landing, dates from the 1880s and is Orcas's business center and largest community. A cozy sort of place, it's ideal for exploring on foot—you can walk from one end to the other in five minutes. Several galleries in town specialize in pottery, limited-edition prints of contemporary Northwest artists, and original sculpture and painting. And you'll see several buildings that remain from the town's early history, including beautiful Emmanuel Episcopal Church, Outlook Inn, and the six log cabins comprising the Orcas Historical Museum. The little village comes alive on Saturdays from

April to October, when local vendors and artisans sell everything from organic produce and flowers to ceramics and watercolors at the farmer's market on the museum grounds. Eastsound also offers some of the best dining in the San Juans.

About three miles beyond Eastsound (follow the only road out of town to the east), you'll find Rosario Resort, the lavish former home of shipbuilder Robert Moran, who made his fortune building riverboats for the Klondike Gold Rush. Moran's 1904 mansion boasts parquet floors, hardwood paneling, stained glass, and a pipe organ that is frequently cranked up for public concerts. Continue into 5,000-acre Moran State Park and follow the park road to the 2,409-foot summit of Mount Constitution for sweeping views of the islands, the Olympic Mountains to the west, and the Cascades to the east. The park has 30 miles of hiking trails, four lovely waterfalls, and two lakes where you can rent canoes and rowboats for trout fishing.

Area Code: 206

DRIVING DIRECTIONS From Seattle follow I-5 north 60 miles to Mount Vernon, then Washington 20 west 18 miles to the ferry landing at Anacortes.

FERRIES During the summer, *Washington State Ferries* schedules 17 departures daily from Anacortes for the San Juan Islands. Two ferries go all the way to Vancouver Island. There are fewer departures in the months after Labor Day and prior to Memorial Day. Not all ferries stop at all the islands. Typical round-trip fares: car and driver to Lopez $13.90, to Orcas $16.60, to San Juan $19. Each passenger $4.65, half fare for children 5–11, seniors 65 and older. For the latest ferry information call 464-6400 or toll-free (in WA) (800) 542-7052, (800) 542-0810.

AIR TRANSPORTATION *Kenmore Air,* (800) 832-9696 (in WA), (800) 423-5526 (outside WA); and *Lake Union Air,* (800) 826-1890 (in WA), offer scheduled floatplane service from Seattle's Lake Union and Lake Washington to several harbors in the San Juans. One-way fares begin at about $50.

SIGHTSEEING *Lopez Island Historical Museum,* Lopez Village, 468-2049. May to September Friday to Sunday noon to 4 P.M. Collection of photographs and memorabilia of early island settlement. *Orcas Island Historical Museum,* Eastsound, 376-4849, 376-2316. Memorial Day to Labor Day Monday to Saturday 1 to 4 P.M. Adults $1, 6–12 50 cents. Modest museum displays nineteenth-century pioneer relics, Indian crafts, basketry. *Lopez Bicycle Works,* Fisherman Bay Road, 468-2847. Rents bicycles on Lopez Island. *Wildlife Cycles,* Eastsound, 376-4708. Rents bicycles on Orcas Island. *Key Moped Rentals* at Eastsound, 376-2474. *Black-*

fish, Eastsound, 376-4041. *Island Kayak Guides,* Doe Bay, 376-4755, offers trips from Orcas and Lopez islands. *Shearwater Sea Kayak Tours,* Eastsound, 376-4699, offers single-day kayak trips from Orcas Island with various itineraries. *Custom Design Sailing Charters,* Deer Harbor, Orcas Island, 376-5105. Fishing and sailing charters by hour or day. *Crow Valley School Museum,* 3 miles southwest of Eastsound on Crow Valley Road, 376-4260. Memorial Day to mid-September Tuesday to Saturday noon to 4 P.M.

LODGING Lopez Island (98261): *Inn at Swifts Bay* (bed and breakfast), Route 2, Box 3402, Port Stanley Road, 468-3636. $$–$$$. *The Islander Lopez,* Fisherman Bay, 468-2233. $$. *MacKaye Harbor Inn* (bed and breakfast), Route 1, Box 1940, 468-2253. $$. *Blue Fjord Cabins,* Route 1, Box 1450, 468-2749. $$. Orcas Island: *Rosario Resort,* Eastsound 98245, (800) 542-8820 (in WA). $$$. *Outlook Inn,* P.O. Box 210, Eastsound 98245, 376-2581. Historic inn dates from the 1880s, $$. *Beach Haven,* Route 1, Box 12, Eastsound 98245, 376-2288. $$. *Deer Harbor Resort and Marina,* P.O. Box 176, Deer Harbor 98243, 376-4420. $$$–$$$$. *Kangaroo House* (bed and breakfast), P.O. Box 334, Eastsound 98245, 376-2175. $$. *Orcas Hotel* (bed and breakfast), P.O. Box 155, Orcas 98280, 376-4300. Victorian inn at ferry landing, $$. *Turtleback Farm Inn* (bed and breakfast), Route 1, Box 650, Eastsound 98245, 376-4914. $$.

CAMPING *Spencer Spit State Park,* east side of Lopez Island, 468-2251. 28 sites, $8, no hookups. *Odlin County Park,* northeast corner of Lopez Island near ferry landing, 468-2496. 29 sites, $8, no hookups. *Moran State Park,* Star Route, Box 22, Eastsound 98245, 376-2326. 166 sites, no hookups, $8, May through September, reservations accepted for period from Memorial Day to Labor Day by mail only.

DINING Lopez Island: *Bay Cafe,* Lopez Village, 468-3700. Lunch and dinner Wednesday to Sunday, brunch Sunday; eclectic ethnic menu; $. *Gail's,* Lopez Village, 468-2150. 3 meals daily in summer, dinner Friday and Saturday other seasons; restaurant and deli, local seafood, homemade soups and desserts; $$. *Islander Lopez* (see "Lodging"). 3 meals daily in season, dinner Saturday night in winter; $$. *Wildflower,* Lopez Village, 468-2114. Lunch and dinner daily in summer, Wednesday to Sunday other months; $. Orcas Island: *Bilbo's Festivo,* Eastsound, 376-4728. Lunch Thursday to Saturday, dinner Tuesday to Sunday, brunch Sunday; Mexican menu; $. *Christina's,* Eastsound, 376-4904. Dinner daily summer, Thursday to Monday winter; imaginative Northwest menu using fresh seafood and local ingredients, $$. *Deer Harbor Lodge and Inn,* Deer Harbor Road, 376-4110. Dinner daily in summer, weekends other seasons; family dining in homey atmosphere, menu changes daily, fresh fish, beef, chicken, vegetarian entrées; $$. *La Famiglia,* Eastsound, 376-2335. Lunch Monday to Saturday; dinner daily, Monday to Saturday in winter; Italian cuisine; $. *The Bungalow,* East-sound, 376-4546. 3 meals daily, $$. *Rosario Resort* (see "Lodging"). 3 meals daily, elegant brunch on Sunday, $$$.

FOR MORE INFORMATION Chamber of Commerce, P.O. Box 102, Lopez Island 98261. Orcas Island Chamber of Commerce, P.O. Box 252, East-sound 98245. San Juan Tourism Cooperative, P.O. Box 65, Lopez 98261, 468-3663.

Historic San Juan Island

Nearly as large as Orcas, westernmost San Juan Island is the most populous and has the greatest number of visitor attractions in the San Juan island group. The ferry docks at Friday Harbor (population 1,400), county seat of San Juan County, on the island's east coast. From here, two-lane rural roads fan out to Cattle Point at the southeastern tip, to the sparsely populated west coast around Small Pox Bay and Smuggler's Cove, and to the northern tip at Roche Harbor and Lime-stone Point. In general, San Juan is much less wooded and more open than Orcas and has splendid views of Vancouver Island to the west.

As you head uphill from the ferry dock through Friday Harbor, stop first at the Whale Museum. Devoted to the orca (killer whale), native to these waters, the displays explain that "killer" is a misnomer for this gentle mammal that preys only on fish. Exhibits include recordings of whale sounds for children and a hot line over which the latest whale sightings are phoned in and posted on a map.

At some time during your visit, schedule at least a couple of hours on the water. Whether you rent an outboard or sea kayak for some exploring on your own or join a sightseeing or whale watching cruise, you'll appreciate the serene beauty of these islands a great deal more if you see them from the water. Access to the coast by road is very limited, and sightseeing only by car means you miss much of what lies along the shore.

Two Friday Harbor firms offer whale watching trips to view the three pods of orcas that ply these waters regularly, especially from June through September. Trip leaders can identify the pods on sight and often point out individual members by their distinctive black-and-white markings. It's a real thrill to have three or four of these 25-foot-long, 8-ton leviathans surface near your boat to look you over.

The Whale Museum offers naturalist-led kayak trips with Shearwater Sea Kayak Tours based on Orcas Island.

Friday Harbor is the social center of the island, with its best restaurants, shops, and a lovely harbor busy with commercial fishing boats as well as pleasure craft.

One favorite Saturday or Sunday morning pastime is to pick out a deck table at one of the restaurants overlooking the harbor and watch the dozens of pleasure boats and an occasional seal or otter cavorting in the water. You can fish off the dock, rent a sailboat or powerboat, or join one of the charter fishing boats that depart from here. The island's biggest event, the San Juan Island Dixieland Jazz Festival, takes place here in July.

One of American history's more comic opera events—the Pig War—took place on San Juan Island in 1859. Americans and British both occupied the island in an uneasy truce over disputed ownership. On June 15, an American settler, Lyman Cutlar, shot and killed a pig that had been rooting in his garden and that belonged to the British Hudson's Bay Company. The British tried to arrest Cutler; the Americans responded by sending a company of infantry under Captain George E. Pickett (the same man who was to attain lasting fame for his charge at Gettysburg).

The British, angered by the presence of American troops on the island, sent three warships to chase them off. Each side called for reinforcements until 461 Americans with 14 cannons faced 2,140 British troops and five warships mounting 167 guns, and a stalemate ensued. Alarmed that the simple action of an irate farmer threatened to set the two countries at war, President James Buchanan sent General Winfield Scott to settle the affair. Scott managed to obtain an agreement that a token force of each belligerent would occupy San Juan Island until a proper treaty could be drawn up.

The island remained under joint military occupation for the next 12 years. In 1871 Germany's Kaiser Wilhelm I was asked to settle the dispute and drew the boundary between British Canada and the United States through Haro Strait, west of the island, thereby making San Juan a U.S. possession.

A national historical park preserves both the British and American camps from that farcical war. To reach American Camp on the barren, windswept southeast tip of the island, follow Cattle Point Road about six miles from Friday Harbor. An officers' quarters and a laundresses' building remain, and the locations of other structures are identified. A marked trail leads from an interpretive shelter to the earthen redoubt, a major feature in the American defense lines. South Beach here is the longest public beach on the island and an excellent place for observing numerous shorebirds and bald eagles.

To reach British Camp, about 12 miles away, follow Cattle Point Road to Bailer Hill Road, which becomes West Side Road as it hugs the western shore of the island. Stop at Lime Kiln Point State Park to view sea mammals just offshore. This spot, about 6 miles after you turn onto Bailer Hill Road, is reputed to be the best whale watching location in Washington, with as many as 70 of the mammals passing the park in a single day. Interpretive signs help you identify the various types of whales and describe their behavior.

Continue to Mitchell Bay Road and turn right then left onto West Valley Road and British Camp. A bit more visually dramatic than its American counterpart, this camp features a well-preserved log blockhouse, a barracks, the commissary, and a small formal garden.

Just to the north (West Valley Road to Roche Harbor Road) is Roche Harbor, now a resort town, and one of the most delightful old hotels in the Northwest. Settlement of the area began in the late 1800s with the founding of the Roche Harbor Lime and Cement Company by Tacoma lawyer John Stafford McMillin. The Hotel de Haro has been here since 1886, when McMillin built it around a former Hudson's Bay post to house visitors and business clients.

The hotel is a handsome ivy-clad frame Victorian overlooking the harbor, has a network of piers and docks that extend out into the water, and is a favorite stopping place for yachtsmen sailing to and from Canadian waters. The small lobby looks much as it did in 1906, when Teddy Roosevelt was a guest at the hotel. A five-foot-tall photo of Roosevelt hangs near the front desk over a register bearing his signature. If you stay overnight here, you may want to ask for Suite 2B, with the sleigh bed in which Roosevelt slept.

Pick up a free copy of "A Walking Tour of Historic Roche Harbor" at the front desk. Among the more unusual sites on this tour is the mausoleum McMillin built as a memorial to his family. Located in a stand of Douglas firs about half a mile from the hotel, the mausoleum is a seven-pillared structure in the middle of which are a round table and six chairs representing members of the family. Etched in the back of McMillin's chair are the affiliations he considered important in his life—thirty-second-degree Mason, Knight Templar, Sigma Chi, Methodist, Republican.

In summer the resort stages a delightfully quaint sunset flag ceremony, with the lowering of the American, Canadian, British, Washington, and house flags accompanied by the appropriate recorded music. The next morning you return to Friday Harbor, about 12 miles away, via Roche Harbor Road.

Area Code: 206

AIR TRANSPORTATION Both *Kenmore Air,* (800) 832-9696 (in WA), (800) 423-5526 (outside WA), and *Lake Union Air,* (800) 826-1890 (in WA), serve San Juan Island with floatplane service from Seattle.

SIGHTSEEING *Whale Museum,* 62 First Street, 378-4710. Call Whale Hot Line, (800) 562-8832 (in western WA) to report whale sightings. Museum hours: June to September daily 10 A.M. to 5 P.M., other months daily 11 A.M. to 4 P.M. Adults $3, over 55 and students $2.50, ages 6 to 11 $1.50. *San Juan Boat Rentals* *and Tours,* Friday Harbor, 378-3499. Three-hour whale watching tours, $40 per person including admission to Whale Museum. *Western Prince,* Friday Harbor, 378-5315. Four-hour whale watching tours, $40 per person including admission to Whale Museum. *Suzie's Mopeds,* Churchill Square, Friday Harbor near ferry landing, 378-5244. Rentals, $10 an hour, $40 a day. *San Juan Island National Historical Park,* two locations—American Camp, 6 miles south of Friday Harbor, and British Camp, 10 miles northwest, 378-2240. Hours: daily sunrise to sunset. Free. *San Juan Historical Museum,* 405 Price Street, 378-4587. Hours: Memorial Day through Labor Day Wednesday through Saturday 1 P.M. to 4:30 P.M. Free. *San Juan Island Tour & Transit Co.,* 470 Hillcrest Drive, 378-3550. Narrated 2½-hour island tours from Friday Harbor, three departures daily, Memorial Day through Labor Day. $10 per person. *Island Bicycles,* 380 Argyle, 378-4941. Rents bicycles, including tandems. $1.50 to $5 per hour, $7.50 to $15 per day.

EVENTS *San Juan Island Dixieland Jazz Festival,* Friday Harbor, 378-5509, every third weekend in July.

LODGING *Hotel de Haro,* P.O. Box 4001, Roche Harbor, 378-2155. $$$. *Olympic Lights* (bed and breakfast), 4531-A Cattle Point Road, 378-3186. Victorian farmhouse, lovely views, $$. *Lonesome Cove Resort,* 5810 Lonesome Cove Road, 378-4477. 6 cabins at water's edge, $$. *Blair House Bed and Breakfast Inn,* 345 Blair Avenue, 378-5907. $$. *Moon and Sixpence* (bed and breakfast), 3021 Beaverton Valley Road, 378-4138. $$. *Wharfside Bed and Breakfast,* on K Dock at Friday Harbor, 378-5661. The moored 60-foot sailboat *Jacquelyn* offers 2 cabins with standard beds, $$. *Island Lodge,* 1016 Guard Street, 378-2000. Scuba diving package available, $. *San Juan Inn,* 50 Spring Street, 378-2070. $.

CAMPING *Lakedale Campground,* 2627 Roche Harbor Road, Friday Harbor 98250, 378-2350. 95 sites on lake stocked with trout, hookups, boats, fishing; $8–$11.

DINING *The Blue Heron,* 1 Front Street, 378-3995. 3 meals daily; overlooking the harbor; $–$$. *Downrigger's,* Front Street at ferry landing, 378-2700. Lunch and dinner daily, view dining with emphasis on seafood; $$. *Cafe Bissett,* 170 West Street, 378-3109. Dinner daily July through September, Thursday through Monday other months; nouvelle Northwest cuisine; $$. *Duck Soup Inn,* 3090 Roche Harbor Road, 378-4878. Dinner Wednesday to Sunday, summer only; menu focusing on fresh local seafood, changes daily; $$$. *Springtree Eating Establishment and Farm,* 310 Spring Street, 378-4848. Breakfast, lunch, dinner daily; fresh local seafood, vegetables, and poultry; $–$$.

FOR MORE INFORMATION San Juan Island Historical Park, P.O. Box 429, Friday Harbor 98250. Chamber of Commerce, P.O. Box 98, Friday Harbor 98250, 378-5240. San Juan Tourism Cooperative, P.O. Box 65, Lopez 98261, 468-3663.

In Seattle's Backyard

When it comes to outdoor recreation, few cities in the country have as much to offer as Portland and Seattle. In the backyards of both lie hundreds of square miles of national forest, mountains, lakes, and rivers. Within a half-hour or 45-minute drive of either city, you can hike, mountain climb, ride horseback, raft a white-water river, ski, fish, bicycle, or camp. With recreational facilities so close, many business travelers schedule their meetings in Portland or Seattle to allow time for hiking or fishing in the summer, night skiing under lights in the winter.

King County, in which Seattle is located, stretches east from Puget Sound some 50 miles to the summit of the Cascades, covering 2,134 square miles (an area larger than Delaware). Because of Seattle's very liberal reputation, many assume the county was named for the late Reverend Martin Luther King. Actually, it was named for an obscure and long-forgotten vice president (under Millard Fillmore) from Alabama, William Rufus de Vane King.

You can make the trip suggested in this section in one or more single-day country drives or, if you're looking for a getaway weekend, stay overnight at the elegant Salish Lodge or one of the bed-and-breakfast inns around North Bend. You'll be surprised how easy it is to create the illusion of a remote forest retreat just a few minutes from the city.

Begin by heading east on I-90. As you emerge from the Mount Baker Tunnel onto the new bridge opened across Lake Washington in 1989, you will be driving across one of only four floating bridges in the world—of which Washington has three, two of them across Lake Washington. To the north you can see Evergreen Point, the second floating bridge. These massive structures are actually huge hollow concrete pontoons linked together and anchored to the floor of the lake by cables. Seemingly much too heavy to float, they respond to the same principle of displacement that allows a battleship of many thousand tons to float. You can still see the approaches to the third Lake Washington floating bridge that sank in a storm in November 1990.

On a clear morning or evening the view from either of these bridges is stunning. The snow-capped peak far to the north is 10,778-foot Mount Baker. On the eastern side of Lake Washington the glittery new bronze towers of Bellevue, Washington's fourth largest city, rise from the wooded shoreline. Ahead on I-90 lies Mercer Island, an affluent suburb. To the southeast 14,411-foot Mount Rainier rises like a giant snow cone, pink, white, or purple, depending on the time of day.

Four miles east of the lake, I-90 tops Eastgate Hill and you start down the long slope into Issaquah. On the left, the other big lake you see is Lake Sammamish, a favorite destination for trout and bass fishing, boating, swimming, water sports, and picnics on the broad lawns of Lake Sammamish State Park. On your right rise Cougar, Squak, and Tiger mountains, together known as the Issaquah Alps. Though the local name "Alps" is a bit pretentious for these forested slopes, West Tiger Mountain does reach 3,004 feet.

Small-town Issaquah is rapidly disappearing. For nearly a century, it has dozed in its splendid mountain and lakeside setting, first as a hop-farming center and later as a coal-mining town. But the 1980s caught up with Issaquah, and shopping centers, parking lots, commercial buildings, and thousands of new homes are replacing scenes of pastoral beauty.

Still, the mountains and forests around Issaquah offer the best opportunities for hiking close to Seattle. The Issaquah Alps Trails Club schedules hikes nearly every weekend. They're free and vary in difficulty from walks suitable for the elderly and the handicapped to difficult work-up-a-good-sweat climbs. You don't even need a car to participate; hikes start at the Municipal Parking Lot one block south of the City Hall on East Sunset Way in Issaquah, reached on the number 210 bus line from downtown Seattle.

One development that stands above the usual anonymous shopping centers is Gilman Village. A collection of vintage wooden stores and homes moved to its present location on Gilman Boulevard from elsewhere in town and connected by boardwalks, the village houses boutiques, small restaurants, and craft shops. Also along Gilman Boulevard is Boehm's Chocolates, founded by Austrian candy-maker Julius Boehm and a must-stop for chocoholics. Housed in a replica of a Tyrolean chalet, the shop dispenses gourmet-quality European-style chocolate and ice cream.

Downtown, just off Front Street, the old Issaquah railroad depot has been spruced up and now serves as a museum. A few blocks away, you'll find the Issaquah Historical Museum in the old Gilman Town Hall (Issaquah was originally named Gilman). Behind the building is the old town jail.

Issaquah is known locally for its spectacular salmon run. Each fall, from mid-September to mid-October, thousands of salmon return home to the Issaquah hatchery through the Ballard Locks (see "On Foot Through the Heart of Seattle"), the Lake Washington ship canal, Lake Washington, Sammamish Slough, and Lake Sammamish to Issaquah Creek. The big fish fill the narrow creek from bank to bank. It's difficult not to get a lump in your throat as you watch them thrash out the last of their energy in this elemental battle to travel upstream to lay eggs. You can best watch them from a bridge over the creek adjacent to the hatchery (see "Sightseeing"). Salmon Days, the town's biggest annual event, celebrates the run and draws thousands.

Our vote for the best Chinese restaurant in the Puget Sound area goes to Issaquah's Mandarin Garden. It's unpretentious, but the cuisine is authentic enough that delegations visiting Seattle from China often come here to eat. Proprietor Andy Wang, a native of Shanghai, does most of the cooking himself and offers a varied menu that includes Szechuan, Mandarin, and Hunan dishes.

Continue east on I-90 four miles to the Preston–Fall City exit and follow the Preston–Fall City road north along the Raging River to Fall City. At the western edge of Fall City, you'll find the Herbfarm—a commercial herb grower with a small restaurant (reservations a must)—where you can purchase any of hundreds of varieties of herbs and get advice on their culture. Picking your own strawberries and raspberries is a long-standing tradition in the Northwest, where Oregon and Washington produce more than 90 percent of the nation's edible berries. The season begins in June and there are several U-pick farms here in the Snoqualmie Valley.

Cross the Snoqualmie River, noted for its winter steelhead fishing, at Fall City and turn right (east) onto Washington 202. The highway follows the river for a couple of miles to Snoqualmie Falls. According to the brochure you pick up at the interpretive display, Snoqualmie Falls is second only to Mount Rainier in annual attendance among Washington's tourist attractions. At any rate, there always seems to be plenty of room to view the 268-foot falls from the cantilevered observation platform that hangs 300 feet over the gorge.

The falls are awesome, throwing up enough spray to fog your glasses as far away as the observation walk. There's also a steep (and sometimes slippery) half-mile trail that leads to the riverbank for close-up views. If photographs are important, you'll want to schedule your trip so that you're here in the late afternoon for the best lighting. If you've brought a picnic lunch, you'll find several tables under the trees; if not, there's a fast-food stand next to the parking lot.

Salish Lodge, perched on the rim of the gorge, is one of the most elegant retreats in the state. Popular for honeymoons and romantic getaways, it also features a gourmet restaurant. Breakfast at the lodge, known as Snoqualmie Falls Lodge before its recent remodeling and name change, has been a tradition with Seattleites for generations. The breakfast is enormous and features several kinds of fruit, oatmeal, ham, sausage, eggs, honey and biscuits, and more. Reservations are a must.

Snoqualmie and North Bend were the locations for the popular television show "Twin Peaks," now discontinued. Fans will recognize the Salish Lodge as the Great Northern Hotel and the Mar-T Café in North Bend as the RR Diner in Twin Peaks. The café is famous for its cherry pie and sells dozens of them every week to hungry fans.

Just up the road is the little lumber mill town of Snoqualmie, home of the

Puget Sound and Snoqualmie Valley Railroad. During the summer and on off-season weekends, the railroad runs a steam locomotive and vintage passenger coaches on a ten-mile round trip to North Bend. The historic depot (1890) houses a museum of railroadiana; the railroad also has an extensive collection of equipment including 15 steam engines, trolleys, freight and passenger cars, cabooses, cranes, and work cars dating from 1881.

The valley from here to North Bend, five miles distant, including numerous side roads, is ideal for bicycling—nearly level, without much traffic.

North Bend has one of the most spectacular settings of any town in the country. Nestled at the foot of the rocky bulk of 4,167-foot Mount Si, with 4,787-foot Mount Teneriffe rising in the background, it resembles a village in the Swiss Alps. If you're in the mood for a little back road exploring, take the Taylor River Road (leave Old Snoqualmie Pass Highway, also known as North Bend Way, at Southeast 140th Street, about 2½ miles east of town). It follows the middle fork of the Snoqualmie River for some 15 miles through fine forested backcountry to forest service campgrounds and good spots for river trout fishing between mid-April and October. You can get information on camping, hiking, fishing, and back roads in the area from the North Bend Ranger District office of the Mount Baker–Snoqualmie National Forest, located on North Bend Way at the eastern edge of town.

From North Bend retrace your route to Fall City and drive west on Washington 202 to Redmond (15 miles). Big Marymoor Park is a great place to spread a picnic lunch. The 500 acres were landscaped by the famous Olmsted brothers, designers of several Seattle boulevards and parks. The 1904 James Clise residence here houses the Marymoor Museum, exhibiting historical photos. Redmond is a town dedicated to the bicycle, and on Friday evenings in summer you can watch cyclists race in Marymoor's velodrome. The Sammamish River Trail, a paved, multiuse trail for pedestrians, bicyclists, and, part of the way, equestrians, starts at Marymoor and extends ten miles to the town of Bothell.

Continue north on Washington 202 for about five miles to Chateau Ste. Michelle Winery, on the outskirts of Woodinville. Open for tours and tasting, the winery spreads over 87 acres of open land and vineyards along the Sammamish River. This is Washington's largest winemaker—including other sites in eastern Washington—and it produces virtually every varietal produced elsewhere in the Pacific Northwest. Focal point is the handsome mansard-roofed, French-style château that houses the winemaking facility, visitor center, and retail wine shop. More than 10,000 flower bulbs bloom around the building beginning in April. Across the road, smaller Columbia Winery also offers tours and tasting.

To return to Seattle, continue north to Woodinville and get on the freeway westbound (Washington 522). Within half a mile, take the interchange exit to

I-405 southbound (Bellevue and Renton). In approximately nine miles, turn west onto I-520 and return to Seattle across the Evergreen Point Floating Bridge.

Area Code: 206

DRIVING DIRECTIONS The loop route described above follows I-90, Washington 202, I-405, and I-520. Approximate round-trip mileage is 73.

SIGHTSEEING *Issaquah Historical Society,* 165 Southeast Andrews, Issaquah, 392-3500. Museum in old City Hall, jail behind it. Hours: Saturday and Sunday noon to 4 P.M. Donation. Another museum in refurbished train depot on East Sunset Way. *Issaquah Salmon Hatchery,* 125 West Sunset Boulevard, Issaquah, 392-3180. Self-guided tours. Hours: Building open daily 8 A.M. to 4:30 P.M., grounds open daily. *Issaquah Alps Trails Club,* P.O. Box 351, Issaquah 98027, information hot line 328-0480, message changed weekly. Free guided hikes (see page 57). *The Herbfarm,* 32804 Issaquah–Fall City Road, Fall City, 784-2222. Hours: March through December daily 9 A.M. to 5 P.M., limited hours in winter. Free. *Snoqualmie Falls Forest Theater,* 36800 Southeast David Powell Road, Fall City, 222-7044. Outdoor theater open July and August, adults $7. *Puget Sound and Snoqualmie Valley Railroad,* P.O. Box 459, Snoqualmie, 746-4025. Train excursions: April and October Sunday; May, June, and September Saturday and Sunday; July through August Friday, Saturday, and Sunday. Adults $5 round-trip, seniors $4, children $3. Also operates a Santa Train in December and a Spook Train for Halloween. *Snoqualmie Winery,* 1000 Winery Road, Snoqualmie, 392-4000. Tasting rooms. Hours: Daily 10 A.M. to 4:30 P.M. *Snoqualmie Valley Historical Museum,* 320 North Bend Boulevard South, North Bend (Exit 31 off I-90), 888-3200. Hours: April through October Saturday and Sunday 1 to 5 P.M. Donation. *Mount Baker–Snoqualmie National Forest,* North Bend Ranger Station, 42404 Southeast North Bend Way, 888-1421. Hours: Monday through Friday 8 A.M. to 4:30 P.M. *Marymoor Park:* Marymoor Museum, Marymoor County Park, 6046 West Lake Sammamish Parkway Northeast, Redmond, 885-3684. Occupies north half of historic Clise Mansion. Hours: Tuesday, Wednesday, Thursday 10 A.M. to 3 P.M.; Sunday noon to 4 P.M. Donation. Velodrome has bicycle races Friday night in summer. *French Creek Cellars,* 17721 132nd Avenue Northeast, Woodinville, 486-1900. Tours and tasting daily noon to 5 P.M. *Chateau Ste. Michelle,* 14111 Northeast 145th, Woodinville, 488-1133. Tours and tasting daily 10 A.M. to 4 P.M. *Columbia Winery,* 14030 Northeast 145th, Woodinville, 488-2776. Tours and tasting daily 10 A.M. to 5 P.M.

EVENTS *Heritage Festival,* Marymoor Park (see ''Sightseeing''), Redmond, 296-2964, July. Celebrates the ethnic arts with music, dance, food, and crafts.

Alpine Days, North Bend, 888-1678, August. Lederhosen and other alpine costumes, arts and crafts fair, parade, salmon bake, music, dancing, mini-marathon, and fireworks. *Issaquah Salmon Days,* Issaquah, 392-0661, early October. 2-day festival celebrates annual return of salmon to Issaquah Creek with parade, pancake breakfast, salmon bake, street fair, arts and crafts, entertainment, and food booths. *Redmond Derby Days,* Redmond, 885-4014, mid-July. Celebration features parade, food, arts and crafts booths, and championship bicycle races. *Snoqualmie Days,* Snoqualmie, 888-4440, August. Community festival with parade, food, and arts and crafts booths.

LODGING *Salish Lodge,* 37807 Southeast Fall City–Snoqualmie Road, Snoqualmie 98065, 888-2556. Elegant country inn overlooking Snoqualmie Falls has 90 rooms with fireplaces and whirlpool baths, $$$$. *The Old Honey Farm Country Inn* (bed and breakfast), 8910 384th Avenue Southeast, Snoqualmie 98065, 888-9399. Public dining room open for breakfast, lunch, and dinner. Rural Snoqualmie Valley lodging with tranquil setting, lovely view of Mount Si and the Cascades, $$–$$$$.

DINING *The Roost,* 120 Northwest Gilman Boulevard, Issaquah, 392-5550. Lunch and dinner daily, traditional American food, $–$$$. *Mandarin Garden,* 40 East Sunset Way, Issaquah, 392-9476. Lunch and dinner Tuesday through Saturday, dinner Tuesday through Sunday; outstanding Hunan, Szechuan, and Mandarin cuisine; $. *The Herbfarm* (see "Sightseeing"). Special 6-course fixed-price lunch with emphasis on herbs grown here, includes 15-minute tour; late April through December, Friday, Saturday, Sunday; $$$$. Reservations are a necessity. *Salish Lodge* (see "Lodging"). Open daily for breakfast, lunch, and dinner; Northwest dining with a Continental flair; famous for its belt-bursting farm breakfast; $$–$$$$.

FOR MORE INFORMATION East King County Convention and Visitors Bureau, 515 116th Avenue Northeast, Bellevue 98004, 455-1926.

The Mountain

Puget Sound residents have an expression that denotes clear weather. They say, "The mountain's out." No one ever asks which mountain. That's obvious.

From almost any vantage point between Everett, 27 miles north of Seattle, and Centralia, 83 miles to the south, massive, white Mount Rainier looms like a giant ice-cream cone on the eastern horizon. This is no ordinary mountain. It is, as author Ray Snow put it in his book *Mount Rainier: The Story Behind the Scenery* (KC

Publications, Inc., 1984) "a mountain beyond imagining. A mountain unbelievable. Like fairy tale magic, an aura of myth, fable and gods pervades. The splendor of altitude, the serenity of tall timber, the haunting presence of an explosive time gone by and yet to come are the vivid and abiding impressions given by Mount Rainier."

Sometimes, on a winter morning when the weather is just right, a deck of flat-bottomed stratus clouds hangs over the mountain. The rising sun peeks over the Cascades, shines beneath the clouds, and turns Rainier a dozen shades of pink, purple, and mauve. Seen at sunset from a ferryboat on Puget Sound, the mountain looks like molten gold.

Because of its height (14,411 feet) and singularly imposing appearance, Mount Rainier has always been a source of respect and wonder for all inhabitants of Washington. For the Nisqually, Yakima, Klickitat, and Puyallup Indians, it was "Takhoma," a place where evil spirits dwelled. For today's residents, Mount Rainier is in evidence everywhere, from the logos on beer cans to the names of exclusive private clubs.

Mount Rainier National Park encompasses 378 square miles of mountains, glaciers, forests, lakes, and rivers, the terrain laced with roads, trails, climbing routes, and campgrounds among other means of enjoying the incredible environment. You can circle the mountain in one hard day's drive or you can make a weekend of it with an overnight stay on the 6,000-foot flank of the mountain at Paradise.

Before you set off for Mount Rainier, outfit yourself with a good pair of hiking boots and a warm sweater, and in any months but July and August, a light rainproof poncho or other covering. Take along a good pair of binoculars and regional guides to birds and flowers, available in Seattle bookstores and at Paradise Visitor Center. Photographers will also want a camera with a telephoto lens for photographing wildlife.

Head south to Puyallup—pronounced "pew-a-lup," a tongue twister that often trips up newcomers—and Eatonville on Washington 161 (see "Driving Directions," page 65). In April, hundreds of acres of daffodils carpet the fields around Puyallup with yellow and make a stunning foreground for color photographs of the mountain.

Six miles north of Eatonville lies Northwest Trek, a 600-acre coastal forest of conifers and deciduous trees and the habitat for indigenous animals of the Northwest. A guided tour in an enclosed rubber-tired tram takes you through the preserve to see moose, caribou, elk, buffalo, deer, and scores of birds. May and June, when dozens of newborn animals are on view, are good months to come, especially if you have children along.

The two-lane state highway winds through second-growth forest to the little town of Eatonville, then joins Washington 706 and follows the Nisqually River to

Elbe. As you near the foot of the mountain, your view of it is frequently obstructed by dense forest. At Elbe, the Mount Rainier Scenic Railroad offers excursions from May to September in a train boasting vintage coaches, an open-air gondola with benches, and a steam locomotive. The trip is a delight as the old steam engine whistles and chuffs its way on a 1½-hour trip through the woods over 19 miles of former Milwaukee Road branch line to Mineral Lake. On summer Saturday evenings the railroad runs a 4-hour dinner train to the logging community of Morton.

Fourteen miles east of Elbe lies the southwest Nisqually entrance to Mount Rainier National Park. This entrance is open year-round, and in winter, depending on the severity of recent storms, the park road is plowed as far as Paradise, 19 miles distant. A mile beyond the entrance the West Side Road hugs the flank of the mountain for 15 miles to dead-end at the North Puyallup River. There are excellent trails for day hikes to Emerald Ridge and Tahoma Glacier (2½ miles of trail) and Saint Andrews and Klapatche parks, 1½ and 6 miles respectively, from this uncrowded side of the park. Closed in winter, the West Side Road is a favorite of snowshoers and cross-country skiers. Unfortunately, floods in recent years have washed out the road and the reopening date is uncertain.

To really savor the park, you must forsake the comfort of your car and hit the trail, for it is only away from the busy park roads that you'll encounter the wildflowers, birds, and shy wildlife that make Mount Rainier so special.

The Trail of Shadows, at Longmire, is a good place to begin. This half-mile, self-guiding nature trail loops from the parking lot through historic Longmire Meadow—where the first explorers camped in 1883—past mineral springs, beaver ponds, and cathedrallike virgin forest of Douglas fir, western red cedar, and western hemlock. Also at Longmire are a modest museum, a park information office, a hiker's center (with trail information), and the restaurant and accommodations of the newly refurbished National Park Inn. In winter, Longmire offers ranger-led snowshoe hikes and cross-country ski treks on weekends.

In the next 13 miles, the park road climbs from 2,761 feet at Longmire to 5,400 feet at the Paradise Visitor Center. You loop and wind through the trees, climbing steadily to swing suddenly around a corner face-to-face with the ice-clad mountain before losing the view around the next turn. You will notice a change in the roadside vegetation as you climb through the equivalent in climate zones from Seattle to the Arctic Circle. The rapid elevation and climate changes dictate a rich diversity of plant life that ranges from the spongy mosses, ferns, and gigantic trees of the rain-washed lowlands to the lichens and compact "belly plants" (because you have to get on your belly to see them) of the frigid, wind-whipped Arctic-Alpine Zone. To put Mount Rainier's winters in perspective, you should know that the world's record snowfall, an incredible 93.5 feet, was measured at Paradise in the winter of 1972.

At the Paradise Visitor Center you face the awesome rivers of ice that cover Mount Rainier. This is the most glaciated peak in the United States outside of Alaska, with 26 named glaciers and 50 small, unnamed ones on its flanks. These masses of ice cover approximately 37 square miles, with the largest, Emmons Glacier on the northeast face, covering about 4 square miles.

Where there's a mountain to be climbed, you'll find mountain climbers. The first who made it to the 14,411-foot summit were Hazard Stevens and P. B. Van Trump, on August 17, 1870. In more recent years the mountain has been used as a training ground for Himalayan expeditions. Jim Whittaker, who became the first American to climb Mount Everest in 1962, climbs here frequently, and some of his expedition gear is displayed in the visitor center. His brother Lou runs the climbing school at Paradise and each summer leads several hundred novice climbers to the summit. You can often spot the roped-up climbing parties crossing a glacier through the high-powered telescopes at the visitor center.

The alpine meadows around Paradise begin to bloom around the Fourth of July and continue through mid-September. One especially rewarding hike takes you on a 4½-mile loop through meadows knee-deep in white anemone and avalanche lily, yellow glacier lily and cinquefoil, red paintbrush and heather, purple lupine and aster.

Evenings at Paradise are a special time. It's like being on an island after the last boat has left. Day visitors have since made their way down the mountain, leaving a near-empty parking lot behind. Through the windows of the inn you can see the setting sun paint the sky and mountains with the reddish hues of alpenglow. Guests gather in the lobby after dinner to await the evening program, which may be a slide show, the weekly employee talent show, a movie, or a naturalist-led walk to experience the night environment.

The next day, continue on around the south and east sides of the park. From Paradise the summer-only road descends the steep side of Stevens Canyon, dropping 3,486 feet in 21 miles. In September the autumn foliage along this road is outstanding, with vine maple adding great splashes of red along the mountainsides.

When you reach the Stevens Canyon entrance to the park, at the junction with Washington 123, detour three miles south to Ohanapecosh. Here, the park's largest campground and visitor center nestle dwarfed beneath stately Douglas fir, hemlock, and cedar, all 500 to 1,000 years old and hundreds of feet tall. This is one of the finest and most accessible old-growth forests in the state. Several trails lead away from the road into the cathedrallike groves along the Ohanapecosh River. Both the Grove of Patriarchs Trail and the trail to Silver Falls cover about two miles of easy terrain and take about two hours round-trip.

Follow Highway 123 north as it climbs out of the river valley up the drainage of the Ohanapecosh River and Chinook Creek to crest Cayuse Pass at 4,630 feet. As you climb past 5,846-foot Shriner Peak on your right and loop around into side canyons, you get magnificent views of Mount Rainier to the west and the subranges of the Cascades stretching away to the south. At Cayuse Pass, detour three miles over Washington 410 to 5,440-foot Chinook Pass. Here is one of the great classic views of the mountain that has graced countless postcards, placemats, guidebooks, and brochures. In the foreground, Tipsoo Lake is surrounded by alpine meadows resplendent in wildflowers by mid-summer. The entire western horizon is occupied by the white bulk of Mount Rainier. The Cascade Crest Trail, part of a system that stretches from the Canadian to the Mexican border, crosses the highway just east of the pass and provides easy access to other viewpoints. It's a favorite summer route for backpackers as well as for horsepacking trips.

Descend to Cayuse Pass and turn right to descend the Mather Memorial Parkway (Washington 410). At three miles a summer-only side road leads west to the visitor center at Sunrise. From the parking lot at 6,400 feet, numerous trails lead closer to the mountain. From Sunrise Point, you're nearly face-to-face with massive, 4½-mile-long Emmons Glacier; you can watch mountaineers scaling the glaciers and mountain goats climbing on Goat Island Mountain. In late September, the haunting bugling of bull elk during mating season sometimes echoes across the mountain.

Returning to Washington 410, continue north out of the park. Just beyond the park boundary, the road to Crystal Mountain detours three miles to the right. Set in a bowl between the mountains, this ski resort covers some 4,000 acres with a top elevation of 7,002 feet (the highest ski slope in Washington) and a vertical drop of 3,100 feet. Nine lifts serve 31 different runs. During the summer, one chair lift operates as a sightseeing lift to the Summit House mountaintop restaurant and magnificent views of Mount Rainier.

Washington 410 continues north then west following the White River. The milky color that gives the White its name comes from finely ground rock dust produced by Mount Rainier's glaciers and suspended in the water. At Enumclaw, 41 miles northwest of Cayuse Pass, you have your choice of turning north on Washington 169 to return to Seattle via Black Diamond, Maple Valley, and Renton or continuing west on Washington 164 to link up with Interstate 5 just west of Auburn.

Area Code: 206

DRIVING DIRECTIONS To reach Mount Rainier's southwest (Nisqually) entrance from Seattle, drive south on I-5 to Exit 142, follow Washington 161 south through Puyallup, Graham, and Eatonville to its junction with Washington 7. Turn east to Elbe and continue to the park entrance on Washington 706. Approximate round-trip mileage is 216.

SIGHTSEEING *Northwest Trek,* 17 miles south of Puyallup on State Route 161, Eatonville 98328, 832-6116. Hours: mid-February through October daily from 9:30 A.M., rest of year Friday, Saturday, Sunday. Adults $6.50, seniors 62 and over $5.50, 5–17 $4.50, and 3–4 $2. *Mount Rainier Scenic Railroad,* P.O. Box 921, Elbe 98330, 569-2588. Hours: April through Memorial Day and mid-October through November, Sunday afternoon dinner train; June 15 through Labor Day, daily plus Saturday night dinner train. Dinner train $45, reservations required; regular rides: adults $6.75, seniors 60 and over $5.75, juniors 12–17 $4.75, and under 12 $3.75. *Mount Rainier National Park,* Tahoma Woods Star Route, Ashford 98304, 569-2211. Cayuse and Chinook passes are normally closed from late fall to late spring. Winter access, only as far as Paradise, through the Nisqually entrance at the southwest corner of the park. Ohanapecosh Visitor Center: mid-June through September daily 9 A.M. to 6 P.M.; Memorial Day through early June and the month of October, weekends 9 A.M. to 5 P.M. Paradise Visitor Center: mid-June to Labor Day 9 A.M. to 7 P.M.; mid-May through mid-June and post–Labor Day through October, 9 A.M. to 6 P.M.; rest of year weekends only 10 A.M. to 5 P.M. Sunrise Visitor Center: July to mid-September daily 9 A.M. to 6 P.M. Longmire Museum: June through September daily 9 A.M. to 5:30 P.M., rest of year weekends 9 A.M. to 4:15 P.M. Admission: $5 per vehicle, good for a 7-day period. *Crystal Mountain,* Crystal Mountain 98022, 663-2265. *Crystal Mountain Corral,* 663-2589. Trail rides.

LODGING *Alexander's Country Inn,* State Route 706, Ashford 98304, 569-2300. 12 rooms in historic inn, $$. *Growly Bear* (bed and breakfast), P.O. Box 103, Ashford 98304, 569-2339. Rustic 1890 homestead 1 mile from Longmire entrance to Mount Rainier National Park, $$. *National Park Inn,* Mount Rainier Guest Services, Star Route, Ashford 98304, 569-2275. Open year-round. Newly remodeled lodging in the park near Longmire entrance, $–$$. *Nisqually Lodge,* State Route 706, Ashford 98304, 569-8804. $$. *Paradise Inn,* Mount Rainier Guest Services, Star Route, Ashford 98304, 569-2275. Open late May through September. Classic national park lodge built in 1916 with commanding view of the mountain, $–$$. *Village Inn Hotel,* Crystal Mountain 98022, 663-2558. Open summer and winter only. 20 units at Crystal Mountain Resort, $$.

CAMPING *Mount Rainier National Park,* Tahoma Woods Star Route, Ashford 98304, 569-2211. No hookups, 14-day limit, 5 campgrounds. *Cougar Rock:* 200 sites, dump station, $6, open mid-May through September. *Ipsut Creek:* 29 sites, no RVs over 20 feet, $5, open late May through September. *Ohanapecosh:* 205 sites, dump station, no RVs over 30 feet, $6, open mid-May through September. *Sunshine Point:* 18 sites, no RVs over 20 feet, $5, open year-round. *White River:* 117 sites, no RVs over 20 feet, $6, open late June to mid-September.

DINING *Alexander's*, Alexander's Country Inn (see "Lodging"). Lunch and dinner daily, weekends only in winter; fresh trout and homemade pies; $$. *Mount Rainier Scenic Railroad* (see "Sightseeing"). *National Park Inn* (see "Lodging"). Breakfast, lunch, and dinner; traditional American fare, $–$$. *Paradise Inn* (see "Lodging"). Breakfast, lunch, and dinner, Sunday brunch; traditional American fare; $–$$$. *Summit House*, Crystal Mountain Resort (see "Lodging," Village Inn Hotel). Breakfast and lunch during ski season, summer sunset dinners Friday, Saturday, and Sunday nights; incredible views of Mount Rainier and the Cascades from this restaurant at the 6,872-foot level, reached by chair lift; $–$$. *Wild Berry Restaurant*, State Route 706, Ashford, 569-2628. Breakfast daily in summer, weekends only rest of year; lunch and dinner daily year-round; famous for its wild blackberry pie; $.

FOR MORE INFORMATION Mount Rainier National Park, Tahoma Woods, Star Route, Ashford 98304, 569-2211. Guest Services, Star Route, Ashford 98304, 569-2275.

Mount Saint Helens: An Awesome Destination

On a quiet Sunday morning, May 18, 1980, Mount Saint Helens blew its top in a tremendous explosion that made headlines (and carried volcanic ash) around the world. Within seconds 1,277 feet of the mountaintop vaporized in a billowing cloud of steam and ash. The statistics are staggering. The eruption lasted nine hours and had a force equal to about 400 million tons of TNT. Four billion cubic yards of mountain were displaced, enough to provide one ton of ash for every person on earth. Timber downed came to 3.2 billion board feet, or enough to build 640,000 homes. At least 57 lives were lost.

In the years since, the devastated landscape around the mountain has started to revive with the regrowth of plants and the return of animals and birds. Now a national volcanic monument, the area is one of the most popular destinations in the Northwest, attracting more than 600,000 people annually.

The trip to view Mount Saint Helens makes a good weekend jaunt with an overnight stop at Morton or one of the small towns along Interstate 5. This is a summer or early-fall trip because the back roads are closed by snow from late October until about mid-May. This is also the time when you're most likely to have clear weather for viewing the mountain from a distance. This trip naturally divides itself into two distinct parts: the visitor center and then the drive to Windy Ridge.

Begin your visit at the new (1986) $5.3-million Mount Saint Helens National Volcanic Monument visitor center on Washington 504, five miles east of I-5 at Castle Rock (Exit 49). Built of stone and huge timbers, the imposing center houses an array of interpretive exhibits that do an excellent job of translating and illustrating the scientific data surrounding the eruption in a manner easily understandable to the layperson. Youngsters particularly enjoy a walk-in model of the volcano.

Dramatic side-by-side photos picture the mountain before and after the eruption. A map shows how far the ash was carried and how deep it collected—from .1 inch in Montana to 1.57 inches at Ritzville in eastern Washington. On display are tools and instruments used to monitor volcanoes, including a working seismograph with its sensitive needle recording current earthquake activity. It is an eerie sensation to watch the needles moving jerkily along, monitoring tremors within the mountain, and realize it's a bit like a giant heartbeat signifying that Mount Saint Helens, though now quiet, is very much a live volcano. Outside, telescopes trained on the mountain give close-up views on clear days. While you're here, pick up maps and the latest forest service information on road conditions around the mountain. The mountain is open to climbers; you'll need a permit from monument headquarters from May through October.

The massive mudflows that buried roads, houses, and logging camps just after the eruption came rushing down the Toutle River (you can still see mountains of ash excavated from the river where I-5 crosses it). Highway 504 leads about another 16 miles up the North Fork of the Toutle River, where structures are half buried from the mudflow. Scheduled for completion in 1992 is the 22-mile Spirit Lake Highway from the confluence of the Green and Toutle rivers to Coldwater Lake. When it's finished, you'll be able to drive within 10 miles of the northwest side of the mountain and look into the crater.

Helicopter services along Highway 504 and around Castle Rock, as well as light plane flights from airports around Kelso and Chehalis, will take you up for aerial views of the crater.

You get the best views of the mountain from the northeast side via roads out of Randle, but including both the visitor center and a trip to this side in a single day is difficult. If your schedule gives you some time to kill, nearby Chehalis offers some worthwhile sightseeing. At Lewis County Historical Museum, housed in the old train depot, the exhibits focus on local history as far back as the pioneer days. The Chehalis and Centralia Railroad operates steam train excursions between the two cities on weekends from mid-May through September. Claquato Church, three miles west on Highway 6, is the state's oldest (1858).

From I-5 turn east on U.S. 12 for 49 miles to Randle. At Mary's Corner, 2½ miles east, a side road to the right takes you several hundred yards to Jackson House Historic Site, an 1844 log cabin and pioneer home once used as a courthouse. Following the Cowlitz River, U.S. 12 passes Mayfield and Riffe lakes, impoundments behind dams on the river that offer rustic resorts, campgrounds, and trout fishing from May to October. Three miles west of Morton, Short Road leads south a half mile to a viewpoint where, with binoculars, you can look into the Mount Saint Helens crater and see the lava dome.

Often, visitors from the East to cities of the Northwest are amazed at how little poverty is visible. But the absence of squalid city ghettos is deceptive. Much of the poverty in the Northwest is rural poverty, and the "stump" ranches along U.S. 12 are typical of what you'll find on many back roads on the west side of the Cascades.

The stump ranch is a phenomenon peculiar to western Washington and Oregon. Typically it denotes a relatively small, marginal subsistence type of farm where the trees have been felled and removed but the stumps remain. The land between the stumps is not cultivated and is usually used for grazing. Historically, the land owner paid less taxes on land that had not been cleared than on land under cultivation.

Morton is another typical logging town, and the main street is often lined with logging trucks, some carrying their rear wheels piggyback fashion. There's a chain saw sculpture of a logger at the entrance to town. Morton is locally noteworthy for the zany quality of its annual Loggers Jubilee. In addition to the traditional lumberjack competitions—tree topping, speed chopping, ax throwing, chain saw and hand saw bucking, and log rolling—the celebration features an unusual event: riding lawnmower races. Locals say the races evolved from the loggers' habit of emerging from the taverns on Saturday night and drag racing riding lawnmowers down the main street. City fathers decided it might be safer to formalize and regulate the event. Several motels and restaurants in Morton make the town a good choice (as is Randle) for an overnight stay on this two-day excursion.

Fill your gas tank in Randle, 17 miles east on U.S. 12, as there are no facilities in the national monument. The round trip to Windy Ridge will take several hours, so you may want to pick up a picnic lunch (try Tilton River Deli in Morton near the corner of Second and Main). There's also a modest restaurant in a mobile home, Crater House—about six miles before you reach Windy Ridge— where you can get sandwiches and fish and chips.

Turn south on the well-marked Forest Service road just beyond Fischer's Shopping Center in Randle. At one mile you'll come to the junction of Roads 23 and 25. Bear right on 25. At ten miles, stop at the information station just beyond Iron Creek campground. There's a ranger on hand here to answer your questions and a lovely trail through virgin forest just off the parking lot.

Nothing prepares you for the shock of seeing the devastation of Mount Saint Helens for the first time. Despite the thousands of words that have been written, the movies and the television coverage, it's an overwhelming experience.

You approach the Windy Ridge viewpoint on the north side through miles of lush green forest. Magnificent virgin timber, 650-year-old Douglas firs stretch over 200 feet into the sky. Velvety moss covers the forest floor, huge sword ferns grow in abundance, sunlight filters through the trees. There's a hushed quality to this land, which looks the way much of western Washington probably did before the advent of logging.

Suddenly you come around a bend in the road and the entire scene changes. Minutes earlier, you were deep in the green forest; now you are out in the open with a view that extends from horizon to horizon.

And all of it is gray. Gray tree trunks, gray mountains, gray valleys. Without its forest cover, the landscape is naked.

At road's end at Windy Ridge, you are within four miles of Mount Saint Helens and can see the side of the mountain blown away in the eruption. The ridge is well named, for the wind blows nearly constantly. A log-and-gravel path anchored by cables climbs the ridge for outstanding views of the mountain and the new Spirit Lake. Below, the lake is jammed with thousands of floating gray logs. A descriptive plaque at the overlook points out the location of Harry Truman's lodge (he was the old caretaker who refused to leave before the eruption and died), highlights of the eruption, and the original Spirit Lake. Your visit to Mount Saint Helens is likely to stick in your mind long after you return home.

Area Code: 206

DRIVING DIRECTIONS From Seattle drive south on I-5 116 miles to Castle Rock and 5 miles east on Washington 504 to the visitor center. From Castle Rock to Windy Ridge, go north on I-5 19 miles to U.S. 12, then 49 miles to Randle and south on Forest Service roads about 35 miles. To vary the trip back to Seattle, follow U.S. 12 east from Randle through Packwood, then Washington 123 up the east side of Mount Rainier National Park (see page 65) and Washington 410 into Enumclaw.

Approximate round-trip mileage via I-5 in both directions is 410.

SIGHTSEEING *Mount Saint Helens National Volcanic Monument,* Amboy 98601, 247-5473. Visitor center on State Route 504, 5 miles east of I-5, Exit 49 at Castle Rock, 274-4038. Hours: April to mid-September daily 9 A.M. to 6 P.M., rest of year 9 A.M. to 5 P.M. *Mount Saint Helens Scenic Flights: Pacific West Aviation,* 748-0035. Small planes. *North Toutle 19 Mile House,* 274-8779, (800) 422-5792 in summer (in WA). Helicopter trips. *Cougar's Bluebird Helicopters,* 238-5326. *Lewis County Historical Museum,* 599 Northwest Front Street, Chehalis 98532, 748-0831. Tuesday through Saturday, 9 A.M. to 5 P.M., Sunday 1 to 5 P.M.; Housed in historic Burlington Northern Railroad Depot. Donation. *Chehalis–Centralia Railroad,*

Main Street east of I-5, Exit 77, Chehalis, 748-8885. Steam train excursions mid-May through September. Adults $6, under 16 $4. *Claquato Church,* State Route 6, 2 miles west of I-5, Exit 77. Washington's oldest church, built 1857. *Jackson Prairie Courthouse,* .25 mile south on Jackson Highway, 2.6 miles east of I-5 at Exit 68. Historic homestead, built in mid-1800s, was first U.S. district court north of the Columbia River.

EVENTS *Loggers Jubilee,* Morton, 496-5289, second weekend in August. *Southwest Washington Fair,* Chehalis, 748-6771, third weekend in August.

LODGING *Best Western Pony Soldier Motor Inn,* 122 Interstate Avenue, Chehalis 98532, 748-0101. Moderate-priced chain motel, $–$$. *Ferryman's Inn,* 1003 Eckerson Road, Centralia 98531, 330-2094. Newer well-maintained motel, $. *Hampton House* (bed and breakfast), 409 Silverbrook Road, Randle 98377, 497-2907. $. *Hotel Packwood,* 104 Main Street, Packwood 98361. $. *The Seasons,* 200 Westlake, Morton 98356, 496-6835. Conveniently located adjacent to U.S. 12, $. *Timberland Motor Inn,* 206 Spirit Lake Highway, Castle Rock 98611, 274-6002. Small lodging, $.

CAMPING *Lewis and Clark State Park,* 4583 Jackson Highway, Winlock 98596, 864-2643. 33 sites, no hookups, $8. Open May through September. *Ike Kinswa State Park,* Harmony Road, Mossyrock 98564, 983-3402. On Lake Mayfield. 101 sites, 41 with full hookup, $8 for tent sites, $12 for full hookup. *Mossyrock Park,* 202 Ajlune Road, Mossyrock 98564, 983-3900. On Riffe Lake. 60 sites, 24 with full hookup, $4–$8. *Maple Grove RV Park and Campground,* 175 Cispus Road, Randle 98377, 497-2741. On the Cowlitz River. Fishing, store, laundry, clubhouse, recreation room. 159 sites, 27 full hookups, 34 water-electricity only, 89 water only, $8–$12.50.

DINING *Casa Ramos,* 929 Harrison, Centralia, 330-2045. Lunch, dinner; Mexican food; $. *Mary McCrank's Dinner House,* 2923 Jackson Highway, Chehalis, 748-3662. Lunch Tuesday through Saturday, dinner Tuesday through Sunday; home-style cooking; $. *Roadhouse Inn,* U.S. Highway 12 and Crumb Road, Morton, 496-5029. Breakfast, lunch, and dinner; American/Italian; $–$$. *Saint Helen's Inn,* 440 North Market, Chehalis, 748-1487. Breakfast; steaks, seafood, pasta at lunch and dinner, $. *Wheel Cafe,* 145 Main Street, Morton, 496-3240. Breakfast, lunch, and dinner; American; $.

FOR MORE INFORMATION Mount Saint Helens National Volcanic Monument, Amboy 98601, 247-5473. Twin Cities Chamber of Commerce, P.O. Box 1263, Chehalis 98532, 748-8885.

Portland for First-Time Visitors

Many newcomers to the Pacific Northwest assume that Portland and Seattle are near-twin sisters, the one a bit smaller than the other, but essentially very similar. True, they're both on the water. They both have the same cool, maritime climate. They both have spectacular forest and mountain scenery visible from downtown. Portland's population (at the 1990 census) is 437,000 covering an area of 103 square miles; Seattle's is 516,259 covering 84 square miles. Pretty similar.

But when you've visited both you begin to notice the differences. Prices of accommodations, meals, and just about everything else are lower in Portland, and Oregon has no sales tax (Seattle's is 8.1 percent). The Seattle skyline is studded with glittering new skyscrapers, some over 50 stories tall. Portland's skyline is more modest, the result of height limits on downtown buildings. Traffic congestion is an increasing problem in Seattle. In Portland, you'll seldom encounter a traffic jam even at rush hour, and the city has a light rail transit system that works. Seattle has more hotels, elegant restaurants, major league sports, and theater. Portland has more crime. Both have their problems with street people. As one writer put it: "There's no question that Seattle has more energy and wields more economic muscle than Portland. But Portland has an elegance and ambience Seattle will never attain."

The pioneers who founded the town here in the 1840s could hardly have picked a more splendid site. The original city and today's business district lie along the west bank of the Willamette River, just a few miles upstream of its confluence with the Columbia. Wooded hills rise steeply to the west, and it's here that Portland's most affluent neighborhoods have been built overlooking the city. On the eastern banks of the Willamette, industrial sites along the river trail off eastward into modest neighborhoods of single-family houses extending to the suburbs of Gresham, Troutdale, and Boring. The pristine white slopes of 11,235-foot Mount Hood punctuate the eastern horizon.

The story of how Portland got its name concerns two New Englanders who, among thousands of others, came west on the Oregon Trail and founded the city. A. J. Lovejoy of Boston and Francis Pettygrove of Portland, Maine, each wanted to name the new 16-block townsite on the west bank of the Willamette River after his own hometown. They flipped a coin to decide; fortunately, Pettygrove won. Somehow, Boston, Oregon, just wouldn't ring true.

Ten bridges, each distinctively different, stitch the east and west sides of the city together. You'll quickly earn the admiration of the natives if you can name them all. From the north they are: Saint Johns, which looks like something out of Camelot; Five Point One, named for a milepost on the railroad, and the highest and widest vertical lift span in the world; Fremont; Broadway, painted red; Steel; Burnside, with twin green turrets; Hawthorne; Marquam, the soaring new freeway bridge; Ross Island; and Sellwood.

Getting around in Portland is easy. Downtown is pedestrian scale and the city has a fine transit system called Tri-Met. Buses in the downtown area are free and depart from shelters along automobile-free Southwest Fifth and Sixth avenues. Stops and shelters are marked with the symbols (trout, raindrops, leaves, a rose, an elk, a snowflake, and a beaver) of the seven areas served, and fares to outlying areas range from 85 cents to $1.15, with an all-day tourist ticket good on all routes for $3. MAX, Portland's nifty new light rail transit, circles through the downtown area, then crosses the river on the Steel Bridge to Lloyd Center and Gresham. For $2 you can buy a comprehensive guide to the whole system from the Tri-Met office in Pioneer Courthouse Square.

If you insist on driving (and raising your blood pressure trying to find a place to park), you'll find it useful to know that the five areas into which the city is divided are designated on the street signs by the prefixes NW, N, NE, SE, or SW. The river is the dividing line between east and west; Burnside Street divides north from south.

On your first visit try to stay at a downtown hotel or around Lloyd Center and the new convention center, from where you can ride MAX across the river into downtown. On your first morning don your comfortable walking shoes (and take an umbrella if the skies are gray) and begin your exploring at Pioneer Courthouse Square in the heart of the city. Powell's Bookstore (see page 80) publishes a free walking map that you can pick up at the Tri-Met office, the visitor center, or numerous locations downtown. Powell's Travel Store, at one side of the square, is an excellent source of maps and reference books on Portland. The square is a delightfully open place with a waterfall, a coffeehouse, a machine that forecasts the weather, and thousands of paving bricks inscribed with the names of Portlanders who contributed to the building of this square. The 1868 Pioneer (Federal) Courthouse and Post Office flanks the east side of the square. Behind the courthouse is the multistoried Pioneer Place, with dozens of shops and restaurants. Saks Fifth Avenue borders Pioneer Place on the south. On the west side of the square is Nordstrom, the Seattle-based apparel store that in recent years has become synonymous with outstanding service. On the north side is Portland's leading department store, Meier & Frank.

Head south on SW Broadway two blocks to the Heathman Hotel, at the corner of SW Salmon. The hotel serves high tea every afternoon and also has one of the best restaurants in town. The Arlene Schnitzer Concert Hall in the elegant, restored Paramount Theater adjoins the Heathman. B. Moloch/Heathman Bakery & Pub, just behind the hotel, is a great place to breakfast if you've started out on an empty stomach. A block to the south is Portland's sparkling new Performing Arts Center. At SW Madison, turn west one block to the Park Blocks, one of the open-space features that make Portland such a remarkable city. In 1852, the city fathers set aside 25 contiguous blocks to remain a park stretching from the hills to the river. Seven of the blocks have since been built upon, the other 18 remain serene islands of lawns, shrubbery, towering elms, and sculpture. At SW Jefferson Street, the Portland Art Institute (with excellent collections of Northwest Coast Indian art, Asian art, and twentieth-century European and American sculpture) and the Oregon Historical Center (pioneer exhibits) face each other across the Park Blocks.

Turn east on SW Madison Street and walk three blocks to the handsome 1895 City Hall. Just to the north is Portland's most striking ediface, the Portland Building (1982), designed in Post-Modern style by Michael Graves. Over the SW Fourth Avenue entrance a massive copper statue of Portlandia, the second largest hammered copper sculpture in the world (the Statue of Liberty is the largest), kneels to welcome visitors. Across the street, the Plaza Blocks, public squares dedicated in 1852, were originally segregated into men's and women's parks. The Justice Center, at SW Second and SW Madison, houses the Police Museum on the sixteenth floor, exhibiting a vintage motorcycle, traffic signals, criminals' weapons, and police radios.

Zigzag north two blocks and east two blocks to SW Salmon and SW Front. The visitor information center here is an excellent place to pick up maps, brochures, and advice on what to see and do in Portland. Another delightful people-pleasing feature of Portland is the Portland Guides. These two-person teams, garbed in distinctive uniforms with green jackets and caps, walk the downtown streets to answer questions and offer assistance. They're great sources of tips, from where to get a vegetarian burrito to where to get your film developed in an hour.

Across SW Front Avenue is Tom McCall Waterfront Park, a two-mile stretch of greensward converted from a four-lane freeway several years ago to provide access to the Willamette River. (Has any other city in the country ripped up freeway to create open space?) Appropriately, it was named for Oregon's maverick governor (1967–75), who took many courageous stands in support of the environment. The park is a peaceful place to walk, jog, picnic, and watch the vessel traffic on the busy river.

The city has preserved much of its past in historic districts, two of which—Yamhill and Skidmore/Old Town—feature dozens of handsome nineteenth-century commercial buildings, examples of the finest remaining cast-iron architecture in the country. You'll see block after block of three- and four-story buildings with ornate scrollwork, filagree, and other details, all cast in iron.

Stroll through the Yamhill Marketplace, on SW Yamhill between SW First and SW Second. The multilevel building with an atrium center is crammed with produce stands, fish markets, bakeries, and dozens of shops and restaurants. You can pick up the makings for a picnic lunch here or, if you're exploring on a weekend from March to December, wait until you reach the Saturday Market a few blocks away.

Continue north along SW First Avenue, detouring a block or two west on the side streets as you spot something interesting. In addition to the handsome photogenic old buildings (morning light is best to photograph most of them), there are scores of one-of-a-kind shops in the historic districts. The Photographic Image Gallery, at 208 SW First, sells museum-quality photos including signed prints by Ansel Adams, Imogen Cunningham, and Oregon photographer Ray Atkeson. On Front and Ash streets is the Oregon Maritime Museum and, nearby, the mast from the battleship *Oregon*. The painstakingly restored rococo New Market Theatre (1892), at First and Ankeny, offers several galleries and shops. The small Jeff Morris Fire Museum, at Ankeny Park, traces the history of the Portland Fire Bureau and displays vintage equipment. At 10 NW First, the Made In Oregon Shop specializes in products from all over the state, such as smoked salmon, jams, cheese, fudge, Pendleton woolen shirts and blankets, and myrtlewood carvings, while the Import Plaza, in the old Globe Hotel at 1 NW Couch, sells products primarily from Asia. You can pick up a wallet, purse, sheepskin coat, or raw leather for crafts at Oregon Leather Company, NW Second and NW Couch. The American Advertising Museum, in the next block on NW Second, displays vintage print and broadcast advertising including more than 200 artifacts on loan from the Smithsonian Institution. The Couch Street Fish House and Dan & Louis' Oyster Bar, where you can watch them shuck oysters in the window, are local seafood institutions. Portland's modest Chinatown occupies several blocks on NW Third, NW Fourth, and NW Fifth immediately north of Burnside.

The Saturday Market is a Portland phenomenon. Between Skidmore Fountain, which in 1888 was the center of town, and the Burnside Bridge, scores of purveyors of pottery, woven goods, paintings, metal sculpture, wood carvings, knickknacks, and ethnic fast food set up shop every Saturday and Sunday from March to December 24. The place has the atmosphere of a street fair with musicians, dancers, jugglers, and other performers putting on their impromptu acts for anyone who will watch.

The quadruple bronze drinking fountains you'll notice on street corners in this part of town are another Portland curiosity. Millionaire lumber tycoon and philanthropist Simon Benson, for whom the Benson Hotel is named, among other things, gave 20 of the fountains to the city in the early 1900s and the city has since added more. Whether it's myth or fact no one seems to know, but the story is that Benson hoped his hard-drinking loggers would choose the fountains for quenching their thirst rather than the town's saloons.

SW Broadway, lined with upscale shops, is a good choice for your return route to Pioneer Courthouse Square. You may also want to pop into the lobby of the

Benson Hotel, at SW Broadway and SW Stark, for a look at the splendid Circassian walnut paneling and crystal chandeliers in the lobby. If breakfast is a major event with you, the London Grill here is a good choice. Some say they serve the best bagels, lox, and cream cheese in the Northwest.

Save most of your second day in town for Washington Park. This splendid 145-acre park perches on the west hills overlooking downtown and is the location of Portland's world-famous zoo, the Oregon Museum of Science and Industry, the World Forestry Center, a rose garden, a Japanese garden, and a miniature steam train. Take Tri-Met bus number 63 from SW Fifth Street or, if you're driving, take SW Jefferson Street west to Canyon Drive (U.S. 26) and follow it for about one mile to the clearly marked exit for "Zoo-OMSI."

The Washington Park Zoo has the largest breeding herd of Asian elephants in the world outside of Asia. In keeping with the new style of zoos all over the country, this one features animals in simulated native habitats including African, Night Country—for nocturnal animals—and Cascade Stream and Pond. Polar bears can be seen through underwater viewing windows, and penguins have their own climate-controlled beach that includes waves.

The Oregon Museum of Science and Industry (say "OMSI" and the locals will know what you're talking about) is a fascinator, especially for children. It's a hands-on museum with a walk-in heart that actually beats, a replica of a space station, hurricane and tornado simulators, a planetarium, and regular science shows. Across the parking lot, the World Forestry Center presents exhibits on trees and the wood products industry. Board the miniature train that winds for four miles through the forested park to the International Rose Test Gardens and the Japanese Garden.

Area Code: 503

GETTING THERE Interstate 5 connects Seattle and Portland. You can make the 172-mile trip in about 3½ hours.

RAIL AND AIR TRANSPORTATION *Amtrak* provides excellent 4-hour service on Superliner equipment between the two cities with 3 departures daily in each direction. The round-trip coach fare is $54, with a special off-season excursion fare of $34.

American, Continental, Delta, Horizon, Northwest, TWA, and *United Airlines* also connect the two cities, and transcontinental flights bound for either Seattle or Portland will often call at the other city before continuing to their destinations. Horizon Air offers departures every half hour from both cities on weekdays. Round-trip fare is from $108 to $254.

SIGHTSEEING *American Advertising Museum,* 9 NW Second Avenue, 226-0000. Hours: Wednesday to Friday 11 A.M. to 5 P.M., Saturday and Sunday noon to 5 P.M. Adults $3, seniors and 6–12 $1.50. *James F. Bybee House,* Howell Park, Sauvie Island, 222-1741. Hours: June to Labor Day daily noon to 5 P.M. Donation. *The Old Church,* 1422 SW 11th Avenue, 222-2031. Hours: Tuesday to Saturday 11 A.M. to 3 P.M. Free. *Oregon Art Institute,* 1219 SW Park Avenue, 226-2811. Hours: Tuesday to Saturday 11 A.M. to 5 P.M., Sunday 1 to 5 P.M., first Thursday open to 9 P.M. Adults $4, students $2, 6–12 $1, under 6 free, seniors free on Thursday; free admission for all from 4 to 9 P.M. on the first Thursday. *Oregon Historical Center,* 1230 SW Park Avenue, 222-1741. Hours: Monday to Saturday 10 A.M. to 4:45 P.M. Donation. *Oregon Maritime Center and Museum,* 113 SW Front Avenue, 224-7724. Hours: Memorial Day to Labor Day Wednesday to Sunday 11 A.M. to 4 P.M.; rest of year, Friday, Saturday, and Sunday 11 A.M. to 4 P.M. Adults $2, 8–18 and over 62 $1.75. *Police Museum,* 1111 SW Second Avenue, 796-3019. Tuesday to Friday, 10 A.M. to 3 P.M. Free. River cruises: *The Rose,* 286-7673. 49-passenger sternwheeler cruises Willamette River from downtown Portland. $7.50 to $10. *Columbia Gorge,* 223-3928. Operates 599-passenger sternwheeler leaving from downtown Portland for 2-hour cruises on the Willamette, some with meals served. October through mid-June Fridays and weekends. $7.50 to $49.95. *Saturday Market,* downtown at the west end of the Burnside Bridge, 222-6072. March to Christmas, Saturday 10 A.M. to 5 P.M., Sunday 11 A.M. to 4:30 P.M. *Washington Park:* International Rose Test Gardens, 796-5193. Free. Japanese Gardens 223-4070. Hours: April to September daily 7 A.M. to 9 P.M., rest of year 10 A.M. to 4 P.M. Adults $3.50, students and over 62 $2. Oregon Museum of Science and Industry, 222-2828. Hours: Daily 9 A.M. to 5 P.M., Friday to 8 P.M. Adults $5.25, 3–17 $3.50, and over 65 $4.25. Zoo, 226-1516. Hours: Daily from 9:30 A.M., closing time according to season. Adults $4.50, 3–11 $2.50, and over 65 $3, under 3 free; railway: adults $2.50, 3–11 and seniors $1.75. World Forestry Center, 228-1367. Hours: Daily 9 A.M. to 5 P.M. Adults $3, 2–18 and over 62, $2.

EVENTS *Artquake,* Pioneer Courthouse Square, 227-2787. Visual arts, juried show. *Chamber Music Northwest,* 223-3202. 5-week summer music festival at Reed College and Catlin Gabel School, pre-concert picnic suppers. *Mount Hood Festival of Jazz,* Mount Hood Community College in Gresham, 666-3810. Variety of jazz performed by national and international artists every August. *Portland Center for the Performing Arts,* SW Broadway and Main Street, 248-4496. Variety of performing arts and entertainment activities throughout the year. Box office hours: Monday to Saturday 10 A.M. to 5:30 P.M. *Oregon Shakespeare Festival,* 1111 SW Broadway, 248-6309. Branch of Ashland's renowned Shakespeare Festival. Performances from November to February. *Portland Marathon,* downtown, 226-1111,

September. *Portland Rose Festival,* 227-2681. City's biggest annual event, citywide in June. *Rose City Blues Festival,* McCall–Waterfront Park, July, 239-1010. *Summer Classics in the Square,* Pioneer Courthouse Square Plaza, 223-1718. Monday evening series of eight classical music performances in June and July. *The Bite!!! A Taste of Portland,* McCall–Waterfront Park, 248-0600. Annual August food festival, dozens of booths. *Your Zoo and All That Jazz Summer Concerts,* Washington Park Zoo outdoor amphitheater, 226-1561. Wednesday nights in summer. *Zoograss Bluegrass Concerts,* Washington Park Zoo outdoor amphitheater, 226-1561. Thursday nights in summer.

LODGING *Benson Hotel,* 309 SW Broadway at Oak, 97205, 228-2000. The city's grand old landmark hotel, $$$$. *Heathman Hotel,* SW Broadway at Salmon, 97205, 241-4100. Elegantly restored 1927 hotel, afternoon tea, $$$$. *Hotel Vintage Plaza,* 422 SW Broadway, 97205, 228-1212. 107-room hotel in renovated historic downtown building, business center, gym, $$$$. *Imperial Hotel,* 400 SW Broadway at Stark Street, 97205, 228-7221, (800) 547-8282. Reasonably priced alternative in the heart of downtown, $–$$. *Portland Hilton Hotel,* 921 SW Sixth Avenue, 97204, 226-1611. Convenient location, $$$$. *Portland Inn,* 1414 SW Sixth Avenue, 97201, 221-1611. (800) 648-6440. Convenient location with free parking, $$. *Portland Marriott Hotel,* 1401 SW Front Avenue, 97201, 226-7600. Attractive hotel overlooks Willamette River, $$$–$$$$. *Red Lion Inn/Coliseum,* 1225 N Thunderbird Way, 97227, 235-8311, (800) 547-8010. Adjacent to Memorial Coliseum on east side of Willamette River, $$. *Red Lion Inn/Downtown,* 310 SW Lincoln, 97201, 221-0450, (800) 547-8010. $$$–$$$$. *Red Lion Inn/Lloyd Center,* 1000 NE Multnomah Street, 97232, 281-6111, (800) 547-8010. Adjacent to huge Lloyd Center shopping complex on east side of Willamette, $$$$. *RiverPlace Alexis,* 1510 SW Harbor Way, 97201, 228-3233. Luxurious riverside lodging adjacent to McCall–Waterfront Park, $$$$. *Riverside Inn,* 50 SW Morrison Street, 97204, 221-0711, (800) 648-6440. Heart of historic Yamhill District overlooking the river, free parking, $$.

DINING *Alexis Restaurant,* 215 W Burnside, 224-8577. Lunch Monday to Friday, dinner daily; Greek cuisine; $–$$. *Atwater's,* 111 SW Fifth Avenue, 220-3600. Dinner Monday to Saturday, Sunday brunch; elegant dining on thirtieth floor of U.S. Bancorp Tower; $$$. *Bijou Cafe,* SW Third and Pine, 222-3187. Breakfast (hearty) and lunch daily; simple, tasty fare; $. *B. Moloch/Heathman Bakery & Pub,* 901 SW Salmon Street, 227-5700. Breakfast, lunch, dinner daily; casual eclectic place with a coffeehouse atmosphere, wood-burning brick oven produces notable pizzas and breads; $. *Couch Street Fish House,* NW Third and Couch, 223-6173. Dinner daily, award-winning restaurant known for its seafood, $$–$$$. *Dan & Louis Oyster Bar,* 208 SW Ankeny Street, 227-5906. Lunch and dinner daily; a

Portland tradition in Skidmore/Old Town Historic District, funky atmosphere; $–$$. *Esplanade Restaurant,* in RiverPlace Alexis Hotel (see "Lodging"). Breakfast, lunch, and dinner daily; elegant setting overlooking the Willamette River; $$–$$$. *Heathman Restaurant,* in Heathman Hotel (see "Lodging"). Breakfast, lunch, and dinner daily; classic regional Northwest cuisine elegantly presented; $$–$$$$. *Hunan,* 515 SW Broadway, 224-8063. Lunch and dinner daily; spicy Hunan and Szechuan Chinese specialties, $–$$. *Jake's Famous Crawfish,* 401 SW 12th, 226-1419. Lunch Monday to Friday, dinner daily; century-old seafood restaurant; $–$$$. *London Grill,* in Benson Hotel (see "Lodging"). Breakfast, lunch, and dinner daily; long-standing Portland reputation for fine dining in Old English setting; $$–$$$. *Macheesmo Mouse,* 719 SW Salmon, 228-3491. Lunch and dinner daily, healthy Mexican fast food, $. *Rose's,* 315 NW 23rd, 227-5181. Breakfast, lunch, and dinner daily; plenty of nostalgia in this New York–style deli right out of the 40s; $–$$.

FOR MORE INFORMATION Portland/Oregon Visitors Association, 26 SW Salmon 97204, 222-2223.

Portland: The Second Time Around

Part of getting to know Portland is getting to know its neighborhoods. On the east side of the river two are especially worth your attention.

Most of Portland's antiques shops (the greatest concentration in the Northwest) are clustered in Sellwood in 13 blocks of SE 13th Avenue, between Malden and Marion streets. The easiest way to get here is to cross the river on the Sellwood Bridge, then follow Tacoma Avenue until you reach SE 13th. The number 40 Tri-Met bus follows the same route.

Once an independent town, Sellwood became a Portland neighborhood around the turn of the century. Many of the antiques shops are housed in the shingle- and clapboard-sided wooden frame residences and Victorians typical of that era. You're unlikely to find any truly rare antiques here, since much of what is sold could more accurately be described as nostalgia, but the relatively quiet streets and small-town atmosphere make it a good choice for a couple of hours of browsing.

The Hawthorne District—reached via the Hawthorne Bridge east to Hawthorne Boulevard between SE 34th and SE 40th avenues—has been described as "the place where old buildings meet new ideas." Because its population was largely Italian at one time, it has also been called "Garlic Gulch," and its main street was once "Asylum Avenue" because it was the principal road to the Oregon Hospital for the Insane.

Start your exploring here with breakfast at the Bread and Ink Cafe, located at 3610 SE Hawthorne and a neighborhood social center noted for its crusty fresh-baked bread and innovative breakfast dishes. Other highlights include Artichoke Music, at number 3522, which sells all manner of sheet music and musical instruments; the Perfume House, number 3328, with an incredible selection of 600 women's and 200 men's fragrances, probably the largest such inventory in the country; and Murder by the Book, number 3729, with in excess of 15,000 mystery volumes for sale. Pastaworks, number 3735, is a delightfully fragrant Italian delicatessen with pasta, cheeses, unusual sauces, and 350 different Italian wines, and right next door, Powell's Books for Cooks has just the recipes you need for using these foods.

Bibliophiles will want to schedule at least a couple of hours for browsing through Powell's Books, back on the west side of the river at 1005 W Burnside. Covering an entire block, this may be the largest bookstore in the West, with an astonishing million-plus volumes. As one wag put it, "If you can't find it at Powell's, you probably don't need it." And, if you tire of browsing, you can take one of your purchases to a table in the Annie Hughes Coffee Room, located in one corner of the store, sip a cup of espresso, and read all afternoon. No one will disturb you.

The Nob Hill neighborhood, just up from Powell's, between W Burnside and NW Kearney, NW 21st, and NW 23rd, may remind you of similar neighborhoods in San Francisco. Big old Victorian and Georgian mansions, now apartment buildings or multiple-family dwellings, crowd the narrow streets that rise to the slope of the West Hills. Sometimes referred to as "Gourmet Gulch," it's an area of specialty food shops, restaurants, sidewalk cafés, gift stores, and boutiques. If you're a "foodie" looking for something unusual to take home, try Elephant's Delicatessen, 13 NW 23rd Place; Coffee People, 722 W Burnside; Gabriel's Bakery, 2272 NW Kearney Street; Hartung Meat Company, 2131 W Burnside; or Blue Herring Fish Market, 2108 NW Glisan Street.

Portland is known as the City of Roses, but from April through June it might just as well be known as the City of Rhododendrons and Azaleas. In late spring the city is ablaze with the pinks, reds, oranges, and purples of these blooming shrubs. Hundreds of well-tended residential gardens, especially in the West Hills, compete visually with immaculate public gardens.

Schedule a drive through the West Hills residential neighborhoods in the morning when the east-facing slopes get the sun, making for the best photographic conditions. Handsome old homes perch on winding streets that wrap around the hillsides. There is no best route, just meander as the mood strikes you. Some of the more popular routes include SW Terwilliger Boulevard, SW Cascade Drive, SW Fairview Boulevard, SW Kingston Drive, and SW Vista Avenue and Greenway Road to Council Crest Park, at 1,073 feet the highest point in the city, with sweeping views of the Willamette River below, Mount Hood to the east, and Mount Saint Helens to the north.

While you're up here in the hills, be sure to visit the handsome old Pittock Mansion. Henry Pittock, Portland newspaper tycoon, built the 22-room, French-style château in 1914 on 46 parklike acres overlooking the city. It's furnished with seventeenth- and eighteenth-century art, Tiffany tiles, and a grand marble staircase. The mansion was about to be torn down and the land subdivided for development in 1964 when, in a move typical of Portland, it was preserved by public subscription.

One of the city's real treasures is Crystal Springs Rhododendron Garden, on SE 28th across from Reed College. Started in 1950 as a joint effort between the Portland Bureau of Parks and the local chapter of the American Rhododendron Society, it is considered by horticulturists to be one of the finest in the country. The six-acre wooded site has more than 2,500 rhododendrons. From the parking lot on SE 28th, walk the high bridge across the ravine. A second bridge leads you to Garden Island, where children delight in feeding the recently hatched duck-lings at the waterside feeding stations.

Reed College, with only about 1,000 students attending classes on its 98 acres, is known for its academic excellence. It has a remarkable student-teacher ratio of about 12 to 1 and ranks first (for its size) in numbers of Rhodes scholars grad-uated. In 1911, Reed's first president established its enduring reputation for iconoclasm and liberal thinking when he said, "Hallowed traditions are petrified errors." Chamber Music Northwest (223-3202) holds a series of evening summer concerts on the campus.

Three other Portland parks are worthy of your attention if you have the time. Hoyt Arboretum, a 214-acre park with tree specimens from all over the world, has the world's largest collection of conifer varieties and nine miles of trails. The fall foliage show here is a stunner, usually beginning about mid-October. Lilacs are the attraction at Duniway Park located at SW Sixth and SW Sheridan. In May several hundred mature shrubs are covered with fragrant white and purple blossoms. Peninsula Park's sunken rose garden, at North Albina and North Ainsworth, is the city's largest, with 10,000 bushes providing a show of blossoms from June to November.

Though Portland doesn't have as many opportunities for water sightseeing as Seattle does, two harbor tours cruise the Willamette River for water-level views of the city and its bridges, docks, grain and petroleum terminals, and shipyards. If you're at RiverPlace Marina—at the south end of Tom McCall Park—early most any morning, you can watch competitive rowers practicing in their slender wooden shells. The Rowing Shop here (223-5859) has rentals. To explore the river on your own, you can rent canoes from Brown's Landing at Sauvie Island (227-6283).

For visitors used to the nocturnal excitement of New York, San Francisco, or Los Angeles, Portland may seem pretty dull except for those interested in music or the theater. Portland has about two dozen nightclubs and lounges, most featuring rhythm-and-blues or jazz, plus a couple of comedy clubs. Noteworthy are the Dakota Cafe, Key Largo, Brasserie Montmartre, and the Last Laugh comedy nightclub. The Rimsky-Korsakoffee House, at 707 SE 12th, is locally known for its classical music served up in a Victorian-style coffeehouse setting.

As hoary liquor laws are gradually changed and micro-breweries (less than 10,000 gallons annual production) have sprung up all over the Northwest, producing high-quality specialty beers, the brewpub has emerged in both Portland and Seattle. Typically, the decor is lots of brass and wood, and the ambience that of a European pub. Some serve the product of just one brewery; others offer a selection of Northwest micro-brews. Five of the better known include: BridgePort Brewpub, 1313 NW Marshall; Heathman Bakery & Pub, 901 SW Salmon; Hillsdale Brewery & Public House, 1505 SW Sunset Boulevard; Portland Brewing Company, 1339 NW Flanders; and Widmer Brewing Company, 1405 NW Lovejoy.

Portland is a delight in summer for music lovers. Portlanders are outdoor people, and the city is alive with music in July, August, and September. Pioneer Courthouse Square offers noon and early evening concerts; Portland State University hosts free indoor lunchtime ("brown bag") concerts; Washington Park Summer Stage features theater, dance, and music in the park; classical and pop music is scheduled summer evenings in Tom McCall Park, and the Washington Park Zoo has a summer series of jazz concerts called Your Zoo and All That Jazz and another of bluegrass music called Zoograss. Mount Hood Community College, in suburban Gresham, holds the two-day, three-night Mount Hood Jazz Festival in August.

Area Code: 503

SIGHTSEEING (See also page 66.) *Crystal Springs Rhododendron Gardens,* S.E. 28th Avenue near Woodstock, 796-5193. Daily from 8 A.M. to dark. Free. *Duniway Park,* SW Sixth and SW Sheridan. Free. *Hoyt Arboretum,* 4000 SW Fairview Boulevard, 228-8732. Visitor center, guided walks. Hours: daily 10 A.M. to 4 P.M. Free. *Peninsula Park,* N Albina and N Ainsworth, 285-1185. Free. *Pittock Mansion,* 3229 NW Pittock Drive, 248-4469. Hours: daily 1 to 5 P.M. Adults $3, seniors over 65 $2.50, 6–18 $1, under 6 free.

EVENTS *The Portland Center for the Performing Arts,* SW Broadway and Main, 248-4496. Hosts regular traveling companies year round, plus the Oregon Shakespeare Festival in winter. *The Arlene Schnitzer Concert Hall,* 813 SW Alder, 228-

1353. 2,700-seat home to the Oregon Symphony, conducted by internationally known James DePriest year round. *The Portland Youth Philharmonic,* 1119 SW Park, 223-5935. 4 concerts a year. *The Portland Opera Association,* Civic Auditorium, 1530 SW Second, 241-1401. 4 operas in spring and fall. *The Portland Civic Theater,* 1530 SW Yamhill, 226-3048. Thursday through Sunday year round; the city's oldest live theater. *The Portland Repertory Theater,* 25 SW Salmon, 224-4491. 6 productions a year; the city's only resident regional theater.

DINING (see also page 78.) *Bread and Ink Cafe,* 3610 Hawthorne, 234-4756. Breakfast, lunch, and dinner Monday through Saturday, Sunday brunch; imaginative Northwest nouvelle menu in a casual setting; $–$$. *Genoa,* 2832 SE Belmont Street, 238-1464. 4-course and 7-course fixed-price dinners Monday through Saturday, northern Italian cuisine, $$$–$$$$. *L'Auberge,* 2601 NW Vaughn, 223-3302. 6-course fixed-price dinners served Monday through Saturday, country French cuisine, $$$$. Bar menu Sunday evenings, $–$$. *Papa Haydn,* 701 NW 22nd, 228-7317. Lunch and dinner Monday through Saturday, known for its lavish desserts, $. *Vista Spring Cafe,* SW Spring and Vista, 222-2811. Lunch and dinner daily, cozy neighborhood restaurant in the city's West Hills, good pizza, $–$$. *Zell's: An American Cafe,* 1300 SE Morrison, 239-0196. Breakfast and lunch daily, imaginative breakfasts at this east side neighborhood restaurant, $.

East of the Cascades

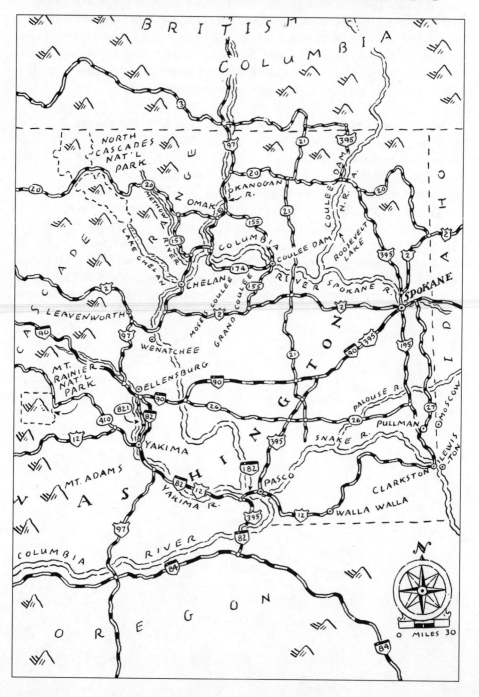

Cascade Loop: Is This Bavaria?

The Cascade Loop is one of the finest scenic mountain routes in the country. In just over 400 miles it takes in the lush greenery of the western part of the state, two crossings of the Cascades, the broad expanses of eastern Washington, and a splendid recreational lake.

The route comprises U.S. 2 east over Stevens Pass to Wenatchee, U.S. 97 north to Washington 153 through the Methow Valley, and Washington 20 to Winthrop and over the North Cascades Highway. You could cover all 423 miles in one hard-driving two-day weekend, but you wouldn't get to see very much. We recommend scheduling three or four days, with overnight stops at Leavenworth, Chelan, and/or Winthrop. Although you can drive the loop in either direction, we recommend driving east from Seattle on U.S. 2 and returning west on Washington 20. As we explain on page 97, there are good reasons for choosing this routing. We've spread the Loop over three sections because the itinerary in each will make a good weekend in itself.

Head north from Seattle on I-5 27 miles to Everett and turn east onto U.S. 2. Make your first stop the little town of Snohomish, the self-proclaimed Antiques Capital of the Northwest. If you're interested in browsing for antiques and collectibles, pick up a free map at the Chamber of Commerce (116 Avenue B), then begin your excursion on First Street, which runs along the Shohomish River. Most of the old buildings here date from the 1870s and 1880s when steamboats from Puget Sound came this far upriver carrying passengers and freight. There are antiques stores just about everywhere you look, each with a different specialty. Dollhouse Cottage, at Avenue A, displays hundreds of dolls while Rocking Chair Antiques, at 908 First Street, has clawfoot bathtubs, razor strops, hundreds of keys of various kinds, cigarette lighters, and harmonicas. The Snohomish Star Center at 829 Second Street, and Old Snohomish Arts & Crafts, at First Street and Avenue C, both include several specialty shops featuring local arts and crafts. Before you leave Snohomish, you might want to stop at the Blackman Museum (118 Avenue B), an ornate 1878 Victorian home built for the first mayor of Snohomish and notable for its 12-foot ceilings, etched-glass windows, and lovely wallpapers and furnishings.

Continue east on U.S. 2 through Monroe (the fortresslike complex you see south of the highway is the state reformatory), and towns with the intriguing names of Sultan, Startup, Gold Bar, and Index. The awesome north face of Mount Index—elevation 5,979 feet—looms over the town and is one of the great challenges for local rock climbers. If you have time, stop at sleepy little Index, which seems hardly to have changed since the turn of the century. The Bush House Country Inn here has a big stone fireplace to cozy up to on a cold drizzly day and a local reputation for hearty country food.

U.S. 2 follows the original route the Great Northern Railway (now Burlington Northern) pushed across the Cascades in 1893. Skykomish, locally known as "Sky," was formerly a busy railroad town where steam locomotives were changed for electric engines for the climb over the mountains. You'll see the big brick powerhouse still standing across the tracks and the ramshackle railroad hotel where train crews used to bunk. Lovely waterfalls plunge down the sheer rock faces of the mountains on either side of the road to the Skykomish River below. The river is a favorite of white-water rafters who enjoy a bit of a challenge in their sport. Deception Falls, about ten miles east of Skykomish, is a good place to schedule a rest stop and take pictures of the thundering falls.

At Scenic, look to the left as the highway crosses over the railroad tracks and you can catch a glimpse of the western portal of the Cascade Tunnel, until a couple of years ago the longest tunnel—7.8 miles—in North America. Canadian Pacific Railroad's new tunnel under Rodgers Pass in British Columbia now claims that honor.

For the next seven miles the highway climbs steeply in a series of broad sweeping curves to 4,061 feet at Stevens Pass. To the west are broad vistas of conifer-carpeted foothills rolling away toward Puget Sound. Stevens Pass is the site of one of the state's popular ski areas. The slopes, which have a vertical drop here of 1,800 feet, are served by ten chair lifts and three tows, and there are cross-country trails, night skiing, a ski school, rental equipment, and a day lodge. Overnight facilities are not provided.

U.S. 2 drops down the east slope of the Cascades, then follows Nason Creek through Merritt and Coles Corner. Washington 207 leads north five miles to 2,445-acre, five-mile-long Lake Wenatchee, popular for swimming, camping, water sports and trout fishing. Just beyond Coles Corner, U.S. 2 joins the tumbling Wenatchee River to squeeze through Tumwater Canyon. A spectacular stretch of highway, with sheer rock walls on one side and white-water rapids on the other, this is a great place to take photos if you can dodge into one of the few turnouts beside the road. From mid-September into October, the canyon is ablaze with the brilliant red and yellow foliage of vine maples and big-leaf maples, making it one of the best locations in the state for viewing fall color.

Leavenworth is your final destination for this portion of the Cascade Loop. Once a declining lumber town, Leavenworth adopted a Bavarian theme in the 1960s and has since become a roaring success as a tourist destination. Almost every building in town is decorated with ornate woodwork and Bavarian motifs. A German oompah band can frequently be heard in the park, and restaurants feature German cuisine, from sauerbraten to Wiener schnitzel. From spring through fall, hundreds upon hundreds of planter boxes, flower pots, and blossoming gardens turn the town into a riot of color.

Got a yen for a cuckoo clock? You'll find scores of them, as well as antique clocks, at the Clock Shop, 721 Front Street. The Blue Heron, 905 Commercial Street, specializes in fine art. Die Musik Box at 837 Front Street is a fantasy store for music box lovers, with 3,700 of the instruments in stock. At 215 Ninth Street, Hoelgaard's Danish Bakery has a mouth-watering array of European pastries and breads. The Gingerbread Factory, at 828 Commercial, is a seren-dipitous shop for all manner of eats including gingerbread houses and out-of-this-world cookies and pastries. It's a great place to stop for coffee on an early morning walk.

Drive up the Icicle River Road to Homefires Bakery, where a German wood-fired oven is used to produce an incredible array of muffins, cookies, and breads, including sourdough, French, rye, raisin wheat, nine-grain, and sixteen other varieties.

Accommodations are excellent, with a wide choice ranging from bed-and-breakfast inns to motels and mountain lodges. Among our favorites are Moun-tain Home Lodge, an elegant retreat perched on a hilltop three miles from town (in winter you go in by Sno-Cat); Haus Rohrbach, a multi-story alpine-style inn tucked at the foot of Tumwater Mountain; Run of the River, a log home on a quiet stretch of the Icicle River; and Pension Anna, designed to resemble an authentic Bavarian farmhouse-inn.

Four inns have joined together on the Tour de Pomme, a lake-to-lake, inn-to-inn bicycle getaway through this apple-growing region for all levels of cyclists. Rental bikes are available.

A word of caution: If you plan to overnight in Leavenworth, make reservations in advance. The town is nearly always busy, especially on weekends or during any of several annual celebrations.

The Wenatchee River, flowing east from Lake Wenatchee through Leaven-worth to the Columbia River at the town of Wenatchee, is the most popular rafting river in the state, accounting for more than 60 percent of all trips. It's also one of the more versatile, with stretches of calm water that are ideal for drifting and fishing as well as big, roller coaster rapids guaranteed to provide thrills.

Most of the river action centers on Leavenworth, where the dozen or more rafting companies offering guided trips launch for the white-water stretch or meet to shuttle up to Lake Wenatchee's calmer waters. The town is also head-quarters for packers and guides who will take you on horsepacking trips into the Cascades. The Chamber of Commerce provides lists of rafting and mountain guide companies.

In winter, Eagle Creek Ranch and Leavenworth Nordic Center offer cross-country ski rentals and hut-to-hut guided trips. More than 30 kilometers of groomed and marked trails traverse meadows and forests within a few miles of Leavenworth. Mountain Ranch Adventures rents snowmobiles and leads cross-country snowmobile tours. Red Tail Canyon Farm offers sleigh rides in winter and hayrides in summer. Ski jumping is a sometime thing and, as this is written, may be revived as a major winter sport in Leavenworth.

Area Codes: west of Cascades 206, east of Cascades 509

DRIVING DIRECTIONS For the Stevens Pass–Leavenworth portion of the Cascade Loop, head north on I-5 27 miles to Everett, then turn east on U.S. 2 for 100 miles to Leavenworth. The round trip on this route is 254 miles. You can also return via Swauk (U.S. 97) and Snoqualmie (I-90) passes for a round trip of 261 miles.

SIGHTSEEING *Blackman Historic Museum,* 118 Avenue B, Snohomish, 568-2526; June through September daily 12 to 4 P.M., rest of year weekends. Free. Museum of pioneer artifacts and Victorian furniture in 1878 mansion. *Stevens Pass Ski Area,* 973-2441. Open November to April daily 9 A.M. to 10 P.M. *Der Heissluft Balloon Adventures,* 548-4219. Offers hot-air ballooning in the Leavenworth area. *Leavenworth Sports Center,* U.S. 2 at the west end of Leavenworth, 548-7864; and *Ride-N-Glide Sport,* on Washington 207 at Lake Wenatchee, 763-2220. Offer bicycle rentals. Among the many white-water rafting companies that schedule trips on the Wenatchee are: *Downstream River Runners,* 12112 Northeast 195th Street, Bothell 98011, (206) 483-0335 or (800) 732-RAFT; *Northern Wilderness River Riders, Inc.,* 101 Highway 209, Leavenworth 98826, 548-4583; *Wenatchee White Water & Scenic Float Trips,* P.O. Box 12, Cashmere 98815, 782-2254; and *Leavenworth Outfitters, Inc.,* 21588 Highway 207, Leavenworth 98826, 763-3733. *Eagle Creek Ranch,* P.O. Box 719, Leavenworth 98826, 548-7798. Offers trail rides, mountain pack trips, wilderness hikes, high country fishing, horse-drawn hayrides, and sleigh rides. *Red Tail Canyon Farm,* 11780 Freund Canyon Road, Leavenworth 98826, 548-4512. Also has hayrides and sleigh rides. Cross-country skiers can rent equipment in Leavenworth from: *Der Sportsman,* 837 Front Street, 548-5623; *Leavenworth Nordic Center,* Highway 2, 548-7864; and *Gustav's X-C Ski Rentals* (plus surfing lessons and rentals), Highway 2 and Front Street, 548-7330; as well as from *Ride-N-Glide Sport* (see above) at Lake Wenatchee. *Mountain Ranch Adventures,* 9661 Mountain Home Road, Leavenworth 98826, 763-3503 and 763-2713. Rents snowmobiles, clothing, and leads guided tours including night trips. Also offers horse packing trips into wilderness areas mid-July to mid-October. *Tour de Pomme,* 5801 Pioneer Drive, Cashmere 98815, 548-6720. 4 inns in Leavenworth, Cashmere, and Chelan offer inn-to-inn bicycling.

EVENTS *Washington State Autumn Leaf Festival,* Leavenworth, 548-5807, end of September through first week in October. Parade, outdoor music, flea market, pancake breakfasts, fall color auto tours. *Christmas Lighting,* Leavenworth, first 2 weekends in December. Celebrate Christmas with spectacular evening lighting ceremony in the snow, entertainment, sleigh rides. *Maifest,* Leavenworth, second weekend in May, spring celebration.

LODGING *Mountain Home Lodge* (bed and breakfast), P.O. Box 687, Leavenworth 98826, 548-7077. $$$. *Haus Rohrbach Pension* (bed and breakfast), 12882 Ranger Road, Leavenworth 98826, 548-7024. $$. *Pension Anna* (bed and breakfast), 926 Commercial Street, Leavenworth 98826, 548-6273. No smoking, $$. *Mrs. Anderson's Lodging House* (bed and breakfast), 917 Commercial Street, Leavenworth 98826, 548-6173. Downtown 1904 Leavenworth landmark, recently remodeled, $–$$. *Haus Lorelei Inn* (bed and breakfast), 347 Division Street, Leavenworth 98826, 548-5726. Elegant old European-style home on 2 wooded acres next to Icicle River, fine mountain views, children welcome, $$–$$$. *Run of the River* (bed and breakfast), 9308 East Leavenworth Road, Leavenworth 98826, 548-7171. Log inn beside the river, hand-hewn log beds, stitched quilts, no smoking; $$–$$$. *Brown's Farm* (bed and breakfast), 11150 Highway 209, Leavenworth 98826, 548-7863. Log home in the woods, livestock, good choice for children, $$. *Bayern Village Motor Inn,* 1505 Alpensee Strasse, Leavenworth 98826, 548-5875. Riverside location, a good choice for those who prefer a conventional motel to a B&B or inn, $$. *Pine River Ranch* (bed and breakfast), 19668 Highway 207, Leavenworth 98826, 763-3959. Set among alpine meadows with mountain views and fish-filled pond, $$.

CAMPING *Lake Wenatchee State Park,* 22 miles north of Leavenworth on Highway 207, 642-3078. 197 sites, $8. *Icicle River Ranch Trailer Park & Campground,* 7305 Icicle River Road, Leavenworth 98826, 548-5420. 71 full-hookup sites, mid-April to mid-October, $10 to $18.50. *Pine Village KOA,* 11401 River Bend Drive, 548-7709. 117 full-hookup sites on 28 acres, $10.45 to $15.45, seasonal rates.

DINING *Bush House Country Inn,* 300 Fifth Street, Index, 793-2312. Breakfast and lunch Monday to Saturday, dinner daily, brunch Sunday; historic inn offers big cozy fireplace and generous portions; $. *Terrace Bistro,* 200 Eighth Street, 548-4193. Lunch and dinner daily; probably the best restaurant in Leavenworth; upscale non-German cuisine, terrace dining in good weather; $$. *Gustav's Onion Dome Tavern,* 617 U.S. 2, 548-4509. Lunch and dinner daily; hamburgers, fries, and beer with a splendid view of the mountains from the outside tables; $. *Reiner's Gasthaus,* 829 Front Street, 548-5111. Lunch and dinner daily; well-prepared German food from schnitzel to red cabbage to sauerbraten, $. *Cafe Crista,* 801 Front Street, 548-5074. Lunch and dinner daily; Bavarian decor, German/American menu; $$. *Visconti's,* 217 Eighth Street, 548-6391. Lunch and dinner daily, Italian menu, $–$$. *The Soup Cellar,* 725 Front Street, 548-6300. Lunch and dinner daily; the place for hearty soups, especially in winter; also salad bar and desserts; $. *Park Place Cafe,* 902 Front Street, 548-6182. Late breakfast, lunch, and afternoon fare daily; salads, sandwiches, pasta, chili-cheese eggs a specialty; indoor and outdoor dining, $.

FOR MORE INFORMATION Cascade Loop Association, P.O. Box 3245, Wenatchee 98801, 662-3888. Snohomish Chamber of Commerce, 116 Avenue B, Snohomish 98290, 568-2526. Leavenworth Chamber of Commerce, P.O. Box 327, Leavenworth 98826, 548-5807.

Cascade Loop: Washington's Mountain Fjord

From Leavenworth east to Wenatchee, then north on both sides of the Columbia River into the Okanogan as far as the Canadian border, this is apple country. In April, clouds of white blossoms envelop the hillsides, and orchards are filled with the heady scent of apple blossoms and the hum of bees diligently pollinating the trees. Wenatchee is considered the apple capital of the state even though plenty of the fruit is grown around Yakima. The town celebrates the season with the Apple Blossom Festival, a ten-day event in April that includes parades, a carnival, a horse show, and a circus.

In September, Washington's signature fruit, the red Delicious apple, hangs heavy on the trees. Harvest is under way. The commercial apple packers are operating full blast; the apple juicers such as Treetop are pressing to beat the band, and roadside fruit stands all along U.S. 2 and U.S. 97 are laden with fruit awaiting the motorist.

It's just 54 miles from Wenatchee to Chelan, but few similar areas in Washington have so much to lure you off the highway. Make your first detour Cashmere, about 10 miles beyond Leavenworth. If you take the first exit, you'll cross an old concrete bridge over the Wenatchee flanked by sculpted boxes of red and yellow Delicious apples, pass through a spruced-up vintage business district, and drive down delightful tree-shaded streets reminiscent of those of small midwestern towns. At the eastern edge of Cashmere is the Chelan County Historical Society and Willis Carey Historical Museum. The small museum houses typical pioneer household items, farm implements, guns, and dioramas of indigenous birds. The collection of Indian artifacts is excellent, and includes thousands of arrowheads, clothing, basketry, and other craft work. An exhibit of skulls and bones of early Indians, several of which show signs of having met violent ends, fascinates the kids.

Outside, a dozen or so pioneer buildings form a rectangular "village." Some are replicas; some are originals brought here from elsewhere in Chelan County. There's a tiny hotel, a school, a store stocked with nineteenth-century provisions, a barbershop, a blacksmith shop, a saloon, and some cabins. A giant waterwheel stands alongside the Wenatchee River.

When you reach the junction of U.S. 2/97 and U.S. 97A about a mile west of Wenatchee, you may be tempted to swing north and pour on the gas for Chelan, just 35 miles away. But if you detour into town, you'll discover one of America's forgotten heroes.

The North Central Washington Museum, at 127 South Mission Street, has a lot to recommend it—a nifty operating model railroad that recreates the Great Northern's crossing of the Cascades, exhibits of pioneer farm and homestead life, and a wealth of memorabilia of the 1930s and 1940s.

But you may not be aware of Clyde Pangborn, a Wenatchee citizen who in 1931 completed the first transpacific flight between Sabishiro Beach, Japan, and Wenatchee. An entire section of this museum is devoted to this historic, and mostly unheralded, achievement. In his honor, the Wenatchee airport is called Clyde Pangborn Field.

In winter, skiers from the Puget Sound area who take their sport seriously often make the 138-mile drive to Wenatchee to ski at Mission Ridge on the eastern side of the Cascades. Located at 4,600 feet, thirteen miles southwest of Wenatchee, the area has a reputation for dry, powder snow. Skiers familiar with snow conditions in the Rockies should be forewarned: "powder" as it applies to Mission Ridge snow is a relative term meaning it's drier than the heavy, wet snow that is more typical of the western slope of these mountains. It does not compare with powder as you typically find it in Utah and Colorado. Mission Ridge offers four double chairs and two tows serving 33 runs having a vertical drop of 2,140 feet. Facilities include a ski school, rentals, cross-country trails, night skiing, and restaurants. The nearest overnight accommodations are in Wenatchee.

Perched on a hill immediately north of Wenatchee is Ohme Gardens, a particularly refreshing oasis if Wenatchee is experiencing one of its typically sweltering summer days. This nine-acre alpine park looks like something you'd expect to see in Switzerland. Flagstone paths wind through tall evergreens. Tiny high-altitude ground covers and flowers decorate the rocky outcroppings. The paths twist and turn, obscuring your view and giving the impression that the area is much larger than it actually is.

From several promontories, you can see the confluence of the Wenatchee and Columbia rivers below. Round a bend and you'll come upon a waterfall splashing down the rocks into a forest pool surrounded by tall firs. If you're a gardener, you'll appreciate the tremendous amount of care and irrigation these gardens must require to survive in the harsh summer climate of eastern Washington.

Within sight of Wenatchee, on U.S. 97A, is Rocky Reach Dam, one of ten Columbia River hydroelectric facilities between Canada and the Pacific. No matter what you may feel about the effect of these dams on the Columbia's ecology, this one is worth the stop.

The first thing you notice is the splendid landscaping. Formal flower beds (in one of them red, white, and blue form the American flag), broad lawns, and shade trees sprawl over the slopes facing the river. Picnic tables and a children's playground make it a good choice for a lunch stop. There's also a small café here.

At one side of the dam an elevator descends to the fish-viewing room. Strategically placed portholes allow you a close-up look at the fish making their way up ladders en route to their spawning ground. Steelhead, and sockeye and chinook salmon, are the fish most often viewed in summer. Lighted overhead displays help you to identify the various species. Wall murals trace the history of the Columbia and the life cycle of the salmon.

The powerhouse is one large museum, surprisingly extensive given its remote location. The whole building rumbles and shakes from the force of the turbines. You can watch them operate from a gallery in the turbine room. At one end of the powerhouse-cum-museum, regional artists display their works, among them a fine collection of 24 portraits of Nez Perce Indian chiefs. The long main hall offers excellent exhibits, wall diagrams, audiovisual programs, and hands-on items detailing Columbia River history, geology, archaeology, and flora and fauna. The Gallery of Electricity has fascinating collections of such early electrical equipment as generators, light bulbs, transmission lines, and communications gear.

North of Rocky Reach, U.S. 97A hugs the bank of the Columbia for 20 miles or more, passing through the little town of Entiat before climbing away from the river and threading its way through a narrow, timber-lined tunnel. Cresting the hill above Lake Chelan, the highway drops rapidly into the little lakefront resort town of Chelan.

Fifty-five miles long and less than a mile wide, Lake Chelan slices northwestward into the heart of the North Cascades. The fjordlike lake is surrounded by a varied landscape: broad, sandy beaches flanked by low, brown hills and apple orchards near the town of Chelan at the southeastern end; a spectacular retreat ringed by snow-capped peaks reaching more than 8,000 feet at the upper end.

The lake is probably the state's top destination for sun seekers who are chockablock at all available facilities from Memorial Day through Labor Day. The promise of warm, dry weather coupled with sandy beaches and water sports is particularly appealing to residents of western Washington, who endure long, gray winters and springs.

Getting out on the water is easy. Several firms, including Ship-N-Shore and Chelan Boat Rentals, provide Jet Skis, rowboats, Hobie Cats, diving gear, canoes, fishing boats, pontoon boats, and Windsurfers. If you get tired of lying on the beach soaking up the rays, there are bumper boats, tennis courts, an 18-hole municipally owned golf course, go-carts and a water slide.

Accommodations range from bed-and-breakfast lodgings and resort condominiums to campsites. The city operates a large RV park right on the downtown waterfront. Lake Chelan State Park comprises 127 lakefront acres with beach along South Shore Drive nine miles from town. In winter cross-country skiers head for Bear Mountain Ranch, just southwest of town. The ranch provides 50 kilometers of groomed trails plus rentals and instructions.

Chelan's real charms lie hidden uplake in Stehekin, and to reach them you must either cruise or fly. Washington 150 hugs the north shore of the lake to dead-end at the little town of Manson. On the south side a county road follows the shore for 25 miles to Twenty-Five Mile Creek before dead-ending. Beyond is roadless.

Each morning in summer and four times a week in winter, the *Lady of the Lake* leaves the Chelan city dock for its four-hour cruise to Stehekin. A new vessel, *Lady Express,* now makes the same trip in two hours. As you cruise uplake, stopping to pick up passengers at Manson and Fields Point (a good time saver if you want to drive partway), the scenery grows more and more spectacular with each bend in the lake. At 1,486 feet the third deepest lake in the country, Chelan narrows between steep mountain walls and seems to probe like a finger into a wilderness of jagged peaks. Thready waterfalls plunge down sheer cliffs into the water at several spots along the way, and the Forest Service has provided tiny isolated campsites for boaters in a few level places on the shore. If you've brought binoculars, you may spot deer, bear, and other wildlife that have come down to the lakeside to drink or browse. In winter mountain goats also often descend and the captain of the cruiser will steer as close to shore as possible for a look.

You arrive in Stehekin at midday and have an hour and a half layover before the boat departs for Chelan. There really isn't sufficient time to both eat and sightsee; you have to make a choice. The lovely valley of the Stehekin River is served by an unpaved stub road that extends 23 miles more into the mountains and is a gateway to North Cascades National Park. In summer the National Park Service operates a bus that takes backpackers and hikers up the road. To coincide with the boat's arrival in Stehekin, a sightseeing bus makes the jouncy 7-mile round trip to 312-foot Rainbow Falls. Along the way you pass the state's only one-room schoolhouse—still in operation—and several ranches and homesteads that have been here since early in the century. In winter you can make this trip on cross-country skis or snowshoes to view the incredible crystal beauty of Rainbow Falls frozen in ice.

There are limited overnight accommodations at Stehekin, a café, and a National Park Service visitor center for Lake Chelan National Recreation Area. Primitive campsites lie along the Stehekin River Road.

Chelan Airways operates single-engine floatplane service from Chelan to Stehekin and to some remote mountain lakes. The trip is great for sightseeing because the pilot seldom flies above a couple of thousand feet. If you find it daunting just to think of another four hours on the boat back to Chelan, you can opt to return by plane. Advance reservations are a must.

Area Code: 509

DRIVING DIRECTIONS If you choose to make Wenatchee or Chelan a weekend destination rather than to complete the whole Cascade Loop, you can reach both in 3 to 4 hours from Seattle via I-90 to Cle Elum, U.S. 97 to U.S. 2, then U.S. 97A north from Wenatchee. The Seattle-to-Chelan round trip is 360 miles.

AIR TRANSPORTATION *Horizon Air* and *United Express* provide scheduled service from Seattle to Wenatchee. Round-trip fares begin at about $110.

SIGHTSEEING *Chelan County Historical Museum and Pioneer Village,* 5698 Museum Drive, Cashmere, 782-3230. Excellent Indian collection and 18 pre-1900 pioneer structures. Hours: April to October Monday to Saturday 10 A.M. to 4:30 P.M., Sunday 1 to 4:30 P.M. Donation. *North Central Washington Museum,* 127 South Mission Street, Wenatchee, 664-5989. Operating model railway, apple processing, first transpacific flight exhibits. Hours: Monday to Friday 10 A.M. to 4 P.M.; Saturday and Sunday 1 to 4 P.M. Donation. *Mission Ridge Ski Area,* 663-7631. November to mid-April Wednesday through Sunday 9 A.M. to 4 P.M. *Ohme Gardens,* 3 miles north of Wenatchee off U.S. 97, 662-5785. 9-acre alpine garden perched above Columbia River. Hours: April through October daily 9 A.M. to dusk. Admission $4, under 18 $2. *Rocky Reach Dam,* 7 miles north of Wenatchee on U.S. 97A, 663-8121. Fish-viewing rooms, gardens, and picnic facilities; electricity museum. Hours: Memorial Day to Labor Day daily 8 A.M. to 8 P.M., 8 A.M. to 6 P.M. other months. Free. *Bear Mountain Ranch,* Route 1, Box 63A, Chelan, 682-5444. Cross-country skiing. Hours: mid-December to January daily 9:30 A.M. to 4 P.M., weekends in November and January to March. Trail passes $7, under 12 and seniors $5. *Lake Chelan Boat Company,* P.O. Box 186, Chelan, 682-2224. April 15 to October 15 daily departure at 8:30 A.M.; February 16 to April 14, Sunday,

Monday, Wednesday, Friday; rest of year, Monday, Wednesday, Friday. Round-trip fare Chelan to Stehekin *Lady of the Lake* $21, 6–11 $10.50; *Lady Express* $38, 6–11 $19. **Lake Chelan Airways,** 682-5555; and **Stehekin Air Service,** 682-5065. Provide floatplane service up lake, reservations required. **Lake Chelan Museum,** Woodin Avenue and Emerson Street, Chelan, 687-3470. Pioneer and Indian exhibits. Open Memorial Day to October 1 Monday to Saturday 1 to 4 P.M. Donation. **Cascade Corrals,** P.O. Box 67, Stehekin. Operates guided horsepacking trips into the North Cascades. June through October.

EVENTS *Apple Blossom Festival,* last week in April through first week in May. 2-week celebration features parades, white-water events, orchard tours.

LODGING *Cashmere Country Inn* (bed and breakfast), 5801 Pioneer Avenue, Cashmere 98815, 782-4212. Delightful restored 1907 farmhouse, $$. **West Coast Wenatchee Center Hotel,** 201 North Wenatchee Avenue, Wenatchee 98801, 662-1234. New, downtown, multistory hotel, $$. **Campbell's Resort and Conference Center,** 104 West Woodin Street, Chelan 98816, 682-2561. Long-established motel is largest in Chelan and occupies best beach on the lake, $$$. **Caravel Resort Motel,** P.O. Box 1509, Chelan 98816, (800) 962-8723. Lakefront motel is newly refurbished, $$$. **Darnell's Resort Motel,** P.O. Box 506, Chelan 98816, 682-2015. Family lakeshore resort includes tennis, putting green, pool, $$$. **Mary Kay's Romantic Whaley Mansion** (bed and breakfast), 415 Third Avenue, Chelan 98816, 682-5735. Lots of pampering and rich cuisine in this Victorian-theme 1911 home; no children, pets, or smoking; $$$. **River House** (bed and breakfast), 307 Second Avenue, Chelan 98816, 682-5122. Comfortable country inn on quiet side street overlooking river; cross-country ski packages; $$–$$$. **Silver Bay Inn,** P.O. Box 43, Stehekin 98852, 682-2212. Well-appointed retreat on the lakeshore, $$. **North Cascades Lodge,** P.O. Box 1779, Stehekin 98852, 682-4711. Rustic lodge and housekeeping cabins at Stehekin landing, $$. **Stehekin Valley Ranch,** P.O. Box 36, Stehekin 98852, 682-4677. Horseback riding, raft trips; meals, local transportation included in price, $$.

CAMPING *Wenatchee River County Park,* 6 miles west of Wenatchee on U.S. 2/97, 662-2525. 40 full hookups, 24 water-electricity, 41 no hookups, on river, $12. **Lake Chelan State Park,** 9 miles west of Chelan off U.S. 97A, 687-3710. 127 tent sites, 17 with full hookups, lakeshore, reservations in summer $8–$12.50. **Twenty-Five Mile Creek State Park,** 18 miles north of Chelan on southside road, 687-3610. 52 tent sites, 33 with full hookups, swimming pool, $8–$12. **Lakeshore RV Park,** P.O. Box 1669, Chelan 98816, 682-5031. 160 full-hookup sites, beach, boats, $14.

DINING *The Pewter Pot,* 124½ Cottage Avenue, Cashmere, 782-2036. Lunch and dinner Tuesday through Saturday, Sunday buffet; home-cooked American-style food; $–$$. *John Horan House,* 2 Horan Road, Wenatchee, 663-0018. Dinner Tuesday through Saturday; probably Wenatchee's best restaurant, in historic 1890s house; conventional menu of fish, poultry, beef, and pork; $$. *New Orleans Kitchen,* 928 South Mission Street, Wenatchee, 663-3167. Dinner Wednesday through Saturday, spicy Creole and Cajun menu, $$. *El Abuelo,* 601 South Mission Street, Wenatchee, 662-7331. Good Mexican food at reasonable prices prepared by Mexican family, $. *River Park Dining,* 114 East Woodin Street, Chelan, 682-5626. Breakfast and lunch daily, dinner Monday through Saturday; lovely location overlooking the Chelan River; good for lunch; $. *Campbell House,* 104 West Woodin Street, Chelan, 682-4250. Breakfast, lunch, and dinner daily; upscale regional cuisine served in 1901 former hotel; $$–$$$.

FOR MORE INFORMATION Wenatchee Area Visitor & Convention Bureau, P.O. Box 850, Wenatchee 98807, 662-4774. Lake Chelan Chamber of Commerce, P.O. Box 216, Chelan 98816, 682-2022, (800) 4-CHELAN.

Cascade Loop:
The North Cascades Highway

On September 2, 1972, Washington's then-governor Dan Evans cut a tape at Winthrop in eastern Washington that opened the North Cascades Highway, officially designated Washington Highway 20. First authorized by the legislature in 1893, the road had for many years languished in the planning stages. For decades, the only way anyone in the northern third of the state could cross from east to west or vice versa was by using U.S. 2 over Stevens Pass to the south or by detouring far to the north into Canada and traveling via British Columbia 3. Towns in the eastern part of the state, especially, were economically stifled by the laborious roundabout route to markets, railheads, and shipping ports on the west side.

Beginning in 1959, construction through some of the ruggedest terrain in North America proceeded by fits and starts over the next 13 years. Engineers were plagued by landslides and avalanches, and deterred by chasms to bridge, sheer slopes to traverse, and a working season that lasted only a few months each year. But the effort was worth the $23-million price tag.

Today, the North Cascades route is one of the most scenic highways in the country. Slicing through virtual wilderness, it brings you close to magnificent snow-capped spires, peaceful mountain meadows, and a variety of wildlife.

Logic dictates driving the route from west to east, and you can make the crossing a two-day weekend from Seattle rather than part of the Cascade Loop trip we've suggested in the previous two sections. Never mind logic. Go the other way if you have time. The scenic vantage points are much better. But keep in mind that this highway is not accessible all year round. Snow usually closes it from Early Winters campground on the east to the Skagit dams on the west by late October, and it's plowed open again typically in May.

Winthrop and the Methow Valley have good overnight accommodations, putting you close enough to climb the east slope of the Cascades early the next morning when sunrise splashes Liberty Bell Mountain with gold.

If you're in the mood to splurge, try elegant Sun Mountain Lodge. Perched on a mountaintop overlooking the Methow Valley near Winthrop, the lodge offers a wide range of resort facilities and activities including horseback riding and hayrides, tennis courts, a swimming pool, canoeing or kayaking on nearby Patterson Lake, hiking trails, and quality dining and entertainment.

To reach Winthrop and the Methow Valley, continue north from Chelan (page 94) on U.S. 97, which climbs over the rugged dry hills for lofty views of the Columbia River far below. Apple trees flank both sides of the river for the 17 miles to Pateros, where you head into the Methow Valley on Washington 153.

The sunny Methow, like Ellensburg, farther south, is Washington's cowboy country. The jagged Cascades form a backdrop for horses and cattle grazing in the fields, stands of aspen trees, log ranch houses, and the meandering Methow and Chewack rivers.

This, and the Okanogan region just to the north, is prime trout-fishing country. Dozens of lakes dot the area, most having at least one rustic fishing resort and RV campground. From opening day of lowland lake fishing season in late April through June, when the lakes warm up, the trout fishing (mostly for rainbows) is consistently good. Summer months are too hot for trout, but the angling action picks up again after Labor Day and continues through the end of the season in late October.

Plan to arrive early enough in Winthrop to do a little exploring. The town has adopted a Western image and works hard to cultivate it. False-front buildings, old-fashioned streetlights, and wooden sidewalks along the main street make good camera subjects.

You can easily spend an afternoon browsing in the shops along Riverside Street. Stop at the Shafer Museum in the 1897 Guy Waring log cabin, where exhibits of furniture, tools, bicycles, and carriages detail the valley's early days. At the Forest Service smoke jumper base, just east of town, guided tours give you a glimpse of the rugged life and dangerous work of these famous firefighters.

Winthrop was founded in 1891 by Guy Waring, a former Massachusetts resident who named the town after that state's colonial governor, John Winthrop.

Waring's Harvard classmate, Owen Wister, spent his honeymoon here in 1898. It is said that Wister found inspiration in Winthrop for his well-known book, *The Virginian,* published in 1902 and one of this country's first Western novels.

Check your gas gauge before you leave Winthrop. It's nearly 90 miles to the next service station.

As you head west, the highway gradually climbs beside Early Winters Creek. Fields of cattle and scattered groves of pine give way to steeper granite slopes covered with fir and larch as you move up the valley. This is prime country for bird-watching, and you're likely to see hawks, golden and bald eagles, grouse, quail, pigeons, woodpeckers, ravens, and the ubiquitous black-and-white magpie.

As the highway swings south, great walls of granite sweep upward to Kangaroo Ridge, Early Winters Spires, and Silver Star Mountain. Dead ahead the massive bulk of 7,600-foot Liberty Bell Mountain seems to block any passage through this mountain fortress. If you make this drive in the fall, you'll see these slopes lit with the brilliant yellow of larch, giving the appearance of giant candles set amid the darker evergreens.

Just when passage seems impossible, the highway makes a great horseshoe bend and clambers up the face of Liberty Bell. As you reach the top, detour to the off-road viewpoint on your right and walk the short distance from the parking lot to a shoulder of granite for splendid views of the mountain-ringed valley of Early Winters Creek.

The highway crosses two passes—Washington Pass at 5,477 feet and Rainy Pass at 4,860 feet. If you've brought a picnic and have the time, stop at the roadside and hike the one-mile trail from Rainy Pass to Rainy Lake. The alpine meadows all along this crest of the Cascades are resplendent with wildflowers in July and August. Other trails, including the Pacific Crest National Scenic Trail, lead from roadside into North Cascades National Park. None of the park is accessible by road.

You descend gradually for the next 27 miles, following Ruby Creek through thick stands of timber and emerging occasionally into meadows on both sides of the road. Your eye can trace the paths of destructive avalanches on the steep mountainsides and, at one point, you'll see a huge blowdown where trees lie in a circle as if a giant whirlwind had flattened them.

Overlooks above Ross and Diablo lakes make excellent vantage points for photographs. Note the distinctive color of each lake—Ross is teal; Diablo jade. The unusual colors are caused by rock particles ground to a fine powder by glaciers high in the mountains, carried down by streams, and suspended in lake waters where it reflects the green of the surrounding forest and the blue of the sky. There's another excellent picnic spot beside the waters of Thunder Arm. Look for the turnoff to the left as you reach the bottom of the grade. From Colonial Creek campground, Thunder Creek Trail rambles through the forest beside the frigid tumbling creek; the trail stretches 19 miles to Park Creek Pass, but the first three or four miles are gentle enough to make an easy family hike of two or three hours.

Land on both sides of the North Cascades Highway and surrounding Ross Lake all the way to the Canadian border is protected in the federally administered Ross Lake National Recreation Area. The long, narrow lake is accessible by boat and hiking trail, and there is a rustic resort on the lakeshore reached only by boat (see "Lodging"). East Bank Trail follows the shoreline of Ruby Arm and sticks close to Ross Lake, a good and easy route for sampling this wilderness park in an off-the-highway excursion.

Three big dams—Ross, Diablo, and Gorge—plug the narrow rocky gorge of the Skagit River here. They're owned and operated by Seattle City Light and are the prime sources of electric power for the city. They're also the feature of a fascinating public tour.

The four-hour Skagit Tour (see "Sightseeing") is a popular day trip from Seattle and requires reservations and ticket purchase several weeks in advance. There's also an abbreviated 90-minute version in July and August that's easier to include in a long day's drive from Winthrop to Seattle.

The tours started back in 1928 when James Ross, superintendent of the Skagit Hydroelectric Project, invited 35 members of the Seattle Women's Garden Club for a visit. For Ross, an amateur botanist, it was an opportunity to show off the Skagit grounds and a public relations effort to display the potential of the upper Skagit River Valley for generating electricity.

The excursion begins with a multi-projector slide show orientation at the Skagit Tour Center in Diablo, 67 miles east of I-5 and 140 miles from Seattle. You then board an open-platform incline railway (used to move supplies to the upper dams), which lifts you 558 feet up Sourdough Mountain on a 70 percent grade. After a short walk through appropriately named Windy Gap, you board the 70-passenger sightseeing boat *Cascadian* for a 25-minute cruise across green Diablo Lake. You can often spot deer and bear along the lake's rugged forested shoreline. After a tour through Ross powerhouse and a return by boat and railway to Diablo, you sit down to a belt-bursting, all-you-can-eat chicken dinner at the tour center. Kids, often a bit bored by most of the tour, really take to this part of it.

For the next 67 miles, Washington 20 gradually descends beside the turbulent Skagit River through the little towns of Newhalem, Marblemount, Rockport, and Concrete. Lush green stands of alder, big-leaf and vine maple (gold and red in the fall), fir, hemlock, and cedar squeeze in close beside the road. The Skagit is a popular white-water rafting river in June and July. In December and January dozens of bald eagles come here to feed on spawning salmon. You can spot these magnificent birds perched high in the leafless branches of alders and cottonwoods along the river. Rafting companies run bird-watching float trips down the river to where you can get close-up views. It's a chilly but exhilarating experience.

Washington 20 intersects I-5 at Burlington; from here it's 64 miles back to Seattle.

Area Codes: east of the Cascades 509, west of the Cascades 206

DRIVING DIRECTIONS If you're making a day trip to the Skagit dams or a weekend outing to Winthrop without following the entire Cascade Loop, head north from Seattle on I-5 to Burlington, then take Washington 20 east. The round trip to the Skagit Tour Center at Diablo is 262 miles, to Winthrop 392 miles.

SIGHTSEEING *Shafer Museum,* Highway 20 and Castle Avenue, Winthrop, 996-2817. Hours: Memorial Day to mid-October daily 10 A.M. to 5 P.M. Donation. Modest pioneer museum in 1897 cabin built by town's founder. *North Cascades Outfitters,* P.O. Box 97, Brewster 98812, 689-2813; and *Early Winters Outfitters,* Star Route Box 28, Winthrop 98862, 996-2659. Offer guided horse-packing trips into the North Cascades. *Methow Valley Ski Touring Association,* P.O. Box 146, Winthrop 98862, (800) 422-3048. Maintains more than 150 kilometers of cross-country trails, rents equipment, and leads ski tours. *Seattle City Light's Skagit Tours,* 1015 Third Avenue, Seattle 98104, (206) 684-3030 for reservations. Several companies offer float trips on the Skagit River in both summer and winter, including: *Downstream River Runners,* 12112 Northeast 195th, Bothell 98011, (206) 483-0335; *Rivers, Inc.,* P.O. Box 2092, Kirkland 98083, (206) 822-5296; and *North Cascades River Expeditions,* P.O. Box 116, Arlington 98223, (206) 435-9548.

EVENTS *49er Days,* 996-2125; early May in Winthrop. Features parade, dances, rodeos. *River Rat Days,* 996-2125, held on Fourth of July weekend in the Methow Valley. Features a zany race of canoes, tubes, rafts, and just about anything else that will float. *Omak Stampede and Suicide Race,* mid-August in Omak. A traditional rodeo, plus a crazy breakneck race down a sheer bluff and across the Okanogan River.

LODGING *Methow Central Reservations,* P.O. Box 505, Winthrop 98862, 996-2148. Provides information and makes reservations for the whole Methow Valley. *Sun Mountain Lodge,* P.O. Box 1000, Winthrop 98862, 996-2211 or (800) 572-0493. Recently remodeled, this fine resort perches atop a mountain overlooking the Methow Valley and offers a full range of activities including horseback riding, fishing, hiking, and cross-country skiing, $$$. *The Virginian Motel,* P.O. Box 237,

Winthrop 98862, 996-2535. Cedar log construction with balconies overlooking the Methow River, $$. *The Farmhouse Inn* (bed and breakfast), 709 Highway 20, Winthrop 98862, 996-2191. Cozy restored farmhouse on the outskirts of town, $$. *Winthrop Inn,* P.O. Box 265, Winthrop 98862, 996-2217. 1 mile east of town on the river, rural setting, $–$$. *Mazama Country Inn,* P.O. Box 223, Mazama 98833, 996-2681, (800) 843-7951. Handsome country inn with splendid mountain and meadow views, $$. *Diablo Lake Resort,* 503 Diablo Street, Rockport 98283, telephone Everett operator and ask for Newhalem 5578. Rustic housekeeping cabins on Diablo Lake, $$. *Ross Lake Resort,* Rockport 98282, no telephone. Rustic, remote fishing cabins on Ross Lake reached by twice-daily boat from Ross Powerhouse; $–$$. *Cascade Mountain Inn* (bed and breakfast), 3840 Pioneer Lane, Concrete 98237, 826-4333. Spacious log inn makes a good base for watching bald eagles on the Skagit River, $$.

CAMPING *Alta Lake State Park,* 2 miles off Washington 153 at Pateros, 923-2473. 180 sites, 16 water-electricity, $8–$12. *Pearrygin Lake State Park,* 5 miles north of Winthrop off Highway 20. 83 sites, 57 full hookups, $8 and $12. Reservations in Summer. *Derry's Resort and RV Park,* 2½ miles north of Winthrop, 996-2322. 83 sites, 20 full hookups, open April 15 to November 1, $8.50–$12. *KOA Methow River,* 1 mile south on Highway 20, 996-2258. 105 sites, 16 full hookups, 50 water-electricity, open April 15 to November 1, $12.50–$15.50. *Okanogan National Forest,* campgrounds on Highway 20 at Early Winters (13 sites, 16 miles northwest), Klipchuck (46 sites, 17 miles northwest), and Lone Fir (27 sites, 27 miles northwest), $5. *Rockport State Park,* 1 mile west of Rockport on Highway 20, 853-8461. 62 sites on 457 acres of old-growth forest adjacent to the Skagit River, April to mid-November, $8–$12.

DINING *Sun Mountain Lodge* (see "Lodging"). Breakfast, lunch, and dinner daily; dining room and lounge have fantastic views of the valley below; upscale menu with Southwest touches; $$. *The Virginian* (in the Virginian Motel, see "Lodging"). Breakfast, lunch, and dinner daily; regional cuisine, outdoor dining on deck; $$. *Duck Brand Restaurant,* 248 Riverside, Winthrop, 996-2192. Breakfast, lunch, and dinner daily; Mexican food, pasta, sandwiches, full breakfasts, outdoor dining; $. *Methow Cafe,* Highway 153, Methow, 923-2228. Breakfast, lunch, and dinner daily; the only business in Methow, this unpretentious café serves hearty food at reasonable prices, especially recommended for breakfast; $. *Mountain Song Restaurant,* Highway 20, Marblemount, 873-2461. Breakfast, lunch, and dinner daily; just about the only good restaurant on the North Cascades Highway between Winthrop and the lower Skagit, Mountain Song serves soups, sandwiches, salads, berry pies; a good place to schedule a meal stop if you're crossing the Cascades in either direction; $–$$.

FOR MORE INFORMATION Winthrop Chamber of Commerce, P.O.
Box 39, Winthrop 98862, 996-2125. North Cascades National Park, 2105 Highway 20, Sedro Woolley 98284, 856-5700.

Over the Mountains to Miners and Cowboys

It's easy to miss Cle Elum. Heading into eastern Washington on I-90, you top Snoqualmie Pass, then descend swiftly between the mountains past big Keechelus and Easton lakes. The scenery opens up dramatically. Close-packed firs and hemlocks give way to open stands of Ponderosa pine; mountain slopes yield to the broad spreads of cattle ranches. Your inclination is to lay a heavy foot on the gas pedal and hurry into all that wide open country. But don't miss Cle Elum just because you can't see it from the freeway.

Take Exit 84, cross over the freeway, and ease down into a town that looks like it's a couple of blocks wide by a couple of miles long. Cle Elum, which is Indian for "swift water," is one of several coal mining towns in the area that once existed primarily to furnish coal to the steam locomotives of "The Main Street of the Northwest," the Northern Pacific Railroad. There's plenty of coal town evidence left if you look for it. The railroad right-of-way, now the Washington Central Railroad, that passes through town is black with the coal dust spilled from thousands of railroad cars over the years. Other giveaways are the rows of modest look-alike company-built houses that line Cle Elum's back streets.

Even if your destination is somewhere else down the road, Cle Elum makes a great lunch, dinner, or snack stop. Especially good are Mama Vallone's, specializing in upscale Italian cuisine, and the Matterhorn, serving authentic German food.

In addition to several other good family restaurants in town, there's the Cle Elum Bakery, at First and Pennsylvania streets, creator of all manner of savory goodies, most of which are consumed by hungry travelers before noon nearly every day—except Sunday, when the shop is closed. Just across the street is Owen's Meats, a Cle Elum institution since 1887 and one of the few places left where you can buy good old-fashioned country smoked bacon in the Northwest. A couple of blocks up the street, Glondo's Sausage Company makes and sells some unusual meat products including cinnamon-and-fennel salsiccia, Yugoslav sausage, Polish kielbasa, and savory beef jerky that comes in large chunks just right for chewing on while driving down the road. Charlie Glondo will also provide recipes for cooking his sausage.

Across the street the Cle Elum Historical Telephone Museum preserves one of the last manually operated switchboards in the country, in use until the 1960s, when the town changed over to a dial system. The museum also exhibits photos and memorabilia relating to the coal mines.

If you're planning to stay overnight in Cle Elum, make it the Moore House. Located beside the abandoned Milwaukee Road right-of-way (now Iron Horse Trail State Park, part of the cross-state John Wayne Trail), this bed-and-breakfast inn occupies the railroad's former bunkhouse. Railroad buffs will find it paradise, with scores of historic railroad photos and artifacts scattered throughout the building. There are even two cabooses that have been made into well-furnished guest rooms. The B&B is one of a dozen members of the Washington Bed and Breakfast Guild Volksport Club that have set up volksmarching (10-kilometer walking) courses near their establishments. Credit for walking the Moore House course is applied toward completion of the club's total of 120 kilometers and an achievement award. Iron Horse Trail State Park extends 25 miles over the old railroad bed and makes a good route for hiking or horseback riding, as most of it parallels the Yakima River.

If the mining history hereabouts intrigues you, there's a three-mile detour—up Washington 903 to Roslyn—you should take. The ramshackle old place is not a ghost town, but there are enough empty buildings to confirm the suspicion that it's not exactly thriving. Old false-front buildings line Pennsylvania Avenue, and weathered homesteads, most roofed with corrugated metal, stud the hills that flank the town. Residents are a mixture of old-timers, back-to-earth young people, and ex-urbanites, some of them busily restoring old buildings or putting up a few new ones. In recent years the town has been used as the site for the TV show "Northern Exposure."

The cluttered but fascinating Roslyn Museum is loaded with odd artifacts, ranging from the big Carmichael Ice Cream sign to mine hoist signals and a still-working store message trolley that scoots from one end of the building to the other.

The town has a history of labor strife and mine disasters, with 45 men killed in an explosion in 1892 and another 10 in 1910. Black strikebreakers were brought in to thwart the early efforts at unionization. The museum is the place to get the details.

Cemeteries are Roslyn's claim to fame. The little town has 24 of them, with more than 2,500 graves. Why so many? Most of the miners who came to settle Roslyn were European immigrants. For religious and cultural reasons each group insisted on having its own cemetery. Italians, Slavs, Serbians, Poles, English, Scots, Welsh, Germans, and a dozen other nationalities secured their plots on the hillside just west of town. You're free to wander through these cemeteries.

Beyond Roslyn the road continues to Ronald, another defunct mining town hunkered down amid mountains of mine tailings. If you like the down-home atmosphere of old-time taverns, try the Brick in Roslyn and Old Number 3 in Ronald. Lake Cle Elum and Salmon La Sac lie at the end of the road, where you'll find Forest Service campgrounds and a network of trails branching off into the Cascades.

For some reason no one has been able to adequately explain, the Pacific Northwest has very few guest ranches. Two of them lie just east of Cle Elum. Hidden Valley Guest Ranch, eight miles from town and three miles off U.S. 97, is tucked away in a lovely green valley out of sight and sound of the modern world. Homesteaded in 1890, the 800-acre ranch offers trail riding, good trout fishing, swimming, and rockhounding for Ellensburg Blue, a semiprecious stone found in the area. Accommodations are in detached cabins; ranch-style meals are served in the lodge's Western-theme dining room. At Thorp, the Circle H Holiday Ranch offers a full range of activities, including trail riding, fishing, rafting, wildlife viewing, and cross-country skiing in the winter. The owners have a background in New York theater and bring their appreciation of fine cultural tradition to hosting guests.

The quickest way to Ellensburg takes you on I-90 over Indian John Hill for 20 miles. There's a slower, prettier route via Washington 10, a comfortable and mostly traffic-free two-lane highway that winds along with the Yakima River through a wooded canyon. River Raft Rentals offers a four-hour, guided 16-mile raft trip through this scenic canyon and also rents rafts to those who want to do it on their own.

Ellensburg is Washington's cow town, devoted to the production of beef, veneration of the cowboy, and enjoyment of rip-roaring rodeo. The town's two major Western events should determine when you go. In May the National Western Art Show and Auction features the best of Western art, including paintings by Ellensburg favorite son and famous Western artist, John Clymer. On Labor Day weekend the town is totally dedicated to the Ellensburg Rodeo, largest such event in the state and among the top 25 rodeos in the United States.

Spend some time downtown, where a historic district preserves 18 Victorian buildings, all of them described on a free walking tour map available at the Chamber of Commerce. The Kittitas County Historical Museum, at East Third and Pine streets, features the usual pioneer artifacts, plus a collection of gemstones, including a six-pound Ellensburg Blue, and petrified wood. Don't miss the marvelous piece of art at the Rotary Pavilion. Called *The Ellensburg Bull,* the metal sculpture is by artist Richard Beyer, whose work *Waiting for the Interurban* in Seattle's Fremont District has brought such delight to viewers. The massive bull is reclining on a park bench, one hind leg crossed over the other, his tail draped over his lap and a cowboy hat placed strategically to avoid offending spectators.

The former Northern Pacific Railroad station is a classic, built in the early

1900s and now housing the wine sales and tasting room of Cascade Mountain Cellars. You can view the works of regional artists, some of them Western, at Ellensburg Community Art Gallery, 408½ Pearl Street, the new John Clymer Museum at 416 N. Pearl Street, and at the Sarah Spurgeon Art Gallery in Randall Hall on the campus of Central Washington University. Olmstead Place State Park, four miles east of town on Squaw Creek Trail Road, preserves an 1875 ranch with home, barn, and outbuildings typical of this region. Interpretive programs and farm equipment demonstrations are held at various times during the year, and in September the park hosts an old-time threshing bee.

Area Code: 509

DRIVING DIRECTIONS From Seattle, Cle Elum is 81 miles via I-90, Ellensburg another 20 miles.

SIGHTSEEING *Cle Elum Historical Telephone Museum,* 221 East First Street, 674-5958. Hours: Memorial Day to Labor Day Tuesday to Thursday 9 A.M. to 4 P.M., Friday to Monday noon to 4 P.M.; other months Tuesday to Friday 9 A.M. to noon. Free. *Roslyn Museum,* 28 Pennsylvania Avenue, 649-2776. Hours: May to September daily 9:30 A.M. to 4 P.M. Donation. *River Raft Rentals,* Route 4, Box 275, Ellensburg 98926, 964-2145. Runs on the upper Yakima River, also rents rafts. *Kittitas County Historical Museum.* East Third and Pine streets, Ellensburg, 925-3778. Hours: April to October Monday to Friday 1 to 4:30 P.M., Saturday 1 to 4 P.M.; other months Monday to Friday 1 to 4:30 P.M. Donation. *The Olmstead Place State Park,* 4 miles east of Ellensburg on Squaw Creek Trail Road, 925-1943. Hours: Thursday to Monday 8 A.M. to 5 P.M.

EVENTS *National Western Art Show and Auction,* Ellensburg, 962-2934, mid-May. The largest event of its kind in the state. *Ellensburg Rodeo and Kittitas County Fair,* at the county fairgrounds, Labor Day weekend. One of the top rodeos in the country; includes parades, dances. Tickets and information: P.O. Box 777, Ellensburg 98926, 925-5381 or (800) 637-2444.

LODGING *The Moore House* (bed and breakfast), P.O. Box 2861, South Cle Elum 98943, 674-5939. Comfortable, well-restored 1913 railroad bunkhouse beside John Wayne Trail; loaded with railroad memorabilia and includes guest rooms in cabooses; $$. *Hidden Valley Guest Ranch,* HC 61, Box 2060, Cle Elum 98922, 674-5990. Rustic guest cabins and ranch house tucked away in a secluded valley make up the state's oldest guest ranch; offers horseback riding, fishing, swimming pool; $$. *Circle H Holiday Ranch,* Route 1, Box 175, Thorp 98946, 964-2000. Family-oriented guest ranch with riding, swimming, rafting on the

Yakima River; $$–$$$. ***Best Western Ellensburg Inn,*** 1700 Canyon Road, Ellensburg 98926, 925-9801. $–$$.

CAMPING ***Lake Easton State Park,*** 12 miles west of Cle Elum off I-90, 656-2230. 136 wooded sites on 196 acres beside Lake Easton, 45 full hookups, $8–$12. ***Forest Service Campgrounds,*** on Highway 903 to Salmon La Sac. Includes Red Mountain (15 sites), no fee, and Salmon La Sac (110 sites), $6. ***Ellensburg KOA,*** Route 1, Box 202, Ellensburg 98926, 925-9319. 144 shaded sites along the Yakima River, 100 water-electricity, $13.50–$17.

DINING ***Mama Vallone's Steak House and Inn,*** 302 West First Street, Cle Elum, 674-5174. Dinner Tuesday to Sunday, brunch Sunday; quality Italian cuisine and steaks; $$. ***The Matterhorn Restaurant and Beer Garden,*** 212 West Railroad Avenue, Cle Elum, 773-3048. Lunch and dinner daily. $–$$. ***Roslyn Cafe,*** 28 Pennsylvania Avenue, Roslyn, 649-2793. Lunch and dinner Tuesday to Sunday, breakfast Saturday and Sunday; a casual, down-home sort of place with burgers, salads, steak, old-fashioned jukebox; $. ***The Valley Cafe,*** 103 West Third Street, Ellensburg, 925-3050. Breakfast, lunch, and dinner daily; this Depression-era cafe is an Ellensburg tradition, especially good for lunch; $$.

FOR MORE INFORMATION Cle Elum Chamber of Commerce, P.O. Box 43, Cle Elum 98922, 674-5958. Ellensburg Chamber of Commerce, 436 North Sprague Street, Ellensburg 98926, 925-3137.

Washington's Wine Country

With 70-odd wineries, some of them producing international award-winning wines, Washington ranks as the second largest wine state in the country after California. Yet, wine touring is a relatively little-remarked and not-very-well organized passion in the Northwest, certainly an activity in its infancy compared to California, or even New York. Wine touring in Washington has its own rewards: lack of crowds, lots of small wineries where you can discover superb vintages in limited quantities, and an opportunity to meet and talk with the vintners rather than a corporate tour guide. The chief drawback is that you're something of a pioneer and will have to do a bit of research and diligent navigation to ferret out the wineries. For the most part, they are poorly signed and often tucked away down obscure country roads.

But there is help. In our opinion, the best guidebook is *Northwest Wine Country* by Ronald and Glenda Holden (published by Holden Pacific, Inc., 814 35th Avenue, Seattle, WA 98122). You can obtain the latest edition directly from the authors at the above address or at most Northwest bookstores. The guide describes each winery and its products in Washington, Oregon, and Idaho, and gives you directions on how to get there. The Yakima Valley Wine Growers Association (P.O. Box 39, Grandview 98930) also publishes a wine map of the Yakima Valley. You can write to them for a copy or pick one up at Yakima Visitors and Convention Bureau. In addition, the Washington Wine Commission, P.O. Box 61217, Seattle 98121, publishes a guide entitled "Touring the Washington Wine Country."

Although wine is the big attraction, the valley also offers visitors a feast of local cheeses and fresh produce. The Yakima Valley is generally considered to be the valley of the Yakima River extending from the city of Yakima in a southeasterly direction to the river's confluence with the Columbia at the Tri-Cities (Richmond, Pasco, and Kennewick). The valley has been one of the richest and most productive agricultural areas of the Northwest for more than a century. Long before wine grapes became a major crop, the valley led the nation in the production of hops. Yakima County also produces more apples than any other region in the Northwest and is a major source of peaches, pears, cherries, apricots, and mint, not to mention corn, tomatoes, onions, and other vegetables. For the visitor this means a bonanza of fresh fruits and vegetables to purchase. From June through October most trips to the Yakima Valley result in stops at the dozens of roadside produce stands and a car trunk stuffed with everything from fresh peaches to garlic. Another reason to visit the valley is for cultural and historic sightseeing that includes vintage railroads, a major Indian reservation, and a frontier fort.

The quickest way to reach Yakima is via I-90 to Ellensburg, then I-82. This highway climbs over Manastash and Umtanum ridges and crosses the army's Yakima Firing Range, where in the summer you're likely to see some dramatic military maneuvers involving tanks, helicopters, and artillery. If you have the time, take the old State Highway 821 through Yakima Canyon. It leaves the freeway on the south side of Ellensburg and meanders through the rugged canyon following the river for 28 miles, then returns you to I-82 four miles north of Yakima. The canyon route is a delight at any season, providing views of birds and wildlife amid dry brown hills and volcanic outcroppings. There are plenty of places to stop beside the river to picnic or camp. It's a top fly-fishing stream, and from May through September, the calm and relatively shallow waters draw flotillas of rafters who come to drift leisurely down the canyon and soak up its sunshine. The canyon is hot in summer, but the beauty of a float down this river is that you can slip over the side of your raft and cool off when the mood strikes you. On certain Sundays in summer, the canyon road is closed to all vehicles except bicycles.

The Washington Central Railroad, a new shortline operating on the former

Burlington Northern tracks and sporting a spiffy black-white-and-red logo featuring a seahawk, has recently inaugurated the Yakima Dinner Train. Comprising three sleek stainless-steel cars that formerly ran in Canada and a locomotive from the Santa Fe railroad, the train makes weekend evening journeys to Ellensburg. During the slow-paced three-hour round trip through the canyon, you're served a fine meal of beef, chicken, or salmon by uniformed waitresses. The whole trip is a nostalgic experience.

The train departs from the restored Northern Pacific depot in downtown Yakima, a building worth visiting whether or not you take the train. Across the street is the home of the Yakima Brewing and Malting Company, one of the state's best micro-breweries and producer of Grants Scottish Ale, Imperial Stout, and Yakima Hard Cider. They have their own pub complete with dart board.

Across the tracks, a grouping of vintage passenger and freight cars and locomotives has been converted to shops and restaurants, billed collectively as Track 29. There's also a farmer's market in the renovated Pacific Fruit Exchange Building.

In one of the historic early-twentieth-century buildings along Front Street, on the opposite side of the depot, you'll find the rock-walled wine cellar run by Lenore Lambert. She stocks more than 500 different labels, including wines of the Northwest, California, Germany, France, Spain, and Italy. Among them are 11 of the world's 19 leading champagnes and a number of other rare vintages. The cellar is a good place to bone up on Yakima Valley wines before you start your wine tour or to purchase products afterward. In the same building, the Greystone Restaurant is one of the best dining spots in the area and features an upscale menu that includes rack of lamb, Norwegian salmon, veal in a caper cream sauce, and mussels with linguine.

If the Yakima Dinner Train has whetted your appetite for nostalgic rail experiences, schedule a ride on the Yakima Trolley. Several years ago a local group of trolley buffs acquired two turn-of-the-century Brill trolleys that had been built in Saint Louis and operated for 56 years in Oporto, Portugal. The group now runs the trolleys on weekends from May to October from their shop and carbarn at Fourth Avenue and Pine Street. The jouncing, clanging ride over several miles of former electric freight railway track always brings smiles from the passengers.

The Yakima Valley Museum houses an outstanding collection of Indian artifacts; a large number of wagons, buggies, and other horse-drawn vehicles; and the office of the late Supreme Court Justice William O. Douglas, who was a Yakima native. The museum also operates the H. M. Gilbert Homeplace, a Victorian farmhouse typical of those once built by well-to-do farmers in this valley.

If you're going to spend the weekend exploring Washington's wine country, you'll probably want to headquarter in Yakima, which has the best choice of motels as well as several RV parks and a dandy state park with campsites right on the river. Sportsman's State Park is one of the elements in the city's new river greenway that provides a bike and walking trail beside the river and lovely, shaded places to picnic on hot summer days.

You can reach all of the valley's nearly two dozen wineries by driving I-82 the 76 miles between Yakima and Richland (one of the Tri-Cities) and detouring at exits in between as the mood strikes you. These wineries produce a variety of white wines including Johannisberg, white, and pink rieslings; gewürztraminer, chenin blanc, sauvignon blanc, chardonnay, semillon, and muscat. Among the reds, you'll most frequently encounter merlot, cabernet sauvignon, and pinot noir.

Heading down the valley, you have a choice of the following exits (unless otherwise noted, all are on the north side of I-82): Exit 40 for Staton Hills; Exit 44 for Donald Fruit and Mercantile, a cornucopia of fruit, produce, and packaged Northwest gourmet foods (they have fresh peach sundaes in peach season, July to early September); Exit 50 for Bonair Winery and Hyatt Vineyards, and Vin de'L'Ouest Winery to the south; Exit 52 to Zillah Oakes, Covey Run, and Portteus Vineyard (also the exit for an outstanding Mexican restaurant in Zillah, El Ranchito, an unpretentious tortilla factory and cafeteria, but the food is authentic and the place is a must stop for Washingtonians who know this valley, Exit 54 for Horizon's Edge and Eaton Hill; and Exit 58 for Stewart Vineyards to the south. As you near Grandview, you reach Exit 69, Tucker Cellars and Cascade Crest to the north; Yakima Valley Cheese Company in Sunnyside produces a fine Gouda. At Exit 73, Chateau Ste. Michelle is to the south (one of several wineries operated by this—Washington's largest—vintner). At Prosser, Exit 80, Pontin Del Roza is to the north; at Exit 82, Yakima River Winery and Hinzerling Vineyards are to the south, Chinook Wines and Hogue Cellars to the north. The last three wineries—Oakwood Cellars, Kiona Vineyards, and Blackwood Canyon— are located at Benton City, north off Exit 96.

If touring two dozen wineries is a bit more than you had in mind and you'd prefer to sample just one or two, we recommend you stop at Hogue Cellars and Kiona Vineyards. Wine aficionados who know Washington wines and are familiar with this valley rate Hogue Cellars as the area's premium winery. And, to quote one expert, "Kiona has the nicest people to visit. The two families who run the winery are enthusiasts and the quality of their welcome is the best you'll find anywhere."

Like most freeways, I-82 bypasses some of the more interesting stops, in this case those in the Yakima Valley. If you have the time, return to Yakima by way of Washington 22 and U.S. 97 via Toppenish and Union Gap.

Toppenish is headquarters for the vast Yakima Indian Nation, and the cultural center here is well worth a stop. The modern building, in the style of a winter lodge, has an excellent museum, with dioramas depicting the Indian story, a gift shop where you may purchase the handmade beadwork for which the Yakimas are famous, and a restaurant serving such traditional foods as game and fry bread.

If you're a history buff, you'll want to schedule a detour at Toppenish—27 miles westward over Highway 220—to Fort Simcoe State Park. A well-preserved frontier army post dating from 1856, the fort boasts five of the original buildings, all in immaculate condition, flanking a large parade ground. The shade of big oak trees makes this a delightful place for a picnic.

Between Toppenish and Yakima, fruit and vegetable stands line the roadside from June through early October. Among the early vegetables that Seattleites drive all the way over here to obtain are Walla Sweets, big onions so mild you can eat them like apples. By July, another treat, Yakima sweet corn, is being sold at these stands. The Yakima Valley Direct Marketing Association publishes an annual buyers' guide to fresh produce that lists more than two dozen farmers and produce outlets and tells which seasons certain fruits and vegetables are available. You can obtain a free copy at the Yakima Visitors and Convention Bureau office in Yakima or by sending a stamped, self-addressed envelope to Farm Products Map, 1731 Beam Road, Granger, WA 98932. You can also call (509) 575-1300 or 248-2021 to find out what's being harvested.

Area Code: 509

DRIVING DIRECTIONS To reach Yakima and the Yakima Valley from Seattle, follow I-90 east to Ellensburg, then I-82 south through the valley. Seattle to Richland is 412 miles round trip.

AIR TRANSPORTATION *Horizon Air* and *United Express* have frequent flights between Seattle–Tacoma International Airport and Yakima. Round-trip fares from about $120.

SIGHTSEEING *Spirit of Washington Dinner Train,* 32 North Front Street, Yakima 98901, 452-2336 or (800) 876-RAIL. Friday dinner Kennewick to Prosser, April through September, Kennewick departure 6 P.M. Saturday dinner Yakima to Ellensburg, April through September, departs 6 P.M. Sunday brunch, Yakima to Ellensburg, year round, departs Yakima 10 A.M. Dinner fare $45, $50 in dome car; Sunday brunch $35 and $40. Reservations and advance menu selections required. *Tent-N-Tube,* on the campus of Central Washington University in Ellensburg, 963-3537. Rents inner tubes, rafts, and canoes for floating the Yakima River. *Carrot's,* 1107 Fruitvale Boulevard, Yakima, 248-3529. Rents rafts, kayaks, and floating islands (disks that hold up to four people). *Gary's Fly Shop/Yakima*

River Outfitters, 1210 West Lincoln Avenue, Yakima, 457-3474. Provides fishing guide services on the Yakima River. *Yakima Trolleys,* P.O. Box 649, Yakima 98907, 575-1700. Hours: May to mid-October Saturday and Sunday 11 A.M. to 3 P.M.; Monday to Friday 6:30 to 7:30 P.M. in July; departures from Third Avenue and Pine Street. Adults $3, 6–12 and over 60 $1.50, families $6, under 6 free. *Yakima Brewing and Malting Company,* 25 North Front Street, 575-2922. Monday to Saturday 11 A.M. to midnight, Sunday to 10 P.M. *The Wine Cellar,* 5 North Front Street, 248-3590. Monday to Saturday 11 A.M. to 6 P.M. *Tucker Cellars Winery,* 5 North First Avenue, 454-WINE. Monday to Friday noon to 5 P.M., Saturday and Sunday 10 A.M. to 5 P.M. *Yakima Valley Museum,* 2105 Tieton Drive, 248-0747. Tuesday to Friday 10 A.M. to 5 P.M., Saturday and Sunday noon to 5 P.M., closed January. Adults $2.50, students and over 60 $1.25, under 10 free. *H. M. Gilbert Homeplace,* 2109 West Yakima Avenue, 248-0747. Teas and tours March through December Friday 10 A.M. to 3 P.M. $2.50. *Central Washington Agricultural Museum,* 102 West Ahtanum, Union Gap, 248-0432. Open-air exhibits of early Yakima Valley farm machinery. Daily 7 A.M. to 9 P.M. Free. *Yakima Indian Nation Cultural Center,* Highway 97 and Fort Road, Toppenish, 865-2800. April to September Monday to Saturday 10 A.M. to 7 P.M., Sunday 10 A.M. to 5 P.M., other months daily 10 A.M. to 5 P.M. Adults $2, 5–18 and over 55 $1, families $5, Monday free to all. *Donald Fruit and Mercantile,* I-82 Exit 44 at Donald, 877-3115. June through December daily 9 A.M. to 6 P.M. *Yakima Valley Cheese Company,* 100 Alexander Road, Sunnyside, 837-6005. Tuesday through Saturday 9:30 A.M. to 5:30 P.M. *Fort Simcoe State Park,* White Swan, 874-2372. April to mid-October Wednesday to Sunday 6:30 A.M. to 10 P.M.; other months Saturday and Sunday only. Museum and interpretive center: April to mid-October Saturday and Sunday 10 A.M. to 5 P.M. *Benton County Historical Museum,* Seventh Street and Patterson Avenue, Prosser, 786-3842. Tuesday to Saturday 10 A.M. to 4 P.M., Sunday 1 to 5 P.M. Adults $1, under 18 50 cents. *Yakima Valley Wineries: Staton Hills,* 2290 Gangl Road, Wapato, 877-2112. Summer Tuesday to Sunday 11 A.M. to 5:30 P.M., winter Tuesday to Sunday noon to 5 P.M. *Vin de'L'Ouest Winery,* 101 Toppenish Avenue, Toppenish, 865-5002. Daily 10:30 A.M. to 5 P.M. *Bonair Winery,* 500 South Bonair Road, Zillah, 829-6027. Daily 10 A.M. to 5 P.M., Saturday and Sunday only in winter. *Hyatt Vineyards Winery,* 2020 Gilbert Road, Zillah, 829-6333. Daily 11 A.M. to 5 P.M., closed January. *Zillah Oakes Winery,* P.O. Box 1729, Zillah, 829-6990. Monday to Saturday 10 A.M. to 5 P.M., Sunday noon to 5 P.M.; winter Saturday and Sunday noon to 4:30 P.M. *Covey Run,* 1500 Vintage Road, Zillah, 829-6235. Monday to Saturday 10 A.M. to 5 P.M., Sunday noon to 5 P.M.; winter Monday to Saturday 11 A.M. to 4:30 P.M., Sunday noon to 4:30 P.M. *Portteus Vineyards,* 5201 Highland Drive, Zillah, 829-6970. Daily 10 A.M. to 5 P.M., Sunday 12:30 to 5 P.M., call for winter hours. *Horizon's Edge Winery,* 4530 East Zillah Drive, Zillah, 829-6401. Daily 10 A.M. to 5 P.M. *Eaton Hill Winery,* 530 Gurley Road, Granger, 854-

2508. Saturday and Sunday noon to 5 P.M. *Stewart Vineyards,* 1711 Cherry Hill Road, Granger, 854-1882. Monday to Saturday 10 A.M. to 5 P.M., Sunday noon to 5 P.M. *Cascade Crest Estates,* 111 East Lincoln Avenue, Sunnyside, 839-9463. Tuesday to Sunday, 11 A.M. to 6 P.M. *Tucker Cellars,* Route 1, Box 1696, Sunnyside, 837-8701. Daily 9 A.M. to 6 P.M., winter daily 10 A.M. to 5 P.M. *Chateau Ste. Michelle,* West Fifth Street and Avenue B, Grandview, 882-3928. Daily 10 A.M. to 5 P.M. *Yakima River Winery,* Route 1, Box 1657, Prosser, 786-2805. Daily 10 A.M. to 5 P.M. *Pontin Del Roza,* Route 4, Box 4735, Prosser, 786-4449. Daily 10 A.M. to 5 P.M. *Hinzerling Winery,* 1520 Sheridan Avenue, Prosser, 786-2163. Monday to Saturday 11 A.M. to 5 P.M., Sunday 11 A.M. to 4 P.M., closed Sundays December through February. *Chinook Wines,* Wine Country Road, Prosser, 786-2725. Friday to Sunday noon to 5 P.M., closed in January. *The Hogue Cellars,* Wine Country Road, Prosser, 786-4557. Daily 10 A.M. to 5 P.M. *Oakwood Cellars,* Route 2, Box 2321, Benton City, 588-5332. Wednesday to Friday 6 to 8 P.M., Saturday and Sunday noon to 6 P.M., summer only Friday noon to 6 P.M. *Kiona Vineyards,* Route 2, Box 2169E, Benton City, 588-6716. Daily noon to 5 P.M. *Blackwood Canyon,* Route 2, Box 2169H, Benton City, 588-6249. Daily 10 A.M. to 6 P.M.

EVENTS *Yakima Valley Spring Barrel Tasting,* late April. Valley wineries pour samples of their new vintages from the barrel. Contact individual wineries above for dates. *Central Washington State Fair,* 248-7160, Yakima, end of September, first of October. Features award-winning agricultural products, entertainment, livestock show, amusement rides.

LODGING *Best Western Rio Mirada Motor Inn,* 1603 Terrace Heights Drive, Yakima 98901, 457-4444. Prime location on the river, $–$$. *Holiday Inn of Yakima,* 9 North Ninth Street, Yakima 98901, 452-6511. Conveniently located next to Exit 33, restaurant, entertainment, $$. *Red Lion Inn,* 1507 North First Street, Yakima 98901, 248-7850. Landscaped pool and garden courtyard, $$. *Towne Plaza Motor Inn,* North Seventh Street and East Yakima Avenue, Yakima 98901, 248-5900. $$. *Tudor Guest House* (bed and breakfast), 3111 Tieton Drive, Yakima 98902, 452-8112. 5 guest rooms in 1929 Tudor mansion, formal garden, $$. *Rinehold Cannery Homestead* (bed and breakfast), 530 Gurley Road, Granger 98932, 854-2508. 2 guest rooms in early-twentieth-century farmhouse adjacent to Staton Hill Winery, $$. *Harvest House* (bed and breakfast), 1204 Meade Avenue, Prosser 99350, 786-1622. Refurbished vintage 2-story hotel in downtown Prosser, $.

CAMPING *Yakima Sportsman's State Park,* on Yakima River immediately east of I-82, 575-2774. 64 sites, 36 full hookups, trout pond for kids, $8 and $12. *Yakima KOA,* 1500 Keys Road (near state park), 248-5882. 129 sites on 20 acres adjacent to the river, full hookups, store, laundry, bicycles, $13–$16.50.

DINING *Birchfield Manor,* 2018 Birchfield Road, Yakima, 452-1960. Dinner Friday to Sunday; elegant dining in historic home decorated with antiques, French country prix fixe menu, no children; $$$. *The Greystone Restaurant,* 5 North Front Street, Yakima, 248-9801. Dinner Tuesday to Sunday; excellent wide-ranging menu with emphasis on local products, wines; $$. *Gasperetti's,* 1013 North First Street, Yakima, 248-0628. Dinner Tuesday to Saturday; northern Italian cuisine; $$. *Track 29 Dining Company,* 1 West Yakima Avenue, 457-2929. Lunch and dinner daily in restored railroad car adjacent to Washington Central tracks; featuring steak and chicken; $$. *Holiday Inn* (see "Lodging"). Breakfast, lunch, and dinner daily; recommended for breakfast—cinnamon knot rolls, which have to be among the best in the Northwest; $-$$. *El Ranchito,* 1319 East First Avenue, Zillah, 829-5880. Breakfast, lunch, and dinner daily; Mexican fare; $. *Dykstra House Restaurant,* 114 Birch Avenue, Grandview, 882-2082. Lunch Monday to Saturday, dinner on Saturdays; a good choice for a lunch stop while wine touring, home cooking with local products; $$. *The Blue Goose,* 306 Seventh Street, Prosser, 786-1774. Breakfast, lunch, and dinner daily; recommended for filling breakfasts; $.

FOR MORE INFORMATION Yakima Valley Visitors & Convention Bureau, 10 North Eighth Street, Yakima 98901, 575-1300. Yakima Valley Wine Growers Association, P.O. Box 39, Grandview 98030. Washington Wine Commission, P.O. Box 61217, Seattle 98121, (206) 728-2252.

Coulee Country

Twenty million years ago one of the largest basaltic lava flows ever to appear on the earth's surface inundated 200,000 square miles of the Pacific Northwest. Receding glaciers of the Ice Age subsequently carved great gouges in the lava plateau and released monumental floods that etched central Washington into long, slender, straight-sided canyons called coulees. Grand Coulee, the largest (52 miles long and, in some places, 5 miles wide), and Moses, the second largest, slice through rock east of Wenatchee, creating some of the most dramatic scenery in the Northwest. There's a sense of being in touch with the earth's beginnings when you travel through this region. The evidence of the tremendous forces that shaped the land is awe-inspiring.

Probably the most convenient itinerary for exploring coulee country is to drive through Moses Coulee on Friday, make your way north to the towns of Grand Coulee, Electric City, or Coulee Dam to spend the night, then see the laser light show at Grand Coulee on Saturday night. Save Sunday to return south, following the chain of lakes that now fill Grand Coulee, and visit Dry Falls.

Washington 28 parallels the Columbia River east of Wenatchee. Four miles past Rock Island Dam you'll see a sign marking the route to Palisades. Turn left onto the two-lane paved road and be prepared to be overwhelmed.

Suddenly, as if you've gone through a door, dry rolling hills give way to the dramatic walls of Moses Coulee, which rise hundreds of feet from the valley floor. (The coulee is named for Moses, a local Indian chief noted for his fine horsemanship, who lived from about 1829 to 1899 and was a contemporary of the great Chief Joseph. Historians believe Moses Coulee was a major north-south route for Indians traveling on horseback.)

Alfalfa fields and young fruit orchards stretch to the base of the cliffs, which dwarf the scattered ranch houses. There's little traffic along the way. Keep an eye out for stray cattle or pheasant on the road. Pull over, turn off your engine, and listen to the stillness, punctuated only by the chirping of birds. Dozens of species inhabit the fields and roadside. If you're lucky, you may see a golden eagle drop from a cliff top in its quest for prey. Roger Tory Peterson's *Field Guide to Western Birds* and a pair of binoculars make good companions.

Eleven miles farther on you come to Palisades, a tiny community nestled at the bottom of the coulee with a neat brick schoolhouse, shade trees, and a cluster of homes. For a spell the hardtop gives way to gravel. The coulee twists and turns, with different views unveiled at every bend in the road. Green and orange lichen colors its steep sides. An irrigation hose shoots water into the air, creating splendid rainbows. The road hugs one side of the coulee, then climbs steeply for sweeping views of the canyon floor, fields, farmhouses, and trees below. You arrive atop a high plateau where rolling hills stretch away to puffy white clouds on the horizon. Wheat fields alternate with sagebrush. At road's end you join U.S. 2 to head east for Coulee City.

A short detour up a roller coaster road to the north takes you to 2½-mile-long Jameson Lake, popular with anglers. Tiny Jack's Resort is typical of many fishing resorts in this country—café, boat rentals, recreational vehicle camping spots, and open just during the fishing season, April to October.

Just east of Coulee City, turn north on Washington 155. The highway hugs the eastern shore of Banks Lake beneath the beetling brows of Grand Coulee. The 27-mile-long lake is part of the Columbia Basin Project and serves as a reservoir for irrigation water used by central Washington agriculture. Paradoxically, this driest part of the state is a prime destination for those who enjoy water sports. Banks Lake and dozens of other lakes in the area provide the means for everything from waterskiing to scuba diving. For the angler, Banks Lake holds smallmouth and largemouth bass, crappie, kokanee, perch, pike, and whitefish. Steamboat Rock State Park, named for a butte that rises 700 feet above the lake, has hiking trails, a swimming beach, and a boat-launching ramp. Keep an eye out for the aeries of golden eagles high in the cliffs along the lake.

To borrow a phrase from mountain climbers, the reason you visit Grand

Coulee Dam is "because it's there." Grand Coulee is impressive by any measure, at nearly 12 million cubic yards the largest concrete structure in the world. It's also the world's largest hydroelectric facility: 33 turbine generators supply 20 billion kilowatt hours of electricity each year, distributed over 14,000 miles of electric lines. Roosevelt Lake, the impoundment behind the dam, is the largest body of fresh water in the Pacific Northwest, stretching 151 miles.

Grand Coulee was one of the crowning achievements of the Roosevelt administration during the Great Depression. Authorized as an unemployment-solving project in 1933, the original structure took seven years to complete. In addition to supplying power to the Bonneville Power network, the dam provides flood control, water recreation, and enough water to irrigate half a million acres of the formerly arid Columbia Basin.

As you drive north on Washington 155 through the Grand Coulee (the dam is not actually in the coulee), nothing quite prepares you for the immensity ahead. Crest a hill, drop down through Electric City and the town of Grand Coulee, and you're confronted with a structure so big it dwarfs the surrounding landscape. Stop first at the visitor center facing the spillway, where you can watch an interpretive film. There are self-guided tours of the dam as well as guided tours of the third power plant that includes a ride on the glass-enclosed incline elevator for spectacular views of the spillway. In summer operators spill water over the spillway every afternoon from 1:30 to 2:00. Summer evenings here are a delight. The heat of the day is dissipating, the night is velvety and star-filled, and all attention is focused on the broad backdrop of the dam's spillway. Just at dusk, powerful lights focus on the spillway and for the next 36 minutes spectators are treated to a stunning laser light show.

If you're staying overnight here, you might want to try the Coulee House or the Ponderosa Motel, both of which overlook the dam. The Colville Confederated (Indian) Tribes operate a modest museum and gift shop on Birch Street where you can purchase arts and crafts made by local artisans.

Whenever we visit this area, we're always surprised at how few vacationers use the facilities in Coulee Dam National Recreation Area and how few boaters there are on Roosevelt Lake behind the dam. The lake is ideal for summertime cruising, with 27 campgrounds (many of them accessible only by boat) and hundreds of miles of shoreline to explore. Marinas at Seven Bays, Keller Ferry, and Kettle Falls rent houseboats that will sleep as many as 13 for up to $1,600 per week in peak summer season, less in spring and fall. Be forewarned that summers here are hot, with midday temperatures usually reaching anywhere from 90 to 100 degrees. By August, water temperature climbs well into the seventies.

Returning to Seattle, take Washington 155 to Coulee City—a small agricultural town at the foot of Banks Lake—then Washington 17. Just south of town you encounter Dry Falls State Park on the rim of what geologists believe to have been the greatest waterfall of all time. From the parking lot beside the interpretive center you look east across a horseshoe-shaped rocky precipice 3½ miles wide with a drop of 400 feet. There's a steep rocky trail to the two lakes at the bottom if you're in the mood for a hike. Experts estimate that these falls had the power of 100 Niagaras. Today, the steep basalt sides stand silent and the wind sighs around the lichen-covered rocks. Lizards dart here and there and tiny birds plunge to the lakes below, giving the whole prehistoric scene an eerie quality.

A small interpretive museum here tells the Ice Age story of this and other coulees in the area and the history of the Indians that later inhabited caves nearby. A short detour south from Coulee City will bring you to Summer Falls, where overflow irrigation water from the Columbia Basin Project plunges into a lake beside a grass-covered picnic area.

Sun Lakes State Park, nestled at the bottom of Lower Grand Coulee just a couple of miles south of Dry Falls, ranks among the best all-around parks in the Northwest. The setting is impressive, with the sheer basalt walls of the coulee rising on either side and several clear blue lakes tucked between grass-covered hillocks.

The park has just about everything a family would want for an outdoor vacation. A marina rents a variety of crafts, from canoes and rowboats to pedal, tricycle, and tandem boats. Fishing for rainbow and German brown trout is excellent. Hiking trails and horse paths lead to Dry Falls, Perch, Deep, and Rainbow lakes as well as through the coulees. You can join guided trail rides from the stables or take an old-fashioned hayride with campfire cookout lunch included. There are docile ponies for small children. Golfers can try their skill on the nine-hole Vic Meyers Golf Course.

The park has campsites for tents and recreational vehicles and modest housekeeping cabins beside the lake. As you'd expect, it's busy from Memorial Day through Labor Day; reservations well in advance are recommended for overnight accommodations.

Area Code: 509

DRIVING DIRECTIONS Round trip from Seattle to Grand Coulee Dam is about 500 miles via Moses Coulee and returning via Sun Lakes and Ephrata. The quickest route east follows I-90, U.S. 97, and U.S. 2 to Wenatchee. On the return you can save time by heading south to pick up I-90 at George.

SIGHTSEEING *Grand Coulee Dam,* Grand Coulee 99133, 633-9265 or 633-9503. Visitor center and tour hours: Memorial Day to Labor Day daily 8:30 A.M. to 10 P.M., other months 9 A.M. to 5 P.M. Free. Laser light show nightly Memorial Day to Labor Day 9:30 to 10:06 P.M. Free. *Roosevelt Recreational Enterprises,* P.O. Box 587, Grand Coulee 99133, 633-0201 or (800) 648-LAKE (in WA). Rents houseboats on Roosevelt Lake. *Dry Falls,* 4 miles south of Coulee City off Highway 17, 632-5583. Park and overlook open daily April to mid-October 6:30 A.M. to 10 P.M., other months 8 A.M. to 5 P.M. Interpretive center open Wednesday to Sunday 10 A.M. to 6 P.M. *Grant County Historical Museum and Pioneer Village*, 742 North Basin Street, Ephrata, 754-3334. Pioneer exhibits of farm life before the Columbia Basin Project, displays of Indian artifacts, and a collection of 18 vintage buildings. Guided tours May to mid-September Monday, Tuesday, Thursday to Saturday 10 A.M.to 5 P.M., Sunday 1 to 4 P.M. Adults $1.50, under 6 free. *Champs de Brionne Winery*, 98 Road W Northwest, Quincy 98848, 785-6685. Splendid setting overlooking a gorge cut by the Columbia River; monthly concert schedule in summer brings top name performers here. Hours: March to December daily 11 A.M. to 5 P.M., January and February weekends only.

EVENTS *Laser Light Festival*, 633-3074, Memorial Day weekend at Grand Coulee. Celebrates beginning of dam's light show season with arts and crafts fair, food fair, music, and fireworks.

LODGING *Coulee House Motel*, 110 Roosevelt Way, Coulee Dam 99116, 633-1101. Good view of the dam spillway, $–$$. *Ponderosa Motel*, 10 Lincoln Street, Coulee Dam 99116, 633-2100. Excellent views of the dam, $. *Sky Deck Motel*, P.O. Box 325, Electric City 99123, 633-0290. Nice location on the shore of Banks Lake, $. *Crescent Bar Resort*, 864 Crescent Bar Road, Box 29, Quincy 98848, 787-1304. Mediterranean-style resort on the Columbia River features golf (9 holes, tennis, water sports), $$$. *Sun Lakes Park Resort, Inc.*, HCR 1, Box 141, Coulee City 99115, 632-5291. Lakeside housekeeping cabins in Sun Lakes State Park, $.

CAMPING *Jack's Resort*, P.O. Box E, Waterville 98858, 683-1095. 35 sites with full hookups on Jameson Lake, $14. *Coulee Lodge Resort*, 8 miles south of Coulee City on Blue Lake, 632-5565. 60 sites, about half with full hookups, $10. *Steamboat Rock State Park*, P.O. Box 370, Electric City 99123. 100 full-hookup sites on Banks Lake, $12.00. *Sun Lakes State Park*, Coulee City 99115, 632-5583. 175 sites, 18 full hookups, $8 and $12.

DINING *Wildlife Restaurant*, 113 Midway Street, Coulee Dam, 633-1160. Breakfast, lunch, and dinner daily; casual dining, steaks, seafood; $. *Siam Palace*, 213 Main Street, Grand Coulee, 633-2921. Lunch and dinner daily; Chinese, Thai, and American menu; $. *Don's*, 14 Canna Street, Soap Lake, 246-1217. Lunch Monday to Friday, dinner daily; steak and seafood in generous portions, Greek food on Mondays and Fridays; $$.

FOR MORE INFORMATION Grand Coulee Dam Area Chamber of Commerce, P.O. Box 760, Grand Coulee 99133, 633-3074. Coulee Dam National Recreation Area, P.O. Box 37, Coulee Dam 99116, 633-0881.

Into British Columbia

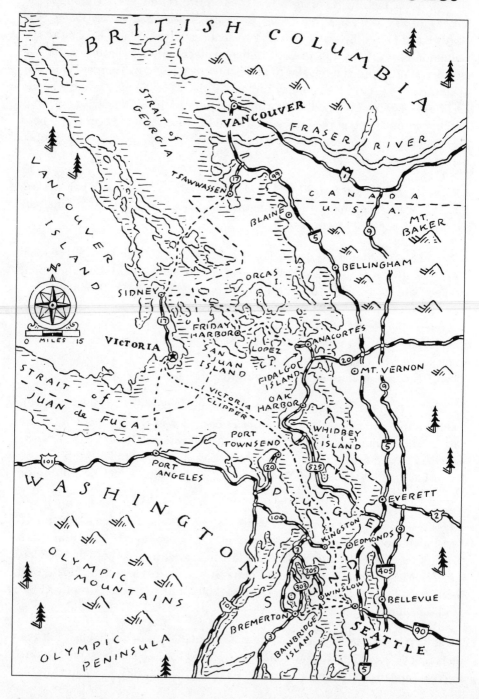

Victoria Without a Car

Victoria, British Columbia, has an image problem. For years tourism promoters have traded on the city's similarities to England—cricket matches, high tea, formal gardens, double-decker buses, and the like. They've reinforced the image with "shoppes" bearing cutesy British names, with some less-than-first-rate tourist attractions, and with hype that ranges from British flags to costumed guides.

The image is not fair to Victoria and it's not fair to visitors. Victoria is an absolutely delightful city with lots of worthwhile attractions, fine accommodations, and, increasingly, some outstanding restaurants. Unfortunately, many visitors never discover the real Victoria because they 1) go in the wrong season, 2) try to see the city on a day trip from Seattle, and 3) don't get much beyond the streets around the Empress Hotel and the Inner Harbour.

If you want to get the most out of a trip to Victoria, don't go in July and August when the city is swamped with tourists. The spring months, April through June, are delightful, with the bonus of blossoms everywhere. September and October are equally fine, with typically clear, sunny days and a city that is recuperating from the tourist invasion of midsummer. We even like winter in Victoria, when you can walk the quiet misty streets, cozy up with the locals in pubs and restaurants, take in one of the fine plays or musical performances, and wander through the museums at your leisure. And, if you're looking for unusual Christmas gifts, November and December shopping can be rewarding.

Getting to Victoria is definitely half the fun. There are several means of reaching Vancouver Island (on which Victoria is located) from Seattle, all involving either a voyage or a flight. Most popular are the vessels that make the daily trip from Seattle's waterfront. Victoria Clipper operates two passenger-only catamarans that make the cruise in 2½ or 3 hours at a speed of 25 to 30 knots. Passengers are seated airline style or on banquettes around tables, depending on the vessel. Picture windows provide good views of the islands and the water traffic. Light meals and beverages are served.

Another option is to drive to Port Angeles on the Olympic Peninsula (see "The Olympic Peninsula: The Northwest Corner") and take the Black Ball Transport ferry, *Coho*, to Victoria. Service is limited on this route, and the demand is high in summer; best plan to arrive in Port Angeles the night before your crossing.

You can also drive north to Anacortes and take the Washington State Ferry through the San Juan Islands (see "The Serendipitous San Juans" and "Historic San Juan Island") to Sidney, B.C., then drive 35 kilometers (22 miles) south to Victoria.

Three British Columbia ferry routes also serve the island and provide good scenic choices for making a loop trip that includes Vancouver. B.C. Ferries has regular service from Tsawwassen, 36 kilometers (22 miles) southwest of Vancouver, to Swartz Bay; 35 kilometers (22 miles) north to Nanaimo, 112 kilometers (69½ miles) north of Victoria. If you're making a loop trip, consider taking the ferry from Nanaimo to Horseshoe Bay, just north of Vancouver. The entrance to the mountain-ringed bay is absolutely spectacular.

If you're in a hurry or like your sightseeing from a low-flying airplane, consider taking a floatplane from Seattle's Lake Union to Victoria's Inner Harbour. If the weather is clear, it's a visually exciting flight.

One last recommendation: Leave your car at home, at least the first time you go. It's fairly expensive to take your car and you won't need it once you get to Victoria. All of the major hotels have vans that will pick you up at the pier if you have reservations. The Victoria Clipper sells packages that include transportation, hotel, and ground transfers. Sightseeing in Victoria seems geared to the pedestrian; most of the attractions are within five or six blocks of the harbor, and walking is on nearly level ground with no hills worthy of the name. Pick up a copy of *Victoria on Foot* at any of the local bookstores; it's an excellent paperback guide to four walking tours. For side trips to Butchart Gardens and sightseeing around Oak Bay and the city's residential neighborhoods, take one of the commercial sightseeing buses that operate from in front of the Empress Hotel. With a single exception, all of the attractions, accommodations, and restaurants we recommend in this section are easily reached on foot.

When you arrive in Victoria by water, you cross the Strait of Juan de Fuca to the outer harbor entrance, swing through the breakwater past Ogden Point (where most cruise ships dock), and pass the Canadian Coast Guard base, where bright red-and-white cutters and a buoy tender or two ride at anchor. As you round Laurel Point and slow to enter Victoria's lovely Inner Harbour, your eyes are met by the massive brick and ivy-covered bulk of the Empress Hotel ahead and, to the right, the whimsical turrets of British Columbia's Parliament buildings. Busy tugs, fishing boats, pleasure cruisers, and sailboats seem to fill the small harbor almost to capacity, yet frequently arriving passenger floatplanes seem to find a place to land without running into anybody.

Since this weekend trip really gives you only a day and a half in Victoria, you need to organize your activities to get the most from it. Sunday mornings are pretty quiet in Canada; we suggest you use the time to take a sightseeing bus to Butchart Gardens. Spend Saturday and Sunday afternoons sightseeing and shopping in Victoria.

Begin with a visit to the Tourism Victoria Information Centre right on the waterfront at 812 Wharf Street (open May through July daily 9 A.M. to 9 P.M. August through September open to 8 P.M.; other months to 5 P.M.) where you can pick up free maps, brochures, and advice. Now head south along the seawall fronting the Empress Hotel (resist the temptation to visit now; wait until tea time, about 4 o'clock). Notice the bronze plaques set in the stones of the wall commemorating the famous ships that have called here. The statue facing the Empress is of English Captain James Cook, who first discovered and explored what is now Vancouver Island.

The city's history is typical of that of other Northwest port cities—first used as a base by fur traders (the Hudson's Bay Company established Fort Victoria here in 1843), then as an arrival port and supply point for the hordes of miners heading inland to the Cariboo gold fields in the 1850s. Americans are often surprised to learn that Victoria and British Columbia were independent British crown colonies, separate from the rest of Canada, until 1871. Victoria has always made its livelihood as a seaport and continues to be an important port of call for cruise ships. From the end of the last century until World War II, the great white *Empress* liners of the Canadian Pacific sailed from here westward across the Pacific to ports (some of which were British) in the Orient. The Empress Hotel, built to serve this traffic, is a visible reminder of those halcyon days.

At the end of the seawall you face British Columbia's Parliament buildings. Victoria, with a population of just 65,000 (276,000 in the metro area), is overshadowed by its big sister, Vancouver, on the mainland, but the seat of government is here. Architect Francis Rattenbury, who designed the Empress, also designed these ornate, turreted buildings, completed in 1897. The gilded figure perched atop the large dome is that of Captain George Vancouver, the British navigator who played such an important role in the discovery of the Pacific Northwest. Thousands of white lights trace the outlines of these buildings at night, giving them a fairy-tale appearance that is reflected in the waters of the harbor. Free tours on weekdays take you inside to view splendid stained-glass windows.

Just across the street is the Royal British Columbia Museum. In our opinion, it's the best museum in the Northwest, with stunning displays depicting the social and natural history of British Columbia. Included are realistic exhibits of the woolly mammoth, the Pacific seashore, nineteenth-century stores, and a fish cannery so true to life you can almost smell the fish. Thunderbird Park, next door, has some fine examples of totem poles, and you might see an Indian carver at work. Behind the museum is the 1852 Helmcken House, once the home of the doctor for the Hudson's Bay Company. Many of the original furnishings and medical instruments are on display.

If you continue south, you'll reach Beacon Hill Park, 183 acres of lawns and gardens with totem poles, a cricket pitch where matches are held on Sunday afternoons in summer, and a splendid, grassy seafront promenade with sweeping views across the Strait of Juan de Fuca to the snow-capped Olympic Mountains in the distance. (If you are staying downtown, the walk here is a delightful early morning option.)

If you have the time, you can return via Cook Street, then detour uphill on

Courtney or Fort streets to ornate Craigdarroch Castle and the Art Gallery of Greater Victoria, which houses an outstanding Asian collection, and paintings by Emily Carr, one of Canada's most notable artists. From there, it's about ten blocks back to the Empress Hotel.

If you're not staying at the Empress, be sure to visit. Call it what you will—pompous, pretentious, a heroic monument—it is impressive and reminiscent of the era when travel was the province of the wealthy and they traveled in style. It was the westernmost of a series of hotels built in the twentieth century by the Canadian Pacific Railway (and steamship line) that included Chateau Lake Louise and Banff Springs Hotel in the Canadian Rockies, Chateau Frontenac in Quebec City, and the Royal York in Toronto. Guests of the Empress have included the Duke of Windsor, Winston Churchill, King George VI, Queen Elizabeth II, and the King and Queen of Siam, who brought 56 attendants and 556 pieces of luggage. Recently refurbished to the tune of 45 million Canadian dollars, the Empress is a veritable museum of fine old woodwork, brass fittings, and fussy details. Don't miss the stained-glass ceiling in the Palm Court. Afternoon high tea at the Empress was a Victoria tradition and it's still as elegant, served by waitresses in black uniforms with white collars. Reservations are a must. Another good choice for afternoon tea is Crystal Garden, on Douglas Street behind the Empress. Once a glass-enclosed natatorium (swimming pool), it's now a conservatory of lush tropical plants, rare and colorful birds, and the world's smallest monkeys.

Few destinations have as much appeal for the serious shopper as Victoria. Downtown shops, especially along Government Street, are good places to look for English tweeds, fine china, English candies, British Columbia Indian arts and crafts (including the famous Cowichan sweaters), English pipes and tobacconist's supplies, hand-woven woolens, Scottish tartans, cashmere sweaters, and teas and coffees. One good route takes you north on Government Street from the Empress Hotel for ten blocks or so to Fisgard and Herald streets and Victoria's modest Chinatown, marked by the red Gate of Harmonious Interest, then back on Douglas (the main commercial street) or Wharf streets. Victoria's major department stores are Eaton's, at 1150 Douglas Street; Simpson-Sears, at 3190 Shelbourne Street; Woodward's, at 3125 Douglas Street; and the Bay, formerly Hudson's Bay Company, at 1701 Douglas Street.

Along the way, stop at Bastion Square, once the scene of public hangings and now the location of the Maritime Museum of British Columbia, which displays ships' models, uniforms, marine paintings, and naval uniforms.

Victorians have an absolute passion for gardening. Everywhere you look, from spring through fall, there are flowers blooming—in formal gardens, on windowsills, in 800 baskets hanging from the lampposts. But the pièce de résistance when it comes to horticulture is Butchart Gardens, located 21 kilometers (13 miles) north of Victoria. Getting there is easy: Gray Line and other sightseeing companies run several tours a day on red double-decker London buses.

Butchart comprises 35 acres of a former rock quarry that have been transformed into a magnificent floral display. Critics compare it favorably to London's Kew Gardens. The most dramatic display is the Sunken Garden, with Ross Fountain programmed to create ever-changing patterns of water. In the afternoon, you can sit among the flowers in the conservatory and take tea. Gardening enthusiasts will find Butchart a great source of ideas, and seeds and garden literature can be purchased at the gift shop.

Area Code: 604

SEA TRANSPORTATION *Black Ball Transport,* 106 Surrey Building, Bellevue, WA 98004, (206) 622-2222; Port Angeles, 457-4491. Port Angeles to Victoria; crossing time 1 hour, 35 minutes. 4 daily summer departures from 8:20 A.M. to 9:30 P.M., October to mid-May 2 daily departures at 8:20 A.M. and 2 P.M. Car and driver $23, passengers $5.75. *British Columbia Ferries,* 1112 Fort Street, Victoria V8V 4V2, 386-3431; Vancouver, 669-1211. Tsawwassen to Swartz Bay, Tsawwassen to Nanaimo, and Horseshoe Bay to Nanaimo; crossing times 1 hour, 35 minutes. Departures from 7 A.M. to 9 P.M. Car C$17.50, driver or passenger C$5. *Clipper Navigation,* 2701 Alaska Way, Pier 69, Seattle 98121, (206) 448-5000, (800) 888-2535. Seattle to Victoria, crossing time 2½ or 3 hours. June to mid-September departures at 7:45 and 8:45 A.M., 3:30 P.M. mid-April to May and mid-September to October no afternoon departure; other months 8 A.M. departure. $43 to $49 one-way and $69 to $79 round-trip, depending on season; less for children, seniors, and advance purchase. *Washington State Ferries,* Colman Dock, Pier 52, Seattle 98104, (206) 464-6400, (800) 542-7052 (in WA), (800) 542-0810. Anacortes to Sidney; crossing time 3 hours. Departures July through Labor Day at 8 A.M. and 2:15 P.M., other months single morning departure. Reservations available from mid-May to September.

AIR TRANSPORTATION *Lake Union Air,* (800) 826-1890. Seattle's Lake Union to Victoria's Inner Harbour. From about $69 one-way. *Air BC,* (800) 776-3000; and *Horizon Air,* (800) 547-9308. Seattle–Tacoma Airport to Victoria Airport. From about $92 one-way.

SIGHTSEEING *Gray Line of Victoria,* 700 Douglas Street, 388-5248, (800) 663-8390 (from U.S.). Operates a variety of Victoria City and upisland tours, including Butchart Gardens. *Black Beauty Line Carriage Tours,* 381-8717; *Victoria Carriage Tours,* 382-8509; and *Tallyho Horse-Drawn Tours,* 479-1113. All operate horse carriage rides around the Inner Harbour area from carriage stands at

Menzies and Belleville streets, adjacent to Parliament, between May and September. Cost ranges about C$7 to C$10 for a 15-minute ride. *Harbour Scooter Rentals,* 1223 Wharf Street, 385-2314. Operates a city tour by motor scooter. *Budget Rent-a-Car,* 757 Douglas Street, 388-5525. Rents scooters, mopeds, and bicycles for touring on your own. *Parliament Buildings,* Belleville between Menzies and Government streets. Tours May to Labor Day daily Monday to Friday; other months, call 387-3046 for times. *Royal British Columbia Museum,* 675 Belleville Street, 387-3701. Daily May to Labor Day 9:30 A.M. to 7 P.M., other months 10 A.M. to 5:30 P.M. Adults C$5, seniors and 13–18 C$3, 6–12 C$2, family C$10. *Helmcken House,* behind Royal B. C. Museum, 387-4697. Mid-June to mid-September daily 10 A.M. to 5 P.M., other months Thursday to Monday noon to 5 P.M. Donation. *Royal London Wax Museum,* 470 Belleville Street, 388-4461. May to October daily 8:30 A.M. to 10:30 P.M., other months 9:30 A.M. to 5 P.M. Adults C$5, seniors and 13–19 C$4.50, 5–12 C$2.40, family C$17. *Pacific Undersea Gardens,* 440 Belleville Street, 382-5717. June to September daily 9 A.M. to 9 P.M., other months daily 10 A.M. to 5 P.M. Adults C$5.50, seniors C$5, 12–17 C$4, 5–11 C$2.50. Underwater viewing windows show harbor marine life. *Crystal Garden,* 713 Douglas Street, 381-1213. June to mid-September daily 9 A.M. to 9 P.M., other months 10 A.M. to 5:30 P.M. Adults C$5.50, seniors and 6–16 C$3.50, families C$14.50. *Emily Carr Gallery,* 1107 Wharf Street, 387-3080. Mid-May to September daily noon to 8 P.M., other months Tuesday to Saturday 10 A.M. to 4:30 P.M. Adults C$2. *Miniature World,* in Empress Hotel, 721 Government Street, 385-9731. May to October daily 8:30 A.M. to 10 P.M., other months 10 A.M. to 5 P.M. Adults C$6, 12–18 C$5, 5–11 C$4, families C$19. Dollhouses, miniature soldiers in mock battle, operating miniature railway. *Maritime Museum of British Columbia,* 28 Bastion Square, 385-4222. July to Labor Day daily 10 A.M. to 6 P.M., other months Monday to Saturday 10 A.M. to 4 P.M. and Sunday noon to 4 P.M. Adults C$4, seniors C$3, 6–12 C$1. *Craigdarroch Castle,* 1050 Joan Crescent Street, 592-1225. Mid-June to Labor Day daily 9 A.M. to 9 P.M., other months 10 A.M. to 5 P.M. Adults C$4, seniors and students C$3. *Butchart Gardens,* 21 kilometers (13 miles) north off Highway 17 at Brentwood, 652-4422. July and August daily 9 A.M. to 11 P.M., June and September 9 A.M. to 9 P.M., March to May and October 9 A.M. to 5 P.M., other months 9 A.M. to 4 P.M. Adults C$9.50, 13–17 C$5, 5–12 C$1. *Art Gallery of Greater Victoria,* 1040 Moss Street, 384-4101. Monday to Saturday 10 A.M. to 5 P.M., Thursday 5 to 9 P.M., Sunday 1 to 5 P.M. Adults C$3, seniors and students C$1, Thursday evenings free.

EVENTS *Victoria Day,* May 24 or the closest prior Monday. A national holiday with special celebrations in Victoria including teacup races, a boat parade, and the Victoria Day parade. *Swiftsure Race,* weekend following Victoria Day. An international race in the Strait of Juan de Fuca. *Victoria International Festival,* second week in July to mid-August. 32 classical music concerts around the city. *First Night,* December 31. New Year's Eve celebration, includes fireworks, performing arts, children's parade. For events information call Tourism Victoria at 382-2160.

LODGING Toll-free accommodations number from all of North America, (800) 663-3833, provides current rates and availability of Victoria's numerous accommodations. *James Bay Inn,* 270 Government Street, Victoria V8V 2L2, 384-7151. Older hotel in quiet neighborhood near Beacon Hill Park, $–$$. *Holland House Inn,* 595 Michigan Street, Victoria V8V 1S7, 384-6644. Sophisticated 10-room inn 2 blocks from Royal B. C. Museum, $$$$. *Huntingdon Manor Inn,* 330 Quebec Street, Victoria V8V 1W3, 381-3456. 3-story, 116-room motor hotel overlooking harbor, $$$–$$$$. *Harbour Towers,* 345 Quebec Street, Victoria V8V 1W4, 385-2405. Modern 184-room hotel near Parliament buildings, $$$$. *Hotel Grand Pacific,* 450 Quebec Street, Victoria V8V 1W5, 386-0450. Elegant new hotel overlooking Inner Harbour, large indoor pool and health club, $$$$. *Embassy Motor Inn,* 520 Menzies Street, Victoria V8V 2H4, 382-8161. Near Parliament buildings, $$–$$$. *Laurel Point Inn,* 680 Montreal Street, Victoria V8V 1Z8, 386-8721. Full-service hotel on waterfront, $$$$. *Captain's Palace,* 309 Belleville Street, Victoria V8V 1X2, 388-9191. Elegant 1897 house overlooking harbor, $$$–$$$$. *The Empress,* 721 Government Street, Victoria V8V 1W5, 384-8111. *The* grand old hotel in Victoria, newly refurbished, $$$$. *The Beaconsfield Inn,* 998 Humboldt Street, Victoria V8V 2Z8, 384-4044. Fine old Edwardian mansion near Beacon Hill Park, $$$$. *Victoria Regent Hotel,* 1234 Wharf Street, Victoria V8W 3H9, 386-2211. Suites on harborfront, $$$$. *The Bedford Hotel,* 1140 Government Street, Victoria V8W 1Y2, 384-6835. Elegant small European-style hotel, $$$$. *Abigail's Hotel,* 906 McClure Street, Victoria V8V 3E7, 388-5363. Refurbished Tudor mansion, $$$$. *Oak Bay Beach Hotel,* 1175 Beach Drive, Victoria V8S 2N2, 598-4556. Fine old English-style seaside hotel with pub, $$–$$$$. *Sooke Harbour House,* 1528 Whiffen Spit Road, Sooke V0S 1N0, 642-3421. Highly rated inn on secluded bluff above ocean, 28 kilometers (17 miles) from town; a great getaway spot, but you'll probably need a car; rate includes breakfast and lunch for two; $$$$.

DINING *Prima's on the Wharf,* 218 Wharf Street, 381-2112. Dinner Monday to Saturday; Italian cuisine, seafood; $$. *Taj Mahal,* 679 Herald Street, 383-4662. Lunch Monday to Saturday, dinner daily; African and Indian food; $–$$. *The Grape Escape,* 506 Fort Street, 386-8466. Dinner Tuesday to Sunday; wide-ranging menu includes seafood, game, beef; $$. *Chandlers,* 1250 Wharf Street, 386-3232. Dinner daily, seafood, $$. *La Cucina,* 920 Gordon Street, 381-4556. Lunch and dinner daily, Italian menu, $–$$. *Smitty's,* 850 Douglas Street, 383-5612. Breakfast, lunch, and dinner daily; noted for robust breakfasts; $. *Causeway Restaurant*, 812 Wharf Street, 381-2244. Lunch and dinner daily; seafood, great view of harbor and Parliament buildings lit at night; $$. *Harbour House*, 607 Oswego Street, 386-1244. Lunch and dinner daily; overlooks harbor, outdoor dining in summer; $$. *Periklis Restaurant*, 531 Yates Street, 386-3313. Dinner daily, Greek cuisine, $$. *James Bay Tea Room*, 332 Menzies Street, 382-8282. Breakfast, lunch, and dinner daily; cozy English-style tea room; $$. *Sooke Harbour House*, (see "Lodging"). Dinner daily by reservation; consistently rated among the top restaurants in western Canada; emphasis on fresh local products, especially seafood; $$$.

FOR MORE INFORMATION Tourism Victoria, 812 Wharf Street, Victoria V8W 1T3, 382-2127.

Up Vancouver Island from Victoria

Beyond Victoria, Vancouver Island stretches more than 450 kilometers (280 miles) northward along the west coast of British Columbia. It's a rugged island for the most part, with dense rain forests where 600-year-old spruce and Douglas fir trees grow to 70 meters (230 feet) or more and a coast so fierce and wave-pounded you can traverse it only on foot. A steep mountain spine, more than 2,000 meters (6,561 feet) high, confines most of the population to a scattering of small waterside towns that line the only north-south highway, Trans-Canada 1/British Columbia 19, along the east coast. At several places, cross-island roads penetrate to the fjordlike inlets from the sea along the west coast. The waters off both coasts of Vancouver Island provide some of the best salmon fishing anywhere in the world, which is the reason most people come here. But even if you're not interested in fishing, the drive upisland will provide an interesting glimpse of Canadian small-town life. Along the way there are museums, Indian settlements, and sweaters to buy, and there is a nifty all-day boat ride you can take on the west coast. And, if you're a hiker, good trails abound.

You could do this trip in a two-day hard-driving trip from Seattle, but we suggest you add at least another day to give you a three-day, two-night trip. You can also include this drive in a longer loop to Vancouver on the mainland.

Just north of Victoria, the highway, known as Malahat Drive, climbs through thickly wooded country to 353-meter (1,156-foot) Malahat Summit. Though it isn't very high compared to Cascade mountain passes, the views nonetheless are breathtaking. There's a viewpoint at the top that gives you sweeping vistas of the Gulf Islands spread out in the Strait of Georgia to the east.

Just north of Mill Bay, you can detour down to the water at the little fishing town of Cowichan Bay. At the north side of town at a roadside rest, there's a touching tribute to Robert W. Service, "the Bard of the Yukon," who published a poem in the local press in 1903.

At Duncan, 61 kilometers (38 miles) north of Victoria, stop at the British Columbia Forest Museum. Located in a fine stand of old-growth Douglas firs, the museum features an old-time logging camp, logging equipment, and a steam train ride. A local curiosity, the Glass Castle, 3 miles south on Trans-Canada 1, is constructed of more than 200,000 bottles!

One product produced locally and coveted by Northwesterners is the Cowichan sweater. Knitted of unbleached wool by the women of the Cowichan tribe, the bulky sweaters come in shades of brown and tan, are decorated with Indian designs, and are as warm as toast—and proof against the worst weather a Northwest winter can throw at you. You'll find them in local shops in Duncan, Cowichan, Ladysmith, and Nanaimo, as well as in stores in Victoria, where they're generally more expensive. Some Cowichan sweaters are now being mass-produced but are of poorer quality.

A new Native Heritage Center in Duncan does a splendid job of explaining the North Coast Indian culture through totems, a replica cedar longhouse, typical Indian food, and programs that include interpretive dancing and a dinner theater that features the traditional potlatch ceremony. This is also a good place to pick up Indian arts and crafts, including Cowichan sweaters. Big Lake Cowichan, just to the west, is a favorite destination for hiking and camping.

Chemainus, known as "The Little Town That Did" (owing to its successful economic endeavors), features 21 large-scale murals painted on the walls of its buildings. Started as a project to revive a moribund town, these works of art attract more than 300,000 tourists annually and have resulted in 45 new businesses to serve the visitors.

The east coast of Vancouver Island is dotted with elegant lodges, most of them tucked away off the main roads. If you're looking for a quiet retreat, Yellow Point Lodge, on the water near Ladysmith, offers the tranquility of 180 secluded acres and more than a mile of waterfront.

Nanaimo, 120 kilometers (74½ miles) north of Victoria, is a bustling waterfront town founded on coal mining. A distinctive and photogenic bastion, built in 1853 as a defensive fort, perches above the harbor. The Nanaimo Centennial Museum houses Indian artifacts and displays detailing the region's coal mining history. You can join charter boats here for a day of salmon fishing; other operators offer wildlife cruises to view eagles and sea lions. If you're looking for an unusual spot to picnic, board the little ferry that runs from the wharf at Maffeo-Sutton Park across to Newcastle Island. A provincial marine park, the island is home to deer, raccoons, rabbits, beavers, and lots of birds; there are trails and picnic facilities.

At Parksville, 35 kilometers (22 miles) north of Nanaimo, turn inland onto Provincial Highway 4 and drive 47 kilometers (29 miles) to Port Alberni. Billed as "the salmon capital of the world," Port Alberni is devoted to the wood products industry, with a large (and odoriferous) pulp and paper mill and a plywood mill dominating the town. Salmon fishing charter boats depart from here, the action culminating in the annual Salmon Festival on Labour Day weekend with $25,000 in prizes for the winning anglers. During the summer, a 1912-vintage Shay steam locomotive carries passengers along the waterfront. World War II airplane buffs will be interested to know that several Martin Mars, the massive four-engine flying boats, are used as firefighting aerial tankers and make their home base on nearby Sproat Lake.

The real treat at Port Alberni is the M.V. *Lady Rose,* a diminutive coastal passenger-freighter that makes single-day voyages down Alberni Inlet to the coast. Scottish-built and sturdy, the jaunty little vessel with a canvas canopy sheltering the afterdeck is reminiscent of the *African Queen,* though it's a bit larger, carrying 100 passengers.

If you arrive early for the scheduled 8 A.M. departure, you can watch deckhands loading groceries and miscellaneous cargo for the Indian villages and logging camps along the route. In summer there's always a generous load of canoes, kayaks, outboards, camping gear, and passengers for the isolated Broken Islands in Pacific Rim National Park.

According to the skipper, "Departure is more or less on time. We always tell people to take their watches off and drop them into their pockets if they are going with us. The world worships time so much, you know. What time do we leave? What time do we get there? Sometimes *Lady Rose* is early, sometimes late."

For 25 miles you cruise down Alberni Inlet, a slender channel ranging from two miles to half a mile wide and flanked by steep mountains. Passengers gather in the tiny coffee shop for refreshment and conversation, or if it's sunny, strip down to bare essentials and sprawl about the deck. You chug past salmon boats, and along the shoreline you're likely to spot bald eagles perched in the trees waiting to dive on an aquatic meal.

Emerging from the inlet, the *Lady Rose* picks her way among the Broken Islands (there are more than 100 of them), stopping every now and then to offload campers and boats at remote beaches. Seabirds of every description can be seen, as well as sea lions perched on rocks to watch you pass. Porpoise and black and gray whales surface off the bow and play games with one another by plunging through the ship's wake.

The *Lady Rose* alternates trips to Bamfield and Ucluelet. On Tuesday, Thursday, Saturday, and Sunday, she goes to Bamfield, terminus of the challenging West Coast Trail. On Monday, Wednesday, and Friday, it's Ucluelet. The skipper guarantees you at least an hour ashore for lunch or a stroll before departure for the return to Port Alberni.

Provincial Highway 4 crosses another 91 kilometers (56½ miles) of rugged, forested landscape to reach the coast. Ucluelet has a substantial commercial fishing fleet, fish-processing plants, and logging operation. Dozens of charter fishing boats are also based here as well as sightseeing vessels that cruise offshore on whale-watching expeditions in March and April. One of the most unusual accommodations in this part of the world is the *Canadian Princess,* a former coastal passenger ship, now beached and serving as a hotel.

The Long Beach section of Pacific Rim National Park stretches most of the 42 kilometers (26 miles) between Ucluelet and Tofino. Miles of deserted sandy beach, headlands, and offshore islands, sea caves, and tidal pools invite you to walk, jog, beach-comb, or just relax and watch the sea. There are modest overnight accommodations in Tofino if the lure of the sea makes you want to stay a while.

Area Code: 604

DRIVING DIRECTIONS It's 318 kilometers (198 miles) from Victoria to Tofino via Trans-Canada Highway 1 and Provincial Highways 19 and 4.

SIGHTSEEING *British Columbia Forest Museum,* Trans-Canada Highway 1, 1 mile north of Duncan, 746-1251. May to September daily 9:30 A.M. to 6 P.M. Adults C$4.75, seniors and 13–18 C$3.50, 6–12 C$2.40, families C$12. *Native Heritage Centre,* 200 Cowichan Way, Duncan, 746-8119. May to September daily 10 A.M. to 6 P.M. Adults C$5.50, seniors and children under 13 C$3.75; potlatch dinner theater, adults C$39, seniors and children C$32. *Glass Castle,* Trans-Canada 1, 3 miles south of Duncan, 746-6518. Mid-March through October, daily 9 A.M. to dusk. Adults C$3.50, over 65 and students C$2.50, 5–11 C$1.50. *Nanaimo Centennial Museum,* 100 Cameron Street, Nanaimo, 753-1821. May to August Monday to Friday 9 A.M. to 6 P.M., Saturday and Sunday 10 A.M. to 6 P.M., other months Tuesday to Saturday 9 A.M. to 4 P.M. Donation. *Alberni Valley Museum,* 4255 Wallace Street, Port Alberni, 723-2181. Daily 10 A.M. to 5 P.M. Exhibits focus on Indian culture, lumbering, fishing, and West Coast Lifesaving Trail. Free. **M.V.** *Lady Rose,* P.O. Box 188, Port Alberni V9Y 7M7, 723-8313. Daily departures for Bamfield or Ucluelet at 8 A.M., round trip takes 9 or 10 hours. Round-trip fares C$30 or C$35, 8–15 half fare.

EVENTS *Pacific Rim Whale Festival,* Tofino, 725-3414, mid-March to mid-April. Celebrates annual whale migration. *Great International Bathtub Race,* 754-8474, early July. Contestants in bathtub-size craft race 55 kilometers across the Strait of Georgia from Nanaimo to Vancouver. *Port Alberni Salmon Festival,* 724-6535, Labour Day Weekend. Angling contests for cash prizes, salmon barbecue, bed race.

LODGING *The Aerie,* P.O. Box 108, Malahat V0R 2L0, 743-7115. 12-room inn atop Malahat Summit overlooks Gulf Islands. C$$$$. *Pine Lodge Farm* (bed and breakfast), 3191 Mutter Road, RR #2, Mill Bay V0R 2P0, 743-4083. 2-story home with 7 guest rooms on working farm, $$. *The Inn at the Water Resort,* 1681 Botwood Lane, Cowichan Bay V0R 1N0, 748-6222. Full-service hotel on the waterfront, $$$. *Grove Hall Estate,* 6159 Lakes Road, Duncan V9L 4J6, 746-6152. 3 guest rooms in elegant 1912 Tudor mansion on 17 acres with tennis court, $$. *Cowichan Valley Inn,* 6457 Norcross Road, Duncan V9L 3W8, 748-2722. $-$$. *Yellowpoint Lodge,* Yellow Point Road RR #3, Ladysmith V0R 2E0, 245-7422. American plan, $$$. *Inn of the Sea,* Yellow Point Road RR #3, Ladysmith V0R 2E0, 245-2211. Modern lodge on the water, some fireplaces, kitchens, $$$-$$$$. *Coast Bastion Hotel,* 11 Bastion Street, Nanaimo V9R 2Z9, 753-6601. Full-service hotel on the waterfront, $$$$. *Harbourview Motor Inn,* 809 Island Highway South, Nanaimo V9R 5K1, 754-8171. Modern motel with views of the water, $$-$$$. *Tigh-Na-Mara,* Island Highway RR #1, Parksville V0R 2S0, 248-2072. Log cottages in woods by the water, $$$-$$$$. *Bayside Inn Resort,* 240 Dogwood Drive, Parksville V0R 2S0, 248-8333. Waterfront resort; $$$-$$$$. *Tyee Village Motel,* 4151 Redford Street, Port Alberni V9Y 3R6, 723-8133. Center-of-town location, $$. *Hospitality Inn,* 3835 Redford Street, Port Alberni V9Y 3R6, 723-8111. Central location, $$. *Canadian Princess Resort,* P.O. Box 939, Ucluelet V0R 3A0, 726-7771. Staterooms on former passenger ship, $-$$. *Ocean Village Beach Resort,* 555 Hellesen Drive, Tofino V0R 2Z0, 725-3755. Large facility with housekeeping units on beach, $$$-$$$$. *Chesterman's Beach Bed and Breakfast,* 1345 Chesterman's Beach Road, Tofino V0R 2Z0, 725-3726. On the beach, $$.

CAMPING *Duncan RV Park and Campground,* 2950 Boys Road, Duncan V9L 4T8, 748-8511. 65 sites, 30 full-hookup, C$12-C$16. *4 All Seasons Resort,* 3464 Yellow Point Road, Ladysmith V0R 2E0, 245-4243. 75 sites on 15 acres on the water, C$12-C$21. 5 provincial parks lie along or near Highway 4 between Parksville and Alberni: *Englishman River Falls,* 105 sites; *Little Qualicum Falls,* 91 sites; *Rathtrevor Beach,* 174 sites; *Sproat Lake,* 59 sites; and *Stamp Falls,* 22 sites. None have hookups, fees are C$6 to C$12, information 248-3931. *Green Point Campground,* Pacific Rim National Park, 21 kilometers (13 miles) north of Ucluelet on Highway 4, 726-7721. 94 sites, no hookups, near beach. C$12.

DINING *Richard's Restaurant,* 161 Kenneth Road, Duncan, 748-5702. Lunch and dinner Tuesday to Saturday; eclectic menu; $. *The Inglenook,* 7621 Island

Highway, Duncan, 746-4031. Dinner Wednesday to Sunday; upscale restaurant in Tudor home; $$. *Quamichan Inn,* 1478 Maple Bay Road, Duncan, 746-7028. Dinner daily; another Tudor-style establishment, this one long established and serving traditional empire dishes such as Yorkshire pudding, steak and kidney pie, and Indian curry, plus seafood; $$. *The Oak and Carriage,* 3287 Cowichan Lake Road, Duncan, 746-4144. Lunch and dinner Monday to Saturday; traditional British-style pub, complete with dart boards, serving "pub grub," baron of beef, seafood; $. *Crow and Gate,* 2313 Yellow Point Road, Ladysmith, 722-3731. Lunch and dinner daily; splendid country pub serving steak and kidney pie, Yorkshire pudding, traditional pub food; $. *Katerina's Place,* 15 Front Street, Nanaimo, 753-3512. Lunch and dinner daily, Greek cuisine, $$. *The Grotto,* 1511 Stewart Avenue, Nanaimo, 753-3303. Dinner Monday to Saturday, seafood near B.C. ferry dock, $. *Kalvas Restaurant,* 180 Moilliet Street, Parksville, 248-6933. Dinner daily; extensive seafood menu, beef served in circular log building; $$. *Courtyard Restaurant,* Port Alberni Highway, Port Alberni, 723-9415. Breakfast, lunch, and dinner daily; steak, seafood; $$. *Whale's Tale,* Peninsula Road at Bay Street, Ucluelet, 726-4621. Dinner Wednesday to Sunday; seafood, quiet surroundings; $$. *The Loft,* 346 Campbell Street, Tofino, 725-4241. Breakfast, lunch, and dinner daily; steak and seafood; $$. *Blue Heron Dining Room,* Way West Motel on Highway 4, Tofino, 725-4266. Breakfast, lunch, and dinner daily; views of marina and Meares Island, serves steak and seafood; $$.

FOR MORE INFORMATION Pacific Rim National Park, P.O. Box 280, Ucluelet, B. C. V0R 3A0, 726-4212. Tourism Association of Vancouver Island, 45 Bastion Square, Suite 302, Victoria V8W 1J1, 382-3551.

Vancouver: Hitting the Highlights

Of all the cities of the Pacific Northwest, Vancouver, British Columbia, is by far the most complex, the most cosmopolitan, the most magnificent in its setting. Vancouver is, in fact, frequently ranked right up there with San Francisco, Sydney, Hong Kong, and Paris as one of the world's most beautiful cities. If you approach Vancouver from the south or east, you're deprived of its setting until you're right downtown. But if you approach by ferry from the west, the scenery is absolutely stunning, with great rocky mountains rising sheer from the water in battlements that tower thousands of feet over the city.

If you're in an arguing mood, you can certainly get a rise by comparing Vancouver to San Francisco. The similarities are many. More than any other Western city except San Francisco, Vancouver is a real cultural melting pot. Settled first by the Scots, Irish, and English, its institutions and structures are familiarly Anglo-Saxon. But after both world wars, and increasingly in the last two decades, the city has been a magnet for immigrants. First came citizens of the British Empire—Indians, Pakistanis, Hong Kong Chinese, New Zealanders, Australians, South Africans, and a rainbow of other former colonials. More recently have come Eastern Europeans, mainland Chinese, Japanese, Southeast Asians, Pacific Islanders, and Latin Americans. The city is booming with new development, much of it fueled by investments from businesses fleeing Hong Kong before the colony's impending incorporation into the People's Republic of China in 1997.

The results have produced a bonanza for visitors. To be sure, Canada is no more free of prejudice than anyplace else, and you're likely to hear negative comments about "New Canadians," usually referring to immigrants from Hong Kong or the Asian subcontinent (Pakistan, India, Sri Lanka, and Bangladesh). But for the most part these people have been assimilated remarkably well and have opened hundreds of ethnic restaurants and shops throughout the city. You can sample cuisine and arts and crafts from virtually anyplace in the world in Vancouver. And we'll put Vancouver up against any city in North America, including New York and San Francisco, when it comes to the variety of food available.

Vancouver is too big and diverse to see in just one trip—or even in a half dozen trips. We've been going for nearly 30 years and discover something new and delightful every trip. This section is not, then, a complete guide to Vancouver; there are more comprehensive guides available in local bookstores. We simply suggest some of our favorite things to see and do in a weekend; mix them and match them to suit yourself. The Tourism Vancouver information center (Plaza Level, Four Bentall Centre, 1055 Dunsmuir Street; open daily in summer 8 A.M. to 6 P.M., rest of year Monday to Friday 8:30 A.M. to 5 P.M., Saturday 9 A.M. to 5 P.M.) is an outstanding source, with a wealth of maps, restaurant lists, entertainment guides, brochures, and good advice as well as postal service and hotel reservation service. If you want to do a little research before you go, write them or visit the Tourism British Columbia office in Seattle (Marsh and McLennan Building, 720 Olive Way; open Monday to Friday 8:30 A.M. to 5 P.M.).

One tip: As in most big cities, downtown Vancouver hotels are expensive. You can save a bit on accommodations by staying in New Westminster and taking the SkyTrain downtown. It's fast, clean, safe, and cheap, and will take you right to the SeaBus terminal for a ride across to North Vancouver (see "Vancouver: The North Shore") if you wish.

Our vote for the city's top attraction goes to Stanley Park. Occupying more than a thousand acres on a peninsula flanked by English Bay, Lions Gate, and Burrard Inlet, and adjacent to downtown, the park is a lush combination of dense coastal forest, manicured lawns, and saltwater beaches. More than 80 kilometers (50 miles) of roads and trails crisscross the park, providing plenty of room for jogging, walking, bicycling, and leisurely driving. You can lawn bowl, watch a cricket match (Sunday afternoons in summer), swim, or play golf or tennis. Photographers tend to use up a lot of film in Stanley Park. There are fine views of the downtown skyline and the cruise ship terminal, Canada Place, across Burrard Inlet from the south side of the park (the evening gun is also fired from here at 6 P.M.). There are rose gardens, totem poles, and a tea house, from whose lofty perch you can see one of our favorite views—the big cruise ships passing through Lions Gate. The Vancouver aquarium in the park features white beluga and killer whales, performing dolphins and an Amazon Rain Forest gallery. The city's modest zoo and miniature steam railroad are also here.

One of the best ways to tour Stanley Park is by bicycle; several firms in the area rent them, including Hertz, the car rental people, for about C$5 per hour or C$16 for five hours. One of the firms is located in the Westin Bayshore parking lot and right across the street is another. If you want to spend most of your time in Stanley Park, good hotel choices close by are the upscale Westin Bayshore and the modest Sylvia Beach Hotel on English Bay.

Next on the must-see list are Gastown and Chinatown, cheek-by-jowl neighborhoods on the northeastern side of downtown. Leave your car in the hotel garage and do your exploring on foot; parking in the area is almost nonexistent. Gastown is adjacent to the SkyTrain and SeaBus terminal, making it easy to reach by public transportation.

Gastown is Vancouver's oldest section, replete with cobblestone streets, gas lamps and ornate old commercial buildings that have been gentrified and now house some of the city's trendiest restaurants, shops, and galleries; because it's a historic district and draws so many visitors, shops are open on Sundays. At the corner of Water and Carrall streets you'll find a statue of "Gassy Jack" Deighton, the man who started it all. He opened a saloon here in 1867 for the local sawmill workers, and the district was named for him. The world's first steam-powered clock stands at the corner of Cambie and Water streets; its whistles announce the time every 15 minutes.

The second largest Chinese community in North America (after San Francisco) is concentrated in Vancouver's Chinatown, focused on Pender Street between Carrall and Gore streets. The district is a warren of small shops, Oriental groceries, herbal shops, pagoda-roofed telephone booths, and restaurants. You can shop for anything from herbs, ginseng root, and dried mushrooms, to brocaded silk shawls and carved Chinese puzzles. If you're on a budget, this is a good place to eat your fill quite inexpensively. The restaurants feature mostly Cantonese fare.

Like Victoria, Vancouver is a city of gardens, and one of the best times to visit is in May, when everything is in bloom. Newest is the Dr. Sun Yat-Sen Classical

Chinese Garden at 578 Carrall Street in the heart of Chinatown. The first full-scale garden of its type ever constructed outside China, it reflects the Taoist philosophy of yin and yang, which balances opposites—light with dark, rugged and hard with soft and flowing, small with large. You leave the noise and bustle of Chinatown behind and enter a peaceful world where you are aware of every detail—the shape of a contoured rock, a lacy maple tree, the reflection of a graceful roof line in a tranquil pool of water. Guided tours are available.

If you're planning to do some shopping, best schedule it for Saturday as most major retail stores only open from noon to 5 P.M. on Sunday. A great place to browse is along Robson Street, with its high-fashion boutiques, trendy shops, sidewalk cafés, and public market. Robson Street runs into Robson Square, where you'll find the glass-tiered pyramid of the Law Courts, Eaton's (one of Vancouver's largest department stores), the Bay, and adjoining Granville Mall. If inclement weather precludes outdoor activities, the large underground malls here in the center of Vancouver are good places to while away a Saturday afternoon.

Robson Square is also the location of the Vancouver Art Gallery, another building designed by Francis Rattenbury, architect of the Parliament buildings and the Empress Hotel in Victoria. It houses a large collection of paintings by Emily Carr as well as other regional works and European and American art dating from the seventeenth century to the present.

For shopping or just sightseeing, Granville Island, at the southern edge of downtown, is a worthwhile place to spend some time, especially on a sunny day. It's a people place. It's an unusual waterside combination of a public market, shops and galleries, theaters, restaurants, and a hotel tucked in among boat builders, a cement plant, architects, and a brewery. Dozens of sailboats and motor cruisers lie berthed at the east and west ends of the island. A plank walkway skirting False Creek affords views of the downtown skyline and the former site of Expo 86—the 1986 World's Fair—just across the creek. Diminutive passenger ferries connect the island with the north shore of False Creek.

Stop at the Public Market, where you're greeted by the aromas of baked goods, deli food, a candy kitchen, coffee, and spices. One of our favorite shops here, the Stock Market, makes and sells soups, stocks, and sauces, from bouillabaisse starter to pesto; it's difficult to pass up one or two purchases to take home. The market is also a good place to pick up the makings of a picnic to spread on one of the waterside wooden benches. If you'd rather have a more formal meal, there are eight restaurants on the island and food stands in the public market.

Browsing the shops and galleries can occupy an entire afternoon. Diana Sanderson designs and makes silk dresses, blouses, sweaters, skirts, and jackets from fabric dyed and woven on looms in her shop. Dragonspace specializes in the mythological in jewelry, figurines, pottery, and dragons in all sizes and shapes.

Net Loft houses an assortment of shops, including a bookstore, print gallery, bead shop, glass works, and knife store. Kids Only Market has some two dozen shops selling all kinds of things for youngsters. Granville Island Brewery, brewers of Island Lager and Island Bock, offers free tasting tours daily at 2 P.M. The modernistic Granville Island Hotel at the east end of the island is a good choice for out-of-the-way accommodations with a view of the water.

If you like museums, you'll love Vancouver. There are more than a dozen good ones. Three are tops on our list—the Maritime Museum, Vancouver Museum, and the H. R. MacMillan Planetarium Complex. The planetarium features a laser light show and programs on space exploration and astronomy.

The Museum of Anthropology on the campus of the University of British Columbia at the western edge of the city is the finest museum devoted to North Coast Indian culture extant. Northwest Marine Drive is an especially scenic way to get there. Though you'll encounter totem poles frequently in Washington, British Columbia, and Alaska, many of them have been carved fairly recently. Authentic, historic totems from the nineteenth century are rare, and this museum probably has the best collection to be found anywhere. The museum also boasts extensive exhibits of Indian art, basketry, carvings, clothing, and utensils, as well as artifacts from Africa, the Pacific Islands, and the Americas.

Downtown, the Vancouver Art Museum is housed in the renovated neoclassical law courts building designed by Francis Rattenbury in 1907. The building itself is worth a visit. Four floors of exhibits include eighteenth- and nineteenth-century British artists, contemporary American graphics, Canadian sculpture and folk art, and a children's gallery.

Situated in Vanier Park, overlooking English Bay, the Maritime Museum is small, but houses the *St. Roch,* the schooner on which a crew of Canadian Mounties completed a round trip through the icebound Northwest Passage for the first time in 1944. As you walk the decks and poke about the cabins of the old ship, a tour guide explains the voyage and the various living and work spaces. You'll marvel at the fortitude of the men who survived in such cramped quarters under miserable conditions for many months.

The Vancouver Museum concentrates on the city's history and includes extensive displays pertaining to its Indian culture, fur trading history, and nineteenth-century development, with features on the art, natural history, and anthropology of western Canada.

If you're traveling with restless kids, there is another museum where you can turn them loose and they'll be captivated for hours. Science World, at 1455 Quebec Street, features dozens of hands-on science exhibits and live "gee whiz"– type demonstrations of scientific phenomena. It's housed in a geodesic dome on the former Expo 86 World's Fair site.

Surprisingly for a western Canadian city, Vancouver provides plenty to do at night, whatever your tastes. You'll find jazz clubs with local bands playing rhythm and blues, soul, hard and soft rock, and Dixieland. You can dance at the Commodore Ballroom or listen to the top visiting performers in BC Place Stadium. On the cultural side, Vancouver has a good symphony orchestra that performs at the Orpheum, an opera association that stages productions in the Queen Elizabeth Theater, and a variety of chamber music groups, chorales, and ensembles. The Vancouver Playhouse is the city's leading theater; the Arts Club Theater has its main stage on Granville Island, with additional facilities at the Seymour Street Theater and the Revue Theater downtown. Also on Granville Island is the Waterfront Theater. Tickets and performance schedules are generally available through Ticketmaster, 280-4444.

Area Code: 604

DRIVING DIRECTIONS Vancouver is 141 miles north of Seattle via Interstate 5 and British Columbia Highway 99.

AIR TRANSPORTATION From Seattle, *Air BC, Canadian, Horizon Air, Lake Union Air,* and *United Airlines* serve Vancouver. One-way fares begin at about $70.

SIGHTSEEING *Budget Rent-A-Car,* various locations, 685-0536 *Stanley Park Bike Rentals,* 676 Chilco Street, 681-5581. *Franco's,* on Cardero across from the Westin Bayshore, 681-2453; and *Robson Cycles,* 1463 Robson Street, 687-2777. Both rent bicycles. *Aardvark Tours,* 431-9330; and *Sea & Cycle Adventures,* 1348 Barclay Street, 689-BIKE. Both lead bicycle tours around the city and to other British Columbia destinations. *Vancouver Aquarium,* Stanley Park, 682-1118. July to September daily 9:30 A.M. to 8 P.M., other months 10 A.M. to 5:30 P.M. Adults C$7, seniors and 13–18 C$6, 5–12 C$4.50. *Stanley Park Children's Zoo and Miniature Railroad.* Daily 11 A.M. to 5 P.M. Adults C$1.75 each attraction, seniors and under 13 C$.85, families C$3.40. *Dr. Sun Yat-Sen Classical Chinese Garden*, 578 Carrall Street, 689-7133. May to September daily 10 A.M. to 7:30 P.M., other months daily 10 A.M. to 4:30 P.M. Adults C$3, seniors and 6–11 C$1.50, families C$6. *Vancouver Art Museum,* 750 Hornby Street, 682-4668. Summer Monday to Saturday 10 A.M. to 5 P.M., plus Thursday 5 to 9 P.M., Sunday noon to 5 P.M.; other months closed Tuesday. Adults C$3.50, over 65 and students C$2. Free Thursday 5 to 9 P.M. *Maritime Museum,* 1100 Chestnut Street, 737-2211. Daily 10 A.M. to 5 P.M. Adults C$3.50, seniors C$2, students and children 5–12 C$1.50, families C$7. *Vancouver Museum and Planetarium,* 1100 Chestnut Street, 736-4431. May to September, daily 10 A.M. to 5 P.M., other months Tuesday to Sunday 10 A.M. to 5 P.M. Adults C$5, seniors and 6–18 C$2.50, families C$10, seniors free on Tuesday.

Museum of Anthropology, University of British Columbia campus, 228-3825. Tuesday 11 A.M. to 9 P.M., Wednesday to Sunday 11 A.M. to 5 P.M. Adults C$4, seniors and students C$2, 6–12 C$1.50, families C$10, free on Tuesday. *Science World,* 1455 Quebec Street, 687-7832. Daily 10 A.M. to 6 P.M. Adults C$7, seniors and 13–19 C$4.50, 4–12 C$3.50.

EVENTS *Vancouver Sea Festival,* 683-2000; mid-July. Week-long event features boat races, water shows, fireworks. *Vancouver Chamber Music Festival,* 736-6034; early August. 6 evenings of chamber music outdoors on the campus of Saint George's School. *Pacific National Exhibition* ("the PNE"), 683-2000, late August to Labor Day. Large exhibition equivalent to a U.S. state fair.

LODGING *Four Seasons Hotel,* 791 West Georgia Street, Vancouver V6C 2T4, 689-9333. Elegant member of prestigious Canadian chain, $$$$. *Granville Island Hotel and Marina.* 1253 Johnston Street, Vancouver V6H 3R9, 683-7373. Waterfront hotel away from downtown traffic and noise, $$$$. *Hotel Georgia,* 801 Georgia Street, Vancouver V6C 1P7, 682-5566. Fine older traditional hotel downtown, $$$–$$$$. *Holiday Inn Vancouver Downtown,* 1110 Howe Street, Vancouver V6Z 1R2, 684-2151. Good value for money downtown, $$$$. *Hotel Meridien Vancouver,* 845 Burrard Street, Vancouver V6Z 2K6, 682-5511. Top-of-the-line French chain hotel, $$$$. *Hotel Vancouver,* 900 Georgia Street, Vancouver V6C 2W6, 684-3131. This classic hotel is a city landmark, $$$$. *Pan Pacific,* 999 Canada Place, Vancouver V6C 3B5, 662–8111. Outstanding waterfront location in cruise terminal/trade center, $$$$. *Sylvia Hotel,* 1154 Gilford Street, Vancouver V6G 2P6, 681-9321. Funky, ivy-covered hotel on English Bay near Stanley Park, a favorite of savvy Vancouver visitors, $$. *Wedgewood Hotel,* 845 Hornby Street, Vancouver V6Z 1V1, 689-7777. Small, elegant European-style hotel, $$$$. *Westin Bayshore,* 1601 Georgia Street West, Vancouver V6G 2V4, 682-3377. Waterfront location near Stanley Park gives this upscale hotel the edge, $$$$. *Inn at Westminster Quay,* 900 Quayside Drive, New Westminster V3M 6G1, 520-1776. On the Fraser River, close to SkyTrain terminal, $$$$. *New Royal Towers Hotel,* 140 Sixth Street, New Westminster V3M 1J4, 524-3777. Good choice for economy hotel, near SkyTrain terminal, $$–$$$.

DINING *Ashiana,* 5076 Victoria Drive, 321-5620. Lunch Tuesday to Sunday, dinner daily; spicy East Indian food; $$. *Bishop's,* 2183 West Fourth Avenue, 738-2025. Lunch Monday to Friday, dinner daily; elegant, nouvelle menu; $$$. *Chartwell,* 791 West Georgia Street in Four Seasons Hotel, 689-9333. Lunch Monday to Friday, dinner daily; English club environment, wide-ranging menu; $$$. *English Bay Cafe,* 1795 Beach Avenue, 669-2225. Lunch Monday to Saturday, dinner daily, brunch Sunday; a delightfully airy place in a residential neighborhood across from the beach at English Bay, strong on seafood; $$. *Il Giardino di Umberto,* 1382 Hornby Street, 669-2422. Lunch Monday to Friday, dinner Monday to Saturday; one of several upscale Umberto Italian restaurants; $$$. *Kirin Mandarin Restaurant,* 1166 Alberni Street, 682-8833. Lunch and dinner daily, upscale establishment specializing in Shanghai and Szechuan cuisine, $$. *Le Crocodile,* 818 Thurlow Street, 669-4298. Lunch Monday to Friday, dinner Monday to Saturday; excellent French cooking; $$. *Le Railcar,* 106 Carrall Street, 669-5422. Lunch and dinner daily; dining in 1929 Canadian Pacific passenger car, Gastown; $$. *Quilicum,* 1724 Davie Street, 681-7044. Dinner daily; Native Indian menu including barbecue salmon, steamed fern shoots, bannock bread; $$. *Sawasdee Thai Restaurant,* 4250 Main Street, 876-4030. Dinner Tuesday to Sunday, long-established Thai restaurant, $$. *Szechuan Chongging Restaurant,* 2495 Victoria Drive, 254-7434. Lunch and dinner daily; good, inexpensive northern Chinese food; $–$$. *The Teahouse at Ferguson Point,* Stanley Park, 669-3281. Lunch Monday to Friday, dinner daily, brunch Saturday and Sunday; glassed-in tea house provides spectacular views of English Bay, ship channel at Lions Gate; traditional Continental menu; $$. *Vassilis Taverna,* 2884 West Broadway, 733-3231. Lunch Monday to Friday, dinner daily; traditional Greek menu; $$. *The William Tell,* 765 Beatty Street, in Georgian Court Hotel, 688-3504. Lunch Monday to Friday, dinner daily, brunch Sunday; elegant, long-standing Vancouver restaurant, Continental cuisine with a Swiss accent; $$$.

FOR MORE INFORMATION Vancouver Travel InfoCentre, 1055 Dunsmuir Street, Vancouver V7X 1L3, 683-2000, hotel reservation number (800) 888-8835.

Vancouver: The North Shore

From almost anyplace in downtown Vancouver you can look to the north and see what appears to be mountain wilderness rising just beyond the city's skyscrapers. It's not really wilderness and it's quite accessible.

If you're like most Pacific Northwesterners, big cities are fine as far as they go, but what really makes a vacation is getting out into all that scenery.

All you have to do is venture across Lions Gate Bridge or take the SeaBus to Lonsdale Quay in North Vancouver. And staying in "North Van," as it's known to locals, is a good alternative to staying downtown; it's generally less expensive, and only about a five-minute drive across the bridge to Stanley Park and the heart of the city. One caveat: If you do decide to stay in North or West Vancouver during the week, schedule your trips into Vancouver to avoid the morning and evening commute hours that jam the Lions Gate Bridge.

Enjoying the outdoors doesn't take much doing on a weekend in Vancouver. One good place to start is Capilano Suspension Bridge and Park. The bridge is a real heart stopper. A wood-and-wire affair, it spans lush green Capilano Canyon some 70 meters (230 feet) above the river. It jounces and sways as you cross; kids like to get it bouncing up and down of course, but it's perfectly safe. Nature trails wind through the woods on either side of the canyon and there are totem pole carvers to watch here in summer.

Beyond Capilano Canyon, Capilano Road turns into Nancy Greene Way (named for the Canadian Olympic skier) and leads to the base station of the Grouse Mountain gondola. From here the enclosed car carries you 1,128 meters (3,700 feet) up Grouse Mountain to the restaurant and ski area near the summit. The gondola operates year round and affords absolutely breathtaking views of Vancouver spread below and the Strait of Georgia and the Gulf Islands on the horizon. For a romantic interlude, plan to dine at the Grouse Nest restaurant just as the sun goes down behind the islands to the west.

Paved paths and nature trails radiating from the summit station lead through mountain meadows that are lush with wildflowers in early summer. If you're in the mood for a good hike, you can return to the foot of the mountain by trail. Grouse Mountain is also a favorite spot for launching hang gliders, and a major meet, the World Invitational, is held here in July. If the weather is clear, you can take a short helicopter tour from here; call 525-1484 for prices and reservations.

Grouse Mountain ski area operates four double chair lifts, two T-bars, and two rope tows serving 13 runs with a vertical drop of 366 meters (1,200 feet). The longest run is 2.4 kilometers (1.5 miles). Seven runs are illuminated for night skiing. The area operates every day and night from November to March.

A series of river canyons slices into the mountains north of Vancouver. To the east of Capilano Canyon is Lynn Canyon, which boasts a park, an ecology center, and another suspension bridge. This bridge sways 80 meters (262 feet) above Lynn Creek and provides access to several trails, some of which lead to waterfalls. At the ecology center you can view exhibits detailing the canyon's plant and animal life.

Keep heading east and follow Mount Seymour Parkway, then Mount Seymour Road into Mount Seymour Provincial Park. For 12 kilometers (7½ miles) the road climbs through dense stands of old-growth timber to a viewpoint and visitor center at 1,006 meters elevation (3,300 feet), where a scenic chair lift is in operation in the summer. If you're here then, pack a picnic lunch, or pick up sandwiches at the Seymour Cafe at the parking lot, and ride the lift to flower-bedecked alpine meadows, then hike down. Or, if you're more ambitious, hike the trail to the 1,453-meter (4,767-foot) summit of the mountain. There's also a ski area here with four double chair lifts operating in winter. If you're a white-water rafter, you might want to drive to the Chilliwack River, more than 100 kilometers (60 miles) to the east, and a favorite for rafting from May to mid-summer. Several Vancouver rafting companies offer day trips on the river.

One of the all-time great train trips runs out of North Vancouver from May to September aboard the Royal Hudson, a string of gleaming black, maroon, and gold coaches pulled by a Hudson-class steam locomotive (designated by its 4-6-4 wheel arrangement). The name "Royal" was bestowed when locomotives like this one carried King George VI and Queen Elizabeth from Quebec to Vancouver in 1939.

For the first part of the trip, you wind around curves and through the backyards of West Vancouver. You can open the top half of the Dutch doors at either end of the coaches to watch the locomotive in action as it screeches around the curves ahead. Pistons thrash, side rods flash up and down, smoke and steam plume back along the train, and the Hudson's mournful whistle screams for the crossings. At nearly every crossroad, cars are parked awaiting the train. Photographers snap away and parents hold their kids aloft to wave at the engine crew.

Climbing up to cross Point Grey, the locomotive really knuckles down to work, its staccato exhaust barking off the rocky cliffs beside the track. You plunge into a tunnel, emerge into daylight, then dive into another tunnel. For the last half of the trip the train clings to cliffs above Howe Sound, winding in and out with splendid views of the deep blue waters below and forested mountains across the way.

The northbound trip ends at the little town of Squamish, where you'll have plenty of time to browse in the shops or have lunch. You can return on the Royal Hudson or you can combine the rail trip with a cruise down Howe Sound and beneath the Lions Gate Bridge aboard the M.V. *Brittania,* a big, comfortable excursion ship.

Area Code: 604

SIGHTSEEING *Capilano Park and Suspension Bridge,* 3735 Capilano Road, North Vancouver, 985-7474. June to Labour Day daily 8 A.M. to 9:30 P.M., September 8 A.M. to 7:30 P.M., other months 9 A.M. to 5 P.M. Adults C$5, seniors C$4.50, students C$3.75, 6–12 C$2. *Lynn Canyon Ecology Centre,* 3663 Park Road in Lynn Canyon Park, 987-5922. February through November daily 10 A.M. to 5 P.M., rest of year Monday to Friday. Free. *Frontier River Adventures,* 927 Fairfield Road, 929-7612; *Hyak Wilderness Adventures,* 1928 West Fourth Avenue, 734-8622; and *Kumsheen Adventures,* 8-2475 Manitoba Street, 879-8687. Offer single-day white-water rafting trips on the Chilliwack River. *Grouse Mountain,* 6400 Nancy Greene Way, North Vancouver, 984-0661. Aerial tram daily 9 A.M. to 10 P.M. Adults C$11, seniors C$8.50, and 13–18 C$7.50, 6–12 C$5, families C$29. *Mount Seymour Chair Lift,* 1700 Indian River Road, North Vancouver, 986-2261. July and

August daily 9 A.M. to 5 P.M. September and October Saturday and Sunday. Adults C$3, children C$1.50. *North Shore Museum and Art Gallery,* 209 West Fourth Street and 333 Chesterfield Avenue, 987-5618. Wednesday to Sunday 1 to 4 P.M. Free. *Royal Hudson,* departs from British Columbia Railway station in North Vancouver, 1311 West First Street, 68-TRAIN. Mid-May to July and September Wednesday to Sunday, July and August daily. Adults C$24, seniors and 12–18 C$20, children 5–11 C$14; combination train/cruise C$42, C$38, and C$25.

LODGING *Best Western Capilano Motor Inn,* 1634 Capilano Road, North Vancouver V7P 3B4, 987-8185. Located near Capilano Suspension Bridge, $–$$. *Horseshoe Bay Motel,* 6396 Bruce Street, West Vancouver V7W 2G4, 921-7454. 1 block from the ferry terminal, convenient for salmon fishing charters, $. *Lonsdale Quay Hotel,* 123 Carrie Cates Court, North Vancouver V6M 3K7, 986-6111. Water and city skyline views, $$$$. *Park Royal Hotel,* 540 Clyde Avenue, West Vancouver V7T 2J7, 926-5511. Lovely English-style hotel on landscaped acres by river, lively pub, $$$$. *Vancouver Lions Gate Travelodge,* 2060 Marine Drive, North Vancouver V7P 1V7, 985-5311. Convenient to Lions Gate Bridge and Stanley Park, $$–$$$. *Beachside Bed and Breakfast,* 4208 Evergreen Avenue, West Vancouver V7V 1H1, 922-7773. Cozy bed-and-breakfast inn on driftwood-strewn beach facing south with panoramic views of Vancouver, $$–$$$.

CAMPING *Capilano RV Park,* 295 Tomahawk Avenue, North Vancouver V7P 1C5, 987-4722. 208 sites, full hookups, C$10–C$25.

DINING *Cafe Roma,* 60 Semisch Street, North Vancouver, 984-0274. Dinner daily, unpretentious Italian restaurant with a remarkable variety of pastas, $$. *Chesa Seafood Restaurant,* 2168 Marine Drive, West Vancouver, 922-3312. Dinner Tuesday to Sunday, reputation for very fresh seafood, $$. *Corsi Trattoria,* 1 Lonsdale Street, North Vancouver, 987-9910. Convenient to SeaBus terminal. Lunch Monday to Friday, dinner daily; excellent Italian cuisine includes some uncommon dishes; $$. *Grouse Nest Restaurant,* top of Grouse Mountain gondola, 984-0661. Dinner daily, spectacular views, $$. *Salmon House on the Hill,* 2229 Folkestone Way, West Vancouver, 926-3212. Lunch Monday to Saturday, dinner daily, brunch Sunday; outstanding views of city and harbor; $$. *The Ship of the Seven Seas,* foot of Lonsdale Street, North Vancouver, 987-3344. Lunch and dinner daily, floating restaurant features seafood, $$$. *Tudor Room,* Park Royal Hotel (see "Lodging"). Regional and Continental cuisine, seafood, beef, $$.

FOR MORE INFORMATION North Vancouver Travel InfoCentre, 131 East Second Street, North Vancouver V7L 1C2, 987-4488.

Weekend Trips
from
PORTLAND

West of the Cascades

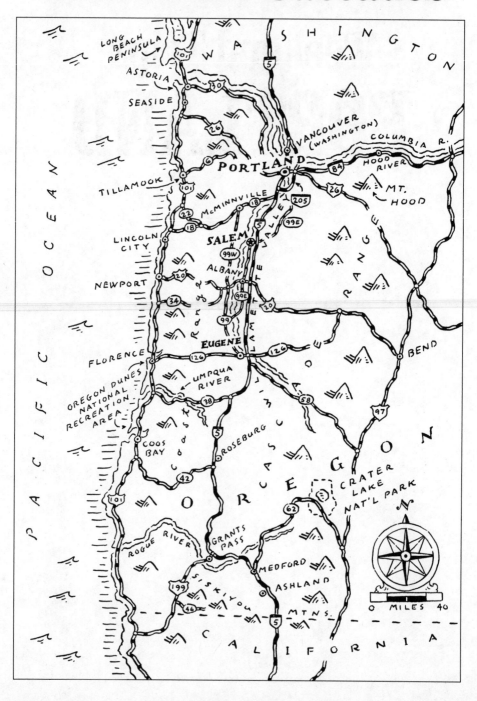

Down to the Mouth of the Columbia

If you visit the mouth of the Columbia River at Astoria, Oregon, you'll wonder how anyone ever could have missed it. More than ten miles wide, it empties more water into the Pacific than any other river in the Western Hemisphere.

For more than two centuries, however, some of Europe's most notable Pacific explorers—Drake, Heceta, Cook, and Vancouver—sailed right by the Columbia without knowing it was there. It was Americans—Gray, Lewis and Clark, and Astor—who discovered and explored this body of water and settled the lands around it. Captain Robert Gray first sailed across the Columbia bar in 1792 with his fur trading ship *Columbia Rediviva,* for which he named the river. Meriwether Lewis and William Clark, leading President Thomas Jefferson's Corps of Discovery, reached the mouth of the Columbia in November 1805 and spent the winter just south of present-day Astoria, before returning to Saint Louis in March 1806. Five years later, John Jacob Astor's American Fur Company founded Astoria, first permanent American settlement west of the Rockies. The whole parade of Northwest history has passed by Astoria's front door.

Today, that history is in evidence in Astoria more than in any other community in the Northwest, most of it linked to the sea. The town has a maritime flavor; the damp air smells of the sea, the waterfront is alive with gulls wheeling and crying, and the mournful sound of foghorns lulls you to sleep at night. Many architectural relics remain from the turn of the century, when the town rivaled San Francisco as a major West Coast port. This is a place for long walks on nearby beaches, for steaming mugs of clam chowder on a chilly afternoon, and for poking about among historic treasures.

As *Sunset Magazine* describes it, "This region's beaches, bays, forested headlands and unassuming towns still offer travelers a sense of discovery, though most tend to bypass the area in favor of better-known destinations.

"That forgotten quality is part of the lower Columbia's appeal. Victorian houses crowd the steep hillsides in Astoria (only a few are elegantly restored). Fishermen's bars, not boutiques, line waterfronts, and commercial boats, not pleasure cruisers, dominate boat basins. After a day's fishing, local families and visitors warm their chilled bones not in hot tubs but in a 50-year-old Finnish bathhouse."

The place to begin your sightseeing in Astoria is atop Coxcomb Hill, surmounted by the 125-foot Astoria Column 625 feet above the Columbia River. From the overlook you have sweeping views of the Columbia River, the Washington shore, the Youngs River delta, and Astoria at your feet. The column, erected by descendants of John Jacob Astor in 1926, is decorated by a frieze depicting the American settlement of the Northwest and is modeled after the famous Emperor Trajan column in Rome. If you're feeling ambitious, you can climb the 164-step circular stairway in the interior to a viewing platform on top.

Crown jewel of Astoria's attractions is the Columbia River Maritime Museum. It's quite simply the finest of its kind in the Northwest and has few rivals on the West Coast. Your visit starts in the soaring Great Hall, with its collection of fishing boats and Coast Guard rescue vessels. Weather-worn river steamer identification boards, bearing nostalgic names such as *Manzanillo, Ione of Portland, Lurline, Relief,* and *Sarah Dixon,* line the walls.

Each of the museum's seven galleries is devoted to a different maritime theme: the fur trade and exploration of the Northwest Coast; navigation and marine safety; fishing, canneries, and whaling; on the river; sailing vessels; steam and motor vessels; and naval history. The lightship *Columbia* that once guarded the entrance to the river is moored outside and open for visitors. When you go aboard imagine what it must have been like to live in these cramped quarters, anchored in stormy seas and tossed about like a cork.

Astoria has many Victorian homes, and one of the best—the elegant 1885 Flavel House—is open to the public. The former home of a pioneer Columbia River bar pilot, it occupies a full city block at the corner of Eighth and Duane. Built in Queen Anne–style architecture with a three-story octagonal tower, it has six fireplaces, three parlors, five bedrooms, and indoor plumbing.

The Heritage Center Museum (included with the Flavel House admission price) is located in Astoria's former City Hall, built in 1903. The museum's permanent exhibits relate to the history of the town's logging, fishing, and shipping industries. Fort Astoria Park, at Fifteenth and Exchange streets, replicates the original fur trading structures built by Astor's American Fur Company on the site in 1811. The Uppertown Firefighters Museum, at Thirtieth Avenue and Marine Drive, occupies an 1896 brick building that has served both as a brewery and a firehouse. Exhibits include an extensive collection of firefighting equipment from horse-drawn pumpers to motorized fire engines of the 1920s and 1930s.

Though Astoria is a town strong on museums, it's also a town with a strong maritime heritage. Take the time to explore the waterfront, feed the gulls, and watch the freighters anchored in the river or on their way upstream or downstream.

Josephson's Smokehouse and Dock, at 106 Marine Drive, is an Oregon institution, famous throughout the Northwest. By way of credentials, Salishan, the elegant Oregon-coast resort, serves Josephson's smoked salmon. Schedule a stop at the store, if only to look. The 1898 building housed the Columbia River Fishermen's Protective Association for 30 years until 1938, when Anton Josephson relocated his smoked salmon business here. You can smell the smoked flavor the minute you open the door. Refrigerator cases display both smoked and fresh fish from cod, tuna, and scallops to sturgeon, oysters, and salmon. If the sight of all that seafood makes you hungry, try munching on a strip of their smoked salmon jerky.

Assuming you'll be spending Saturday night of your weekend in Astoria, schedule Sunday for a trip to Fort Stevens and Fort Clatsop. Head west and south on U.S. 101, cross the bridge over Youngs Bay, then turn right at the signs indicating Hammond and Warrenton.

It's obvious even to the outsider that these are seafaring communities. Rows of weathered clapboard houses line the quiet streets. Now and then you'll pass a fishing boat perched on blocks in a side yard awaiting repair, or nets and buoys strung over frames for drying or mending. Marinas are full of commercial boats bobbing at anchor. The first time we visited this area, in the early 1960s, a whaling station still operated here. Now, the Warrenton marina and the Hammond boat basin are good places to join a deep-sea charter boat going for salmon, sturgeon, halibut, ling cod, shark, or tuna.

Beyond Hammond lies the entrance to Fort Stevens State Park, at 3,760 acres the largest state park in Oregon. The fort itself was a coast artillery installation that defended the mouth of the Columbia from the Civil War until after World War II. The original earthworks were completed the day before General Robert E. Lee signed the surrender at Appomattox on April 9, 1865. Shelled by a Japanese submarine in 1942, it's the only mainland U.S. fortification to be fired upon by a foreign enemy since the War of 1812.

You can explore the old casemates of Battery Russell and visit the modest military museum that traces the fort's history. In summer, guides lead historical walking tours and sightseeing tours in a vintage army truck.

The park features four miles of unobstructed sand beaches, excellent for surf casting, beach-combing, and clam digging. The skeletal remains of the *Peter Iredale,* a 287-foot four-masted British sailing ship that ran aground in 1906, still project from the sand. Although each winter destroys a little more of it, there's still plenty left to see and photograph. If you're really ambitious, you can hike 64 miles of the yet-to-be-completed Oregon Coast Trail from the South Jetty on the Columbia River to Tillamook Bay. The park is also an excellent place to bicycle or walk, with several miles of quiet paved roadway.

Fort Clatsop National Memorial is located four miles south of Astoria off U.S. 101. Several low log buildings forming a closed compound replicate the log fort where the Lewis and Clark expedition spent the winter of 1805–1806. And a miserable winter it was. According to Lewis and Clark's journals, it rained every day but 12 of the 106 they spent here. Clothing and bedding rotted or was infested by fleas. The dampness gave nearly everyone rheumatism or colds. The men (and one woman) lived on elk and deer, spent the winter repairing gear and clothing, and boiled seawater for salt at a site near present-day Seaside.

The National Park Service visitor center at Fort Clatsop details the expedition through displays and audiovisual presentations. During the summer, there are living history programs with park personnel costumed in buckskins demonstrating candle making, hide tanning, woodworking, hand hewing canoes, and other typical chores.

Area Code: 503

DRIVING DIRECTIONS Astoria lies 95 miles from Portland via U.S. 30 along the south bank of the Columbia River.

SIGHTSEEING *Astoria Column,* follow Fifteenth Street to Coxcomb Drive, 325-6311. Daily 8 A.M. to dusk. Free. *Captain Flavel House,* 441 Eighth Street, 325-2203. May to October daily 10 A.M. to 5 P.M., other months 11 A.M. to 4 P.M. Adults $3, seniors $2.50, 6–12 $1, admission includes Heritage Center Museum. *Heritage Center Museum,* 1618 Exchange Street, 325-2203. May to September daily 10 A.M. to 5 P.M., other months 11 A.M. to 4 P.M. Adults $3, seniors $2, 6-12 $1 (includes admission to Flavel House). *Columbia River Maritime Museum,* 1792 Marine Drive, 325-2323. April to October daily 9:30 A.M. to 5 P.M., adults $3, seniors $2, 6–18 $1.50. *Shallon Winery,* 1598 Duane Street, 325-5978. Daily noon to 6 P.M. Small winery, specializes in local wild berry wine. *Fort Astoria,* Exchange and Fifteenth streets. 325-6311. Open daily dawn to dusk, summer (mid-June to Labor Day) living history program 4 times daily Thursday to Monday 11 A.M. to 3:30 P.M. *Uppertown Firefighters Museum,* Thirtieth Street and Marine Drive. 325-6311. May to September daily 10 A.M. to 5 P.M. October to April 11 A.M. to 4 P.M. *Fort Stevens Military Museum,* Historic Area Fort Stevens State Park, 861-2000. June to September daily 10 A.M. to 6 P.M., other months Wednesday to Sunday 10 A.M. to 4 P.M. Donation. Memorial Day to Labor Day walking tours $1.50, truck tours $2.50. *Fort Clatsop National Memorial,* 861-2471. Mid-June to Labor Day daily 8 A.M. to 6 P.M., remainder of year 8 A.M. to 5 P.M. Adults 17–61 $1, others free. *Fishing charters: Corkey's Charter Fishing,* Hammond, 861-2668; *Columbia Pacific Charter,* Hammond, 861-1527 (May to October), 861-3303 (November to April); *Warrenton Deep Sea Fishing,* Warrenton, 861-1233; *Astoria Thunderbird Charters,* Astoria, 325-7990. *Astoria Cruise and Charters,* 352 Industry Street, Astoria, 325-0990. Various river cruises including sunrise-croissant cruise, $45; sunset-champagne cruise, $55; historical river tour, $16; crab and cruise, $45; crab and sturgeon cruise, $55; and salmon and deep-sea charters, $50.

EVENTS *Great Astoria Crab and Seafood Festival,* 325-6311, first weekend in April. 150 seafood booths, wine tasting, arts and crafts, helicopter rides. *Scandinavian Midsummer Festival,* Astoria High School, 325-6311. Mid-June. Festival features folk dancing, parade, food and crafts booths, ethnic music.

LODGING *Crest Motel,* 5366 Leif Erickson Drive, Astoria 97103, 325–3141. East edge of town off U.S. 30, splendid blufftop views, $–$$. *Red Lion Inn,* 400 Industry Street, Astoria 97103, 325-7373. Full-service hotel, waterfront location, $$–$$$. *Franklin Street Station* (bed and breakfast), 1140 Franklin Street, Astoria 97103, 325-4314. 5 guest rooms in faithfully restored Victorian, $$. *Franklin House* (bed and breakfast), 1681 Franklin Street, Astoria 97103, 325-5044. Restored Victorian in quiet neighborhood, $$. *Grandview Bed and Breakfast,* 1574 Grand Avenue, Astoria 97103, 325-0000, 325-5555. 7 guest rooms in restored Victorian, $–$$. *Hammond House* (bed and breakfast), 884 Pacific Avenue, Hammond 97121, 861-0943. Modest accommodations in 1890 home catering especially to anglers, will arrange fishing charters, $.

CAMPING *Fort Stevens State Park,* Hammond 97121, 861-1671. 605 sites, 343 electric-water hookups, of those 224 also have sewer, $8–$10. Reservation system in effect Memorial Day through Labor Day, make reservations directly with the park.

DINING *Columbian Cafe,* 1114 Marine Drive, 325-2233. Breakfast and lunch Monday to Saturday, dinner Wednesday to Friday; wide-ranging vegetarian menu, no smoking; $$. *Dooleys West Texas Bar-B-Que,* 144 Eleventh Street, 325-5534. Lunch and dinner Monday to Saturday, $$. *Pacific Rim,* 229 West Marine Drive, 325-4481. Lunch and dinner daily, best pizza in town, $. *Pier 11 Feedstore and Deli,* 77 Eleventh Street, 325-0279. Breakfast, lunch, and dinner daily, $–$$. *Seafare Restaurant,* in the Red Lion Inn, 325-3551. Breakfast, lunch, and dinner daily; nautical-theme restaurant with waterfront views, children's menu; $$. *The Ship Inn,* 1 Second Street, 325-0033. Lunch and dinner daily; specializes in seafood, fish and chips, chowder; $$.

FOR MORE INFORMATION Greater Astoria Chamber of Commerce, P.O. Box 176, Astoria 97103, 325-6311. Superintendent, Fort Clatsop National Memorial, Route 3, Box 604, Astoria 97103, 861-2471.

The Longest Beach

If you had been living in Portland around the turn of the century and been affluent enough to have time for a summer "holiday," chances are you would have taken it at the seashore. You probably would have boarded a train for Seaside or a paddlewheel steamship for a voyage down the Willamette and Columbia rivers to Megler or Ilwaco on the Washington shore. Then you would have boarded one of the diminutive narrow-gauge passenger trains of the Ilwaco

Railway and Navigation Company to one of the beachside resort communities of Seaview, Long Beach, or Ocean Park that dot the Long Beach Peninsula in Washington.

Jutting north from the mouth of the Columbia River is the Long Beach Peninsula. Twenty-eight miles long and a mile or so wide, low-lying and sparsely forested, this stretch of land forms the longest uninterrupted beach in North America. The barrier of the peninsula shelters the quiet waters of Willapa Bay— and Washington's premier oyster-growing beds—from the ocean.

Back in the 1870s, when entrepreneurs in a growing Portland recognized the peninsula's tremendous potential as a vacation spot and rich real estate market, they formed the IR & N. Variously known as the "Clamshell Railroad," owing to its roadbed of crushed clam and oyster shells, and as the "Irregular Run and Never Get There," because of its cavalier regard of schedules, the little railroad carried generations of Portlanders to vacations at the beach. Typically, the wealthy owned their own beach cottages where mother and the children might spend the summer while father commuted on weekends via steamer from Portland. The less affluent came to spend a few days in rented digs at any of dozens of modest beachfront tourist homes or pitched a tent among the dunes.

By the time of the Great Depression, the Long Beach Peninsula was beginning a long decline as a vacation destination. Few people had much money to spend on vacations. And later, with more families owning automobiles and new highways being built, Portlanders were reaching out to other destinations.

The hiatus lasted until the mid-1970s, when young entrepreneurs, like David Campiche and Laurie Anderson of the Shelburne Inn and others, began to invest their time and capital in rehabilitating or building quality facilities on the peninsula. About that time, Jimella Lucas and Nanci Main (who now own the Ark at Nahcotta) opened a gourmet restaurant in the Shelburne Inn. James Beard discovered it, publicized it, and the rest is history.

Though the peninsula now boasts the best accommodations and restaurants in southwest Washington, it's a quiet, laid-back sort of place except in July and August. The single state highway, two-lane Washington 103, runs the length of the peninsula atop the roadbed of the old railroad. Traffic never moves very fast and there's a "mañana" attitude to everything.

This is a vacation destination for those who don't need a lot of organized activity or entertaining, who are comfortable just relaxing or creating their own fun. Some come to ride horseback on the hard-packed sand beach (horse rentals in Long Beach). Others come to fly kites in the always dependable breezes. During spring low tides, hundreds come to dig clams, buying or renting clam guns and forks in the local shops. As one of the most productive salmon fishing ports on the coast, Ilwaco draws others who come for charter fishing at the mouth of the Columbia. For those who get restless doing nothing, there's plenty of historical sightseeing.

As you reach the northern end of the Columbia River bridge from Astoria, turn left onto U.S. 101, drive through the tunnel (formerly used by the railroad), and turn immediately left into Fort Columbia State Historical Park. Constructed between 1896 and 1904, the fort was one of three coastal defense forts guarding the mouth of the Columbia. A self-guided walking tour takes you around the old gun emplacements, barracks, and other buildings. The fort also includes three museums. At the interpretive center, audiovisual and narrated programs describe early life at the fort. The recorded voice of a messman private of the 1930s describes the enlisted men's mess and the kitchen, with its big old coal-fired stoves. The DAR Museum is the completely furnished commandant's house, and the art museum features works by local artists and a collection of photographs of Northwest Indians.

The weathered little town of Ilwaco is devoted to the sea. The harbor is home to scores of commercial and charter fishing boats. During the season, which lasts from June to October, charters depart daily for salmon, tuna, and bottom fish. The no-nonsense cafés here are good choices if you're in the mood for some clam chowder, broiled salmon, or fish and chips. The murals you see on the walls of some of Ilwaco's buildings were created for the state's centennial in 1989.

Don't miss the Heritage Museum. Exhibits include historic photographs, artifacts, native plants, and clothing, but the highlight is a working model of the Ilwaco Railroad and Navigation Company line up the peninsula, housed in the railroad's former baggage depot.

The mouth of the Columbia is one of the most treacherous stretches of water in the world, known to mariners as the ''Graveyard of the Pacific'' for the many ships it has claimed. Cape Disappointment Coast Guard Station, at the edge of Ilwaco, is nicknamed the ''Home of the Heavy Weather Lifesavers.'' The Coast Guard's Motor Lifeboat School is here, and sometimes you can see the guardsmen practicing with the boats offshore. Bronze memorial plaques and dramatic photographs in the station testify to the hazards of this duty.

On the bluff above, near the Lewis and Clark Interpretive Center in Fort Canby State Park, you have a commanding view of the mouth of the Columbia, and you can sometimes see a pilot bringing a freighter across the bar. Two lighthouses—North Head and Cape Disappointment—stand like white sentinels atop the cliffs to the west; both make great photo subjects. Cape Disappointment, built in 1852, is among the oldest lighthouses on the coast. The cape itself was named by English fur trader Captain John Meares in 1788 for his emotion at failing to find the Northwest Passage. Displays in the interpretive center detail the 1805–1806 Lewis and Clark Expedition between Saint Louis and the Pacific.

On the upper level, there's a history of the Cape Disappointment area, lots of shipwreck photographs and Coast Guard rescue gear. There are some splendid ocean-view walks to both lighthouses from here; inquire about the trails from the state park ranger.

From the park, wander up the peninsula through the little town of Seaview, where several homes dating from the 1880s can be seen along the back streets near the beach. Next comes Long Beach, the largest town in the area and a good place to schedule a lunch stop. Milton York Candy Company here dates from 1882 when York started making his candy in a copper kettle in a tent. Today the company makes candy from original recipes, ice cream, and frozen yogurt, and operates a restaurant.

A few doors away, the Dog Salmon Cafe is a one-of-a-kind place. The modest café doubles as an art gallery displaying the Northwest Indian carvings of Astorian Roger McKay. It's filled with handsome totems, masks, and other Indian art.

Across the street, the Cottage Bakery and Delicatessen is the place to go for a double chocolate chip muffin, a raspberry scone, homemade soups, and sandwiches.

Heading north from Long Beach, you pass through the oceanside communities of Klipsan Beach, Ocean Park, and Surfside. Fronting on Willapa Bay on the east side of the peninsula are Nahcotta and Oysterville. You'll recognize Nahcotta by the piles of oyster shells around it. Two oyster-packing companies operate on the wharf here; both sell fresh oysters, clams, salmon, Dungeness crab, pickled shrimp, rock cod, perch, ling cod, geoduck, and other seafood in season. The award-winning Ark restaurant is adjacent to the wharf. For a more modest seafood lunch, try the tiny (four tables) U.S.S. Andrea restaurant at the East Point Seafood Company.

Oysterville is one of the oldest communities in the state and is a national historic district. It began in 1854 when Chinook Indian Chief Nahcati led Isaac Alonzo Clark and Robert H. Espy to oyster beds on the tidelands of western Willapa Bay. The oyster made wealthy men of Clark, Espy, and others. The highly prized mollusk was harvested and shipped to Gold Rush–wealthy San Francisco, where oysters commanded as much as a dollar apiece. Oysterville prospered and became the county seat.

By the 1880s oyster parasites and new oyster beds in San Francisco Bay spelled the beginning of the end for Oysterville. The final blow was dealt when a group of men rode into Oysterville on a Sunday morning in 1893 and carried off the county records to establish the county seat in South Bend, across the bay. A sign near the old schoolhouse marks the location of the county courthouse and tells the tale of "the South Bend Raiders."

Several photogenic old homes still exist in Oysterville, many of them built of redwood brought in as ballast in the ships from San Francisco. You can pick up a free walking-tour guide in the restored 1892 Baptist church. If you enjoy poking about old cemeteries, Oysterville has a dandy. Chief Nahcati is buried here, along with several generations of Espys and other pioneers. Among the more curious gravestones are those of two men who drowned in Shoalwater Bay on January 1, 1873.

Three miles north is Leadbetter Point State Park, an area of shifting dunes, grasslands, ponds, salt marshes, and forests at the tip of the peninsula. More than 100 species of birds have been recorded here at the Willapa National Wildlife Refuge, a feeding and resting area for migrating and resident birds. You're apt to see black brant, shearwaters, sandpipers, plovers, and other waterfowl. There is a 1¾-mile hiking trail that leads out through the salt grass flats to the end of the point. You may see low-profile oyster dredgers working offshore. The park is a year-round facility close to the peninsula accommodations.

Area Code: 206

DRIVING DIRECTIONS From Portland, take U.S. 30 to Astoria, then cross the Astoria Bridge to Megler and follow U.S. 101 to Ilwaco. This route is 112 miles. If you cross the Columbia at Longview and follow Washington 4 west along the Washington bank of the river, it's a bit longer—125 miles—and slower, but the highway hugs the river most of the way and you may come face-to-face with freighters on the river. Washington's only covered bridge is also on this route, near Grays River.

SIGHTSEEING *Fort Columbia State Historical Park,* 2 miles southeast of Chinook off U.S. 101, 777-8221. April to October daily 6:30 A.M. to dusk, other months 8 A.M. to dusk. Free. *Lewis and Clark Interpretive Center,* Fort Canby State Park, Ilwaco, 642-3029. May to September daily 9 A.M. to 5 P.M. October to April, Saturday and Sunday 10 A.M. to 3 P.M. Free. *Fishing charters* (Ilwaco): *A-1 Tuna-Salmon Charters,* 642-4471; *HoHo Salmon Charters,* 642-2300; *Ilwaco Charter Service,* 642-3232; *Pacific Salmon Charters,* 642-3466. *Ilwaco Heritage Museum,* 115 Southeast Lake Street, 642-3466. Monday to Saturday 9 A.M. to 5 P.M., Sunday noon to 4 P.M., adults $1.25, seniors $1, 6–12 50 cents. *Willapa Bay Kayak Rentals,* P.O. Box 22, Nahcotta 98637, 642-4892. Rents kayaks for use on Willapa Bay and leads guided tours of the bay and uninhabited islands. *Leadbetter Point State Park,* tip of Long Beach Peninsula, no telephone. April to mid-October daily 6:30 A.M. to dusk, other months 8 A.M. to dusk.

EVENTS *Garlic Festival,* Ocean Park and Nahcotta, 665-5477, mid-June. Celebration pays homage to the garlic, including garlic dinner at the Ark Restaurant. *Washington State International Kite Festival,* Long Beach, 665-5744, mid-August.

Weeklong competitions and demonstrations of aerobatic kites including lighted kite night flying. *Cranberry Festival,* Ilwaco, 642-3446, weekend in mid-October. Features food circus, quilt show, old-time fiddle music, bus tours of cranberry bogs.

LODGING *The Inn at Ilwaco* (bed and breakfast), 120 Williams Street Northeast, Ilwaco 98624, 642-8686. Comfortable 9-room inn in former Presbyterian church, shared with performing arts center, $$. *The Shelburne Inn,* P.O. Box 250, Seaview 98644, 642-2442. One of the finest country inns in the Northwest, cozy rooms, antique furnishings, lavish breakfasts, $$$. *Enchanted Blue Wave* (bed and breakfast), 1004 Forty-first Street, Seaview 98644, 642-4900. 5-room B&B catering exclusively to women, $$–$$$. *Super 8 Motel,* 500 Ocean Beach Boulevard, Long Beach 98631, 642-8988, national reservations (800) 843-1991. New 2-story motel on the beach, $. *The Lighthouse Motel,* Route 1, Box 527, Long Beach 98631, 642-3622. Comfortable older motel on beach 2½ miles north of Long Beach, fireplaces, $. *Nendel's Inn,* 409 Tenth Street Southwest, Long Beach 98631, 642-2311. Conventional motel on dead-end street at the beach, $–$$. *Pacific Breakers Condominiums,* P.O. Box 428, Long Beach 98631, 642-2727. 1- and 2-bedroom units with kitchens on the beach, $$. *Chautauqua Lodge,* P.O. Box 757, Long Beach 98631, 642-4401. Units with kitchens, fireplaces on the beach, $$–$$$. *Sunset View Resort/Motel,* P.O. Box 399, Ocean Park 98640, 665-4494. Lodge on 6 wooded acres adjacent to beach, fireplaces, kitchens, $$–$$$.

CAMPING *Fort Canby State Park,* 2½ miles west of Ilwaco, 642-3078. 250 sites adjacent to the beach, 60 full hookups, $8–$12. *Ilwaco KOA,* P.O. Box 549, Ilwaco 98624, 642-3292. 238 sites on 17 acres, full hookups, $13.50–$17.50.

DINING *The Sanctuary,* U.S. 101 and Hazel Street, Chinook, 777-8380. Dinner daily Memorial Day to Labor Day, Wednesday to Sunday other months; local seafood well prepared in former Methodist church; $$. *The Shoalwater Restaurant,* in Shelburne Inn, Seaview, 642-4142. Lunch Tuesday to Thursday, dinner daily, brunch Sunday; award-winning restaurant specializes in seafood, local ingredients; this and the Ark (see below) are the best restaurants in southwest Washington; $$–$$$. *Lightship Restaurant and Columbia Bar,* in Nendel's Inn, Long Beach, 642-3252. Breakfast, lunch, and dinner daily; new restaurant operated by owners of the Shoalwater features grilled seafood, fresh sheet (a sheet inserted into the menu each day listing fresh items), low-cholesterol dishes; $$. *Dog Salmon Cafe,* 111 Highway 103, Long Beach, 642-2416. Breakfast, lunch, and dinner daily; good choice for breakfast; $. *Milton York,* First and Pacific streets, Long Beach, 642-2352. Breakfast, lunch, and dinner daily; lavish ice-cream concoctions, sandwiches, local seafood, also good for breakfast; $. *The Ark,* on the dock at Nahcotta, 665-4133. Dinner Tuesday to Sunday, brunch Sunday in summer, dinner Friday to Sunday other seasons; restaurant with international reputation features extravagant entrées; $$$.

FOR MORE INFORMATION Long Beach Peninsula Visitor's Bureau, P.O. Box 562, Long Beach 98631, 642-2400, (800) 451-2542 (in WA), (800) 451-2540 (in OR, ID, and northern CA).

That Other Vancouver

Vancouver, Washington, labors under a couple of handicaps. Many people confuse it with that other Vancouver up in British Columbia. The local chamber of commerce is trying to overcome that by encouraging people to call this one Vancouver USA. Still, many other Northwesterners envy the residents of Vancouver, who can live in Washington, where they pay no state income tax, and shop in Oregon, where they pay no sales tax.

The other handicap is that the city lies too close to Portland. Travelers heading for Portland are reluctant to stop in Vancouver when they're so close to their destination. On the other hand, Portlanders heading north and eager to be on their way tend to speed right through Vancouver on Interstate 5 without stopping.

But Vancouver, the north bank of the Columbia River, and the attractions in surrounding Clark County are well worth spending a weekend exploring. Schedule Saturday for city sightseeing and drive out to the Lewis and Clark Railroad and other county sights on Sunday.

Vancouver is the oldest city in the state, founded in 1824 when the Hudson's Bay Company established Fort Vancouver, its primary fur trading post in this part of the Northwest. As you will learn if you visit Oregon City and Champoeg (see "At the End of the Oregon Trail"), the Hudson's Bay Company and its fatherly chief factor, John McLoughlin, was vital to the survival of the first American immigrants to this territory arriving over the Oregon Trail. When the Treaty of 1846 established the boundary for the Oregon Territory and validated the American claims to the area, the Hudson's Bay Company withdrew and Fort Vancouver became a U.S. Army post, which part of it remains today.

Fort Vancouver National Historic Site (on the east side of I-5, Mill Plain exit) is a good place to begin your sightseeing. The National Park Service has restored portions of the fort. Begin at the visitor center, where exhibits and a slide show will help you to understand the fort and how it operated. Especially informative are the exhibits explaining the methods of trapping beavers and curing and marketing their pelts. The center also sells Hudson's Bay blankets, candle molds, slates and pencils, lard soap, and other historical items.

The imposing log stockade and five buildings in the fort's compound have been restored; the locations of other buildings are marked. You can climb to the top of the octagonal bastion at the northwest corner and peer through the gun ports to the Columbia River. A blacksmith shop, bakery, trade store, and hospital are all open to the public. Summer interpretive programs conducted by costumed personnel begin in mid-June and last through Labor Day; they include demonstrations of blacksmithing, carpentry, and bread baking as well as narrations in the trade store and hospital.

Centerpiece of the fort is John McLoughlin's white clapboard house, with authentic furnishings of the early nineteenth century. You can visit McLoughlin's office, the family bedrooms, and the parlor. In the big dining hall, the table is set for 16, the normal complement for dinner in those days. Guides explain that a separate table was set whenever an Indian chief was visiting the fort. Indians did not eat with whites.

Vancouver Barracks, adjacent to the park service area, is still an active army post. Officer's Row, a stately collection of 21 homes flanked by big maple trees and with sweeping views to the river, was built for army officers between 1850 and 1906. It has been meticulously restored and is now incorporated in a national historic district operated by the city. Two of the homes—the Grant House and the Marshall House—are open to the public (unfortunately, the Marshall House is frequently closed on Saturdays). George Marshall, chief of staff of the army under Presidents Roosevelt and Truman and author of the Marshall Plan for European recovery, presided here as commandant of the fort from 1936 to 1938. The Marshall House is furnished with antiques, including a stern portrait of the general, who stares down at the reception desk. Guided tours include a 15-minute video. Just down the street is the Grant House. Ulysses Grant never lived there, but he did serve at the fort as a young lieutenant in 1850. The house was named to honor him when he visited the fort after the Civil War. Nearby are a potato patch once cultivated by Grant and what is reputed to be the oldest apple tree in the Northwest, planted in 1829.

Just downhill from Officer's Row is Pearson Air Park, one of the oldest airfields in the West, dating to balloon flights in 1905. In 1937 the airfield became the final destination of the first transpolar flight, piloted by three Soviet aviators who landed here en route from Siberia to San Francisco. There's a monument to the flyers at the south edge of the field off Highway 14. A modest air museum at one side of the field has a handful of permanent aviation displays and sometimes hosts visiting vintage aircraft.

The Vancouver/Clark County Visitors & Convention Bureau, at 404 East Fifteenth Street, Suite 11, distributes free maps with suggested walking, bicycling, or driving routes to see the city's leading historical attractions. Highlights include Providence Academy (circa 1873); the Hidden Houses, dating from the

1860s; the old log Covington House, dating from 1848 and once used as a school; Esther Short Park, the oldest public square in the state; and the white clapboard, Rhode Island–design Slocum House, built in 1867. Clark County Historical Museum features an 1890s store, a pioneer doctor's office, a printing press, a railroad exhibit, Indian artifacts, and historical dioramas.

Vancouver's Open Air Market sets up shop every Saturday from May through October in the academy parking lot at Eleventh and C streets. Vendors sell a wide array of fresh fruits and vegetables, garden and house plants, berries, honey, and other local products.

Vancouver has several excellent restaurants from which to choose for dinner, but we suggest you select one of the places on the Columbia River—either the Chart House or the Red Lion Inn at the Quay. Watching the river traffic as you dine is something special, and on a rainy night the twinkling lights on the bridges and the vessels moving by on the river take on a misty, romantic quality. If you're visiting Vancouver between October and May, check the local listings for live theater. The city boasts a remarkable number of theater companies as well as a music arts series, its own symphony orchestra, and a choral group called the Brahms Singers.

On Sunday head north on I-5 nine miles to the Battle Ground exit and Washington 502. Follow it north and east eight miles to Battle Ground and the boxcar depot of the Lewis and Clark Railroad. Excursion trains depart every weekend of the year for a 21-mile 2½-hour trip through thick evergreen forest along the Lewis River. You ride in coaches with windows that open so you can lean out, or in an open-air car furnished with benches, or in the jaunty red caboose at the end of the train. You thread your way through a 340-foot rock tunnel and cross the river on spindly wooden trestles and steel bridges. At Moulton Falls County Park you detrain for a short walk to Hidden Falls. The railroad operates several trains a day in summer, so you can pack a picnic lunch and stop over at the park, returning on a later train. There's also a "Rib Train" that includes a rib dinner and a moonlight excursion on summer Saturday evenings, a country buffet meal train on Sundays, and a longer 38-mile 5-hour trip on summer Sundays. On December weekends the railroad runs Christmas tree trains to cut-your-own tree farms.

If you're touring on the first full weekend of the month from June through October, head north from Battle Ground on Washington 503 for 5½ miles to Northeast Rock Creek Road and turn right. Follow it and Northeast Lucia Falls Road to Pomeroy Living History Farm, a working farm that depicts life in the 1920s. Costumed interpreters grind corn and coffee, wash clothes on a scrub board, feed the animals, and cut wood with a crosscut logging saw, among other chores and activities typical of a farm of that period. A farm lunch is served on Saturdays.

Return to I-5, drive north to Exit 16, and follow Northwest La Center Road about two miles to La Center. On Fork Road, at the northeastern edge of the little crossroads village, lies Salishan Vineyards, producing premium dry wines, especially pinot noirs and dry rieslings. Tours and tastings are offered on weekend afternoons. Another nine miles northeast is Cedar Creek Grist Mill, tucked away off County Road 16 (ask locally for directions). Now fully restored and operating, the 1876 grist mill is the only one of its kind in the state.

Migratory waterfowl love the marshlands of the Columbia River and stop by the hundreds of thousands on their long migration routes up and down the Pacific Flyway. On your return from La Center detour off I-5 at the Ridgefield exit and follow Washington 501 three miles to Ridgefield National Wildlife Refuge. Here 4,615 acres of river, lake, marsh, and slough are devoted to dozens of species of waterfowl such as mallard and northern shoveler ducks, wigeons, teals, Canada geese, tundra swans, and sandhill cranes, as well as shorebirds and songbirds. Black-tailed deer, coyotes, foxes, raccoons, skunks, beavers, otters, rabbits, and the nutria are abundant. Bring binoculars, a bird book, and walking shoes and follow the two-mile Oaks to Wetlands Wildlife Trail along the shore.

Area Code: 206

DRIVING DIRECTIONS Vancouver lies astride Interstate 5 at the north end of the bridge crossing the Columbia River from Portland.

SIGHTSEEING *Fort Vancouver National Historic Site,* 1501 East Evergreen Boulevard, Vancouver, 696-7655. April to October daily 9 A.M. to 5 P.M., other months 9:30 A.M. to 4 P.M. adults $1, families $3. *Marshall House,* 1313 Officer's Row, Vancouver, 693-3101. Monday to Friday 9 A.M. to 5 P.M., Sunday 11 A.M. to 6 P.M. Donation. *Pearson Air Park Museum,* 101 East Reserve Street, Vancouver, 694-7026. Wednesday to Sunday noon to 5 P.M. Adults $2, children $1. *Clark County Historical Museum,* Sixteenth and Main streets, Vancouver, 695-4681. Tuesday to Sunday 1 to 5 P.M. Donation. *Lewis and Clark Railway,* 1000 East Main Street, Battle Ground, 687-2626. Departures year round Saturday and Sunday at 1:30 P.M.; also a Tuesday and Saturday 10 A.M. departure April to June, September, and October; from mid-June through September daily except Monday; plus dinner specials on weekends in summer. Adults $9, 3–12 $5; dinner trains, adults $25, 3–12 $20. *Pomeroy Living History Farm,* 20902 Northeast Lucia Falls Road, Yacolt, 686—3537. June to October Saturday 11 A.M. to 4 P.M., Sunday 1 to 4 P.M. Adults $3, 3–11 $1.50. *Salishan Winery,* North Fork Road, La Center, 263-2713. May to October, Saturday and Sunday 1 to 5 P.M. Free.

EVENTS *Miss Washington Pageant,* 693-1313, June. 18 to 25 young women compete for the Miss Washington title and the chance to go on to the Miss America finals. *Fort Vancouver Brigade Encampment,* 696-7655, July. Participants in 1840s costumes camp at Fort Vancouver and re-create activities of the period. *Clark County Fair,* at Ridgefield fairgrounds, 573-1921, early August. County fair featuring agricultural exhibits, entertainment, amusement rides, horse shows.

LODGING *Ferryman's Inn,* 7901 Northeast Sixth Avenue, Vancouver 98665, 574-2151, (800) 528-1234. Large motor inn north of downtown, pool, $. *Nendel's Suites,* 7001 Northeast Highway 99, Vancouver 98665, 696-0516. Quiet location north of town, $. *Red Lion Inn at the Quay,* 100 Columbia Street, Vancouver 98660, 694-8341, (800) 547-8010. Prime riverfront location, restaurant, $$$– $$$$. *Shilo Inn Downtown,* 401 East Thirteenth Street, Vancouver 98660, 696-0491, (800) 222-2244. Central location, easy access from freeway, $$.

CAMPING *Battle Ground Lake State Park,* 20 miles northeast of Vancouver on Northeast 244th Street, 753-2027. 50 sites, no hookups, swimming beach, $7. *Big Fir Campground and RV Park,* 4 miles east of I-5 off Exit 14, 887-8970. 80 sites, some hookups on 14 wooded acres, view of Mount Saint Helens, $10– $13. *Lewis River RV Park,* 3125 Lewis River Road, Woodland, 225-9556. 80 sites with hookups, riverside location, golf course, $14. *Paradise Point State Park,* 16 miles north of Vancouver off I-5 Exit 16, 753-2027. 79 sites, no hookups, on Lewis River, $7.

DINING *Chart House,* 101 East Columbia Way, 693-9211. Lunch Monday to Friday, dinner daily; seafood, steaks, prime rib; river view; $$. *Fatty Patty's,* 813 West Main Street, Battle Ground, 687-3904. Breakfast and lunch daily; in shopping center at intersection of Highways 502 and 503; legendary hamburgers, also good for breakfast; $. *Hidden House,* corner of Main and West Thirteenth streets, 696-2847. Lunch Monday to Friday, dinner Tuesday to Sunday; eclectic menu served in 1885 residence; $$$. *Red Lion Inn at the Quay,* 100 Columbia Way, 694-8341. Breakfast, lunch, and dinner daily; outstanding river view; $$. *The Crossing,* 900 West Seventh Street, 695-3374. Lunch Monday to Friday, dinner daily, brunch Sunday; railroad-theme restaurant in complex of vintage railroad cars adjacent to Burlington Northern main line; $$. *Who Song & Larry's Cantina,* 111 East Columbia Way, 695-1198. Lunch and dinner daily, fun-loving Mexican cantina with view of river, $$.

FOR MORE INFORMATION Vancouver/Clark County Visitors & Convention Bureau, 404 East Fifteenth Street, Suite 11, Vancouver 98663, 693-1313.

On Foot Through the Heart of Seattle

If you haven't visited Seattle in a while, you may be in for some surprises. The whole central Puget Sound area, with Seattle as its hub, has been riding a wave of prosperity and rapid growth in the past three or four years. New skyscrapers punctuate the downtown skyline; there's a new bus tunnel beneath downtown; new stores, hotels, and restaurants are springing up everywhere. Dining out has taken on new dimensions with the addition of dozens of upscale restaurants, and Seattle has become a "foodie's" town.

Seattle has also received a great deal of media hype, having been named the number-one vacation destination (by Rand-McNally), "most livable city" (by *Changing Times* magazine, *Places Rated Almanac,* and *Money* magazine), "city with best hotels in the U.S." (by Zagat U.S. Hotel Survey), "best city for bicycling" (by *Bicycling* magazine), and on and on. One Seattleite put it in perspective this way: "Seattle has always been here. We haven't changed. It's other people's perception of us that's changed."

And all the media hype tends to obscure the real Seattle and its attractions, most of which have not changed. As a newspaper columnist put it, "At heart, Seattle is really still a small town."

All this prosperity and growth has brought a few negatives as well. Traffic is congested and getting worse. If you're driving into Seattle, try to time your arrival for midday or after the evening rush hour when bumper-to-bumper commuter traffic on the interstates has subsided. Better yet, leave your car at home and take public transportation.

Prices are up, especially for lodging and meals. If you want to spend your time downtown, but are alarmed by rack rates at downtown hotels, try one of the more modest motels on the Denny Regrade (between downtown and the Seattle Center) or a bed-and-breakfast inn on Queen Anne Hill (just above the Seattle Center).

There are lots of reasons to visit Seattle without a car. Downtown is pedestrian scale and easy to get around on foot (once you learn the best routes around the steepest hills). All Metro buses in the downtown area are free; just step aboard and ride from Pioneer Square to the Regrade, or vice versa. In addition, Gray Line runs a shuttle bus disguised as a trolley that connects the major downtown hotels with Pike Place Market, the waterfront, and Pioneer Square on a frequent schedule in summer. Taxis are relatively inexpensive, $1.20 at the flag drop, $1.40 a mile. Downtown parking is scarce and expensive.

To savor the soul of Seattle, you must begin your morning early. Plan to be on hand at the Pike Place Market—an easy walk from downtown hotels—before 8 A.M. when the "high stall" vendors are setting up for the day.

Pike Place Market, one of the last authentic farmer's markets in the country, has become the city's number-one tourist attraction. But though the tourists may love it, it's the locals who sustain it. Many Seattle restaurants and neighborhood residents do much of their shopping here, and suburbanites put it high on their list of shopping stops in the city.

The market was founded in 1907 and has grown higgledy-piggledy into a three-story warren of fish and meat markets, spice shops, vegetable vendors, delicatessens, craft shops, secondhand stores, and several restaurants. Shops have also spread across the street to neighboring Sanitary Market and beyond. It's a wonderful, funky, very human sort of place.

Early in the morning fruit and vegetable sellers are unloading trucks and building display mountains of tomatoes, cucumbers, carrots, lettuce, apples, oranges, radishes, onions, eggplant, and just about every other kind of fresh produce you can imagine, all the while calling to each other and passersby in accents of Greek, Italian, Japanese, Spanish, and half a dozen other tongues. The fishmongers, clad in white aprons and high rubber boots, are the market's theatrical performers. One will help you select a whole salmon, cod, or Dungeness crab from the scores displayed on hills of ice at the front of his stand, then toss it through the air to the wrapper at the back. You can join a guided behind-the-scenes tour of the market by reservation.

There are a number of good choices for breakfast at the market. Maximilien's, Sound View Cafe, and the Athenian are right in the market and have fine bluff-top views of Elliott Bay. Cafe Sport, one block north, offers fresh fruit and breads and breakfast pastries right from the oven.

It won't take you more than a few minutes strolling Seattle's streets to discover that this is a coffee lover's town. Dozens of coffee bars purveying espresso, latte, cappuccino, and other exotic concoctions are scattered at street level all through downtown. The two principal companies are SBC and Starbucks, and their products are quite different to the discerning coffee drinker. Both have coffee bars in the market area.

Descend the stairs at the back of the market (Pike Place Hillclimb) to the waterfront along Alaskan Way. Directly in front of you is Pier 59, location of the Seattle Aquarium, with its collections of regional and tropical marine species and a glass-domed viewing room beneath Elliott Bay. The Omnimax wide-screen theater is in the same building.

To the north the waterfront extends to Pier 70, a refurbished wharf that houses gift and craft shops, restaurants, and studios. The excursion boat *Spirit of Puget Sound* and visiting navy ships dock here. In between you'll find the Edgewater Inn, Seattle's only waterfront hotel, at Pier 67 and the Victoria Clipper terminal next door at Pier 69.

Plan to spend an hour or more strolling and browsing south along the waterfront as far as Pier 52. If you get tired of walking, you can board one of the green-and-cream trolleys that run along the waterfront and continue to Pioneer Square and the International District. In the summer there are also horse-drawn carriages and pedicabs.

Seattle is a maritime city, and getting out on the water is an essential part of the Seattle experience. The least expensive means is to board a ferry from Pier 52 (Colman Dock) to Winslow, on Bainbridge Island, or Bremerton (see "In the Footsteps of Vikings and Indians" and "Bremerton"). There are several restaurants within an easy walk of the dock at both destinations. Seattle Harbor Tours and Grayline Water Sightseeing run regular narrated excursions of the harbor from Piers 55 and 56. The Gray Line boat, M.V. *Sightseer,* includes a trip through the Hiram Chittenden Locks into Lake Union.

Another excellent choice combines a harbor tour with a salmon dinner and entertainment. Tillicum Village, at Blake Island State Park, features a replica of a cedar Indian longhouse in which guests can watch Indians bake salmon in the traditional way over open alder fires, then sit down to a salmon dinner and a program of costumed Indian dancers.

Though no longer used for commerce, the piers fronting Elliott Bay once played a significant role in Seattle's evolving into a major port city. Pier 58, adjacent to Waterfront Park, was once known as Schwabacher's Wharf, the dock where the steamer *Portland* landed in 1897 with "a ton of gold" from Canada's Klondike. There's a bronze plaque commemorating the event set in the concrete wall near the pier. Seattle became the principal supply and debarkation port in the rush that followed and remains the principal gateway to Alaska. Trade with the Orient began with tea and spices and included the famous silk trains that sped carloads of Asian silk from the waterfront to East Coast markets on passenger train schedules.

Fire Station 5, home of Seattle's fireboats, is located at Pier 53. If you're lucky, you may arrive about the time they conduct their weekly practice in Elliott Bay, creating rainbows as their powerful nozzles jet fountains of water high in the air.

If it's lunchtime, you'll want to begin looking for a restaurant. There are several along the waterfront that specialize in seafood with a view. If you'd prefer a walking lunch, you can pick up a container of clam chowder or some fish and chips at walk-up bars at Ivar's Acres of Clams and Steamers. You can feed the gulls on French fries at Ivar's. Ivar's and Elliott's both offer outdoor dining on the pier in good weather; Elliott's has one of the most extensive fresh sheets (a sheet inserted into the menu each day listing fresh items) in town.

Turn east on Yesler Way and walk two blocks to Pioneer Square, at First

Avenue. As you look up Yesler, you can see the hill on which loggers in the 1860s and 1870s built a corduroy or "skid" road made of logs laid crossways, down which they skidded timber from the hillside cuttings to Henry Yesler's sawmill at tidewater. South of skid road lay the brothels, saloons, and loggers' rooming houses, a rough section of town that became synonymous with skid road. In other cities the name has been changed to "skid row."

Pioneer Square (formerly a streetcar stop), with its handsome iron pergola, totem pole, and red brick and sandstone business blocks, is the heart of old Seattle and now the focus of a historic district. A good time to photograph this area is in the afternoon, when the western light accentuates the rugged old facades, especially that of the Pioneer Building. Many of the old buildings now house art galleries, boutiques, bookstores, taverns, and restaurants. Most galleries are closed on Sunday; best do your browsing on Saturday. In summer, many of the restaurants line the sidewalks with umbrellaed tables screened from street traffic.

Highlights of the district include Occidental Park, a lovely cobblestoned square shaded by London plane trees. Elliott Bay Book Company, at First Avenue and Main Street, is Seattle's equivalent of Powell's in Portland, though not as large. It has a vast collection of books and a coffeehouse downstairs. The Klondike Gold Rush National Historical Park, at 117 South Main Street, is a small museum with artifacts and old films pertaining to the Gold Rush. Park personnel will show you the films on request. Waterfall Garden, at Second Avenue South and South Main Street, commemorates the site where United Parcel Service was founded in 1907.

Bill Speidel's Underground Tour, perhaps the top attraction in Pioneer Square, is also its most curious. Back in 1889 a major fire destroyed most of Seattle. When the city was rebuilt, street levels were raised as much as 35 feet to avoid problems with low-lying land and high tides. The tour explores the fascinating remains of the old city that still lie beneath the streets.

Around Pioneer Square and throughout the downtown area you'll notice distinctive Seattle City Light manhole covers in two designs, one a city map, the other a North Coast Tlingit Indian design of a whale. If you look closely at the map covers, you'll see that each location is pinpointed. Beneath the Pioneer Square pergola, there's a special manhole cover dedicated to Bill Speidel, Seattle historian and founder of the underground tours.

The same features that make Seattle the nation's number-one vacation city also make it an attractive destination for the homeless. Unfortunately, Pioneer Square is one of their favorite haunts, but generally, they are harmless.

If time permits, hop a trolley or walk the few blocks to the International District, the city's large Oriental community. Here, in an area of about 30 blocks (roughly, bounded by Fifth and Eight avenues, and Washington and Dearborn streets), you'll find dozens of small Chinese, Japanese, Filipino, Thai, Korean, and Southeast Asian restaurants, shops, herb stores, Kung Fu parlors, Oriental groceries, and small hotels. Be sure to visit Wing Luke Museum, which details the Asian history of the city; Hing Hay Park, with its dragon mural and pagoda; and Uwajimaya, an incredible Oriental grocery/household goods/clothing store with thousands of exotic items ranging from one-thousand-year-old eggs and kimonos to dried seaweed and teakwood boxes.

Seattle is a city committed to art, both public and private. A city ordinance requires that 1 percent of all capital funding be devoted to the arts. There are splendid pieces of sculpture, especially fountains, all over the city. Seattle has also seen the development of glass sculpture, primarily led by artist Dale Chihuly and the Pilchuck Glass School. You can view two splendid collections downtown, one at the Sheraton Seattle Hotel (in the lobby and in Fuller's restaurant), the other just across the street on the second floor of the Pacific First Centre.

The newly opened Seattle Art Museum, at Second Avenue and University Street, features a major African collection, an Asian-Oceania-American collection, and a collection entitled "Art of the Western Tradition" on five floors. The museum's former building in Volunteer Park has been closed for renovation and will reopen as an Asian art museum.

If shopping is an important item on your agenda, you'll find the major department and high-fashion stores—the Bon, Frederick & Nelson, Nordstrom, I. Magnin—on Fourth, Fifth, and Sixth avenues between Pine and Pike streets. Rainier Square, at Fifth Avenue and University Street, and Westlake Center, on Pine Street between Fourth and Fifth avenues, have dozens of upscale shops selling everything from cookware to books. Eddie Bauer, Fifth Avenue and Union Street, is at the top of the outdoor equipment and clothing list, as is REI, at 1525 Eleventh Avenue (take the number 10 bus from Pike Street).

What to do on a Saturday evening? You may just want to choose a scenic vantage point and relax with a companion to watch the sun set over the Olympic Mountains. Our downtown choices for drinks with a view are the Cloud Room, in the Camlin Hotel; Cutter's Bayhouse, at the north end of the market; Ernie's Bar and Grill, in the Edgewater Inn; the Space Needle; and Prego, in the Stouffer Madison Hotel.

Seattle is not very strong in the nightclub department. The choices generally run to comedy or jazz clubs or piano bars. Several of the hotels offer quiet listening music in the evenings; the Garden Court of the Four Seasons Olympic Hotel offers dancing. Nine clubs and taverns in the Pioneer Square area offer a single admission (called Joint Cover) on Saturday nights.

With eight equity theaters, an opera company, an outstanding symphony, ballet, chamber orchestras, and many other performing groups, the opportunities for a cultural evening are broad. Tickets to most performances are sold through Ticketmaster (628-0888) or at the venue box office. To find out what's playing when, pick up a copy of the *Seattle Post-Intelligencer,* the morning newspaper, or the *Seattle Times,* the evening newspaper, on Friday. Both have extensive entertainment sections. *The Weekly,* Seattle's alternative newspaper, also devotes a lot of space to the performing arts.

Sunday mornings in Seattle are pretty quiet, a good time to sleep late and read the Sunday comics or, if you're an early riser, take a walk around the deserted streets, through Freeway Park adjacent to the convention center or down to Myrtle Edwards Park just north of Pier 70. Several Seattle restaurants serve brunch beginning about 10 A.M., or if you're feeling adventurous, you may want to journey to the International District for the traditional Chinese dim sum breakfast. Our vote for the most lavish brunch in town goes to the Georgian Room at the Four Seasons Olympic Hotel.

Unless it's one of the three big festival weekends—Northwest Folklife, over Memorial Day; Bite of Seattle, in mid-July; or Bumbershoot, over Labor Day—Seattle Center makes a delightful, relatively quiet Sunday destination. To get there, just hop aboard the monorail downtown at Westlake Center for the 90-second ride above Fifth Avenue. Seattle Center is the 74-acre site of the 1962 World's Fair and the cultural heart of Seattle. The Opera House, Coliseum, Playhouse, Bagley Wright Theater, Exhibition Hall, and Arena all are located here. For a bird's-eye view of the city, the Cascade and Olympic mountains, and Puget Sound, take the elevator to the observation deck of the 605-foot Space Needle.

The spacious lawns and tree-shaded walks are ideal for Sunday relaxing. If you have children in tow, you can send them off to the rides at the Fun Forest amusement center while you lie back on the grass and listen to whatever musical group may be performing that afternoon. At one side of the park, the Pacific Science Center is a four-building complex that features a hands-on science museum, laser light show, IMAX theater, replica Indian longhouse, and changing shows and exhibits. Center House has a variety of fast-food stands ranging from Mongolian barbecue and fried chicken to pizza and pie and an outstanding children's museum on the lower level.

Area Code: 206

DRIVING DIRECTIONS Seattle is 172 miles north of Portland via Interstate 5.

RAIL AND AIR TRANSPORTATION Both *Amtrak* and seven airlines provide frequent service between the two cities (see page 76).

SIGHTSEEING *Pike Place Market,* foot of Pike Street, 682-7453. May to December daily, rest of year Monday to Saturday. Tours: 1 hour, Saturday at 9 A.M., reservations required, 682-7453. Free. *Seattle Aquarium,* Pier 59, 386-4320. Memorial Day to Labor Day daily 10 A.M. to 7 P.M., rest of year 10 A.M. to 5 P.M. Adults $5.75, 13–18 and over 65 $3.50, 6–12 $2.50. *Fire Station 5,* Pier 53, 386-1400. Station tours daily 10 A.M. to 7 P.M., by reservation. Free. *Seattle Harbor Tours,* Pier 55, 623-1445. 1 tour, 6 departures daily in summer, fewer rest of year. Adults $8.50, seniors $7.50, 13–19 $6, 5–12 $4. *Gray Line Water Sightseeing,* Pier 57, 623-4252. 2½-hour tour, 3 departures daily in July and August, fewer rest of year. Adults $17, 5–12 $9. *Tillicum Village,* Pier 56, 443-1244. 4-hour round trip including cruise, dinner, dance performance; several departures daily in summer, weekends only spring and fall. Adults $35, over 65 $32, 13–19 $24, 6–12 $14, 4–5 $7. *Major Marine Tours,* Pier 54, 292-0595. 1-hour harbor cruise with barbecue chicken picnic, 6 departures daily in summer months. Adults $7.50, seniors $6, 12–18 $5, under 12 $3. Daily saltwater fishing trips for salmon and bottom fish depart daily at 5:30 A.M. in summer, return at 11 A.M.; include tackle, bait, and lunch; $45. *Spirit of Puget Sound,* Pier 70, 443-1442. Summer schedule of lunch cruises Monday to Friday $19.35, Saturday lunch cruise and Sunday brunch cruise $21.40, dinner cruises Sunday to Thursday $36.70, Friday and Saturday $40.80, moonlight cruise Friday and Saturday $14. *Klondike Gold Rush National Historical Park,* 117 South Main Street, 442-7220. Daily 9 A.M. to 5 P.M. Free. *Bill Speidel Underground Tour,* 610 First Avenue (Doc Maynard's Saloon), 682-4646, 682-1511. Several tours daily, varies by season, call for reservations. Adults $4.75, 13–17 $3.50, 60 and over $3.50, 6–12 $2.25. *Wing Luke Asian Museum,* 407 Seventh Avenue South, 623-5124. Tuesday to Friday 11:30 A.M. to 4:30 P.M., Saturday and Sunday noon to 4 P.M. Adults $1.50, over 62 and 5–18 50 cents. *Seattle Art Museum,* Volunteer Park, 625-8900. Tuesday to Saturday 10 A.M. to 5 P.M., Sunday noon to 5 P.M., plus Thursday to 9 P.M. Adults $2, 6–18 and over 61 $1, Thursdays free. *Space Needle,* Seattle Center, 443-2100. Memorial Day to Labor Day daily 8 A.M. to 1 A.M., rest of year 10 A.M. to midnight. Adults $4.75, 5–12 $2.75. *Pacific Science Center,* Seattle Center, 443-2001. Summer daily 10 A.M. to 6 P.M. Other months Monday to Friday 10 A.M. to 5 P.M., Saturday and Sunday 10 A.M. to 6 P.M. Adults $5, 6–13 $4, 2–5 $3. *Seattle Children's Museum,* Seattle Center, 441-1767. Tuesday to Sunday 10 A.M. to 5 P.M. $3. *Gray Line of Seattle,* desks at all major hotels downtown, 626-5208. 2½-hour Discover Scenic Seattle Tour, several daily departures, hotel pickup; adults $17, 2–12 $9. 6-hour Grand City Tour; adults $27, 2–14 $14. *Chinatown Discovery,* 236-0657. 3-hour guided tours of International District include lunch, reservations necessary, $22.

EVENTS *Northwest Folklife Festival,* on Seattle Center grounds, 684-7300, Memorial Day weekend. The largest folk festival in the country, with dance, music, crafts, and ethnic food. *Bite of Seattle,* at Seattle Center, 232-2982, mid-July. More than 50 restaurants purvey their best from open-air booths. *Seafair,* 623-7000. Seattle's biggest annual event, incorporates dozens of small festivals city wide; high points include torchlight parade, Bon Odori (Japanese) events, Blue Angels aerobatic team show, unlimited hydroplane races on Lake Washington. *Bumbershoot,* at Seattle Center, 684-7200, Labor Day weekend. Arts and crafts displays and demonstrations, performing arts, writers and poets simultaneously on several stages.

LODGING *The Alexis Hotel,* 1007 First Avenue, Seattle 98104, 624-4844. Elegant, small European-style hotel, $$$$. *Best Western Executive Inn,* 200 Taylor Avenue North, Seattle 98109, 448-9444. Near Seattle Center, $$$. *Days Inn Town Center,* 2205 Seventh Avenue, Seattle 98121, 448-3434. Regrade location, $$. *Edgewater Inn,* 2411 Alaskan Way, Seattle 98121, 728-7000. Seattle's only waterfront hotel, newly refurbished, $$$$. *Four Seasons Olympic Hotel,* 411 University Street, Seattle 98101, 621-1700. Seattle's traditional grand hotel, $$$$. *Holiday Inn Crowne Plaza Hotel,* Sixth Avenue and Seneca Street, Seattle 98101, 464-1980. Noted for quality of service, across from Freeway Park. $$$$. *Inn at the Market,* 86 Pine Street, Seattle 98101, 443-3600. Intimate French country-style inn overlooking Pike Place Market, $$$–$$$$. *Mayflower Park Hotel,* 405 Olive Way, Seattle 98101, 623-8700. Quiet, downtown hotel adjacent to Westlake Center, $$$–$$$$. *Sheraton Seattle,* Sixth and Pike Street, Seattle 98101, 621–9000. Seattle's largest hotel, major art collection, award-winning restaurant, $$$$. *Sixth Avenue Inn,* 2000 Sixth Avenue, Seattle 98121, 441-8300. Regrade location, $$$. *The Sorrento Hotel,* 900 Madison Street, Seattle 98104, 583-0300. Elegant hilltop hotel, $$$$. *Stouffer-Madison Hotel,* 515 Madison Street, Seattle 98104, 583-0300. Convenient near-freeway location, outstanding views, $$$$. *Warwick Hotel,* 401 Lenora Street, Seattle 98121, 443-4300. Quiet, comfortable hotel at northern edge of downtown, $$$$. *West Coast Camlin Hotel,* 1619 Ninth Avenue, Seattle 98101, 682-0100. Modest accommodations, rooftop restaurant, downtown location, $$$. *West Coast Roosevelt Hotel,* 1531 Seventh Avenue, Seattle 98101, 621-1200. Modest, refurbished, close to city center, $$$–$$$$. *Westin Hotel Seattle,* 1900 Fifth Avenue, Seattle 98101, 728-1000. Westin's flagship hotel, twin towers, second largest in the city, $$$$.

DINING *Adriatica,* 1107 Dexter Avenue North, 285-5000. Dinner daily; Mediterranean cuisine in an intimate, classy setting; $$–$$$. *The Aegean,* 1400 First Avenue, 343-5500. Lunch Monday to Saturday, dinner daily; Greek menu; $$. *The Athenian,* Pike Place Market, 624-7166. Breakfast, lunch, and dinner daily May to December, closed Sunday rest of year; one of the oldest establishments in the market, wide-ranging menu with many unusual items, fine views; $$. *Cafe*

Alexis, Alexis Hotel, 624-3646. Lunch Monday to Saturday, dinner daily, Sunday brunch; considered one of the best restaurants in the city, innovative menu focuses on seasonal ingredients, regional dishes; $$$. *Cafe Sport*, 2020 Western Avenue, 443-6000. Breakfast, lunch, and dinner daily; Northwest and Pacific Rim dishes; $$. *Campagne*, Inn at the Market, 728-2800. Lunch Monday to Saturday, dinner daily; French provincial cuisine, excellent views; $$$. *Elliott's*, Pier 56, 623-4340. Lunch and dinner daily; one of the best seafood houses in town, outdoor dining, outstanding views; $$. *F. X. McRory's*, 419 Occidental Avenue South, 623-4800. Lunch Monday to Friday, dinner daily; steak and oyster house in the New York tradition, very crowded when there's a game in the nearby Kingdome; $$. *Fuller's*, Sheraton Seattle Hotel, 447-5544. Lunch Monday to Friday, dinner Monday to Saturday; arguably the best restaurant in town, emphasis on fresh local ingredients in regional dishes prepared by bright young female chefs; $$$. *The Georgian Room*, 411 University Street in the Four Seasons Olympic Hotel, 621-1700. Breakfast and dinner Monday to Saturday, lunch Monday to Friday, brunch Sunday; grand dining room with elegant service; $$$. *The Hunt Club*, Sorrento Hotel, 622-6400. Breakfast, afternoon tea, and dinner daily; lunch Monday to Saturday; brunch Sunday; dark wood-paneled intimate restaurant; Northwest dishes prepared by another of the city's star female chefs; $$$. *Italia*, 1010 Western Avenue, 623-1917. Breakfast, lunch, and dinner Monday to Saturday; Italian restaurant with café atmosphere; $$. *Ivar's Acres of Clams and Steamers*, Pier 54, 624-6852. Lunch and dinner daily; long-established family waterfront seafood restaurant with fascinating collection of memorabilia hung on the walls; $$. *Kaleenka Russian Cafe*, 1933 First Avenue, 728-1278. Lunch and dinner Monday to Saturday; storefront restaurant serving authentic Russian dishes; $$. *Labuznik*, 1924 First Avenue, 682-1624. Dinner Tuesday to Saturday; Czech menu, memorable quality; $$$. *Maximilien-in-the-Market*, Pike Place Market, 682-7270. Breakfast, lunch, and dinner Monday to Saturday, brunch Sunday; great views, good for breakfast. *McCormick's Fishhouse*, 722 Fourth Avenue, 682-3900. Lunch Monday to Friday, dinner daily. Emphasis is on seafood. $$. *McCormick & Schmick's*, 1103 First Avenue, 623-5500. Lunch Monday to Friday, dinner daily; among the top 2 or 3 seafood restaurants in the city; $$. *Mikado*, 514 South Jackson Street, 622-5206. Dinner Monday to Saturday; excellent Japanese restaurant, tatami rooms; $$. *The Palm Court*, Westin Hotel, 728-1000. Lunch Monday to Friday, dinner Monday to Saturday; one of the best hotel restaurant menus in the city, Continental, outstanding service; $$$. *Tai Tung*, 659 South King, 622-7372. Breakfast, lunch, and dinner daily; long-established Cantonese restaurant with large Chinese clientele; $. *Thirteen Coins*, 125 Boren Avenue North, 682-2513. 24 hours; favorite haunt of late-night theater crowd and *Seattle Times* newsies from across the street; you can watch the chefs at work from the counter seats; café food, Italian dishes; $$. *Tlaquepaque*, 1122 Post Alley, 467-8226. Lunch Monday to Saturday, dinner daily; authentic Mexican food, including seafood, raucous atmosphere, mariachis; $$. *Trattoria Mitchelli*, 88 Yesler Way, 623-3885. Breakfast, lunch, and dinner daily; lots of earthy Italian food, café atmosphere; $$. *Union Square,* 621 Union Street, 224-4321. Lunch Monday to Friday, dinner daily. Sophisticated Art Deco setting in new downtown highrise, $$. *Von's Grand City Cafe*, 619 Pine Street, 621-8667. Breakfast, lunch, and dinner daily; good choice for breakfast, try the Caesar salad for lunch; $$. *Wild Ginger Asian Restaurant & Satay Bar*, 1400 Western Avenue, 623-4450. Lunch Monday to Saturday, dinner daily; wide-ranging Oriental menu, behind Pike Place Market; $$.

FOR MORE INFORMATION Seattle–King County Convention & Visitors Bureau, 520 Pike Street, Seattle 98101, 461-5840. Walk-in information center is located on the ground level of the Washington State Convention and Trade Center, 800 Convention Place. Hours: 8:30 A.M. to 5 P.M. Monday to Friday.

Seattle: A City of Neighborhoods

Seattle, like New York, is a city of distinctive neighborhoods. Some are ethnic, some focus on a single industry such as fishing, and some are set apart by their geography.

For the visitor, the most interesting neighborhoods lie in a band running across the city just north and south of the Lake Washington Ship Canal from saltwater Puget Sound to freshwater Lake Washington. Beginning with Ballard on the west, they are Fremont, Wallingford and the University District, and, immediately south of the ship canal, Lake Union and Montlake.

You'll need a car for this weekend. Metro buses reach all the important attractions, but going by bus requires a lot of transferring. Accommodations outside the downtown core are somewhat limited (see "Lodging" for our recommendations). For a wider selection try the airport area south of the city. Motels here are handy to I-5 and less expensive than downtown. Some of the city's best restaurants are located north of downtown, so you may want to plan to stay overnight near the airport, drive the 17-or-so miles north the next day for sightseeing and dining, then return south in the evening. Forty-fifth Street (I-5 Exit 169) is the principal east-west arterial that links these neighborhoods.

One major attraction—the Museum of Flight—lies south of the city (Exit 158). Plan to see it on your drive up from Portland or on your way back. The museum is sometimes referred to as the Boeing Museum of Flight because it incorporates Boeing's first airplane factory ("the Red Barn") and because it stands across the street from Boeing's Developmental Center. It is in fact independently run and offers a great deal more than just the history of Boeing.

Twenty-one aircraft hang from the ceiling of the Great Gallery, together resembling some vintage squadron suspended in air beneath the glass of a giant greenhouse. You'll see a DC-3, an early tri-motor, biplanes, military jets, early mail planes, a reproduction of Boeing's first seaplane, a curious combination of automobile and airplane, helicopters, and such legendary greats as the B-17 and B-47. In the Red Barn, displays trace the early history of flight and aircraft manufacture; all the pieces are authentic, many from the very earliest days of flight. The museum's gift shop is a treasure trove of models, reference books, aviation uniforms and patches, leather flight jackets, and all sorts of paraphernalia that will delight airplane buffs. The museum is located at one side of Boeing Field (King County Airport) near the Boeing Flight Test Center, where you can watch many of the latest aircraft taking off and landing.

If you're going to try to visit all these neighborhoods and attractions in one weekend, we recommend you work from east to west. The view of the rising sun dramatically illuminating Mount Rainier is a stunner from the University of Washington campus, while the place to view the sun setting behind the Olympic Mountains is the beach at Golden Gardens Park or one of the upscale restaurants at Shilshole Marina.

The Northwest's largest university spreads over 694 lovely acres of campus accessible from University Way Northeast and Northeast Forty-fifth Street. It is one of the garden spots of the city despite its expansion in several new buildings and enrollment, which has reached about 35,000. The site was the location of the 1909 Alaska-Yukon-Pacific Exposition, with several buildings remaining from that and the late nineteenth century. With its older buildings nestled among huge trees and surrounded by lawns, the university owes its parklike landscaping to those ubiquitous Olmsted brothers, whose designs had such a lasting impact on the rest of the city. Nowhere is the quality of this design more evident than at Drumheller Fountain, where, on a clear day, the arching jets of water and clean bricked corridor lead your eye to a stunning view of Mount Rainier.

You can pick up a free campus map and parking permit ($3) at either of the entrance stations. Campus highlights include the Student Union Building (called HUB); the handsome Gothic buildings of the Fine Arts Quadrangle; Denny Hall, the oldest building on campus (1894); and Red Square.

The university has two outstanding museums. Burke Memorial Washington State Museum is located just to your right as you enter from Northeast Forty-fifth Street. The museum is devoted to natural history and anthropology, with exhibits of dinosaur skeletons and the arts and crafts of Pacific Rim cultures. It contains the best collection of North Coast Indian artifacts in the state, including masks, baskets, and totems. The Henry Art Gallery on the southwestern side of the campus is not very big, but it manages to display a respectable permanent collection of nineteenth- and twentieth-century art, and its rotating exhibits frequently contain the best works of Northwest artists and traveling shows.

One of the abbreviated terms in the Seattle lexicon you'll probably hear is "the Ave," as in "I'm going shopping on the Ave." "The Ave" refers to University Way Northeast and, by extension, to the whole University District. The district, especially University Way Northeast and Northeast Forty-fifth Street, is the hub of student off-campus activity. A warren of fast-food restaurants, bookstores, stereo shops, clothing stores, and art theaters, the district is bustling with activity 16 or more hours a day during the school year. It's a good spot to have breakfast or lunch. At 4326 University Way Northeast, the University Book Store has an incredible array of volumes for sale, plus software, office supplies, and stationery items.

Drive south on Montlake Boulevard Northeast, crossing the ornate green Montlake Bridge over the Lake Washington Ship Canal. This narrow portion of the canal is known as the Montlake Cut and is host to the Opening Day yacht parade the first weekend in May, marking the beginning of boating season. Scores of sail and power boats parade through the cut while spectators crowd the banks and bridge. There's a water-level walking path through the cut that affords close-up views of the passing marine traffic. Seattle's rather neglected Museum of History and Industry lies on the south side of the ship canal. You may find it a disappointment if you've visited similar museums in other cities, but it does have exhibits detailing the Seattle fire of 1889, plus antique automobiles and a famous racing hydroplane among other maritime displays.

Just across I-520 to the south, the Washington Park Arboretum comprises 200 acres of plants and trees, most of them indigenous to the Northwest. You can drive through the grounds on Arboretum Drive, but a much better idea is to park your car and stroll through the groves of giant rhododendrons and the quiet glens beneath the cedars. The park is a riot of color in May, when the hundreds of azaleas, rhododendrons, and flowering trees bloom, and again in fall, when the deciduous trees turn red, orange, and gold. At the southwest corner is the Japanese Garden, where the intricate plantings and designs of classic Japanese landscaping flank a traditional tea house. Perhaps the most delightful way to visit the arboretum is by canoe. You can rent one at the University of Washington Waterfront Activities Center near Husky Stadium and paddle through the arboretum's marshlands.

Just west of the University of Washington, the ship canal opens out into Lake Union, which pokes southward like a giant thumb almost into downtown Seattle. Very much an urban working waterway, the lake is ringed with shipyards, moorings, retired ships, and marine supplies businesses. Floatplanes take off for the

San Juan Islands and other points on Puget Sound, often dodging squadrons of sailboats plying the lake. One of Seattle's two colonies of privately owned houseboats is moored along the eastern shore of the lake (the other is in Portage Bay, just across from the University District). In recent years some of the city's most attractive restaurants have sprung up around the lake, most of them offering outdoor dining on decks overlooking the water in fair weather.

From the university you can loop the lake by crossing the University Bridge and following Eastlake Avenue East, Fairview Avenue North, Westlake Avenue North, and recrossing the ship canal on the Fremont Bridge. The Center for Wooden Boats, at the southern tip of the lake, is an active museum of vintage boats, many of which are under repair or for rent. The collection includes ancient Indian dugout canoes, Polynesian outriggers, and handmade wooden fishing boats. You can watch master boat builders construct classic wooden boats with hand tools. Another curiosity is the M. V. *Challenger*, a venerable tugboat recycled into a "bunk-and-breakfast" inn that is moored nearby.

Lake Union is an excellent place to schedule a lunch break, with several good restaurants from which to choose, including Benjamin's, Franco's Hidden Harbor, Cucina! Cucina!, and Chandler's. One unusual and delightful way to see the lake is from the water itself. The Northwest Outdoor Center rents canoes and kayaks for exploring on your own and leads guided paddle trips around the lake and out through the Ballard locks to Shilshole. Some kayakers paddle from restaurant to restaurant in a progressive dining trip.

North Northlake Way hugs the north shore of the lake leading you past Ivar's Salmon House, a good lunch or dinner choice if you have children along. The restaurant is built of cedar and festooned with Indian artifacts including full-size dugout canoes and dozens of historic photos of Indians. Salmon, the specialty of the house, is barbecued Indian-style over alder fires, and there's a waterside deck for dining outside. Just down the street Gasworks Park affords one of the finest water and skyline views in the city. The big old industrial structures that have been preserved here were once part of a gas-manufacturing plant. Some have called it urban recycling at its best. The city's most popular walking and bicycling trail, the Burke-Gilman Trail, follows an abandoned railroad right-of-way from Gasworks Park, east along the ship canal and past the university, then northward along Lake Washington 13 miles to Logboom Park in Kenmore. Several bicycle shops in the area will rent you bicycles for the trip.

Directly north of Lake Union (take Stone Way) lie Green Lake and the Woodland Park Zoo. Green Lake is one of the most popular parks in the city. A three-mile walking-jogging-bicycling path circles the lake, and at almost any hour of the day or evening you'll find scores of exercise-minded Seattleites "doing their thing" here. Broad sloping lawns surrounding the lake are ideal for spreading a picnic, and if you have any leftover sandwich bread you can feed it to the flocks of ducks and geese looking for a handout.

Woodland Park Zoo has been ranked by zoologists as one of the ten best zoos in the country. That notwithstanding, the zoo is a leader in the evolution that is taking place at zoos all over the country whereby the animals are uncaged and allowed to roam free (relatively) while the spectators are confined to a safe viewing area. Several elements of this zoo are absolutely stunning, among them the African savannah, the lowland gorilla enclosure, and the Asian elephant forest with its impressive new Thai elephant house.

West of Lake Union the ship canal once again squeezes down to a narrow trench until, just beyond the Ballard Bridge, it opens out to Salmon Bay. At this point in your explorations around the city's various waterfronts you may have wondered about the dearth of fishing boats. They're on the south side of Salmon Bay, at Fishermen's Terminal. Hundreds of boats, from diminutive gill netters to big trawlers and crab boats, tie up here, many of them vessels that regularly fish Alaskan waters. Depending on the time of year, you can often watch fishermen mending their nets in the open areas beside the docks or you might stop to chat with them from dockside as they spruce up their boats. If you're looking for marine hardware, nautical books or charts, or decorative items such as ship's chronometers or brass fittings for your home, you'll find them at the several ships' chandlers here.

On the north side of Salmon Bay lies Ballard, Seattle's Scandinavian community. Though the neighborhood is no longer primarily Swedish and Norwegian, it is strong in the traditions of fishing and lumbering and much of the Scandinavian influence remains, evidenced in the names of some of the streets and stores, in the celebration of Norwegian Independence Day, and in such delicacies as lutefisk, available in some fish markets. One of the area's best known microbrews is Ballard Bitter, which sports a label with the Scandinavian slogan "Ya Sure Ya Betcha" prominently displayed. While you're in Ballard, be sure to stop and visit the Nordic Heritage Museum. The museum is modest, but it has some outstanding displays recounting the life of the first Scandinavian immigrants.

Follow Market Street (Ballard's main street) west to the Hiram M. Chittenden Locks, usually referred to as the Ballard locks or, simply, "the locks." When, early in the century, engineers cut the ship canal across Seattle's waist to provide large vessels deep-water access to and from the fresh water of Lake Washington, they had to install locks to compensate for the approximately 21-foot difference between tidal salt water and the canal. These days the locks are a focal point of marine activity, with scores of pleasure craft, fishing boats, tugs and barges, and log rafts "locking through" 24 hours a day. From May through October the locks are busy with floating traffic jams of weekend sailors anxious to be cruising the

Sound or returning to home port. You can stand on the lock rim and watch the boats below you being raised or lowered. The process is endlessly fascinating and can easily lure you away from scheduled sightseeing. On the south side of the locks are fish ladders that enable salmon to swim upstream to spawn, and underwater windows from which you can view them.

At Ballard's western edge lies Shilshole Bay Marina and Golden Gardens Park. The marina provides moorage to hundreds of sail and power boats and the park has one of the two best saltwater beaches in Seattle, the other being Alki Beach in West Seattle. But the main attraction to this western edge of the city is the evening and watching the sun go down over the Olympics. Several excellent restaurants and lounges offer good vantage points where you can wile away a romantic hour or two.

Area Code: 206

SIGHTSEEING *Museum of Flight,* 9404 East Marginal Way South, 764-5720. Daily 10 A.M. to 5 P.M., Thursday until 9 P.M. Adults $5, seniors and 6–16 $3. *Burke Museum,* University of Washington campus, 543-5590. Daily 10 A.M. to 5 P.M., plus Thursday 5 to 8 P.M. Free. *Henry Art Gallery,* University of Washington campus, 543-2280. Tuesday to Sunday 10 A.M. to 5 P.M.; Thursday to 7 P.M.; adults $3, seniors and students $1.50. *Museum of History and Industry,* 2700 Twenty-fourth Avenue East, 324-1126. Daily 10 A.M. to 5 P.M. Adults $3, 6–12 and seniors $1.50. *University of Washington Waterfront Activities Center,* University of Washington campus on ship canal, 543-9433. Spring, summer, and fall 10 A.M. to 8 P.M. or dusk. Canoe rentals $3.50 per hour. *Center for Wooden Boats,* 1010 Valley Street, 382-2628. July and August Wednesday to Monday noon to 8 P.M., rest of year noon to 6 P.M. Free. *Northwest Outdoor Center,* 2100 Westlake Avenue North, 281-9694. Canoe and kayak rentals $5–$7 per hour, single; guided kayak tours $15 for 2 hours to $30 for sunset and through-the-locks tours; classes in sea kayaking, trips to San Juan Islands and other destinations. *Woodland Park Zoo,* 5500 Phinney Avenue North, 684-4800. April to September Monday to Friday 10 A.M. to dusk, Saturday and Sunday 8:30 A.M. to dusk; rest of year daily 10 A.M. to dusk. Adults $4.50, 6–17 and seniors $2.25. *Nordic Heritage Museum,* 3014 Northwest Sixty-seventh Street, 789-5707. Tuesday to Saturday 10 A.M. to 4 P.M., Sunday noon to 4 P.M. Adults $2.50, seniors $1.50, 6–16 $1. *Hiram M. Chittenden Locks,* 783-7059. Visitor center open mid-June to mid-September daily 11 A.M. to 8 P.M.; rest of year Thursday to Monday 11 A.M. to 5 P.M.

EVENTS *Emerald City Flight Festival,* at Museum of Flight/Boeing Field, 764-5720, early July. Air show with vintage airplanes, aerobatics, military demonstrations. *Lake Union Wooden Boat Festival,* 382-2628, Fourth of July weekend.

The Center for Wooden Boats stages rowing, sailing, and boat-building competitions.

L O D G I N G *Tugboat Challenger Bunk & Breakfast,* 809 Fairview Place North, Seattle 98109, 340-1201. 7 cozy rooms aboard former oceangoing tugboat moored on Lake Union, $$. *Chambered Nautilus Bed & Breakfast Inn,* 5005 Twenty-second Avenue Northeast, Seattle 98105, 522-2536. 6 antiques-furnished guest rooms in hillside vintage Georgian home in University District, $$–$$$. *Chelsea Station Bed & Breakfast Inn,* 4915 Linden Avenue North, Seattle 98103, 547-6077. 5-bedroom B&B in quiet residential neighborhood near Woodland Park Zoo, $$. *Doubletree Inn/Doubletree Suites,* 205 Strander Boulevard and 16500 Southcenter Parkway, Seattle 98188, 246-8220, 575-8220. 2 affiliated hotels across the street from each other off I-5 at Southcenter, near airport, $$$–$$$$. *Meany Tower Hotel,* 4507 Brooklyn Avenue Northeast, Seattle 98105, 634-2000. High-rise hotel in University District, $$$. *Red Lion Hotel/Sea-Tac,* 18740 Pacific Highway South, Seattle 98188, 246-8600. 850-room multistory airport hotel with several restaurants, entertainment, $$$$. *Seattle Airport Hilton,* 17620 Pacific Highway South, Seattle 98188, 244-4800. Smaller, cozier airport hotel with secluded inner courtyard, $$$$. *Seattle Marriott Sea-Tac Airport,* 3201 South 176th Street, Seattle 98188, 241-2000. Upscale hotel built around atrium, indoor pool, $$$$.

D I N I N G *Beeliner Diner,* 2114 North Forty-fifth Street, 547-6313. Lunch and dinner daily; basic American food—meatloaf, meat pies, corned beef hash—in an upbeat atmosphere; famous for its coconut cake; $. *Benjamin's,* 809 Fairview Place North, 621-8262. Lunch Monday to Saturday, dinner daily, brunch Sunday; lakeside location, good for brunch; $$. *Burk's Cafe,* 5411 Ballard Avenue Northwest, 782-0091. Lunch and dinner Tuesday to Saturday; this gets our vote for the best Cajun/Creole restaurant in town; $$. *Canlis,* 2576 Aurora Avenue North, 283-3313. Dinner Monday to Saturday; established for decades as one of Seattle's best conventional restaurants, hilltop view of Lake Union; $$$. *Chandler's Crabhouse and Fresh Fish Market,* 901 Fairview Avenue North, 223-2722. Lunch Monday to Saturday, dinner daily, brunch Sunday; seafood served with a view of Lake Union; $$. *Cucina! Cucina!,* 901 Fairview Avenue North, 447-2782. Lunch Monday to Saturday, dinner daily; chain restaurant, sister to Chandler's, trendy Italian menu, Lake Union waterfront; $$. *Franco's Hidden Harbor,* 1500 Westlake Avenue North, 282-0501. Lunch and dinner daily; long-established seafood restaurant tucked beneath a pier among moored pleasure boats; $$. *Hiram's-at-the-Locks,* 5300 Thirty-fourth Avenue Northwest, 784-1733. Lunch Monday to Saturday, dinner daily, brunch Sunday; popular upscale restaurant overlooking the locks and ship canal, Northwest cuisine; $$. *Ivar's Salmon House,* 401 Northlake Way, 632-0767. Lunch Monday to Saturday, dinner daily, brunch Sunday; alder-barbecued salmon served beside the lake, Indian photos and artifacts; $. *Julia's 14-Carrot Cafe,* 2305 Eastlake Avenue East, 324-1442. Breakfast daily, lunch Monday to Saturday, dinner Tuesday to Saturday; breakfast Sunday; health food with an ethnic twist, popular spot for breakfast; $$. *Kamon on Lake Union,* 1177 Fairview Avenue North, 622-4665. Lunch Monday to Friday, dinner daily; Japanese menu, sushi bar, waterside location; $$$. *Lake Union Cafe,* 3119 Eastlake Avenue East, 323-8855. Lunch Monday to Friday, dinner daily, brunch Sunday; pasta, seafood, hillside view of the lake; $$. *Latitude 47,* 1232 Westlake Avenue North, 284-1047. Lunch and dinner daily, brunch Sunday; lakeside location, American menu; $$. *Le Gourmand,* 425 Northwest Market Street, 784-3463. Dinner Wednesday to Saturday; French restaurant tucked among stores of Ballard's main street; $$$. *Ray's Boathouse,* 6049 Seaview Avenue Northwest, 789-3770. Lunch and dinner daily; a near legend in Seattle, this waterfront seafood restaurant burned several years ago, has been rebuilt and is back in business catering to the romantic; $$$. *Rattlers Grill,* 1823 Eastlake Avenue East, 325-7350. Lunch Monday to Friday, dinner daily. Hearty New Mexican–style food, $–$$$. *Saleh al Lago,* 6804 East Green Lake Way North, 522-7943. Lunch Monday to Friday, dinner Monday to Saturday; elegant, intimate Northern Italian restaurant; $$$.

At the End of the Oregon Trail

The Oregon Trail is one of the most romantic and inspiring elements in the story of this nation's westward expansion. From about 1841 to 1869 probably half a million fur traders, missionaries, fortune hunters, and emigrant farmers and merchants trekked over the rugged 2,000-mile route from Independence, Missouri, to the Willamette Valley. Many endured extreme hardship. It is estimated that 30,000 people died along the way. But those who survived staked their claims on the rich promise of the Oregon Country in a bountiful valley just begging to be turned to the plow.

Oregon City was the only incorporated town west of the Mississippi River and the official end of the Oregon Trail. To get in touch with the history of American settlement in the Northwest, schedule a weekend of sightseeing in this small town beside the Willamette River just south of Portland. And plan to include a visit to its neighbor, Champoeg. It was at Champoeg that the first American government in the West was founded in a movement that made Oregon American and not British or Canadian.

Oregon City, with a population of about 15,000, occupies a strategic location at the falls of the Willamette River, a source of power for the early saw mills and flour, wool, and paper mills that were located here. The town is split by a 100-foot bluff with the McLoughlin neighborhood residential district perched atop and the business district, highway, and railroad squeezed onto a narrow shelf alongside the river. Canemah Historic District lies on the lower level and just south of downtown. Steep streets, a series of stone steps built by the WPA in the 1930s, and a curious street elevator connect the two levels.

Much of early Oregon City has been lost to industrial development along the river, but the McLoughlin Historic District atop the bluff preserves more than 80 residences built between 1845 and 1920, several on the National Register of Historic Places. The city publishes an excellent driving tour map that leads past 54 of the most important sites. This map and five walking tour maps of the McLoughlin and Canemah historic districts are available at the Chamber of Commerce and at the End of the Oregon Trail Interpretive Center for a nominal fee.

Begin your sightseeing at the modest interpretive center, located in the basement of the senior center at 500 Washington Street. A video presentation introduces you to the Oregon Trail and the role of Oregon City as terminus. If you're visiting during the summer months, plan to attend one or both of the historical pageants that relate the story of the Oregon Trail and the founding of the first government. The Oregon Trail Pageant is held in Oregon City; the Champoeg Historical Pageant is held at Champoeg State Park.

The next stop of historical importance is the McLoughlin House National Historic Site. John McLoughlin, the chief factor of the Hudson's Bay Company post at Fort Vancouver (see page 155), retired to this trim, two-story home in 1845. Although he was the most powerful man in the Northwest for decades, McLoughlin was by most accounts also a kindly man who assisted the new settlers though their continued immigration doomed British control of the region.

The Ermatinger House, built in 1845 by another Hudson's Bay Company employee, is the oldest in town, predating the McLoughlin House by several months. Nearby, the Mertie Stevens House/Clackamas County Museum (circa 1908) contains 15 furnished period rooms, including a working kitchen, and displays a large doll collection and items used by the Northwest Indians. Because Oregon City was the only seat of American government west of the Mississippi, San Francisco filed the plat for its incorporation here in 1850, a copy of which is also on display in the museum. Possession of the document has been a bone of contention between the two cities for a number of years.

Rose Farm is the oldest American house in Oregon City. Built in 1847, it was the site of the swearing in of the first territorial governor, Joseph Lane. The upstairs ballroom was used by the territorial legislature and for many social events in Oregon City's early settlement period. In the Canemah Historic District the 1867 Fellows House includes an art gallery and restaurant.

West Linn is Oregon City's sister community on the west bank of the river and is dominated by a large paper mill. Willamette Falls Locks, accessible from the

West Linn side of the river, are the oldest multilift navigation locks in operation in the United States, built in 1873 and now a national historic site. You can stand beside the locks and watch boats "locking through," rising or descending 41 feet from one level of the river to the other.

Follow Oregon 99E south along the bank of the Willamette River. The quiet old four-lane highway, one of the two principal U.S. highways through the valley in pre-interstate days, gives you plenty of room to cruise along at leisure, pulling over now and then for a photograph or a view. Just south of town the highway climbs to an overlook for a good view of Willamette Falls. A plaque explains that the first paper mill in the Northwest was built here in 1867 and the first long-distance commercial electric power transmission in the United States was fed to Portland from here in 1889.

It's eight miles to Canby, where you may want to pick up picnic supplies for a lunch beside the river a bit later in this trip. Four miles beyond lies Aurora, the first commune on the West Coast, predating similar experiments in the 1960s by more than a century. German immigrants founded the Christian colony on the banks of the Pudding River in 1856 and it flourished for more than 20 years. Several buildings remain, and the museum in the old ox barn will give you glimpses of what life must have been like for those social pioneers. The site is on the National Register of Historic Places and includes about two dozen buildings. You can get a detailed walking map for 50 cents in the museum at Second and Liberty streets. The old town has also become the antiques capital of Oregon, with nearly a dozen shops tucked in among the old buildings off Highway 99E.

Retrace your route now through Canby and turn left (north) onto Northeast Territorial Road at the signs to Canby Ferry 1½ miles beyond the town. Continue for another 1½ miles, then turn right onto North Holly Street. It always astonishes us that so much unspoiled countryside lies so close to Portland. Commercial flower, fruit, and vegetable farms are interspersed with woodlands and rolling fields of hay and grain.

At 2512 North Holly Street, Leo Garre combines his hobby of miniature railroading with his business of growing and selling flowers and vegetables. About a mile of track, with a scale of 1½ inches to 1 foot, is laid through his growing acres. During the week Garre hauls fertilizer and other supplies with his miniature train. On weekends he allows visitors to ride free. The retail end of the business sells fresh flowers and vegetables, homemade pies and preserves, and dried flower arrangements.

If you've brought a picnic lunch, Molalla River State Park is the place to eat beside the river. You're also likely to catch sight of great blue herons; there's a large rookery here.

The Canby Ferry, one of three remaining cable ferries on the Willamette River, is truly an anachronism. The tiny vessel accommodates only four cars, takes just five minutes to reach the far bank, and costs $1, but even if you have to detour to include it in your plans, the ride is worth the trip. If the ferryman is on the far side of the river when you arrive at the landing, just honk your horn and he'll putt-putt across. If you plan to use the ferry again, save your receipt. With ten receipts you get a free ride.

Continue 1.2 miles north from the ferry landing and turn left on Southwest Mountain Road at the sign to Wilsonville. It's four miles to Wilsonville and I-5, another 12 miles to Oregon 219 and a final 2 miles into Newberg. This north bank road meanders past truck farms, hazelnut orchards, and the lush green pastures and white fences of horse farms. These are the hobby farms of the wealthy, as one sign attests: "Whip N' Spurs, A Rich Feller's Place." The Portland Opera's elegant Country Classic, a combination horse show, grand prix, art show, musical event, and wine and food festival, is held here annually in mid-July.

Though overnight accommodations on our suggested route are sparse, you may want to stay overnight in Oregon City or Newberg, especially if you're attending either of the evening historical pageants. Newberg is at the edge of Oregon's wine country (see "Wine Touring in Yamhill County") and the little town makes a good base for visits to nearby wineries, one of which, Rex Hill Vineyards, lies just northeast of town. If you're a honey fancier, stop at Oregon Apiaries to sample their smooth, semisolid form of honey, which they blend with hazelnuts and various berries. On a historical note, the Hoover-Minthorn House Museum in Newberg is the boyhood home of our thirty-first president and is open to the public.

Head south on Oregon 219 for 3½ miles to the Champoeg (pronounced "Cham-poo-ey") turnoff, then left 2 miles to Champoeg State Park. Aside from its historical significance, the park is one of Oregon's loveliest, with 567 acres of fields and forest on the Willamette River. The name Champoeg has both French and Indian origins and is thought to mean "blue flowers of the Camas," a bulb native to this region.

The North West Company's Willamette Post was established near the present-day park in 1814 to serve trappers in the area. Pioneers had constructed the first permanent homes and were clearing and planting the fields as early as 1831. Champoeg evolved into a village that functioned as the chief gathering spot of the Americans in the valley and in 1843 became the site of the first American government west of the Mississippi when the settlers voted 52 to 50 to establish their American identity. The seat of government moved to Oregon City the next year, but Champoeg continued to play an important role in agriculture and river commerce until it was obliterated in a flood in 1892.

The sense of history here is almost palpable. Grazing sheep dot the fenced fields and, aside from paved roads, there's little to remind you that you're not in the nineteenth century. Walking trails and bicycle paths wind through the park, and the site of the annual historical pageant is a grassy amphitheater next to the river. The park's visitor center displays artifacts excavated from the site and explains the archaeological techniques used for excavation; there's also a short history of the resident Kalapuyan Indians, the fur trade, and the river steamboats. Just outside the gate the Newell House Museum is the reconstructed home of Robert Newell, an early settler. The home is furnished in the period and contains a collection of inaugural gowns worn by the wives of Oregon governors. Down near the river in a lovely grove of trees is Pioneer Mother's Memorial Cabin, operated by the Daughters of the American Revolution. This replica of a typical pioneer log cabin houses artifacts of the fur trading period and a fine collection of guns and muskets dating from 1777.

Area Code: 503

DRIVING DIRECTIONS From Portland take Southeast McLoughlin Boulevard to Oregon City. Then follow the directions above to Canby, north across the Willamette River on the Canby Ferry, west through Wilsonville to Newberg. You can drive directly from Champoeg State Park 5½ miles to Interstate 5 for your return to Portland. Round-trip mileage for this itinerary is about 86 miles.

SIGHTSEEING *End of the Oregon Trail Interpretive Center,* 500 Washington Street, Oregon City, 657-9336. Tuesday to Saturday 10 A.M. to 4 P.M., Sunday noon to 4 P.M. Adults $2, seniors $1.50, 18 and under $1. *McLoughlin House National Historic Site,* 713 Center Street, Oregon City, 656-5146. Tuesday to Saturday 10 A.M. to 4 P.M., Sunday 1 to 4 P.M. Adults $2.50, seniors $2, 6–17 $1. *Ermatinger House,* Sixth and John Adams streets, Oregon City, 656-1619. Thursday to Sunday noon to 4 P.M. Adults $1.50, 12 and under 75 cents. *Mertie Stevens House/ Clackamas County Museum,* 603 Sixth Street, Oregon City, 655-2866. February to December Tuesday to Saturday 10 A.M. to 4 P.M., Sunday 1 to 4 P.M. Adults $1.50, seniors $1.25, under 18 50 cents. *Rose Farm,* 536 Holmes Lane, Oregon City, 656-5146. March to mid-December Sunday 1 to 4 P.M. Adults $1.50, seniors $1.25, students 50 cents. *John Inskeep Environmental Learning Center,* 19600 South Molalla Street, Oregon City, 657-6958. Daily 9 A.M. to dusk. Donation. 8-acre demonstration wildlife habitat on former industrial site. Tours and interpretive programs Sunday afternoons. *Old Aurora Colony Museum,* Second and Liberty streets, Aurora, 678-5754. June through August Tuesday to Saturday 10 A.M. to 4:30 P.M., Sunday 1 to 4:30 P.M.; closed Tuesday March to May and September to December, open Thursday to Sunday only January and February. Adults $2.50, 6–18 $1. *The Flower Farmer,* 2512 North Holly Street, Canby, 266-3581. May to November daily 9 A.M. to 6 P.M. *Canby Ferry.* Operates daily 6:45 A.M. to 9:15 P.M. $1 per car. *Oregon Apiaries,* 1306 North Harmony Lane, Newberg, 538-8546.

Monday to Friday 9 A.M. to 4:30 P.M. *Rex Hill Vineyards,* 30835 North Highway 99W, Newberg, 538-0666. April to December daily 11 A.M. to 5 P.M., February and March Friday to Sunday 11 A.M. to 5 P.M. Winery specializes in pinot noir, chardonnay, white riesling, pinot gris, and symphony. *Veritas Vineyard,* 31190 Northeast Veritas Lane, Newberg, 538-1470. May to Labor Day daily 11 A.M. to 5 P.M., rest of year weekends. Small 20-acre vineyard specializes in pinot noir, white riesling, Müller-Thurgau, and chardonnay. *Hoover-Minthorn House Museum,* 115 South River Street, Newberg, 538-6629. March to November Wednesday to Sunday 1 to 4 P.M., December and February Saturday and Sunday 1 to 4 P.M. Adults $1.50, seniors $1, students 50 cents. *Champoeg State Park Visitors Center,* 678-1251. Memorial Day to Labor Day Monday to Friday 8 A.M. to 4:30 P.M., Saturday and Sunday 9:30 A.M. to 5:30 P.M., rest of year Monday to Friday 8 A.M. to 4:30 P.M. Saturday and Sunday 1 to 4 P.M. Free. *Robert Newell House,* Champoeg State Park, 678-5537. February to November Wednesday to Sunday noon to 5 P.M. Adults $1.50, under 12 50 cents. *Pioneer Mothers' Memorial Cabin,* Champoeg State Park, 633-2237. February to November Wednesday to Sunday noon to 5 P.M. Adults 75 cents, under 12 50 cents.

E V E N T S   *The Oregon Trail Pageant,* Oregon City, 656-1619, after May 1 through run of pageant 657-0988, mid-July to first week in August. Outdoor history, drama, music, and dancing depicts pioneer trek. *Champoeg Historical Pageant,* at Champoeg State Park, Newberg, 245-3922, Thursday through Sunday in July. Outdoor pageant depicts settlement of Oregon Country.

L O D G I N G   *Jagger House* (bed and breakfast), 512 Sixth Street, Oregon City 97045, 657-7280. 3 guest rooms in 1880s home in historic district, easy walk to museums, $$. *Val-U Inn,* 1900 Clackamette Drive, Oregon City 97045, 655-7141. Conventional motel overlooking Willamette River, $$. *Best Western Willamette,* 30800 Southwest Parkway Boulevard, Wilsonville 97070, 682-2288, (800) 528-1234. Large units, tree-shaded grounds, close to freeway, $$. *Hess Canyon Estate Bed and Breakfast Extraordinaire,* 712 Wynooski Street, Newberg 97132, 538-1139. 4 guest rooms in 1903 home on 4 wooded acres, $$. *Littlefield House Bed and Breakfast,* 401 North Howard Street, Newberg 97132, 538-9868. 2 rooms in elegant 1909 home; hosts take guests on wine-tasting tours; $–$$. *Owl's View Bed & Breakfast,* P.O. Box 732, Newberg 91732, 538-6498. 2 guest rooms in contemporary home overlooking valley, $$–$$$. *Secluded Bed and Breakfast,* 19719 Northeast Williamson Road, Newberg 97132, 538-2635. 2 guest rooms with decks on 10 acres, $$. *Spring Creek Llama Ranch B&B,* 14700 Northeast Spring Creek Lane, Newberg 97312, 538-5717. Ranch with 2 guest rooms on 40 acres, raises llamas that guests are permitted to take on walks, $$. *Shilo Inn,* 501 Sitka Avenue, Newberg 97132, 537-0303. New 3-story motel on quiet side street, best in Newberg, $$.

CAMPING *Champoeg State Park,* 7 miles west of Newberg, 678-1251. 48 sites on the river with electrical hookups, hot showers, $11.

DINING *Fellows House Restaurant,* 416 South McLoughlin Boulevard, Oregon City, 656-2089. Breakfast and lunch Monday to Saturday, brunch Sunday; restaurant in historic 1867 house features sandwiches, garden vegetables; $$. *J's Family Restaurant and Pie House,* 2017 Portland Road, Newberg, 538-5925. Breakfast, lunch, and dinner daily; reputation for excellent pies made with local fruit; $. *Pasquale's,* 111 West First Street, Newberg, 538-0910. Lunch and dinner daily; cozy family spot with Italian dishes, pizza, takeout; $. *Horseless Carriage,* 607 East First Street, Newberg, 538-2600. Breakfast, lunch, and dinner daily; family restaurant specializing in steak and mushrooms; $–$$.

FOR MORE INFORMATION Tri-City Chamber of Commerce, 500 Abernethy Road, Oregon City 97045, 656-1619. Newberg Chamber of Commerce, 115 North Washington Street, Newberg 97312, 538-2014.

Wine Touring in Yamhill County

Wine touring is a fairly recent pastime in Oregon, but one that brings with it the rewards of discovery and the opportunity to get out into the countryside close to Portland.

If you've ever been wine touring elsewhere—in France, perhaps, or California—you'll find that in Oregon it is quite a different animal indeed. The wineries here are not big commercial establishments where you'll encounter hordes of tourists, or find professional guides and tasting rooms that include major retail outlets.

Oregon wineries are small—tiny, in fact—compared to the better-known California and Washington wineries. Typically, they're mom-and-pop affairs, producing a few thousand bottles a year. The wineries are often located in modest sheds or industrial buildings, tucked away on back roads with few signs to tell you how to get there. When you drive up, the winemaker may come out to greet you, offer a glass of his best, and lead you on a personal tour of his facilities trailed by a friendly dog or two. Frequently, you're the only visitors in sight.

Unlike Washington, where the wines are predominantly white, Oregon produces primarily reds, especially those made from the pinot noir grape. Yamhill County, southwest of Portland, is reminiscent of the Burgundy region of France in the red wines it produces and in its lush, green farmlands, set among the rolling hills of the Coast Range. In recent years the reds of Yamhill County have walked away with award after award in blind tastings, not only against other

Northwest wines but against some of France's best as well. The county produces about 32 percent of Oregon's wines.

The county is ideally suited for a leisurely weekend of wine touring. Two-lane country roads meander through the hills, passing fields of hay, truck crops, commercial nurseries, hazelnut orchards, and grazing cattle, then plunge briefly into tiny towns studded with turn-of-the-century architecture that have a frozen-in-time quality.

The loop route we suggest will take you to eight of the county's 17 wineries, a couple of museums, a tasting room, and a handful of antiques shops. Best plan to base yourself in McMinnville, because it has the best choice of accommodations and restaurants. Newberg (see "At the End of the Oregon Trail") is a second choice. Plan to pick up the ingredients of a picnic lunch in one of the delis in McMinnville. Most of the wineries are perched atop hills—lovely spots to enjoy local bread, cheese, and wine—and have shaded picnic tables with splendid views of the surrounding countryside.

The Yamhill County Wineries Association publishes an excellent free brochure listing all the county wineries. You can pick up one at either the Newberg or McMinnville Chamber of Commerce, or in many of the county's stores and restaurants, or you can write to the association at P.O. Box 871, McMinnville, OR 97218.

Take Highway 47 north out of McMinnville to Carlton and Yamhill. The road wanders five miles to Carlton through fields of grain and hay, past small farms with big barns similar to those in New England and small orchards lined with neat rows of filbert trees. Filberts (hazelnuts) are ubiquitous hereabouts; Yamhill County produces 90 percent of the nation's crop.

Pause a while and drive around the back streets of Carlton (population 1,285). You'll discover fading two-story brick business blocks dating from the nineteenth century, a butterscotch-colored railroad station from about the same period, the Portland Glove Company, and an imposing feed and grain elevator where, if you ask, they'll tell you all about the barley, wheat, oats, and alfalfa growing just beyond the edge of town. This is also a good town for a bit of browsing for antiques or collectibles. Carlton owes its claim to fame to William Anderson Howe, the inventor of the baseball catcher's mitt.

A detour of about three miles east via the Carlton–Newberg Road, then Mineral Springs Road, will bring you to Chateau Benoit Winery, known for its sauvignon blancs and sparkling wines, but also producing pinot noir, chardonnay, and Müller-Thurgau. The winery is located atop a hill with a commanding view.

Continue north to Yamhill (population 700), where you'll find several ornate old Carpenter's Gothic residences on the back streets. If you have the time and/or it's mealtime, detour west ten miles on Oak Ridge Road to Flying M Ranch, the only guest ranch in this part of Oregon. Run by the Mitchell family since 1922, the big spread offers trail rides, its own airstrip, good hearty meals in the massive main lodge, and entertainment on weekends. It's worth the drive just to see the peeled-log interior of the lodge decorated with mounted hunting trophies, a full-size buggy suspended from the ceiling, and photos of celebrities who have stayed here. Meals and riding are available to nonguests.

From Yamhill, turn east on Highway 240, which traces the Chehalem Valley to Newberg. At approximately six miles, turn onto Ribbon Ridge Road and drive north two miles to Autumn Wind Vineyard. The 52-acre vineyard and winery, established in 1987 and with 14 acres planted in grapes thus far, is new enough so that it's not listed on some maps of the area. The owners, the Kreutner family, produce altogether about 6,500 gallons of pinot noir, chardonnay, Müller-Thurgau, sauvignon blanc, and pinot noir blanc annually. When you return to Highway 240, stop several hundred yards west of the intersection at the historical marker designating the nearby grave of Ewing Young. Young was notable as the first U.S. citizen in the Oregon Country to die and leave an estate, necessitating the election of a judge with powers to probate his large herd of cattle. The election signified the first step in forming an Oregon provisional government, which eventually led to statehood.

Continue to Newberg, then south on Highway 99W to Dundee, named for Dundee, Scotland, the hometown of an early Oregon railroad builder, William Reid. Elk Cove Vineyards has a tasting room beside the highway in Dundee, and three other wineries—Lange, Cameron, and Knudsen Erath—are located a short distance over the rolling hills to the west via Worden Hill Road. Cameron Winery is devoted to pinot noir and chardonnay; Lange Winery specializes in those wines as well as pinot gris. Dick Erath is one of Oregon's wine pioneers, having established Knudsen Erath in 1968, and he is one of the state's largest producers. The winery is famous for its pinot noir and also produces chardonnay and white riesling. If the weather is drizzly, as it often is in the Willamette Valley, the winery's covered patio is an ideal spot for a picnic.

Just south of Dundee off Oregon 99W is Sokol Blosser Winery, another pioneer winemaker and one of the state's largest producers. Surrounded by orchards and vineyards, the winery makes chardonnay, pinot noir, white riesling, gewürztraminer, and Müller-Thurgau.

From June through October, shopping for fresh fruit, vegetables, and nuts is excellent in the Willamette Valley, with roadside stands scattered along virtually every road. Laube Orchards operates one such stand just south of Dundee. There are also several U-pick farms around McMinnville. At Lafayette, four miles south of Dundee, the big white schoolhouse beside the road is now a mall served by 90 antiques dealers and probably the best place in the county for comprehensive antiques shopping.

Just beyond the intersection of Highway 47 from the north, detour left onto

Lafayette Avenue to reach both the Eyrie Vineyards and Arterberry Winery. The first vinifera vineyard in Yamhill County, established in 1966, Eyrie is small (20 acres) and specializes in pinot noir, pinot gris, muscat ottonel, and pinot meunier. More than half the production of Arterberry Winery is devoted to pinot noir with the rest divided among chardonnay, sauvignon blanc, and white riesling.

It all comes together in McMinnville. An unpretentious country town with quiet, tree-lined streets and a small college, McMinnville has some surprisingly good restaurants. Most have extensive lists of local vintages. Tops in our book is Nick's Italian Cafe, a small, dimly lit place with simple decor and fantastic food. Fully 21 Oregon, 10 California, and 12 Italian wineries are represented on its wine list. Dinners are prix fixe and typically include five courses. What more fitting end to a day of wine touring than a fine Italian meal and a bottle of pinot noir?

The crusty bread they serve at Nick's is to-die-for. If you want to buy some, you'll have to drive 15 miles west to Willamina and Piontek's Breadworks, at 212 Northeast D Street, which also features baguettes and hearth-baked breads— wheat, rye, and challah. Get there before noon because they sell out early. Along the way, you may want to drop in at the Lawrence Gallery and Oregon Wine Tasting Room in Sheridan to view local art and sample local vintages.

Area Code: 503

DRIVING DIRECTIONS From Portland take Oregon 99W 40 miles southwest to McMinnville. Mileage for our suggested loop route is 35.

SIGHTSEEING *Chateau Benoit Winery,* 6580 Northeast Mineral Springs Road, Carlton, 864-2991, 864-3666. Daily 10 A.M. to 5 P.M. *Autumn Wind Vineyard,* 15225 North Valley Road, Gaston, 538-6931. April to November Saturday and Sunday noon to 5 P.M. *Elk Cove Vineyards Dundee Wine Cellar,* 691 Southwest Highway 99W, Dundee, 538-0991. Daily 10 A.M. to 5 P.M. *Lange Winery,* 18380 Northeast Buena Vista Road, Dundee, 538-6476. Call for appointment. *Cameron Winery,* 8200 Worden Hill Road, Dundee, 538-0336, 232-6652. Call for appointment. *Knudsen Erath,* Worden Hill Road, Dundee, 538-3318. Daily 11 A.M. to 5 P.M. *Sokol Blosser Winery,* Sokol Blosser Lane, Dundee, 864-2282. Daily 11 A.M. to 5 P.M. *Laube Orchards,* 18400 North Highway 99W, Dundee, 864-2672. Daily 9 A.M. to 5 P.M. *Lafayette Schoolhouse Antique Mall,* 748 Highway 99W, Lafayette, 864-2720. Daily 9 A.M. to 5 P.M. *The Eyrie Vineyards,* 935 East Tenth Street, McMinnville, 472-6315, 864-2410. Call for appointment. *Arterberry Winery,* 905 East Tenth Street, McMinnville, 472-1587, 244-0695. April to December daily noon to 5 P.M. *Lawrence Gallery,* Highway 18, Sheridan, 843-3633. Daily 10 A.M. to 5:30 P.M.

EVENTS *International Pinot Noir Celebration,* Linfield College Campus, McMinnville, 472-6196, late July. An afternoon of tasting more than 50 pinot noirs from several countries. *Yamhill County Fair,* McMinnville, 472-6196, early August. 4 days of traditional rural fair exhibits and events. *Wineries Open House,* 434-5814, Thanksgiving weekend. Wineries all over Oregon put on special displays and tastings for visitors.

LODGING *Safari Motel,* 345 North Highway 99W, McMinnville 97128, 472-5187. Good value, north end of town, $. *Flying M Ranch,* 23029 Northwest Flying M Ranch Road, Yamhill 97148, 662-3222. Full range of guest ranch activities, 28 rooms and 7 cabins in wooded foothills, $$. *Paragon Inn,* 2065 South Highway 99W, McMinnville 97218, 472-9493. Modest motel with swimming pool, laundry facilities, in town, $. *Steiger Haus* (bed and breakfast), 360 Wilson Street, McMinnville 97218, 472-0821. 3 guest rooms in contemporary home, 1 with fireplace, $$. *Youngberg Hill Farm Bed and Breakfast,* 10660 Southwest Youngberg, McMinnville 97128, 472-2727. 5 guest rooms, 2 with fireplaces, on 700-acre farm overlooking Willamette Valley, $$. *Mattey House* (bed and breakfast), 10221 Northeast Mattey Lane, McMinnville 97128, 434-5058. 4 guest rooms in 1890s Victorian house with its own small vineyard, $$.

CAMPING *Mulkey RV Park,* 14325 Southwest Highway 18, McMinnville 97128, 472-2475. 80 sites, about half with hookups, $10–$12.

DINING *Alice's Restaurant,* 976 Highway 99W, Dundee, 538-8224. Breakfast and lunch daily, 26 different kinds of hamburgers, $. *Alfie's Wayside Country Inn,* 1111 Highway 99W, Dundee, 538-9407. Lunch and dinner daily; wide-ranging menu including frogs' legs, veal chasseur, and quiche; $$. *Flying M Ranch* (see "Lodging"). Breakfast, lunch, and dinner daily, brunch Sunday; classic ranch menu of beef, chicken, and ribs includes roast buffalo; $$. *Roger's Seafood,* 2121 East Twenty-seventh Street, McMinnville, 472-0917. Dinner daily, seafood in nautical-theme restaurant, $$. *La Maison Surrette,* 729 East Third Street, McMinnville, 472-3787, 635-5836. Dinner Friday and Saturday, reservations required, French-style prix fixe meal served in restored Victorian home, $$. *Nick's Italian Cafe,* 521 East Third Street, McMinnville, 434-4471. Dinner Tuesday through Sunday, reservations advised; prix fixe Italian meals, extensive local wine list, probably the best restaurant in town; $$$. *Safari Restaurant* (in Safari Motel, see "Lodging"). Breakfast, lunch, and dinner daily; good choice for breakfast; $. *Mazatlan,* Highway 99W and McDonald Lane, McMinnville, 472-9771. Lunch and dinner daily; Mexican menu, good value; $. *Farmstead,* 319 North Baker Street, McMinnville, 472-8742. Breakfast, lunch, and dinner Monday to Saturday; barbecue specialties; $. *Country Cottage Restaurant,* 825 South Baker Street, Mc-

Minnville, 434-6249. Breakfast, lunch, and dinner daily; traditional American menu, good choice for breakfast; $.

FOR MORE INFORMATION Greater McMinnville Chamber of Commerce, 417 North Adams Street, McMinnville 97218, 472-6196.

Meandering Through the Willamette Valley

Once upon a time, before the advent of interstates, a system of U.S. highways crisscrossed the country bringing travelers to all the large cities and many of the smaller ones. You knew you were on a U.S. highway because a large shield with the highway number on it was displayed beside the road. Many of these highways were two lanes, widening to four lanes as they approached populated areas, then narrowing again as they left the towns behind. They were high-speed for the time—55 miles per hour maximum—and you could get off on the spur of the moment to pull up to a vegetable stand or (in California) a giant orange juice stand, or just to stop under a shade tree.

Most of those old highways are gone now, replaced by interstates, torn up by the bulldozers or truncated by more expedient routes. One of the best, however, still stretches along the Willamette Valley.

Oregon 99W lies west of Interstate 5 and leads from Portland to Eugene. Within our memory, this highway and its sister, U.S. 99E, were once the principal routes from the Pacific Northwest to California. Now, Oregon 99W is one of the most delightful routes in the Northwest, connecting Newberg, McMinnville, Monmouth, Corvallis, and Junction City with another dozen or so "wide spots" in the road. Newberg and McMinnville have been covered in previous sections; we're going to begin this Willamette Valley sojourn just south of McMinnville.

This is farming country, the rich land at the end of the Oregon Trail. As you head south, you pass through mile after mile of fields growing mint, hops, oats, beans, corn, cabbage, barley, wheat and alfalfa, bluegrass and ryegrass, peppermint, groves of hazelnut trees, orchards, and nurseries. Dozens of small roadside stands are scattered all along this route, and if you're traveling between June and October you can shop for a variety of fresh vegetables, local honey, jams and jellies, pickles, and other products, all reasonably priced. Local farm organizations have encouraged many farmers to label their crops with roadside signs so you can identify them. Jade green, purple, and white signs with a barn silhouette are marked "99W Scenic Route."

You can best savor this route at a leisurely pace, just meandering along and stopping when the mood strikes you. As one local bumper sticker sums it up: "Life begins at 40 miles per hour."

In the little town of Amity, stop first at the fire station, bank, or post office for a map and directions to the Brigittine Monastery, located about five miles west of town. The detour is a delightful experience.

Sixteen monks live in the large gray monastery set in a grove of trees and surrounded by fields of grain. If you're lucky, you'll arrive to the sound of male voices celebrating the liturgy of the hour in song, as the monks do seven times daily beginning at 4:30 A.M. They welcome visitors and will take you on a tour of the parts of the monastery that aren't cloistered, including a beautiful small church with stained-glass windows. The public is welcome to attend mass on Fridays and Sundays at 11:30 A.M. and on other days at various times depending on the schedule of visiting local priests. The monks support themselves by making candy, eleven different kinds of some of the richest, tastiest truffles and fudge you're likely to run across. You can purchase it at the monastery or at Made in Oregon stores.

Two wineries are located near Amity. Amity Vineyards, to the north, specializes in pinot noir, white riesling, chardonnay, gamay noir, gewürztraminer, and Oregon blush. Hidden Springs Winery, east of town in the Eola Hills, produces white riesling, pinot noir, chardonnay, pinot noir blanc, and Pacific Sunset. One of the Willamette Valley's diminutive ferries is located at Wheatland, about five miles east of Amity.

The valley is great bird-watching territory with scores of species resident here because of the abundant food—grain and insects—available. If you're traveling here in the fall especially, bring along binoculars and bird guidebooks for identifying the thousands of Canada geese and other waterfowl that make the valley a rest and feeding stop in their migrations along the Pacific Flyway. Two national wildlife refuges just off Highway 99W offer rewarding and convenient bird-watching. Baskett Slough National Wildlife Refuge lies near the junction of Highways 99W and 22 south of McCoy. William L. Finley National Wildlife Refuge is located between Corvallis and Monroe. Both have signed trails that lead to good observation points near fields, marshes, or ponds.

Detour east on Highway 22 for about four miles to the Harrison Brunk House, built in 1861 and now operated as a museum by the Polk County Historical Society. The big two-story clapboard house, with its wide front porch and overhanging balcony, is typical of homes built by the more prosperous of the valley's early settlers. It's furnished with period pieces including brass beds, a rolltop desk, a treadle sewing machine, and portraits of the original owners.

Turn south on Highway 51 to return to the main route via the towns of Independence and Monmouth, named by their pioneer founders after the Midwestern towns they came from—Independence, Missouri, and Monmouth, Illinois. The Heritage Museum in Independence is located in an 1888 Baptist church. The Paul Jensen Arctic Museum in Monmouth features more than 3,000 cultural items from Indians and Eskimos of the far north. If you're in the mood for a picnic, stop at Riverview Park in Independence, with a vintage railroad caboose and lawns and picnic tables fronting on the Willamette River. Wooded Helmick State Park, on Highway 99W five miles south of Monmouth, is another good choice for a picnic.

While you're in Independence, don't miss Taylor's Fountain and Gifts, an old-fashioned ice-cream parlor at 296 Main Street. Sit up at the counter on one of the 17 red stools and read the menu, which proclaims, "It's great to be alive and live in Independence, Oregon, the nicest place in the world." Choose from banana splits, shakes, sodas, floats, phosphates, and sarsaparilla. Taylor's is open Monday through Saturday 7 A.M. to 6 P.M., Sunday 8 A.M. to 6 P.M.

Seven miles south of Monmouth, Airlie Road leads six miles west to the little community of Airlie. Just south of town, on Dunn Forest Road, Airlie Winery and Serendipity Cellars Winery are open to visitors. Serendipity makes Muller-Thürgau, chenin blanc, chardonnay, cabernet sauvignon, zinfandel, and the award-winning Marechal Foch. Airlie makes riesling, gewürztraminer, and pinot noir.

Corvallis, population 45,000, is the largest city on this route and your best choice for an overnight stop. Home of Oregon State University, it's a pleasant place with a comfortable small-town feeling, yet it's big enough to offer a variety of restaurants and lodgings.

Spend some time touring the university. You can pick up a self-guided walking tour brochure at the information kiosk at Fourteenth and Jefferson streets. The Horner Museum has exhibits on natural science, world cultures, and history. Fairbanks Gallery, in Fairbanks Hall; Guistina Gallery, in LaSells Stewart Center; and the Memorial Union Concourse Gallery all have displays of fine art, both traditional and contemporary. The photogenic Irish Bend Covered Bridge spanning Oak Creek is located on the bike path just west of the OSU campus.

Downtown, the landmark Benton County Courthouse, built in 1888, is a classic Victorian building complete with clock tower. You can pick up a self-guiding walking tour brochure of the historic downtown at the convention and visitors bureau. Corvallis Art Center, housed in an 1889 church at Seventh and Madison streets, features a central gallery with wood-beamed ceiling and arched windows. The sales shop offers a good selection of crafts and fine arts by Oregon artisans and artists.

Assuming you're spending Saturday night in Corvallis, there are a couple of short excursions you should consider on Sunday morning before you head back to Portland. One leads farther down the Willamette Valley through rural landscapes and the small towns of Peoria, where there's a delightful riverside park, and Harrisburg, where you may see Mennonite women on the streets in long dresses and bonnets, to Coburg (see "Eugene") and Interstate 5. Follow Highway 34 east from Corvallis and just after you cross the Willamette River, turn south onto Peoria Road. About ten miles north of Harrisburg, watch for American Drive and an unmarked dirt road on the opposite (west) side of Peoria Road. Pine Grove Cemetery, one of the oldest in Oregon, with graves dating from 1853, lies about half a mile down this road.

The other route leads west on U.S. 20 to Philomath, Wren, and two of Benton County's three covered bridges. The Harris bridge, built in 1929, is located on Harris Road, 2½ miles west of Wren. Just beyond Philomath turn southwest on Highway 34 and follow it to Alsea, about 19 miles. Hayden covered bridge (circa 1918) spans the Alsea River, about 1½ miles west of town. Between Philomath and Alsea, you'll pass the spur road that leads up 4,097-foot Mary's Peak, highest in the Coast Range. There are several good hiking trails around its slopes, and its summit provides picnickers with sweeping views of the Willamette Valley and flanking mountains. In Philomath, the Benton County Historical Museum in the 1867 Philomath College Building has some excellent historical and art exhibits, but if you're traveling on Sunday, you'll have to wait until afternoon to visit; it opens at 1 P.M.

Area Code: 503

DRIVING DIRECTIONS To reach Amity and the start of this excursion, you can follow Highway 99W south from Portland through Newberg and McMinnville. A slightly longer, but quicker, route takes you via I-5 to Salem, then Highway 22 west to Rickreall, where you backtrack approximately 13 miles north to Amity. The round trip from Portland to Corvallis, not including detours, is 162 miles.

SIGHTSEEING *Brigittine Monastery,* 23300 Walker Lane, Amity, 835-8080. The monastery is open to visitors most hours daily, but courtesy dictates you call before you go to avoid disrupting religious activities. *Amity Vineyards,* 18150 Amity Vineyards Road Southeast, Amity, 835-2362. June to October daily noon to 5 P.M. November to May weekends only. *Hidden Springs Winery,* 9360 Southeast Eola Hills Road, Amity, 835-2782. March to November Saturday and Sunday noon to 5 P.M. *Harrison Brunk House,* Highway 22, Rickreall, 623-4643. June to September Wednesday 9 A.M. to noon, Saturday and Sunday 1 to 5 P.M. Free. *Heritage Museum,* Third and B streets, Independence, 838-4989. Wednesday and Saturday 1 to 5 P.M., Thursday and Friday 1 to 4 P.M. Free. *Paul Jensen Arctic Museum,* 590 West Church Street, Monmouth, 838-1220. Tuesday to Saturday 10 A.M. to 4 P.M. Free. *Airlie Winery,* 15305 Dunn Forest Road, Monmouth, 838-6013.

March to December Saturday and Sunday noon to 5 P.M. *Serendipity Cellars Winery,* 15275 Dunn Forest Road, Monmouth, 838-4284. May to October Wednesday to Monday noon to 6 P.M. November to April Saturday and Sunday. *Horner Museum,* Gill Coliseum, Oregon State University, Corvallis, 754-2951. Tuesday to Friday 10 A.M. to 5 P.M., Saturday 10 A.M. to 2 P.M., Sunday 2 to 5 P.M., closed Saturday in summer. Donation. *Oregon State University galleries,* 737-4745: *Fairbanks Gallery,* Fairbanks Hall, Monday to Friday 8 A.M. to 5 P.M.; *Guistina Gallery,* LaSells Stewart Center, Monday to Friday 8 A.M. to 5 P.M.; *Memorial Union Concourse Gallery,* Monday to Sunday 8 A.M. to 11 P.M. All are free. *Corvallis Art Center,* 700 Southwest Madison Street, Corvallis, 754-1551. Tuesday to Sunday noon to 5 P.M. Free. *Benton County Historical Museum,* 1101 Main Street, Philomath, 929-6230. Tuesday to Saturday 10 A.M. to 4:30 P.M., Sunday 1 to 4:30 P.M. Free.

EVENTS *Festival Corvallis,* 754-1551, mid-July. Series of indoor and outdoor concert performances. *Da Vinci Days,* Corvallis, 757-1544, second half of July. Festival celebrates art, science, and technology.

LODGING *Grand Manor Inn,* 925 Northwest Garfield Street, Corvallis 97339; 758-8571. New hotel close to downtown, $$–$$$. *Motel Orleans,* 935 Northwest Garfield Street, Corvallis 97339, 758-9125. Another new hotel close to downtown, $. *Nendel's Inn,* 1550 Northwest Ninth Street, Corvallis 97339, 753-9151. Large motor inn features jogging track, restaurant, $$. *Huntington Manor* (bed and breakfast), 3555 Northwest Harrison Boulevard, Corvallis 97330, 753-3735. 3 elegant guest rooms upstairs in vintage Williamsburg Colonial home in quiet neighborhood near university, $$. *The Hanson Country Inn* (bed and breakfast), 795 Southwest Hanson Street, Corvallis 97333, 752-2919. 4 guest rooms in 1928 home on 5-acre estate, near university, $$. *Madison Inn* (bed and breakfast), 660 Madison Avenue, Corvallis 97330, 757-1274. 7 guest rooms in 5-story Tudor home near university, $$. *Davidson House* (bed and breakfast), 887 Monmouth Street, Independence 97351, 838-3280. 2 guest rooms in 1880s Gothic Revival farmhouse, $.

CAMPING *Corvallis–Albany KOA,* 33775 Oakville Road, Albany, 5 miles east of Corvallis, 967-8521. 53 sites, about half with full hookups, $12–$15.50.

DINING *Veracruz Cafe,* 226 South Main Street, Independence, 838-1348. Breakfast, lunch, and early dinner Monday to Saturday; simple Mexican menu, specialty coffees; $. *The Class Reunion,* 777 Northwest Ninth Street, Corvallis, 757-1700. Lunch and dinner daily; casual dining for seafood, salads, pasta, and beef in spacious loft of rebuilt cannery downtown; $$. *Papagayo,* 550 Northwest Harrison Street, Corvallis, 757-8188. Lunch and dinner daily, Mexican menu, $$.

Michael's Landing, 603 Northwest Second Street, Corvallis, 754-6141. Lunch and dinner daily, brunch Sunday, in former railroad depot overlooking Willamette River, $$. *The Gables,* 1121 Northwest Ninth Street, Corvallis, 752-3364. City's most upscale restaurant, American menu, large portions, $$. *Oscar's,* 559 Northwest Monroe Street, Corvallis, 753-7444. Breakfast and lunch Monday to Saturday, brunch Sunday, dinner Tuesday to Sunday; good spot for big breakfasts; $.

FOR MORE INFORMATION Corvallis Convention & Visitors Bureau, 420 Northwest Second Street, Corvallis 97330, 757-1544.

Eugene: Bicycling Capital of the Northwest

Several years ago, *New West* magazine devoted an issue to the best cities in the West. In the mid-size population category—between 75,000 and 300,000—Eugene, Oregon, was number one. "The residents of Eugene," said *New West,* "believe it's not simply the best in its category, or the West, but the best place to live in America." Now, according to the 1990 *Money* magazine study of the best places to live, Eugene ranks sixth nationally and was the only Oregon city to make the top ten.

If you're looking for a weekend that combines culture with some outdoor activity, and you want to get out of town without spending a lot of time on the road, there's no better choice than Eugene. The same things that make it so livable make it a good place to visit.

Just two hours south of Portland, this city of 110,000 people seems to have it all. It's ideally located just at the point where the Willamette Valley gives way to the foothills. It straddles one river, the Willamette, and is adjacent to another, the McKenzie. One of the reasons Eugene is consistently ranked among the best small cities in the country is because of what it has done to preserve open space. Parks and greenways abound, with jogging and bicycle paths along the river and out into the countryside. The University of Oregon's lovely green campus lies close to a downtown that is not dominated by automobiles. Some of the streets have even been closed off into pedestrian malls.

Eugene is devoted to the bicycle, which is one of the best ways to get around the city. That's what the locals do. In fact, thousands of people here bicycle to work regardless of the weather. One locally popular T-shirt is emblazoned with "Last year in Oregon, 677 people fell off their bikes and drowned!"

Eugene is a biker's paradise. The terrain is relatively flat, and a network of designated bicycle paths crisscrosses the city. In addition, most streets have bicycle lanes. Paths line both sides of the Willamette River. Three pedestrian-bicycle bridges cross the river, versus just two for cars. Bicycle touring of the adjacent Willamette Valley is popular, and several Eugene tour operators lead groups that overnight at bed-and-breakfast inns. You can get details from the convention and visitors bureau. The place to rent a bicycle is Pedal Power, downtown at 535 High Street across from the Fifth Street Market. Rates are $2.50 per hour, $12 per day, or $15 for 24 hours. They have tandems and mountain bikes as well. At least one of the major hotels, Valley River Inn, rents bikes to its guests. You can obtain lists of tour operators and bike rentals and a bicycle map of the city ($3) at the Eugene–Springfield Convention & Visitors Bureau. The map is plasticized for all-weather use.

If you've started your weekend in Eugene by overnighting on Friday, rise early on Saturday and head for the Saturday Market at Eighth and Oak streets downtown to watch the vendors set up their stalls. Open from April through December, and a forerunner of Portland's Saturday Market, this market is where artists and craftspeople display and sell their works, from high-quality jewelry and ceramics to sculpture, painting, weaving, and food products. You may think you've stepped back into the 60s. The counterculture is alive and well in Eugene, and the market is a magnet for former flower children, many of whom look just about like they did 20 years ago, except their hair is a bit grayer.

Nearby, Fifth Street Public Market is a delightful collection of more than 70 shops, food stores, and a dozen restaurants housed in a 1929 chicken processing facility. Focal point of the three-story building is a brick fountain in the center courtyard surrounded by pots of brightly colored flowers. It's a people place. You're apt to hear musicians performing and see patrons reading their newspapers at outdoor tables. The crafts area features artists who work with glass, clay, leather, wood, silver, fibers, and other mediums. In dozens of shops you'll find everything from mandolins, balalaikas, and folk harps (at Balladeer Music) to Key lime pie and Amaretto cheesecake (at the Metropol Bakery). Try a belt-bursting breakfast at *Terry's Diner.* Their specialty is imaginative omelets such as the Swisshroom, with Swiss cheese and mushrooms, and Rancheros Supreme, consisting of cheddar, green pepper, mushrooms, onions, avocado, hot salsa, sour cream, and olives. Shops are open daily from 10 A.M. to 6 P.M.

While you're in the neighborhood, wander down by the railroad depot to discover the handsome old Oregon Electric Station, now a restaurant. Across the street the powder blue Lane Building houses Escape Books, which specializes in science fiction, fantasy, and mystery, and the Monster Cookie Company, named for the size of their peanut butter, Tollhouse, chocolate chip, and oatmeal delights. They also prepare a superb drink for a cold day, called a "steamer," consisting of steamed milk combined with vanilla, hazelnut or chocolate mint flavoring. Just up the street, at Fifth and Willamette streets, the Smith Family

Bookstore and Delbert's Cafe combine in the same room to allow you to browse your favorite volumes while having lunch or a cup of coffee.

The University of Oregon's 250-acre campus is a must-see. Big trees (2,000 varieties), spacious lawns, and handsome old stone buildings make this a tranquil place to stroll or cycle. Be sure to see ivy-covered Deady and Villards halls, both built in 1876; the Museum of Art, with its fine Murray Warner Oriental collection and a Northwest collection; and the Museum of Natural History. Two giant bronze statues on the campus depict a pioneer mother and father. Legend has it that if you flip a coin into the lap of the mother on your way to final exams and the coin stays put, you're going to do well.

Two other museums in Eugene make worthwhile stops. At WISTEC (Willamette Science and Technology Center), across from the university's Autzen Stadium, youngsters can measure their energy output on a bicycle generator and take tests for color blindness and peripheral vision.

The Lane County Museum, next to the Lane County Fairgrounds, displays a collection of historical memorabilia including an elegant 1890 hearse.

It won't be difficult to decide what to do for evening entertainment. Just check what's going on at "The Hult."

The Hult Center for the Performing Arts, a multiroofed glass and concrete structure, is quite remarkable. Not only is it one of the finest theaters in the Northwest, it was built totally by Eugenians, who voted a bond issue for its construction and raised the rest of the money through private contributions. Performances here are worthy of any major city stage.

The handsome lobby, with its green floral carpeting and 70-foot-high Douglas fir columns, has the feel of a Northwest coniferous forest. The building also houses "please touch" artwork, most of it by Oregon artists. Groups of masks decorate the walls on each level. We especially like the masks of six black female jazz singers which include one of Billie Holiday with a rose and a tear. Whimsical green frogs with bulging eyes atop concrete columns at the Sixth Street entrance are sure to bring a smile to your face.

Two halls cater to different needs. Soreng Theater, with seating for 493, is modernistic and functional, and is most often used for plays and small musical performances. Silva Concert Hall, seating 2,503, is reminiscent of an eighteenth-century baroque European opera house. Its two outstanding features are the curved basket-weave ceiling and the ethereal stage curtain silk-screened by two local artists. Here you can see symphony, ballet, opera, and performances by nationally known artists.

If you're looking for simple dining close to the theater, try Poppi's Anatolia. The menu is Greek and Indian and the character of the place is expressed by a note on the menu that reads, "As much as possible we use organic local produce and only free-range eggs. And, if you raise chickens, ask us for the leftovers."

When you arise Sunday morning, climb into your car or on your bike and head for Coburg, about seven miles north on the Coburg Road. It's a gem of historical architecture, with more than 60 percent of the homes dating from before World War I. Once a lumber mill town, it was named by a local blacksmith for his favorite horse. All this is delightful, but the real reason you go to Coburg on a Sunday morning is to have breakfast at the Coburg Cafe. It's a little hole-in-the-wall sort of place—nine seats at the counter and three tables—where the locals gather, including a group of men who play cards every morning in the back room. The breakfast specialty of the house is the garbage omelet, a concoction of eight eggs, ham, bacon, sausage, mushrooms, onions, bell peppers, two kinds of cheese, and sliced tomatoes, served with hash browns and toast, all for $10.50.

Eugene's top natural treasure is the McKenzie River, flowing swift and icy from the Cascades east of town. And a quiet Sunday morning is an ideal time for a drive up the McKenzie River Road, Oregon 126.

Shortly after you leave the outskirts of Springfield behind, road, river, and valley come together in a narrow course pointed straight into the mountains. You drive so close to the river you can almost reach out and touch it in places, and lush green foliage closes in on all sides. You're likely to see a curious wooden boat with high, pointed bow and stern carrying anglers down the river while they cast into the shallows or troll through the deeps. Such boats are indigenous to this river and are called McKenzie River Dories. If you get a chance to look at one up close, you'll see that these boats are works of art, with hundreds of individual pieces of wood cut and shaped to make their graceful curves. Generations of river guides and fishermen have used them and, these days, people come from all over the country to have them custom-built by the master boat builders who construct just one boat at a time. (One boat builder, Whitewater Woodworks, on Highway 126 2½ miles east of Walterville, welcomes guests to come and watch when they're open.) The unusual design, with its high sides and ends, is especially suited to the white water on the McKenzie. The high sides help keep waves from swamping the boat as it moves through rapids, and the high ends mean there is little bottom surface in contact with the river, making it easy for the boatman, seated in the center, to turn the craft on its axis with two oars. You can run the McKenzie's white water with any of the many licensed guides, who use either dories or rafts. The season begins in April and lasts through midsummer. The Eugene Springfield Convention & Visitors Bureau can supply a complete list of guides.

Probably the most photographed covered bridge in Oregon is the Goodpasture (1938), spanning the river 22 miles east of Eugene and 1 mile west of Vida. At Rainbow detour onto McKenzie River Drive and follow it to the intersection with King Road to view the Belknap Covered Bridge (1966).

If you've brought a picnic lunch to eat beside the river, try Ben and Kay Dorris

State Park, 31 miles east of Eugene on Highway 126. Another good choice for lunch is the Whitewater Cafe in Blue River, a favorite breakfast gathering spot for rafters and fishermen.

If you continue on Highway 126, you'll eventually reach Bend, but if you're returning to Portland on the same day, the little town of McKenzie Bridge, 53 miles east of Eugene, is probably a good place to turn around. Beyond there the highway begins its climb to 5,325-foot McKenzie Pass.

Area Code: 503

DRIVING DIRECTIONS The round trip from Portland to Eugene is 220 miles via Interstate 5.

RAIL TRANSPORTATION *Amtrak* serves Eugene with the daily *Coast Starlight* between Seattle, Portland, San Francisco, and Los Angeles.

AIR TRANSPORTATION Eugene is served by *American Airlines, Horizon Air, United Airlines,* with flights from Portland, San Francisco, and Midwest cities.

SIGHTSEEING *Oregon University museums*: Art, 686-3027, Wednesday to Sunday noon to 5 P.M., free; Natural History, 686-3024, Wednesday to Sunday noon to 5 P.M., free. *Willamette Science and Technology Center* (WISTEC), 2300 Centennial Boulevard, 484-9027. June, July, and August, noon to 6 P.M. Other months reduced hours. Adults $2, seniors and college students $1.50, 4–11 $1, $1 more on weekends. *Lane County Historical Museum,* 740 West Thirteenth Avenue, 687-4239. Tuesday to Friday 10 A.M. to 4 P.M., Saturday and Sunday 11 A.M. to 4 P.M. Adults $1, seniors 75 cents, under 18 50 cents. *Kerns Art Center,* 1910 East Fifteenth Avenue. 345-1571. Monday to Saturday 10 A.M. to 5 P.M., Sunday 1 to 5 P.M. $1. *Hult Center for the Performing Arts,* Willamette Street between Sixth and Seventh avenues, 687-5000 for performance and ticket information. Guided 1-hour tours, reservations required, phone for times 687-5087. *McKenzie River Rafting: Downstream Discoveries,* 1864½ Moss Street, Eugene 97403, 484-9763; *Sierra Whitewater Expeditions,* P.O. Box 1330, Springfield 97477, (800) 937-7300; *Oregon Whitewater Adventures,* 660 Kelly Boulevard, Springfield 97477, 746-5422; *Spencer Guide Service* (fishing also), 656 North Seventy-first Street, Springfield 97478, 747-8153.

EVENTS *Oregon Bach Festival,* 687-5000, Eugene, last week in June and first week in July. 2 weeks of classical performances in the Hult Center. *Summer Park Concerts,* Eugene, 687-5303, July. Delightful series of concerts, many of them outdoors. *Eugene Festival of Musical Theater,* the Hult Center, July. 345-0028, theater, performances.

LODGING *Best Western New Oregon,* 1655 Franklin Boulevard, Eugene 97440, 683-3669. Well-run motel near UofO campus, indoor pool, 2 saunas, 2 racquetball courts, $$. *Eugene Hilton,* 66 East Sixth Street, Eugene 97401, 342-2000. 275-room hotel adjacent to Hult Center, restaurant, indoor pool, $$$. *Red Lion Inn,* 205 Coburg Road, Eugene 97401, 342-5021. Restaurant, convenient to freeway, $$–$$$. *Valley River Inn,* 1000 Valley River Way, Eugene 97401, 687-0123. Located right on the Willamette River with access to bicycle, jogging, and walking paths, $$$–$$$$. *Campus Cottage* (bed and breakfast), 1134 East Nineteenth Avenue, Eugene 97403, 342-5346. Cozy, antiques-furnished home 1 block from university campus, $$. *Mapletree Inn* (bed and breakfast), 412 East Thirteenth Avenue, Eugene 97401, 344-8807. Victorian home in heart of West University Historic District, $$. *The Shelley Guest House* (bed and breakfast), 1546 Charnelton Street, Eugene 97401, 683-2062. 2 large guest rooms in 1928 home with garden, $–$$. *McGillivray's Log Home Bed & Breakfast,* 88680 Evers Road, Elmira 97437, 935-3564. Unusual log home with wood-burning stove, on 5 wooded acres, $–$$.

CAMPING *Eugene KOA,* west of I-5 Exit 199, 343-4832. 144 sites with hookups, $12–14.50. *Sherwood Forest KOA,* Creswell exit 182 from I-5, ½ block west on Oregon Avenue, 895-4110. 126 sites, 104 full hookups, $10–$17. *Patio RV Park,* 6½ miles east of Blue River off Highway 126, 822-3596. 40 full hookups, 25 water-electricity, $10. Superb site right on the McKenzie River.

DINING *Terry's Diner,* Fifth Street Public Market, 683-8196. Breakfast, lunch, and dinner daily; known for burgers, omelets; $. *Chanterelle,* 207 East Fifth Avenue, 484-4065. Lunch Tuesday to Friday, dinner Tuesday to Saturday; European-style cuisine, one of Eugene's best; $$. *Coburg Cafe,* 230 North Willamette Street, Coburg, 342-3828. Breakfast and lunch daily; known for their breakfasts, served all day; $. *Holiday Farm,* 54455 McKenzie River Drive, Blue River, 822-3715. Breakfast, lunch, and dinner daily; a special place with breakfast or lunch beside the McKenzie River, dinner in Farmhouse Restaurant, reservations required; $$. *Oregon Electric Station,* 27 East Fifth Avenue, 485-4444. Lunch Monday to Friday, dinner daily, brunch Sunday; prime rib, fish, and salad bar in historic train station and railroad cars; $$. *Poppi's Anatolia,* 992 Willamette Street, 343-9661. Lunch Monday to Friday, dinner daily; ethnic restaurant specializing in Greek and Indian food; $$. *The River Room,* Valley River Inn (see "Lodging"). 341-3462. Breakfast, lunch, and dinner daily; fine dining overlooking the Willamette River; $$–$$$.

FOR MORE INFORMATION Eugene–Springfield Convention & Visitors Bureau, 305 West Seventh Avenue, Eugene 97440, (800) 547-5445 (outside OR), (800) 452-3670 (in OR).

In the Heart of Covered Bridge Country

You don't have to look much beyond an Oregon highway map to realize the tremendous legacy the pioneers from New England and New York left to the Willamette Valley. The place names alone—Portland, Salem, Albany, Springfield—are a revealing litany of the homesick transplants. If you poke about the Willamette Valley towns, you'll also note the predominance of neat white-steepled Protestant churches, trim gabled clapboard or board-and-batten houses, brick business buildings, town squares (sometimes with a bandstand), and wool and flour mills. Perhaps the most curious legacy is the covered bridge. Nowhere else outside of New England were so many covered bridges built. And, curiously enough, they were not built in any great numbers in adjacent Washington and northern California, whose rainy coastal conditions are similar to Oregon's.

The weekend we suggest in this section takes you into the heart of Oregon's covered bridge country, where in addition to these handsome old structures you'll discover some of the best examples of the pioneer legacy in the state. We suggest you base yourself in either Salem or Albany and make excursions from there, setting aside enough time to see the attractions in those cities as well. Though accommodations and restaurants in Salem and Albany are somewhat limited, they represent a virtual plethora of choices compared to what's available in most of the small towns.

Covered bridges are romantic anachronisms, some of the few reminders of a time when life was slower and simpler. Their wooden decks once echoed to the clip-clop of horses' hooves and the rumble of wagon wheels. Known as "kissing bridges" in the East, they were favorite spots for "spooning" in the days before the sexual revolution.

The state's first covered bridge was constructed at Oregon City in 1851. By 1925, about 450 of them spanned Oregon streams. Later, when the early roads graded for horse-drawn vehicles were widened from their original 16 feet to handle two-way motorized traffic and heavier loads, many of the old bridges were torn down.

Oregon still has 53 of the charming old structures spanning creeks and rivers and the back roads west of the Cascades, the largest remaining concentration west of the Mississippi. Linn County, east of Albany, has seven of them and two others are located east of Salem.

The oldest existing in Oregon today date from the time of World War I, with most having been built in the 1920s and 1930s. All of the roads they carry are now little used, and some bridges have been preserved intact but without connecting approaches as new roads bypassed them. The bridges were originally covered to protect them from the wet and freezing weather in an era before creosoted and chemically treated lumber was available. Timber was handy and inexpensive and the sheathing often doubled the life of the bridge. In some instances bridge timbers even gained strength as they aged.

Though no two of the remaining bridges are identical, most are sturdy, wood, Howe truss designs. Their appearance varies from county to county, but all have signs identifying them by name and with the date they were built. Some have rounded portals, some square or angled ones. Some have solid walls, either vertical or flaring toward the bottom; others have windows or open sides that enable drivers to see approaching traffic when the road curves just beyond the bridge, and small boys use them for diving platforms above the old swimming hole.

When you come upon these bridges, take the time to get out of your car and savor their nostalgia. Youngsters especially delight in exploring their dim interiors and listening for the echoes of footsteps and voices. Some of the handsome bridges are obscured by foliage during the summer months, making good camera angles difficult, but the rest of the year you can photograph them through bare branches.

Between Salem and Albany, the loop route to the east off I-5 provides access to seven of them; plan on spending about three hours to cover this loop. Some of the bridges can be a bit difficult to find so don't hesitate to ask directions locally. Valley residents are used to encountering tourists looking for covered bridges. There are also two free publications that will help. One is distributed by the Covered Bridge Society of Oregon and details all the state's bridges; it's available in most visitor information centers or by writing the society (see "For More Information"). The other provides a map and data on the covered bridges near Albany and is distributed by that city's convention and visitors bureau.

Detour onto Oregon 22 (North Santiam Highway) and follow it 11 miles to Stayton. The 18-by-90-foot Jordan Bridge (1937), which was moved here from Thomas Creek in Linn County, connects Pioneer and Wilderness parks in Stayton.

Continue another 11 miles east on Highway 22 to Mehama. Turn southwest on Oregon 226 and continue through Lyons and Jordan to view the 105-foot-long Hannah Bridge (1936), which crosses Thomas Creek on Camp Morrison Drive. This bridge is one of those unusual designs with the sides exposed. Keep to the north bank of the creek as you head west on Highway 226 and follow Shimanek Bridge Drive to its namesake bridge, distinctive for its red paint and louvered windows.

Larwood Bridge is a bit out of your way, so you can skip it if you're in a hurry. If not, follow Richardson Gap Road south to Larwood Drive, then turn east to the bridge near the confluence of Roaring River and Crabtree Creek. There's an old waterwheel here as well as a shaded picnic spot beside the road.

Backtrack now via Larwood Drive and Richardson Gap Road to Highway 226 and take it west to the little community of Scio. Just west of town on Goar Road, Gilkey Bridge (1939), another open-sided structure, spans Thomas Creek. Continue south on Goar and Gilkey roads until you intersect Highway 226, turn east into Crabtree and left again onto Hungry Hill Drive on the north side of town. The Hoffman Bridge (1936) across Crabtree Creek is a classic design with flared skirts, Gothic-style windows, and suspended approaches painted a dazzling white.

The last bridge lies just on the outskirts of Albany. Bohemian Hall Bridge (1947) was moved from Crabtree Creek to its present location over Cox Creek. To reach it continue west on Highway 226 and U.S. 20 until you reach Price Road about two miles east of I-5. Turn north on Price Road.

Albany was founded by two brothers, Walter and Thomas Monteith, who named it for their hometown in New York. During the second half of the nineteenth century, the city grew and prospered as a commercial center at the confluence of the Calapooia and Willamette rivers. More than 500 of the original residences and business buildings, many of them handsome old Victorians, still stand. The city has three historic districts and claims more historic buildings per capita than any other town in Oregon. Albany also has an astonishing six public rose gardens. You can pick up free walking-tour maps of the historic buildings and gardens from the historic information gazebo at the corner of Ellsworth Street and Eighth Avenue. Many of the Victorian homes are open to the public annually on the last Saturday in July and the second Sunday in December. Horse-drawn carriage tours of the city are sometimes available from the Fourth of July weekend to the Labor Day weekend; check with the convention and visitors bureau for details.

But Albany is probably best known for its annual World Championship Timber Carnival, a rip-snortin' event that is the best of its kind in the country. Few events are as typically Northwest as this, the logging show. Like the rodeo, the logging show evolved from the working skills of loggers. Back in the days when timber was felled with ax and handsaw and teams of oxen supplied the horsepower, loggers in remote forest camps began competing to amuse themselves on off-duty Sundays. Today, chain saws and mechanical cutters have replaced the handsaw, diesel trucks haul the logs, and most loggers commute to the woods from homes in town, but the old skills are kept alive in shows like the Timber Carnival.

Main events, all held outdoors in a natural amphitheater just east of I-5, fall into five general categories—chopping, bucking (sawing), log rolling, ax throwing, and climbing. Professionals supply their own gleaming and perfectly balanced axes for the chopping events, the blades so sharp they must be carried in specially padded boxes to avoid dulling. Standing astride a 14-inch-diameter log and slicing within inches of his feet, a veteran axeman can cut it through in less than 30 seconds.

Brute force is needed in the bucking event, where loggers use old handsaws, known as "misery whips," to cut through logs in record time. Log rolling is a descendant of the early-day log drives on the rivers of the Northeast, and its object is to topple your opponent from a floating, spinning log. Losers go for a swim.

The climbing events are the heart stoppers of the show. Two 100-foot-tall spar trees are erected side by side. In the speed contests, climbers using tree-encircling belts and spikes affixed to their caulked boots race to the top, ring a bell, and drop down again. Record times for the round trip are just over 30 seconds, and the fastest climbers will touch the tree only half a dozen times on the descent, free-falling for 15 or 20 feet at a time. In the topping event, the climber must saw completely through the tree once he has reached the top.

Salem, Oregon's state capital and third largest city, has more than enough attractions to keep you occupied for an entire weekend. But assuming you've already toured the covered bridges and spent some time in Albany on Saturday, we recommend you just hit the Salem highlights on Sunday.

You can stretch your legs with a walk through the wooded campus of Willamette University, bounded by Twelfth, State, Winter, and Trade streets downtown. Founded in 1842, it's the oldest university in the West. Waller Hall here dates from 1867. Mark O. Hatfield Library honors the former university president who went on to become Oregon's senior senator.

One of the oldest cities in the state, Salem boasts more than two dozen structures listed in the National Register of Historic Places. Most are located in a compact nine-square-block area around the capitol and are easy to see on foot. The handsome white Vermont marble capitol building is open to visitors. Shunning Greco-Roman columns, domes, and other traditional capitol styles, Oregon designed its capitol to reflect the period in which it was built, 1936 to 1938. Massive sculptures beside the north entrance depict the covered wagon era and explorers Lewis and Clark. The huge bronze-and-gold statue surmounting the tower represents the Oregon pioneer. Inside, splendid murals on the walls of the rotunda and above the main stairs depict Oregon's history and industry.

Across Twelfth Street to the east, Mission Mill Village preserves the big red-brick buildings of the Thomas Kay Woolen Mill, now a woolen museum. Built in

1889, the mill produced fine wool blankets and fabrics for 70 years. Guided tours show the step-by-step process from picking the fleece to shipping the finished product. There are also several other historic buildings on the 4½-acre grounds. The white clapboard Jason Lee House (1841) was built the year before Lee founded Willamette University. Locals say it is the oldest known wood frame house in the Northwest. You can tour the house, as well as the Methodist Mission Parsonage (1841) and the John D. Boon House (1847). While you're at the Village, browse through the arts and crafts shops adjacent. There's also a deli where you can pick up a picnic lunch then dine with the ducks beside the pleasant mill stream that meanders through the village.

Deepwood Estate, a marvelous old mansion in the Queen Anne Victorian style, sits amid two acres of gardens just a few blocks away at Twelfth and Mission streets. The mansion and adjacent carriage house were built by a prominent Salem doctor in 1894 and reflect all the architectural opulence of the period.

Salem's historical crown jewel is Bush Pasture Park, once the country estate of Asahel Bush, a prominent citizen of the 1870s. His Victorian country mansion perches on a low hilltop from which, it's easy to imagine, he must have had an imperial view of the fledgling city, pastures, and orchards spread below. The grounds are now a 100-acre public park with some of the oldest trees in the West and rose gardens that are among the most beautiful in the Northwest. The estate's barn has been converted into a working art center where you can see exhibits by regional artists and craftspeople.

The Bush House is one of the best examples of Victoriana in this part of the country. Built in 1878 in Victorian Italianate style, the home incorporates such innovations as a central heating system, a gas-generating system for illumination, and lavatories in all the upstairs bedrooms. There are also ten marble fireplaces and a wood-burning kitchen stove built by the inmates of the state penitentiary. The home is completely furnished in the period and much of the original wallpaper remains.

If you have children along, consider cutting short this historical sightseeing and spending a couple of hours at Enchanted Forest, a storybook theme park. We usually shun these sorts of places and rank most of them in the ripoff category, but this one is an exception. It's a delight. The park was the dream of Roger Tofte, an Oregon State Highways employee and father of four who bought some property just off the freeway, then spent seven years developing it. You can walk into the open jaw of a witch's head, crawl down a rabbit hole like Alice in Wonderland, and make your way through a wonderfully scary haunted house. Enchanted Forest is an experience that kindles the imagination and makes you wish you were a kid again.

Area Code: 503

DRIVING DIRECTIONS Salem and Albany are both located on Interstate 5, 47 and 69 miles south of Portland, respectively. The suggested covered bridge loop will add about another 60 miles to your trip.

SIGHTSEEING *Chuck's Jet Tours,* 928-2200. Willamette River historical tours by boat. *State Capitol,* between Court and State streets, 378-4423. Monday to Friday 8 A.M. to 5 P.M., Saturday 9 A.M. to 4 P.M., Sunday noon to 4 A.M. Tours Memorial Day to Labor Day hourly Monday to Saturday 9 A.M. to 3 P.M. *Mission Mill Village,* 1313 Mill Street Southeast, 585-7012. Year-round Tuesday to Saturday 10 A.M. to 4:30 P.M., May through September Sunday 1 to 4:30 P.M. Adults $2, 12–18 and seniors $1.50, 6–11 $1. *Deepwood Estate,* 1116 Mission Street, 363-1825. May to September Sunday to Friday noon to 4:30 P.M., rest of year Sunday, Monday, Wednesday, and Friday 1 to 4 P.M. Adults $2, students and seniors $1.50, under 12 75 cents. *Bush Barn Art Center,* 600 Mission Street, 581-2228. Tuesday to Friday 10 A.M. to 5 P.M., Saturday and Sunday 1 to 5 P.M. Free. *Bush House Museum,* 600 Mission Street, 363-4714. June to August Tuesday to Sunday noon to 5 P.M., rest of year 2 to 5 P.M. Adults $1.50, seniors $1, students 75 cents, children 50 cents. *Enchanted Forest,* I-5 at Exit 248, 8462 Enchanted Forest Way, 363-3060. Mid-March to September daily 9:30 A.M. to 6 P.M. Adults $4, 3–12 $3.50.

EVENTS *World Championship Timber Carnival,* Albany, 926-1517, Fourth of July weekend. *Victorian Week,* Albany, 926-1517, end of July and beginning of August. Week of festivities includes covered bridge tours, Victorians open house, walking tours. *Oregon State Fair,* Salem, 378-3247, mid-August. Traditional state fair includes horse show, floral displays, agricultural exhibits, big-name entertainment, horse racing.

LODGING *Best Western Pony Soldier Motor Inn,* 315 Airport Road, Albany 97321, 928-6322, (800) 634-PONY. Convenient location off I-5 Exit 234, $$. *Comfort Inn,* 251 Airport Way, Albany 97321, 928-0921. Indoor pool, some kitchens, $$. *Lilla's Bed & Breakfast & Cafe,* 206 Seventh Avenue Southwest, Albany 97321, 928-9437. 4 guest rooms in restored Victorian close to downtown, restaurant, $$. *Best Western New Kings Inn,* 3658 Market Street, Salem 97301, 581-1559. Convenient to freeway, indoor pool, $$. *Chumaree Hotel,* 3301 Market Street, Salem 97301, 370-7888. Convenient to freeway, restaurant, free happy hour, $$–$$$. *State House Bed and Breakfast Inn,* 2146 State Street, Salem 97301, 588-1340. On mill creek with gazebo, hot tub, ducks, and geese; noted for outstanding breakfasts; $.

CAMPING *Silver Falls State Park,* 26 miles east of Salem via Highways 22 and 214, 873-8681. 104 sites, 53 electricity-water, $9–$11. Oregon's largest state park and one of its finest features 14 waterfalls, woodland trails, bike paths. *Salem KOA,* 1595 Lancaster Drive Southeast, 581-6736. 128 full-hookup sites, $11.

DINING *Novak's Hungarian Paprika's,* 2835 Santiam Highway Southeast, Albany, 967-9488. Lunch and dinner Sunday to Friday, Saturday dinner only; goulashes, Eastern European dishes in only Hungarian restaurant between San Francisco and Vancouver, British Columbia, $. *Buzz Saw Restaurant,* 421 Water Street, Albany, 928-0642. Dinner daily, overlooking river, $$. *Lilla's Bed & Breakfast Inn & Restaurant* (see "Lodging"). Dinner daily, lunch Tuesday to Saturday, brunch Sunday; intimate dining in restored Victorian; $$. *Inn at Orchard Heights,* 695 Orchard Heights Road Northwest, Salem, 378-1780. Dinner Monday to Saturday; upscale menu, excellent local wine list, overlooking Salem; $$. *Alessandro's Park Plaza,* 325 High Street, Salem, 370-9951. Lunch Monday to Friday, dinner Monday to Saturday; dining on the formal side overlooking Mill Creek Park, Northwest entrées with an Italian twist; $$. *Kwan's,* 835 Commercial Street, Salem, 362-7711. Lunch Sunday to Friday, dinner daily; Chinese menu strong on seafood, prepared to health standards (no fat, no MSG); $. *Pilar's* 189 Liberty Street North, Salem, 363-7578. Lunch and dinner Tuesday to Saturday, pasta specialties, $.

FOR MORE INFORMATION Covered Bridge Society of Oregon, P.O. Box 1804, Newport 97365, 265-2934. Albany Convention & Visitors Bureau, 435 West First Avenue, Albany 97321, 926-1517, (800) 526-2256. Salem Convention & Visitors Bureau, 1313 Mill Street, Salem 97301, 581-4325, (800) 874-7012.

Sunsets and Sand Castles

The Oregon coast, the state's most popular tourist attraction, is often compared with the seacoast of Maine as the finest in America. For more than 400 miles, all but 21 of them public property, the coast stretches from the mouth of the Columbia River to the California border in a series of magnificent seascapes, rugged headlands, offshore monoliths, long beaches washed by endless ranks of waves, and small rock-bound harbors.

Each part of the coast has a distinctly separate character, and where you go depends largely on what you want to do. Take Seaside and Cannon Beach, for example. The closest coastal resorts to Portland, they're as different from each other as Eugene is from Salem.

Seaside might be described as the dowager with a face lift. The grand old lady of the coast has been a popular family destination since 1898, when the first through train brought Portlanders down the Columbia River to Astoria, then south 17 miles to Seaside. The town was beginning to look a bit down-at-the-heels a few years back, but with some major refurbishing and the opening of new hotels, restaurants, and a new convention center, it has become one of the best family destinations on the coast.

Cannon Beach, just nine miles south, can be characterized as an exuberant youngster, full of fun. It has a reputation as an upscale artsy-craftsy town and also boasts one of the loveliest settings on the coast.

Before you go, one caveat about the Oregon Coast—especially the Cannon Beach and Lincoln City–Newport areas—it is overrun by people in July and August. If you don't mind traffic jams, standing in line for meals, and competition for every square inch of beach, by all means, go in midsummer. But if you'd prefer a slower pace and fewer people, consider spring or fall, or even winter. All three seasons are delightful at the coast, each with its own rewards.

You'll probably take U.S. 26 from Portland to reach either Seaside or Cannon Beach. If you're making the drive around mealtime, check out the Helvetia Tavern, two miles north from the Helvetia Road Exit. *Oregon* magazine declared its hamburger-and-French-fries combo the best in the state. It's a funky place perched beside a country road with everything from pickup trucks and motorcycles to BMWs and Mercedes parked in front. It's been there as long as anyone can remember, at least long enough for the proprietors to have collected hundreds of billed caps, which hang from the ceiling.

Some things never change. One feature that has always made Seaside special for us is the broad 8,000-foot beachfront promenade. You can almost imagine ladies in hoop skirts strolling under their parasols beside the sea. The broad beach seems to stretch forever, and at almost any hour of the day is busy with sun worshipers, strollers, joggers, and people playing catch or Frisbee with their dogs while gulls wheel overhead in search of an easy meal. About two blocks north of Broadway on the promenade, the modest Seaside aquarium exhibits regional marine life, including harbor seals. Several blocks south, also along the promenade, a replica of the Lewis and Clark salt cairn marks the spot where members of the expedition spent the winter of 1805–1806 boiling seawater down for salt.

The beach is ideal for kite flying, and you can often see two or more of the fancy Oriental fighting kites sparring in the air. There are several kite shops that carry everything from the simplest models to multiwinged fancy kites and replicas of World War I fighter planes. At The Sky's the Limit, on Broadway, the shop is crammed with kites from wall to wall and the owner will teach buyers how to fly them.

Broadway is the main street, running at right angles to the beach. There's a turning circle at the end, and on weekends teenagers continuously cruise the street up one side and down the other. Everybody enjoys the arcades along Broadway. Filled with old-fashioned games and mechanical devices, they provide good entertainment at a low price. Our favorite is a game of skill in which you release a spring-loaded platform to fire a rubber chicken into a revolving stew pot.

Shoppers can visit the Town Center Mall and Heritage Square plus dozens of shops along Broadway. Cannon Beach's famous bakery has an outlet here, as does Josephson's, the Astoria-based company known for its smoked salmon and other seafood. You'll find bookstores, agate shops, clothing emporiums, and arts and crafts galleries. Tucked away in an alley off Broadway, the Weary Fox features a wide variety of Northwest art, including jewelry, pottery, and fine art. A Seaside institution is Terhar's for quality women's clothing. And no trip to Seaside is complete without buying some saltwater taffy. Try Phillips Candies.

There is no shortage of choices when it comes to dining. For a great view, try the Shilo Inn dining room on the promenade. Norma's is known for its Crab Louis, Lumpy's for its clam chowder. The Channel Club has a wide variety of seafood, and you can specify the way you want it cooked. Dooger's Seafood & Grill is small, unpretentious, and popular with locals for its fresh fish, the selections listed on a blackboard and changed daily. Locals also say the German-Hungarian menu at the Alpine Gardens is great.

Cannon Beach fronts on seven miles of sandy beach dominated by 235-foot Haystack Rock, one of the world's largest monoliths, hulking just off shore. Beachfront motels face the massive rock, which, at sunset, is silhouetted against an orange sky. The base of the rock is a favorite spot for tide pool exploring, with plenty of starfish, anemones, sea cucumbers, crabs, and shellfish to discover. The beach is also great for walking and kite flying. Once Upon a Breeze and other kite shops are located in town. Cannon Beach's biggest annual event, held in May, is a sand castle contest that features incredibly elaborate structures built entirely of sand.

The town gets its name from the small cannon of the U.S. Navy schooner *Shark* that was washed ashore when the ship was wrecked in 1846 off Tillamook Head, just to the north. The cannon is still there. If you hike the Pacific Coast Trail over Tillamook Head, you'll see Tillamook Head Lighthouse perched on a rock offshore. Built in 1879, it warned ships away from these treacherous rocks until 1957, when it was replaced by an automatic beacon. The lighthouse is now privately owned and used as a columbarium.

The center of town is only a few blocks from end to end, easy to cover on foot. You can walk it in less than ten minutes, but you have a great deal of willpower if you can resist browsing in the boutiques, galleries, bookstores (there are at least three excellent ones), and candy shops along the way. The town is also a haven for artists; at last count, there were about 18 galleries displaying everything from traditional seascapes to driftwood sculptures, stained glass, fabric art, photography, jewelry, and works done in other media.

Especially noteworthy is the White Bird Gallery, which specializes in original art with the emphasis on coastal scenes. At Worcester Glass Works you'll find one-of-a-kind blown and etched glass vases, bowls, paperweights, and sculpture, some with Northwest themes. Cannon Beach Art Center features the works of prominent Northwest artists. Bill Steidel, one of Cannon Beach's most prominent artists, displays and sells his work at the gallery in Sandpiper Square that bears his name. You'll find natural-fiber clothing, much of it imported, for both men and women at El Mundo.

The goodie shops tempt at every turn. At Bruce's Candy Kitchen, you can watch them making saltwater taffy. Among their other treasures are sand dollars made with white chocolate, starfish composed of dark chocolate and almonds, and coconut (what else?) haystacks. Don't miss Cannon Beach Bakery, an Oregon institution. Get there early because the place is so popular they need a rope barrier to control the eager shoppers. Plump pecan caramel squares, custard-filled German chocolate cakes, poppyseed cakes, cream cheese Danish, fagosa (a cheese-egg-onion bread), and their famous haystack bread are among their more popular offerings. And, lest you forget Jonathan and his friends, pick up a sack of "Seagull Supper" (day-old bread).

If you're settled in for the weekend and looking for a short, scenic excursion, consider driving south about four miles to Arch Cape for a splendid seascape. Or pack a picnic lunch and drive north two miles to Ecola State Park, with its fine views of offshore islands, the resting places for sea lions and shorebirds. For a bit longer excursion drive east 23 miles on U.S. 26 to Elsie and the Camp 18 Logging Museum, where you'll find a collection of old-time logging equipment, a gift shop, and a restaurant.

Where to dine? The Wayfarer, on the beach at Surfside, with splendid views of Haystack Rock and the setting sun, offers such dishes as sole Florentine, chicken Dijonnaise, and rack of spring lamb. *Oregon* magazine called Cafe de la Mer the finest seafood restaurant in Oregon. For breakfast or lunch try the Lemon Tree Inn, featuring 12 different omelets and a "hand sammich" for kids.

Except for a few lounges with music, nightlife is almost nonexistent in these beach towns, but if live theater tickles your fancy, check out what's playing at the Coaster Theater, (436-1232), one of the oldest community theaters on the coast.

Area Code: 503

DRIVING DIRECTIONS For either Seaside or Cannon Beach take U.S. 26 west from Portland. It's 79 miles to Cannon Beach, 81 miles to Seaside.

SIGHTSEEING *Seaside Aquarium,* Second Avenue and the Promenade, Seaside, 738-6211. Mid-June to August daily 9 A.M. to 6 P.M., Friday and Saturday to 8 P.M.; rest of year 9 A.M. to 5 P.M.; closed November to February Monday and Tuesday. Adults $4.50, 6–11 $2.25. *Camp 18 Logging Museum,* Elsie, 755-2476. Monday to Thursday 7 A.M. to 9 P.M., Friday to Sunday 7 A.M. to 10 P.M. Free.

EVENTS *Miss Oregon Pageant,* Seaside, 738-6391, mid-July. Determines Oregon's entrant in the Miss America contest. *Sand Castle Contest,* Cannon Beach, 436-2623, May. Features elaborate structures of sand.

LODGING *Best Western Ocean View Resort,* 414 North Promenade, Seaside 97138, 738-3334. Upscale lodgings on oceanfront, some with fireplaces, $$$–$$$$. *Seashore Resort Motel,* 60 North Promenade, Seaside 97138, 738-6368. On the beach, $$–$$$. *Shilo Inn,* 30 North Promenade, Seaside 97138, 738-9571. Best hotel in town, prominent beachfront location at Broadway turnaround, $$$–$$$$. *Sundowner Motor Inn,* 125 Ocean Way, Seaside 97138, 738-8301. Modest motel with some kitchens, near the beach, $–$$. *Gilbert Inn* (bed and breakfast), 341 Beach Drive, Seaside 97138, 738-9770. Cozy 1885 home 2 blocks off the beach, $$. *Gaston's Beachside Bed & Breakfast,* Avenue I and the Promenade, Seaside 97138, 738-8320. Just 2 rooms, but good value for money near the beach, $. *Riverside Inn* (bed and breakfast), 430 South Holiday Drive, Seaside 97138, 738-8354. 11 guest rooms adjacent to Necanicum River, good value, $$. *New Surfview Resort Motel,* 1400 South Hemlock Street, Cannon Beach 97110, 436-1566. Handsome 3-level cedar-shake motel perched on bluff overlooking the beach and Haystack Rock, $$$. *Viking Motel,* Matanuska and Ocean Front streets, Cannon Beach 97110, 436-2268. Located on the south, quiet side of the beach, $$–$$$. *Sea Sprite Motel,* 280 Nebesna Street, Tolovana Park 97145, 436-2266. Quiet, small (6 units), tidy and on the beach (Tolovana Park is the south end of Cannon Beach), this is a delightful discovery, $$. *Tolovana Inn,* South Hemlock Street and Warren Way, Tolovana Park 97145, 436-2211, (800) 333-8890. Large beachfront motel with some kitchens, fireplaces, $$–$$$.

CAMPING *RV Resort at Cannon Beach,* 345 Elk Creek Road, Cannon Beach 97110, 436-2231, (800) 452-4470 (in OR), (800) 547-6100 (outside OR). 100 sites with hookups on 11 acres, $17–$22.

DINING *Helvetia Tavern,* Helvetia Road, Hillsboro, 647-5286. Lunch and dinner daily; funky atmosphere, terrific hamburgers; $. *Dooger's,* 505 Broadway, Seaside, 738-3773. Lunch and dinner daily, popular seafood spot on Seaside's main drag, $$. *Crab Broiler,* junction U.S. 26 and U.S. 101, Seaside, 738-5313. Lunch and dinner daily, long-established seafood restaurant on Coast Highway,

$$$. *Norma's,* 20 North Columbia Street, Seaside, 738-6170. Lunch and dinner daily March to October, noted for seafood salads, $$. *Lumpy's Fishworks,* 104 Broadway, Seaside, 738-7176. Breakfast, lunch, and dinner daily, closed Tuesday in winter; good variety of seafood reasonably priced; $$. *The Channel Club,* 521 Broadway, Seaside, 738-8618. Lunch and dinner daily, closed Tuesday in winter; imaginative seafood menu; $$. *Alpine Garden,* 412 Broadway, Seaside 738-8530. Lunch and dinner daily, European menu, $$. *Shilo Inn,* 30 North Promenade, Seaside, 738-8481. Breakfast, lunch, and dinner daily; upscale restaurant with outstanding ocean view; $$$. *Lemon Tree Inn,* 140 South Hemlock Street, Cannon Beach, 436-2918. Breakfast, lunch, and dinner daily in summer; breakfast and lunch other seasons; great breakfasts; $. *Cafe de la Mer,* 1287 South Hemlock Street, Cannon Beach, 436-1179. Lunch and dinner Wednesday to Sunday; best restaurant in Cannon Beach, imaginatively prepared seafood; $$$. *The Bistro,* 263 North Hemlock Street, Cannon Beach, 436-2661. Lunch Saturday and Sunday, dinner Thursday to Tuesday; pasta, Italian, and French accents; $$$. *Wayfarer,* 1190 Pacific Drive, Cannon Beach, 436-1108. Breakfast, lunch, and dinner daily; splendid views of Haystack Rock; $$$. *The Brass Lantern,* 1116 South Hemlock Street, Cannon Beach, 436-2412. Dinner Tuesday to Saturday; wide-ranging international menu, seafood; $$. *Lazy Susan Cafe,* 126 North Hemlock Street, Cannon Beach, 436-2816. Breakfast and lunch daily, dinner summer only; local breakfast hangout; $$.

FOR MORE INFORMATION Seaside Chamber of Commerce, 7 North Roosevelt Way, Seaside 97138, 738-6391, (800) 444-6740. Cannon Beach Chamber of Commerce, P.O. Box 64, Cannon Beach 97110, 436-2623.

The Riviera of the Oregon Coast

The central Oregon Coast, comprising 30 miles that stretch from Lincoln City to Newport, is just about as popular with Northwesterners as the French and Italian Rivieras are with Europeans. And for good reason. Those 30 miles are packed with spectacular scenery plus hundreds of acres of beaches and some of the niftiest little towns and harbors to be found anywhere on the coast. This is also where the best and the widest variety of accommodations on the coast are located. Just about two hours' drive from Portland, it's an ideal weekend choice. Once a summer-only destination, the area is now busy year-round; reservations are mandatory in summer and highly recommended for any weekend in the year.

Lincoln City, stretching for several miles in a narrow band along U.S. 101, is relatively new, created in 1964 by the banding together of the cities of Oceanlake, Delake, and Taft, and the unincorporated communities of Cutler City and Nelscott. The city has the best range of accommodations on the coast, with many, at reasonable prices, fronting its 7½ miles of uninterrupted beach. Highlights of a visit should include Lacey's Doll House Museum, where there's a collection of more than 4,000 dolls, and Alder House II, the oldest glassblowing studio in the state. Other attractions include the "world's shortest river" (the D River, about 200 yards long), and the resident colony of sea lions that hangs out on the sandbars at the mouth of the Siletz River.

Heading south along U.S. 101, you pass through Gleneden Beach, location of elegant Salishan Lodge and Golf Course, the Northwest's five-diamond resort property. Boiler Bay Wayside, a good choice for a picnic lunch, is named for the steam boiler of the *J. Marhoffer*, a ship that exploded here in 1910. The boiler is still visible at low tide.

Tiny Depoe Bay claims to be the "world's littlest harbor," and there are no others in this part of the world that would dispute the title. Covering a mere six acres, the tiny rock-bound harbor is home to an intrepid fishing fleet that puts to sea through a tidal channel just 50 feet wide. It'll give you goose bumps to stand on the highway bridge above the channel or on the breakwater and watch the fishing boats thread their way between the rocks, especially if there's a high sea running. Channel House, a bed-and-breakfast inn perched on the south side of the channel, also provides excellent views of the action. If you visit in winter, you'll be treated to two spouting horns that shoot geysers 50 feet or more in the air with each surge of the surf against the breakwater. You can join a charter boat trip that leaves from Depoe Bay for salmon, tuna, or bottom fishing. In whale season, from February to May, some of these boats take visitors out for close-up views of the whales.

In the past several years storm watching has become a major winter activity along this coast. A plummeting barometer and the twin red gale-warning pennants flapping atop the weather bureau are the signals for many Northwest families to climb into the car and head for the coast. Between November and April the winter storms that batter the North Pacific Coast from Cape Flattery in Washington to California's Mendocino County attract hundreds of adventurous souls anxious to sample the twin pleasures of storm watching and beachcombing.

Winter storms in this part of the world originate in the Gulf of Alaska, sweep unhindered across the empty North Pacific, and hit the coast with a fury of pounding waves and wind-driven spume. Storm watchers seek the security of the numerous oceanfront cottages or motels, from where, snug by a crackling driftwood fire, they can view the drama of wind and surf. At night, or when visibility is limited, the mournful call of foghorns or the winking beam of a lighthouse add other dimensions to the experience. Bring along a pair of binoculars or a telescope for spotting a coastal freighter plying the shipping lanes a few miles offshore, or the whales that pass close to the coast in places on their annual late winter migration from Baja California to the Arctic. You can also frequently hear the bellowing call of the Steller and California sea lions and see their colonies on the rocks offshore.

Our choices for cozy storm watching accommodations with good vantage points include the Nordic Motel and the Inn at Spanish Head in Lincoln City, the Channel House at Depoe Bay, the Inn at Otter Crest at Otter Rock, the Moolack Shores Motel and the Hotel Newport.

Not all winter weather is violent, however. Typically, a series of squalls will be broken by periods of sunshine and relative calm, inviting even the most timid to get out and explore the beaches. Winter is the best season for beach-combing, as each new storm deposits all manner of flotsam on these shores. Top on the beach comber's list are the colorful Japanese glass fishing floats. They are used to support the nets of commercial fishermen, but often break loose and are carried across the Pacific by wind and current.

Driftwood collectors, too, have a field day immediately following a storm. The bleached chunks of fir, cedar, and hemlock come in an endless variety of contorted shapes and sizes. Dedicated collectors make lamp bases, paperweights, sculptures—even outdoor furniture—from their treasures.

Hunting for agates (a variety of quartz) is another favorite winter pastime. Rough waves wash sand off the beaches, exposing untouched deposits, and high water in coastal streams carries other specimens down to the sea beaches. Central Oregon beaches are particularly noted for agates, jaspers, Oregon jade, and petrified wood. Seashells, too, are here for the collecting, though these waters don't yield the rainbow hues and bizarre forms found on warmer coasts. And if you happen to come up empty-handed, dozens of souvenir shops along this coast are ready to sell cleaned and polished specimens.

Continuing south on U.S. 101 from Depoe Bay, you reach a turnoff to the Otter Crest Loop Road in 1½ miles. The road takes you around Cape Foulweather (named by the English explorer Captain James Cook when he encountered storms here in 1778) and past Rocky Creek State Park, Devil's Punchbowl, and Otter Crest Wayside (perched 500 feet above the sea). There are magnificent viewpoints all along this road. At Devil's Punchbowl you can look down into a seething cauldron of surf-pounded cove. The Inn at Otter Crest clings stair-step fashion to the face of the bluff and affords outstanding views of the wave-washed cape. Return to U.S. 101 and continue south past Beverly Beach, Moolack Beach, and Agate Beach into Newport.

Situated on lovely Yaquina Bay, Newport, with a population of about 9,000, is the largest city on the coast, not counting Astoria, which is on the Columbia River. The ramshackle old waterfront is an authentic curiosity. Park your car and make your way past the tall stacks of crab rings and fishing buoys that jam Bay Boulevard. If your accommodations have a kitchen, here is the place to get fresh crab, oysters, salmon, and clams from streetside fish stalls. Mo's, a funky old café here, is known all along this coast for its delicious clam chowder. Undersea Gardens features underwater windows for viewing marine life and schedules scuba diving shows. Charter boats moored along this waterfront offer fishing trips and whale-watching cruises.

Mark O. Hatfield Marine Science Center (named for Oregon's senior senator) lies across the bay. This coastal research station specializes in marine biology, geology, weather conditions, and other sciences as they apply to this coast. There's a small aquarium that includes a tide pool "touch" tank for children and a friendly octopus with which you can shake tentacles. Idaho Flats, adjacent to the center, is one of the best shorebird-watching spots on the coast.

Newport's best beaches lie out of sight of town to the west. There are state parks located at One Beach, South Beach, Beverly Beach, and Agate Beach. Beverly Beach is noted among collectors for its abundant supply of fossils embedded in the sandstone cliffs at the south end of the beach. Yaquina Bay State Park, on the north side of the entrance channel to Yaquina Bay, features the old Yaquina Bay Lighthouse, built in 1871, now restored and open as a museum. Drive north to the edge of town, then take Ocean Drive out to Yaquina Head, a popular spot for tide pool exploring and whale watching. Try to time your arrival for an hour or so before low tide (all fishing supply shops on the coast have tide tables) and take the steep trail at the edge of the parking lot.

Area Code: 503

DRIVING DIRECTIONS An easy loop route that takes you from Portland to Lincoln City, Newport, and the coast in between leads southwest on Highways 99W and 18 to U.S. 101 and returns via U.S. 20 to Corvallis, Albany, and I-5. The round-trip mileage is 249.

SIGHTSEEING *Lacey's Doll House and Museum,* 3400 Northeast U.S. 101, Lincoln City, 994-2392. May to September daily 8 A.M. to 5 P.M., other months 9 A.M. to 4 P.M. Adults $2, under 15 50 cents. *Alder House II,* Immonen Road near Gleneden Beach, 996-2483. Mid-March to November, 10 A.M. to 5 P.M., Tuesday to Sunday. Free. *Thundering Seas* (Oregon State University School for the Crafts), South Point Street, Depoe Bay, 765-2604. Wednesday to Saturday 9 A.M. to 4 P.M., tours on Wednesday and Saturday. Donation. Watch goldsmiths and silversmiths at work; museum and mineral display. *Maveety Gallery,* Salishan Marketplace, Gleneden Beach, 764-2318. Monday to Saturday 10 A.M. to 6 P.M., Sunday 10 A.M. to 5 P.M. Free. Northwest fine arts and crafts. *Mark O. Hatfield Marine Science*

Center, Marine Science Drive, Newport, 867-3011. Mid-June through Labor Day daily 9:30 A.M. to 6 P.M., rest of year 10 A.M. to 4 P.M. Free. *Lincoln County Historical Museum,* 545 Southwest Ninth Street, Newport, June to September Tuesday to Sunday 10 A.M. to 5 P.M., other months 11 A.M. to 4 P.M. Free. Modest museum of pioneer, logging, and maritime exhibits includes historic Burrows House. *Ripley's Believe It or Not,* 250 Southwest Bay Boulevard, Newport, 265-2206. June to Labor Day daily 9 A.M. to 8 P.M., rest of year 10 A.M. to 5 P.M. Adults $5, seniors $4, 12–17 $3, 5–11 $2. Displays of strange objects, people, events. *Undersea Gardens,* same address, phone, hours, and fees as Ripley's Believe It or Not. *The Wax Works,* same as Ripley's. Displays of animated wax figures. *Yaquina Art Center,* Nye Beach Turnaround, Newport, 265-5133. Daily noon to 4 P.M. Exhibits of local arts, crafts, and photography. Free. *Yaquina Bay Lighthouse,* Yaquina Bay State Park, Newport. June to Labor Day daily noon to 5 P.M., rest of year Saturday and Sunday noon to 5 P.M. Admission 50 cents, under 6 free. *Fishing/Whale Watching Charters: Jimco Dock,* Pier 1, Depoe Bay, 765-2713, 765-2382; *Tradewinds,* P.O. Box 123, Depoe Bay, 765-2345; *Sea Gull Charters,* 343 Southwest Bay Boulevard, Newport, 265-7441; *South Beach Charters,* P.O. Box 1446, Newport, 867-7200; *Newport Tradewinds,* 653 Southwest Bay Boulevard, Newport, 265-2101; *Newport Sportfishing,* 1000 Southeast Bay Boulevard, Newport, 265-7558.

EVENTS *Seafood and Wine Festival,* Newport, 262-7844, February. Northwest's oldest and largest wine festival. *Memorial Day Fleet of Flowers Sailing,* Depoe Bay, 765-2889, Memorial Day. Flower-laden boats put to sea after shoreside ceremony honoring those who have lost their lives at sea.

LODGING *Coho Inn,* 1635 Northwest Harbor Avenue, Lincoln City 97367, 994-3684. On the beach, kitchens, fireplaces, $$. *The Inn at Spanish Head,* 4009 South U.S. 101, Lincoln City 97367, 996-2161. Multistory hotel built into cliff face, $$–$$$$. *Nordic Motel,* 2133 Northwest Inlet Avenue, Lincoln City 97367, 994-8145, (800) 452-3558. Overlooking beach, very clean and neat, $$. *Channel House* (bed and breakfast), P.O. Box 56, Depoe Bay 97341, 765-2140. Exceptional location overlooking harbor channel, $$–$$$$. *Salishan Lodge,* P.O. Box 118, Gleneden Beach 97388, 764-2371. Top-rated resort in the Northwest; has golf course, nature trails, exercise rooms, indoor pool, indoor tennis, fireplaces; not on beach; $$$$. *Inn at Otter Crest,* P.O. Box 50, Otter Rock 97369, 765-2111, (800) 547-2181 (outside OR). Condominium-style lodging on 84 acres facing ocean and Cape Foulweather, $$$–$$$$. *Moolack Shores Motel,* Star Route North, Box 420, Newport 97365, 265-2326. On the beach away from other lodgings, attractive themed rooms, good value for money, $$–$$$. *Best Western Windjammer Hallmark Resort,* 744 Southwest Elizabeth Street, Newport 97365, 265-8853. Oceanfront, fireplaces, $$$. *Embarcadero Resort Hotel & Marina,* 1000 Southeast

Bay Boulevard, Newport 97365, 265-8521. Upscale lodgings on Yaquina Bay, not on beach, $$$–$$$$. *The Hotel Newport,* 3019 North Coast Highway, Newport, 97365, 265-9411. Multistory hotel on Agate Beach, $$$. *The Sylvia Beach Hotel,* 267 Northwest Cliff Drive, Newport 97365, 265-5428. Unusual, historic hotel for book lovers, with rooms named for authors; on the beach; $$–$$$$. *Ocean House Bed & Breakfast,* 4920 Northwest Woody Way, Newport 97365, 265-6158. Cozy B&B overlooking Agate Beach, $$.

CAMPING *Devil's Lake State Park,* off U.S. 101, 2 miles east of Lincoln City, 994-2002. 100 sites, 32 with full hookups, $8–$11. *Lincoln City KOA,* 5298 Northeast Park Lane, Lincoln City, 994-2961. 76 sites, 38 with hookups, $12. *Holiday RV Park,* 1 mile north of Depoe Bay on U.S. 101, 765-2302. 110 sites with full hookups overlooking ocean, $12–$20. *Beverly Beach State Park,* 7 miles north of Newport on U.S. 101, 265-9278. 279 sites, 127 with hookups, $8–$11. *South Beach State Park,* 2 miles south of Newport on U.S. 101, 867-7451. 254 sites with hookups, $8–$11. *Pacific Shores RV Resort,* 6225 North Coast Highway, Newport, 265-3750, (800) 666-6313. High-quality new RV resort with clubhouse, cable TV hookups, overlooking ocean, 287 sites with full hookups, $13–$27.

DINING *Cafe Roma,* 1437 Northwest Highway 101, Lincoln City, 994-6616. Breakfast, lunch, and dinner daily; cozy coffeehouse and bookstore featuring gourmet coffees; good place for light breakfast; $. *Bay House,* 5911 Southwest Highway 101, Lincoln City, 996-3222. Dinner daily; upscale seafood restaurant, views of Siletz Bay; $$$. *Lighthouse Brew Pub,* 4157 North Highway 101, Lincoln City, 994-7238. Lunch and dinner daily; first brewpub on the coast, featuring ales brewed on the property, light tavern meals; $$. *Pier 101,* 415 Southwest Highway 101, Lincoln City, 994-8840. Lunch and dinner daily, excellent seafood served in funky nautical atmosphere, $$. *Chez Jeanette,* 725 Old Highway 101, Gleneden Beach, 764-3434. Dinner Tuesday to Sunday, closed Sunday in winter; Northwest cuisine, local seafood in French country inn; $$$. *Salishan Lodge,* U.S. 101, Gleneden Beach, 764-3535. Breakfast, lunch, and dinner daily; 4 award-winning restaurants, outstanding wine list; $$$–$$$$. *Sea Hag,* 58 East Highway 101, Depoe Bay, 765-7901. Breakfast, lunch, and dinner daily; long a favorite hangout on the coast for fishermen and kindred souls; seafood, sack lunches if you're going on a charter boat; $$. *The Flying Dutchman,* Inn at Otter Crest (see "Lodging"), 765-2060. Breakfast, lunch, and dinner daily; brunch Sunday; Northwest cuisine, local seafood, ocean view; $$$. *Champagne Patio Restaurant,* 1630 North Coast Highway, Newport, 265-3044. Lunch Monday to Saturday, dinner Friday and Saturday; intimate restaurant with eclectic, innovative menu featuring seafood, and homemade desserts; $$. *Mo's,* 622 Southwest Bay Boulevard, Newport, 265-2979. Breakfast, lunch, and dinner daily; a tradition on the coast for seafood, especially clam chowder; $. (For some reason this, the original Mo's, is much better than their newer clones in other coastal towns.) *Canyon Way Restaurant and Bookstore,* 1216 Southwest Canyon Way, Newport, 265-8319. Lunch Monday to Saturday, dinner daily in summer, closed Sunday and Monday other seasons; small restaurant, within a book and gift store, serving seafood and pasta; $$. *The Whale's Tale,* 452 Southwest Bay Boulevard, Newport, 265-8660. Breakfast, lunch, and dinner daily; especially good for breakfast; $$.

FOR MORE INFORMATION Visitor and Convention Bureau of Lincoln City, 3939 Northwest Highway 101, Lincoln City 97367, 994-8378. Newport Chamber of Commerce, 555 Southwest Coast Highway, Newport 97365, 265-8801, (800) COAST-44.

Roseburg: A Family Destination

Nestled in the rolling oak-studded hills where the Umpqua River rushes down from the Cascades, Roseburg is about an hour south of Eugene and an ideal destination for an easygoing family weekend. For children, this is where they'll have the best close-up encounters with exotic animals north of San Francisco. For adults, there's some excellent low-key wine touring, the best summer steelhead fishing in the state, and a bit of historical sightseeing. Another plus is the climate, which is generally sunnier, warmer, and drier than that of any of the cities along I-5 to the north, including Eugene, Portland, and Seattle.

You can make a getaway weekend of it and stay at Steamboat Inn on the North Umpqua River, or make reservations for a night or two in Roseburg and set off on excursions from there. Another alternative is to stay at a working farm in the area. Country Host Registry places visitors as paying guests on local sheep ranches and other rural properties.

On your way to or from your destination, take the time to detour off the Interstate at Oakland, about 14 miles north of Roseburg. The first pioneers to come over the Oregon Trail and settle in this part of Oregon built their cabins about a mile north of the present-day main street in 1846. The original waterwheel from the first grist mill, built by one of the pioneers, Dr. Dorsey S. Baker, is located in Oakland's city park. Oakland is a gem of a town filled with vintage architecture that has not yet been discovered by the gentrifiers. Substantial brick business buildings, dating from the 1890s, line Locust Street, the main thoroughfare. Walking-tour maps are available at the museum and at most of the shops. Be sure to stop at Tolly's, where you'll find an old-fashioned soda fountain and row upon row of jars of hard candy. The restaurant upstairs has an eclectic menu that ranges from sautéed chicken breasts to rack of lamb. The Pringle

House, at the head of Locust Street, offers bed-and-breakfast accommodations in an 1893 Victorian home.

Wildlife Safari is the high point of this trip for youngsters—and for many adults, too. Unlike many of the "wildlife" parks where you view a collection of often sad-looking critters confined by chain link fences, this park is a quality experience. It's run by a nonprofit corporation dedicated to preserving endangered species, many of which can be seen here.

Located out of sight of Highway 42 in the hills southwest of Roseburg, the park is divided into two segments. The first is rather typical of small zoos, with enclosures housing various animals from monkeys to exotic birds. But there are significant differences. Youngsters have exciting firsthand encounters with animals usually just seen behind bars. They can have their picture taken sitting beside—and petting—a full-size adult cheetah. They, and their parents, can ride atop a lumbering African elephant or a camel. A sign beside the elephant enclosure, reading "Only elephants should wear ivory" reinforces the park's preservation theme. There's also a petting area where small children can touch pigmy goats, Rocky Mountain sheep, potbellied pigs, llamas, and donkeys. In this area, near the gate, there's also a restaurant and gift shop.

The second segment of the park, and the essence of the experience, is a drive-through area—a graveled three-mile road that winds among more than 500 animals of about 40 species. The animals roam free; you stay in your car. Fences separate predators from prey and wardens in towers open gates to let cars, but not animals, through. The park is divided into geographical habitats. In the Asian portion, for example, you view indigenous animals and birds likely to be found coexisting in the wilds of Asia. There are rental cars available at the gate if you're driving a convertible, not permitted in the park. If you have a pet along for the weekend, you may not take it through the park (for obvious reasons); Wildlife Safari provides a free kennel at the entrance.

Cars move at a walk and drivers seem to mind their manners and stay in line; still, the park tends to get a bit crowded on summer weekend afternoons. If you're spending the weekend in Roseburg, make this stop the first on your agenda and schedule it for before noon. That way you'll have more time to linger and photograph the animals without the distraction of many other cars. The animals also tend to be more lively before the heat of midday. Plan on spending about 1½ hours on the drive-through.

There are zebras, elephants, yaks, lions, various apes and monkeys, water buffalo, bison, oryx, kudu, dromedaries, moufloun sheep, gazelles, gnus, and wildebeest, among many other animals. As you ease up beside them, the tiny fallow deer seem as gentle as house pets. The big cats seem docile enough, still . . . Curious ostriches may reach over to peck at your windshield or poke their heads in your car. If your first drive-through has just whetted your appetite to linger and observe more, you can make the loop again the same day at no additional charge.

Wine touring in Douglas County around Roseburg is the same low-key activity it is farther north in the Willamette Valley. Like those in Yamhill and Washington counties, the wineries here are small family-run operations tucked away on back roads. Their landscapes resemble those in parts of northern California—rolling grass-covered hills studded with oak and pine trees. Seven wineries are located on county roads west of Roseburg and I-5. The wines are both reds and whites. Six of the wineries have regular hours for tasting; the seventh requests that you call for an appointment. The county roads noted in the following pages are marked by signs with yellow numbers on a blue background.

Head directly west from downtown Roseburg for about three miles on Garden Valley Road then Melrose Road, cross the South Umpqua River, and turn right on Busenbark Lane to Callahan Ridge Winery. They specialize in white wines, including gewürztraminer, white zinfandel, white riesling, and chardonnay.

Backtrack to Melrose Road, turn west to Melqua Road, and follow it north to its intersection with Fort McKay Road (County Road 9), about 13 miles northwest of Roseburg. Turn west and cross the Umpqua River to Henry Winery, located in a lovely river valley flanked by low hills. This winery has collected its share of gold medals for its pinot noir as well as awards for its chardonnay and gewürztraminer.

Retrace your steps now, returning to the intersection of Melqua and Melrose roads, then turn west and continue to Doerner Road. Turn right on Doerner to Elgarose and follow it north and west to Vineyard Lane and HillCrest Vineyard, about ten miles west of Roseburg. HillCrest, established in 1962, is the oldest vinifera vineyard in Oregon. It produces about 20,000 gallons annually of riesling, cabernet sauvignon, and pinot noir from about 35 acres of grapes.

Back to Melrose Road again, and follow it west and south as it becomes Flournoy Valley Road (County Roads 51 and 5) to Reston Road and turn south. Davidson Winery and Girardet Wine Cellars are located on this road. Davidson produces pinot noir and cabernet sauvignon and is open by appointment only. Girardet specializes in riesling, chardonnay, and pinot noir and features a picnic pergola with views of the Umpqua Valley.

Continue on Reston Road to the little community of Tenmile and the junction of Oregon 42. Turn back toward Roseburg, drive through Winston, and turn left at the signs to Wildlife Safari. Continue to Lookingglass Road, where you'll find Lookingglass Winery, a small, new establishment that released their first wine, a white riesling, in 1990. Return to Roseburg via Winston or continue on Lookingglass Road. A seventh, new winery, Umpqua River Vineyards, is located on Hess Lane off Garden Valley Road to the northwest and produces cabernet, sauvignon blanc, semillon, chenin blanc, and cabernet franc.

If there's still time left at the end of a busy day, stop to visit the Douglas County Museum adjacent to I-5 Exit 123 a mile south of town. The handsome museum features exhibits on county history and natural history, including some fine mounted animals. The Mill-Pine District, a historic district of modest working-class homes, is located near the railroad yards where many of the original residents once worked. There are more than 180 buildings spread over 21 blocks bracketed by Southeast Mill and Pine streets. The county museum is the place to get directions to Roseburg's several historic homes. The most unusual is the Parrott House, with its three-story octagonal tower, at 1772 Southeast Jackson Street. The only one open to the public is the 1853 Floed-Lane House.

Railroad buffs may want to wander down to the old Southern Pacific depot in Roseburg. This railroad line was the first to connect the Pacific Northwest with California in the 1870s. The substantial Craftsman-style depot was built in 1912, the third to serve Roseburg. Passenger trains disappeared years ago, but the line still carries considerable freight and Roseburg is the main crew-change point between Eugene and Ashland. There are usually a few locomotives on hand and a freight train or two coming or going. The venerable lower-quadrant semaphore signals used on this line are real anachronisms, among the oldest in the West.

Reserve Sunday morning for a drive up the North Umpqua River to breakfast or lunch at the Steamboat Inn. Heading east from Roseburg on four-lane Highway 138, you quickly reach the foothills, where sheep graze in the fields and fir tree farms line the road. At Glide, 18 miles east of Roseburg, stop at Colliding Rivers Viewpoint, where the North Umpqua River and Steamboat Creek meet head-on, an unusual phenomenon. A short detour south at Glide on Little River Road (County Road 17A) will bring you to the Cavitt Creek Covered Bridge, a 70-foot Howe truss span built in 1943. Beyond Glide, the North Umpqua and the two-lane highway twist and turn between steep, densely forested slopes where you can see some magnificent stands of old-growth timber across the river. At almost every turnout you'll see cars or pickup trucks parked, their owners standing hip-deep in the river casting for steelhead.

The North Umpqua River is one of the Pacific Northwest's legendary fishing streams. Wherever anglers gather in this part of the world, they're sure to talk about the summer steelhead runs on this river. The elusive steelhead (an ocean-going trout) make this a prime destination from July through September. The river also hosts spring (mid-May to July) and fall (September to December) salmon runs, as well as a winter steelhead run (December to March). For 31 miles, from Soda Springs to Rock Creek, the river is open to fly-fishing only for steelhead and trout. The North Umpqua Trail hugs the river, providing good access for both anglers and hikers. You can obtain maps of the river and its best fishing holes from the Umpqua National Forest North Umpqua Ranger District

Office in Glide or the Bureau of Land Management office in Roseburg, at 777 Garden Valley Boulevard. The Roseburg Visitors & Convention Bureau or Steamboat Inn can give you advice on how to hire a fishing guide.

About 40 miles east of Roseburg you reach Steamboat Inn, long known by anglers as *the* place to stay on the North Umpqua. But in the last few years, under the guidance of owners Jim and Sharon Van Loan and manager Patricia Lee, the inn has secured its reputation as a prime getaway spot with good accommodations and excellent meals. Nestled beneath tall firs right beside the river, the inn is an ideal retreat whether or not you intend to fish. There are plenty of hiking trails in the area, several waterfalls to view, and a covered bridge just half a mile east of the inn. It's popular enough to make reservations a necessity.

On your return, take North Bank Road at the west end of Glide for a 16-mile route on the north bank of the river and over the hills to Wilbur, then north to I-5 at Sutherlin.

Area Code: 503

DRIVING DIRECTIONS Roseburg is located 177 miles south of Portland via I-5.

SIGHTSEEING *Oakland Museum,* 140 Southeast Locust Street, Oakland. Inquire locally about hours. *Wildlife Safari,* off Highway 42 and Lookingglass Road outside of Winston, 679-6761. Summer daily 8:30 A.M. to 8 P.M., rest of year 9 A.M. to 4 P.M. Adults $8.50, seniors $7, 4–12 $5.25, plus $1 per car; half price after 6 P.M. in summer. *Callahan Ridge Winery,* 340 Busenbark Lane, 673-7901. April to October daily 11:30 A.M. to 5:30 P.M. *Henry Winery,* County Road #9, Umpqua, 459-5120, 459-3614. Daily 11 A.M. to 5 P.M. *HillCrest Vineyard,* 240 Vineyard Lane, 673-3709. Daily 10 A.M. to 5 P.M. *Davidson Winery,* 2637 Reston Road, 679-6950. Open by appointment. *Girardet Wine Cellars,* 895 Reston Road, 679-7252. May to September daily noon to 5 P.M., October to April, Saturdays noon to 5 P.M., closed mid-December to January. *Lookingglass Winery,* 6561 Lookingglass Road, 679-8198. April to December daily noon to 5 P.M. *Umpqua River Vineyards,* 451 Hess Lane, 673-1975. Saturdays 10 A.M. to 6 P.M. *Douglas County Museum,* Exit 123 from I-5, 440-4507. Tuesday to Saturday 10 A.M. to 4 P.M., Sunday noon to 4 P.M. Free. *Floed-Lane House,* 544 Southeast Douglas Avenue, 459-1393. Daily 1 to 4 P.M. Free.

EVENTS *Timber Days,* Sutherlin, 459-2236, mid-July. 4 days of traditional loggers' competitions. *Douglas County Fair,* county fairgrounds in Roseburg, 440-4505, early August. Week of carnival rides, agricultural and food exhibits, country-western entertainment.

LODGING *Pringle House Bed & Breakfast,* Seventh and Locust streets, Oakland 97462, 459-5038. Guest rooms in 1893 Victorian in historic Oakland, $. *Steamboat Inn,* Steamboat 97447, 496-3495, 498-2411. Woodsy country inn beside the North Umpqua River, $$$–$$$$. *Sonka's Sheep Station Inn,* 901 Northwest Chadwick Lane, Myrtle Creek 97457, 863-5168. Guest rooms in main house and private guest house on 300-acre sheep ranch, $–$$. *Umpqua House Bed & Breakfast,* 7338 Oak Hill Road, Roseburg 97470, 459-4700. Country home on 6 wooded acres overlooking Umpqua Valley, $$. *The Woods Bed & Breakfast,* 428 Oakview Drive, Roseburg 97470, 672-2927. 2 guest rooms in 3-story home on 7 wooded acres 6 miles northwest of Roseburg, $$. *Windmill Inn,* 1450 Mulholland Drive, Roseburg 97470, 673-0901. Best conventional motel in Roseburg, near freeway, pool and restaurant, $$–$$$. *Best Western Douglas Inn,* 511 Southeast Stephens Street, Roseburg 97470, 673-6625, (800) 528-1234 (outside OR). Good budget choice, $–$$. *Best Western Garden Villa Motel,* 760 Northwest Garden Valley Road, Roseburg 97470, 672-1601, (800) 547-3446 (in OR), (800) 528-1234 (outside OR). Good budget choice, $–$$. *Country Host Registry,* 901 Northwest Chadwick Lane, Myrtle Creek 97457, 863-5168. Write or call for free brochure on member properties.

CAMPING *Amacher County Park,* off I-5 at Winchester (Exit 129), 5 miles north of Roseburg, 672-4901. 10 tent sites, 20 RV sites with full hookups, on North Umpqua River, $9. *Douglas County Fairgrounds RV Park,* 2110 Frear Street, Roseburg, 440-4505. 50 hookups, $10. *Twin Rivers Vacation Park,* 433 River Forks Park Road, Roseburg, 6 miles west of town at confluence of North and South forks of Umpqua, 673-3811. 85 sites, $10–$14. The Bureau of Land Management and Umpqua National Forest operate several campgrounds (no hookups) along Little River Road southeast of Glide, including: *Cavitt Creek Falls* (8 sites), *Wolf Creek* (9 sites), *Coolwater* (7 sites), and *White Creek* (4 sites); $3–$4. Off Highway 138 between Glide and Steamboat, you'll find *Susan Creek* (33 sites), *Bogus Creek* (15 sites), *Island* (7 sites), and *Canton Creek* (5 sites); $4–$5. Most of these campgrounds are open only from May to October; check at the ranger station in Glide.

DINING *Brutke's Wagon Wheel,* 227 Northwest Garden Valley Road, 672-7555. Lunch Monday to Friday, dinner daily; casual dining; steak, prime rib, seafood; $$. *P. B. Clayton's,* 968 Northeast Stephens Street, 672-1142. Dinner daily, Italian menu, $$. *Sandpiper Restaurant,* located in Windmill Inn (see "Lodging"), 673-0021. Dinner daily; part of small-city chain started in Boise, upscale, good quality; beef, seafood, pasta; $$. *Dynasty Restaurant,* 1790 Northwest Garden Valley Road, 673-1323. Lunch and dinner daily, Cantonese menu, $$. *Steamboat Inn* (see "Lodging"). Breakfast, lunch, and dinner daily; elegant prix fixe dinner, reservations required; in winter call first for all meals to see whether or not they're serving that day, $$$.

FOR MORE INFORMATION Roseburg Visitors & Convention Bureau, 410 Southeast Spruce Street, Roseburg 97470, 672-9731.

Oregon Dunes National Recreation Area

As we mentioned in an earlier section (see "Sunsets and Sand Castles"), the 400-mile Oregon coast has many faces, many moods—dramatic seascapes and rugged headlands, broad sandy beaches, resort towns with nonstop activity, and quiet secluded retreats where nothing much happens but the play of wind and waves. What part of the coast you choose for a weekend depends largely on what you want to do.

The Oregon dunes, a 40-mile stretch of giant sand dunes, saltwater bays, and freshwater lakes anchored by the towns of Florence and Reedsport, offers more activity concentrated in a relatively small area than anywhere else on the coast north of California. A partial list of what you can do might include fishing (deep-sea, freshwater, or surf), horseback riding on the beach, riding speedy dune buggies over the dunes, sailboarding, swimming, hiking, wildlife viewing, crabbing and clamming, and historical sightseeing. There's even a smattering of nightlife.

The dunes themselves, vast shifting mountains of sand sculpted by coastal winds, are unusual in that they cover so large an area. Between the Siuslaw River and Coos Bay more than 40 miles of them rise as high as 500 feet and extend inland from one to three miles. Oregon Dunes National Recreation Area, administered by Siuslaw National Forest, preserves 32,000 acres of dunes and regulates the activities within the area, setting aside portions for the wild and noisy antics of the dune buggies and other portions for the more contemplative pursuits of walking and nature study.

If you're interested in understanding the ecology of the dunes, stop early in your weekend at the recreation area visitor center, at the intersection of Highways 101 and 38 in Reedsport. Exhibits and audiovisual programs here explain that the dunes resulted from millions of years of glacial activity that ground rock into sand high in the Cascade and Coast ranges, where rivers washed it down to the sea. Waves then pushed the sand onto the beaches, where wind shaped it into dunes. The landscape you view today evolved about 6,000 years ago around the mouths of the Siuslaw, Umpqua, and Coos rivers. Highway 101 runs through the dunes paralleling the beach, providing easy access at many points. You'll notice how the dunes are constantly moving, in places burying large, mature trees in the coastal forest that flanks the area to the east.

The recreation area provides viewpoints, boat-launching ramps, hiking and riding trails, and beach facilities. There are 16 public campgrounds and 30 miles of hiking trails. The Oregon Dunes Overlook, 12 miles south of Florence, provides three elevated platforms from which to view the dunes and the ocean. Forest Service rangers conduct regular interpretive walks through the dunes daily during the summer months and on weekends during the winter. The best spots for walking are in the north dunes, north of Jessie M. Honeyman State Park, because dune buggies are confined to the areas south of the park, except for an area near the South Jetty. One of the bonuses of dune and beach walking, in addition to the shells for collecting and the birds and mammals on view, is the berries, available for gathering. From June into September, you'll find salmon berries, thimbleberries, blue elderberries, blackberries, huckleberries, and wild strawberries beyond road's end. All are delicious fresh or made up into jams and jellies.

If your time is limited, the Forest Service recommends South Jetty Road, off U.S. 101 just south of the Siuslaw River crossing, as a good place to watch people landing their catch at the crabbing and fishing dock. The Umpqua Dunes Trail, a ¼-mile trail that starts from the North Eel Campground, gives you spectacular views of the dunes. And you can see the highest dunes in the recreation area from the second and third parking lots on County Road 251 from Winchester Bay.

If you want to try your hand at buzzing over the dunes on four wheels, you can rent various kinds of vehicles, including all-terrain vehicles (like motorcycles with three or four wheels), dune buggies, and modified Jeeps. Fees run from about $25 to $45 per hour, plus a hefty deposit. You'll find the rental locations along U.S. 101 between Florence and North Bend. Several firms also offer guided tours where someone else does the driving. You can rent horses for beach riding or join guided trail rides along the beach and through the dunes for about $13 to $20 per hour. Chambers of commerce in Florence and Reedsport can furnish lists of dune buggy operators and stables.

When it comes to fishing, you can have it just about any way you want. Right behind the dunes is a chain of approximately two dozen lakes, many of which are stocked each spring with legal-size trout, mostly cutthroat. The larger lakes— Woahink, Siltcoos, Tahkenitch, and Tenmile—have marinas where you can rent boats and tackle. Charter boats operate out of Florence and Winchester Bay and will take you out off the coast for salmon or bottom fishing or in one of the bays for crabbing. They also offer scenic cruises when they're not fishing. Cost ranges from about $45 per person for five hours up to about $100 for 12 hours of bottom fishing, and includes bait, tackle (including crab pots), and cleaning; you bring your own lunch and license for bottom fish. If you're adept at surf or rock fishing, try the jetties and beaches for rockfish, greenling, yellow perch, perch, and ling cod.

If you've set aside some of your weekend for sightseeing, you may want to begin at Sea Lion Caves, 12 miles north of Florence. The caves have been a visitor attraction since 1932. An elevator takes you down 208 feet through a rocky headland to a fenced-off observation area overlooking a large cavern. From here you have a good view of dozens of giant Steller sea lions, some as large as 2,000 pounds, being swept up on the rocks by the force of water entering the cave. The cacophony of barking is deafening, but it's fascinating to get a glimpse of how seals behave on their territory, in a setting where they feel perfectly at home. Just to the north is Heceta Head Lighthouse, probably the most photographed beacon on the coast. The headland on which it stands was named for Spanish explorer Bruno Heceta, who sailed along this coast in 1775.

A few miles south of the caves is Darlingtonia Botanical Wayside. In a boggy area thick with cedars, rhododendrons, and ferns grows a concentration of the exotic Darlingtonia plant, sometimes known as the cobra lily, a carnivorous species that traps and digests insects lured by its nectar. A raised wooden path leads you through the area and interpretive displays explain this curious plant's role in the environment.

If you're an ice cream lover, stop at BJ's, at 2930 U.S. 101 North, just outside of Florence. The ice cream they make has a reputation as the best on the coast, with a rich butterfat content of 14.2 percent. You can have it in any of 48 flavors.

Florence is known as "the Rhododendron City" for the thousands of wild rhododendrons that burst into blossom here in May. Detour off U.S. 101 to visit Old Town, a three-block stretch of Bay Street along the Siuslaw riverfront that has been refurbished to house touristy restaurants and shops. Noteworthy here are Incredible Edible Oregon, at 1350, featuring gifts, wines, and food products made in Oregon; a branch of BJ's Ice Cream, at 1441; the espresso bar at Old Town Coffee Co., at 1269; and Catch the Wind Kite Shop and Old Town Books, at 1250 and 1340, respectively. Around the corner, at 280 Nopal Street, stands the Fly Fishing Museum. And, miracle of miracles, praise to the city fathers of Florence for putting up public rest rooms; they're just off Mo's parking lot.

Rhododendron Drive makes a rewarding scenic loop west along the river to Harbor Vista County Park, overlooking the mouth of the Siuslaw River, then north along the coast to Heceta Beach. If you're staying in Florence and it looks like there's going to be a worthwhile sunset, drive out to the South Jetty at the end of the day, climb a sand dune, and watch the sun go down over the Pacific. Nightlife in Florence is pretty tame by big-city standards, but curiosity may tempt you to try the latest fad, the Japanese sing-along known as "karaoke," staged evenings at the Lotus Seafood Palace.

Heading south from Florence, you encounter the Siuslaw Pioneer Museum and Gallery of Local Arts about a mile south of the Siuslaw River Bridge. The museum focuses on the area's pioneer history, with particular attention to logging, Indians, and natural history; the gallery exhibits and sells works by local artists and artisans. Stop on the Umpqua riverfront at Reedsport to view the *Hero*, a former Antarctic research ship, unusual in that it incorporates both sail and diesel for propulsion and has a stout oak hull for protection against the floe ice encountered in southern seas. The Coast Guard icebreaker *Glacier* has been donated to Reedsport and will soon be open to visitors as well.

A detour three miles east of Reedsport on Highway 38 will bring you to Dean Creek, where you can view a herd of about 55 Roosevelt elk. The best time to see them is in winter; the peak of bugling season, when you can hear the mating calls of the bulls for miles, is from mid-September to early October.

Little Winchester Bay, three miles south of Reedsport, is the home of a small commercial fishing fleet and the departure point for charter fishing trips off the coast. Another two miles south, Umpqua Lighthouse State Park embraces an 1892 lighthouse, some lofty sand dunes, and a platform that is a splendid spot for watching the seasonal migration of gray whales from March through May. The Douglas County Coastal Historical and Information Center nearby occupies the former U.S. Coast Guard Umpqua River Station. Displays deal with coastal shipping and the timber industry.

Area Code: 503

DRIVING DIRECTIONS It's 328 miles round-trip from Portland to Florence, 370 miles round-trip to Reedsport. There are several ways to go, but the quickest and easiest is to take Interstate 5 to Eugene, then Oregon 126 west to Florence. For an alternate route on your return, take Oregon 38 to Interstate 5 at Curtin.

SIGHTSEEING *Sea Lion Caves,* 91560 U.S. 101, Florence, 547-3111. Daily 9 A.M. to dusk. Adults $5, 6–15 $3. *Dolly Wares Doll Museum,* U.S. 101 and 36th Street, Florence, 997-3391. Tuesday to Sunday 10 A.M. to 5 P.M. Adults $3.50, 5–12 $2. Collection of more than 2,500 dolls. *Siuslaw Pioneer Museum,* 85294 U.S. 101 South, Florence, 997-7884. Tuesday to Sunday 10 A.M. to 4 P.M. Donation. *Siuslaw Gallery of Local Arts,* same address and phone. Mid-May to October Wednesday to Monday 10 A.M. to 5 P.M., rest of year noon to 4 P.M. *Hero,* Umpqua River waterfront, Reedsport. Memorial Day to Labor Day daily 10 A.M. to 4 P.M. Adults $5, 4–18 $2.50, families $10. *Douglas County Coastal Visitor Center,* 1½ miles south of

Winchester on Lighthouse Road adjacent to Umpqua Lighthouse State Park, 271-4631. May to September Wednesday to Saturday 10 A.M. to 5 P.M., Sunday 1 to 5 P.M. *Fishing Charters: Siuslaw Pacific Charters,* Harbor and First streets, Florence, 997-7995; *Holiday Charters,* Winchester Bay, 271-3702, 271-3175; *The Main Charters,* Fourth Street and Beach Boulevard, Winchester Bay, 271-3800; *Gee Gee Charters,* "B" Dock, Winchester Bay, 271-3152; *Becky Lynn Charters,* Beach Boulevard, Winchester Bay, 271-3017.

EVENTS *Rhododendron Festival,* Florence, 997-3128, third weekend in May. Includes carnival, barbecue, soap box derby, sailboarding, Heceta Lighthouse tours, floral parade, arts and crafts show. *Ocean Festival,* Reedsport and Winchester Bay, 271-3495, last weekend in July. Arts and crafts fair, beer garden, live entertainment, lighthouse tours, parade.

LODGING *River House Motel,* 1202 Bay Street, Florence 97439, 997-3933. At the edge of Old Town on the river, built in 1989, $$. *Driftwood Shores Surfside Resort Inn,* 88416 First Avenue, Florence 97439, 997-8263, (800) 824-8774 (outside OR), (800) 422-5091 (in OR). The only motel on Heceta Beach, $$–$$$. *Best Western Pier Point Inn,* 85035 U.S. 101 South, Florence 97439, 997-7191. Balconies and views of the bay, $$. *Johnson House Bed & Breakfast,* 216 Maple Street, Florence 97439, 997-8000. 5 guest rooms in Victorian home in Old Town, plus 2 beachside cottages north of town, $$. *Gardiner Guest House,* 401 Front Street, Gardiner 97441, 271-4005. 2 guest rooms in lovely 1883 Victorian built by the founder of Reedsport and perched on a hill overlooking Gardiner, $–$$. *Tropicana Motel,* 1593 U.S. 101, Reedsport 97467, 271-3671. Good bargain choice in town with limited accommodations, $.

CAMPING *Oregon Dunes National Recreation Area,* operates 16 campgrounds ranging from 11 sites to more than 100 sites with various facilities, some open only in summer. For campground information and/or reservations write to the headquarters office in Reedsport or call (800) 283-CAMP. *Carl G. Washburne State Park,* 14 miles north of Florence, 547-3416. 66 sites, 58 with full hookups, $8–$11. *Jessie M. Honeyman State Park,* 3 miles south of Florence, 997-3851. 382 sites, about half with hookups, $8–$11. *Umpqua Lighthouse State Park,* 6 miles south of Reedsport off Highway 101, 271-4118. 41 sites, half with hookups, $7–$9. *Woahink Lake Resort,* 83570 Highway 101 South, Florence, 997-6454. 40 sites on lake with full hookups, $12.

DINING *The Windward Inn,* 3757 U.S. 101 North, Florence, 997-8243. Breakfast, lunch, and dinner daily; good selection of seafood, good choice of Oregon wines; $$. *Bridgewater,* 1297 Bay Street, Florence, 997-9405. Lunch and dinner daily; seafood, beef, salad bar, tropical decor in Old Town; $$. *Lotus Seafood Palace,* 1150 Bay Street, Florence, 997-7168. Lunch and dinner daily; unusual combination of Chinese and Pacific Northwest menu with wide selection of seafood, overlooking river; $$. *Surfside Restaurant,* in Driftwood Shores Surfside (see "Lodging"), 997-8263. Breakfast, lunch, and dinner daily; upscale dining on seafood and steaks with splendid views of the surf on Heceta Beach; $$. *Seven Seas Cafe,* Fourth Avenue and Beach Boulevard, Winchester Bay, no telephone. Breakfast and lunch Tuesday to Saturday, a good choice for breakfast before an early morning fishing charter departure, $.

FOR MORE INFORMATION Florence Area Chamber of Commerce, P.O. Box 712, Florence 97439, 997-3128. Lower Umpqua Chamber of Commerce, P.O. Box 11, Reedsport 97467, 271-3495. Oregon Dunes National Recreation Area, 855 Highway Avenue, Reedsport 97467, 271-3611.

Browsing the Quiet Coast

At the other end of the spectrum from the busy pace of the Oregon dunes, there's an area just a few miles south that is so lovely and so quiet you'll wonder why it's not overrun with tourists. The area lies west and south of Coos Bay, and the reason it hasn't been overrun is because U.S. 101 bypasses it and the growth of tourist facilities has been minimal. It's a great choice for a romantic getaway.

We'd recommend staying in Bandon. The little town, 23 miles south of Coos Bay, has several good and remarkably inexpensive motels on a bluff overlooking the beach about a mile west of town. And the beach here is absolutely magnificent—big offshore rocks, cliffs jutting into the water, all dramatically silhouetted at sunset. In between there are secluded stretches of beach where you're likely to find only a handful of early morning walkers or evening strollers, even in midsummer. The beaches offer the conventional pastimes—chasing the surf, throwing Frisbees, building sand castles. Where the cliffs meet the sea, you'll discover excellent tide pools filled with saltwater critters, from anemones and urchins to starfish and crabs. Some of the best tide-pooling is at Bandon Beach and Bullard's Beach State Park. Stables located just south of town rent horses for riding on the beach.

Winter storm watching has been elevated to a major activity in Bandon by a group called the Storm Watchers. Every Saturday in winter they organize field trips to tide pools and shorebird colonies (there are two national wildlife refuges within the city limits), or engage in educational sessions on meteorology, geology, or wildlife. If you're lucky enough to be in Bandon when one of the big winter storms arrives, head for Face Rock Viewpoint just south of town or for other cliff-top viewpoints along Beach Loop Drive. The South Jetty, where the Coquille River meets the sea, provides good views of boats crossing the bar and lots of action as the breakers crash against the rocks on stormy days. Winter is also a good time for beach-combing, and you'll find some of the best hunting for shells and agates on the beach adjacent to the South Jetty.

Bandon's Old Town (every Oregon coast town seems to have one) is a great place for browsing and dining. Low-key and laid-back, it invites you to stroll and poke about without any pressure to try or buy. There are a dozen or more small shops selling everything from driftwood to beachwear. Poke your head into Big Wheel Farm Supply, at First and Baltimore streets, which houses the extensive Driftwood Museum, part of the private collection of a late Bandon resident. The Bandon Historical Society Museum is in the old Coast Guard station and features exhibits on the area's maritime history and the Coast Guard lifesaving service. Also on display are Indian artifacts and photographs of the 1936 fire that destroyed much of the town.

If you're having dinner in Old Town, walk down to the little harbor just about sundown to watch the fishing boats coming home into the mouth of the Coquille River. You can watch them unload their catch at the fish buyer's dock, where salmon, cod, halibut, and other fresh fish are iced down in big boxes. The sternwheeler *Rose* ties up here and offers 1¾-hour cruises of the harbor and river. Charter boats also operate out of this marina.

While you're exploring Bandon, don't miss the Coquille River Lighthouse, on the north side of the river adjacent to Bullard's Beach State Park. The weathered old lighthouse was built in 1896 and served until it was replaced by an automated light in 1939. It's now a public museum. Among the unusual tales this old lighthouse could tell is the one about the night in 1903 when it was rammed by an abandoned schooner driven ashore by a storm. The lighthouse and the former keeper's house once stood on an island in the middle of the river, but silt deposits and a change in the river's course eventually placed it on the mainland.

Bandon is a center for cranberries and cranberry products, with more than 100 local growers producing about 180,000 barrels of the fruit a year. Stop in at CranBerry Sweets, at First and Chicago streets, for a sample of some unusual cranberry products including fudge, nougat, craisins (we're not going to explain; you'll have to go see for yourself), and all sorts of confections, jams, and fruit pâtés, also available by mail order.

If you schedule a day to explore the coast just north of Bandon, as we suggest, you may want to consider packing a picnic lunch—there aren't many restaurants handy to the route but there are a number of splendid spots to spread a picnic with a view of the sea. One of the places to start your picnic shopping should be the Bandon Cheese Factory, on U.S. 101 in the center of town. Here you can sample and purchase a variety of cheddars, Jack, Colby, and specialty cheeses. If you happen to be here on a weekday, you can watch the cheesemaking process. You can pick up fresh crab, smoked salmon, and other seafood, as well as meats and local Oregon wines, at several stores around town.

For your Saturday or Sunday exploring the coast, set off early and check a local tide table for the time of low tide if you want to go beach-combing. Head north on U.S. 101 for about five miles and turn left—west—on the secondary road at the signs to Seven Devils Wayside. The wayside is a state park day-use area on an arc-shaped sandy beach in a cove. It's typically very quiet and a good spot for a picnic or to stroll the beach without being disturbed. If you're a serious rock-hound, you'll want to detour at the sign to Whiskey Run Beach; it's about three miles to road's end and was once the site of a minor gold rush. You can still find gold, if you're persistent, and plenty of good-quality agates.

Continue north, through some shady forested coastal glens and some ugly scarred areas of clear-cutting, on a narrow gravel road (it has a good hard surface) for 4½ miles until you reach pavement once again.

In about two miles you'll come to South Slough National Estuarine Reserve, a real treasure tucked away off the road. The visitor center perches on a hill overlooking several arms of Coos Bay and has exhibits and films on the region's wetlands, seabirds, geology, and hydrology. The exhibits are cleverly arranged so the ecological interdependence of the wetlands is easy to understand. One display, called "Cafe Estuary," consists of four different dinner plates filled with the fish, shellfish, and other creatures indigenous to the Coos Bay tide lands. Nature trails of varying lengths lead down to the water, and the park personnel lead interpretive canoe trips (or you can go on your own) into the bay. For visitors, U-Haul in downtown Coos Bay rents canoes, paddles, and life jackets if you want to participate.

Continue north on the Seven Devils Road to the signs designating the Cape Arago Highway and turn left to Sunset Bay, Shore Acres, and Cape Arago state parks. This trio of parks preserves some of the finest portions of the Oregon coast. Sunset Bay is a gorgeous beach park where the sun shimmers off the sea in a cove rimmed with sandstone bluffs. The swimming is safe here, with relatively little undertow and a beach with a gradual slope. The chilly water is a bit daunting, however. At the base of the cliffs there are tide pools to explore.

Just to the south, Shore Acres State Park preserves the coastal estate of lumber baron Louis J. Simpson. The mansions are gone now, but beautiful formal gardens spread over several acres and nearly always seem to have something in bloom. They're a riot of color in midsummer. There's a Japanese garden built around a 100-foot lily pond. At Christmastime the garden is strung with 40,000 lights. On the site of the former Simpson mansion, on a promontory that juts toward the sea, the state park has constructed a glassed-in shelter where you can stay dry in the worst of weather and still have a good view of the waves pounding the sandstone cliffs in front of you. Because the sandstone is relatively soft, the ceaseless action of the sea has worn dramatic caves and arches in the rock that make fine photographic subjects. If the wind is right, you'll hear the noisy barking of hundreds of sea lions that occupy the rocks offshore.

As you drive south to Cape Arago State Park, you'll pass a pulloff and viewpoint on the right where you can get a good look at these sea lions offshore, especially if you've brought binoculars. In December and January and again in March and April migrating gray whales often pass close enough to shore that you can see them from this viewpoint.

Cape Arago is the place to ready your camera for the fine seascapes of rugged headlands bordered on the north and south by shallow, protected coves. Simpson Reef, a sea lion habitat, is just offshore. Steep trails lead down to the beach here.

Reverse your route and drive the six miles or so to the little fishing town of Charleston. A photogenic commercial fleet ties up here, and several charter operators will take you out for salmon, bottom fish, crab, or whatever is available for very reasonable prices (much less than we've encountered elsewhere on the coast). Charleston is also a good place to stop if you're in the mood for a seafood lunch, or to pick up seafood for dinner if your Bandon lodgings include cooking facilities. As you'd expect, the seafood is outstanding in almost any restaurant in the area, usually caught that day right off the coast. One delicacy you might want to try is the Oregon scallop, abundant in the waters just off Coos Bay. When you're back on the road, it's nine miles from Charleston to the city of Coos Bay and U.S. 101.

Coos Bay and its neighbor city, North Bend, are major ports and mill towns, their primary industry the manufacture of wood products. Although there is little of interest to the vacationer in either city, there are, however, three stops worth considering. In North Bend the Coos County Historical Museum displays a vintage steam locomotive and has exhibits relating to Indian, logging, and farming history. The Coos Art Museum in Coos Bay features works by contemporary Northwest artists, many of them influenced by their coastal surroundings. The Coast Guard Cutter *Citrus*, located on U.S. 101 between the two cities, is open for tours.

From Florence southward to the California border you'll encounter shops advertising myrtlewood. The Oregon myrtle grows along the coast of southern Oregon and reaches a height of from 50 to 150 feet and an age of from 250 to 500 years. The long, flat leaves, much like those of the bay tree common in California, are used for seasoning; the oil of the leaf is used in perfume, incense, and candle scents. Because of its slow growth, the myrtle produces a very close-grained, fine-textured wood. Another result of slow growth is the development of burls, which when removed and polished reveal intricate and delicate markings referred to as birdseye, ribbon, and fiddleback. Color typically varies from light tan to deep golden brown, shades of gray, and even a velvety black. In the stores you'll find these burls crafted into jewelry, clocks, serving bowls, furniture, sculpture, and a number of other items. House of Myrtlewood, just off U.S. 101 at 1125 South First Street in Coos Bay, is one of the larger and better manufacturers and retailers of these products. If things are not too busy, they'll usually let you have a look at their factory where they craft the myrtlewood.

One longer and slower way to get home to Portland on Sunday is via Highway 42 to Roseburg and I-5. This green, winding route through the Coast Range is a real treat if you're not in a hurry. One stop to consider along the way is the Coos County Logging Museum in Myrtle Point. You'll spot the curious dome-shaped and shingled building from several blocks away. It resembles a Russian Orthodox church and was originally built as a church in 1910. Inside are displays of tools and artifacts from the era before logging became mechanized, and you immediately gain an appreciation for what a rugged life the logger's must have been.

Area Code: 503

DRIVING DIRECTIONS Portland to Bandon is 236 miles, with the most convenient route taking you south on I-5 to Eugene or Curtin, then west on Oregon 126 to Florence or on 38 to Reedsport, then south again on U.S. 101.

SIGHTSEEING *Bandon Beach Riding Stables,* Beach Loop, Bandon, 347-3423. *Driftwood Museum,* in Big Wheel Farm Supply, First and Baltimore streets, Bandon, 347-3719. Monday to Saturday 9 A.M. to 6 P.M., Sunday 10 A.M. to 5 P.M. Free. *Bandon Historical Society Museum,* Coast Guard Station in Old Town, 347-2164. Tuesday to Sunday 10 A.M. to 4 P.M. Donation. *The Rose Riverboat Trips,* 315 First Street Southeast, Bandon, 347-3942. In summer, cruises Monday to Saturday at 11 A.M. and 2 P.M., Sunday at 12:30 and 2:30 P.M., telephone for schedule at other times of the year. Adults $7, 5–11 $5, 4 and under $3. *Coquille River Lighthouse,* adjacent to Bullard's Beach State Park, off U.S. 101. Daily 8 A.M. to 5 P.M., 7 A.M. to 8 P.M. in summer. Free. *South Slough National Estuarine Reserve,* Seven Devils Road, Charleston, 888-5558. Daily 8:30 A.M. to 4:30 P.M. Free. *Bob's Sport Fishing,* 7960 Kingfisher Drive, Charleston, 888-4241. *Betty Kay Charters,* Guano Rock Avenue, Charleston, 888-9021. *Charleston Charters,* 5100 Cape Arago Highway, Charleston, 888-4846. *Coos Art Museum,* 235 Anderson Avenue, Coos Bay, 267-3901. Tuesday to Friday 11 A.M. to 5 P.M., Saturday and Sunday 1 to 4 P.M. Free. *Coast Guard Cutter Citrus,* U.S. 101 between North Bend and Coos Bay, 269-5859. Tours daily 1 to 7 P.M., call for reservations. Free. *Coos County Historical Museum,* Simpson Park on U.S. 101, North Bend, 756-6320. Memorial Day to Labor Day Tuesday to Saturday 10 A.M. to 4 P.M., Sunday noon to 4 P.M., rest of year Tuesday to Saturday. *Coos County Logging Museum,* Seventh and Maple streets, Myrtle Point, 572-3153. Monday, Wednesday, and Friday 10 A.M. to 4 P.M., Saturday noon to 4 P.M., Sunday 1 to 4 P.M. Donation.

EVENTS *Oregon Coast Music Festival,* Coos Bay, 267-0938, mid-July. Musical performances range from bluegrass and jazz to chamber and symphonic music. *Cranberry Festival,* Bandon, 347-9616, late September. Parade, barbecue, harvest ball.

LODGING *Sunset Motel,* 1755 Beach Loop Road, Bandon 97411, 347-2453, (800) 842-2407. Splendid location on cliff face above beach, quality accommodation; $–$$$$. (The owners also act as agents for rental homes, condominiums.) *The Inn at Face Rock,* 3225 Beach Loop Road, Bandon 97411, 347-9441. Newer property across the street from the beach, kitchens, fireplaces, $–$$$$. *Windermere Motel,* 3250 Beach Loop Road, Bandon 97411, 347-3710. On cliff above beach, kitchens, $–$$. *Cliff Harbor Guest House* (bed and breakfast), Beach Loop Road at Ninth Street, Bandon 97411, 347-3956. Modern home on bluff top above beach, $$$. *Tintagel,* 1455 Beach Loop Road, Bandon 97411, 347-9234. Private house and apartment on the beach, $$$. *Lighthouse Bed and Breakfast,* 650 Jetty Road Southwest, Bandon 97411, 347-9316. Lovely modern home overlooks harbor and lighthouse, $$–$$$. *Sea Star Hostel,* 375 Second Street, Bandon 97411, 347-9632. The niftiest hostel we've seen, in Old Town adjacent to coffeehouse, caters to bicyclists, $.

CAMPING *Bullard's Beach State Park,* U.S. 101, Bandon, 347-2209. 192 sites, 92 with full hookups, $9–$11. *Driftwood Shores RV Park,* U.S. 101, Bandon, 347-4122. 40 spaces with full hookups, walking distance to Old Town, $12. *Sunset Beach State Park,* on Cape Arago Road southwest of Charleston, 888-4902. 109 sites, 29 with full hookups, $9–$10. *Bastendorff Beach County Park,* off Cape Arago Highway 1½ miles southwest of Charleston, 888-5353. 81 sites, 56 water-electricity, $7–$9. *Charleston Marina Complex Trailer Park,* Charleston, 888-9512. 104 sites, 65 full hookups, graveled park adjacent to harbor, $7–$12.

DINING *Andrea's Old Town Cafe,* 160 Baltimore Street, Bandon, 347-3022. Breakfast and lunch Monday to Saturday, dinner Friday and Saturday, brunch Sunday; good choice for breakfast, seafood dinner; $$. *Boatworks Restaurant,* on the South Jetty, Bandon, 347-2111. Lunch and dinner Tuesday to Saturday, dinner Sunday; splendid ocean/river view, seafood, Mexican; $$. *Sea Star Bistro,* Second Street adjacent to hostel in Old Town, 347-9632. Breakfast, lunch, and dinner daily; coffeehouse atmosphere, healthy food well prepared; $. *Lloyd's of Bandon,* Old Town, 347-4211. Breakfast, lunch, and dinner daily; seafood, steaks, chowder; $$. ***Lord Bennett's at the Sunset,*** at Sunset Motel (see "Lodging"), 347-3663. Lunch and dinner daily; upscale menu, fabulous ocean view; $$–$$$. ***The Inn at Face Rock*** (see "Lodging"), 347-9441. Breakfast, lunch, and dinner daily in summer, may be closed some weekdays in winter; fresh seafood, ocean view; $$–$$$. ***Portside,*** Charleston Boat Basin, Charleston, 888-5544. Lunch and dinner daily; freshest seafood on this part of the coast, caught by the restaurant's own fishing boat; $$.

FOR MORE INFORMATION Bandon Chamber of Commerce, P.O. Box 1515, Bandon 97411, 347-9616. Coos Bay/North Bend/Charleston Bay Area Chamber of Commerce Visitor and Convention Bureau, P.O. Box 210, Coos Bay 97420, (800) 824-8486, 269-0215, 756-4613.

The Play's the Thing

Ask most Northwesterners what they know about Ashland, Oregon, and they'll probably mention Shakespeare. In the last couple of decades that little town (population about 16,000) in the Rogue River Valley just north of the California border has become synonymous with some of the best Shakespearean theater offered anywhere in the country. The Oregon Shakespeare Festival runs from February to October and includes a variety of other theatrical productions ranging from the classics to the avant-garde. With theater running all but three months of the year and matinees as well as evening performances throughout the season, you can choose almost any time to go, but spring or fall are preferable if you want to avoid summer's crowds.

But there's a great deal more to see and do in the Rogue River Valley, including historical sightseeing, fishing, and river rafting. Just over the hill from Ashland, the outstanding Peter Britt Festivals take place in historic old Jacksonville in July and August. To get the most from what should be a three-day weekend, we suggest you schedule your trip to include both theatrical and musical performances.

From its beginnings in 1935 as a small community celebration, the Oregon Shakespeare Festival has grown to encompass three theaters that often run simultaneously. On summer evenings playgoers sit under the stars to enjoy Shakespeare performed on the stage of the Elizabethan Theater, modeled after the seventeenth-century Fortune Theater in London. Evenings in Ashland can be chilly, but you can rent seat cushions and blankets at the theater. Two indoor theaters, the 600-seat Angus Bowmer (named for the festival's founder) and the 140-seat Black Swan, complete the trio. If you go, don't miss the two-hour backstage tour conducted by members of the theater company. It's a wonderful way to enhance your theater experience.

Though Ashland has a range of conventional accommodations, consider staying in a bed-and-breakfast inn. Not only are some of the top-rated inns in the Northwest located in Ashland (the city has nearly 100 B&Bs), but the experience is likely to broaden your knowledge of and interest in what is being performed at the festival. At the Chanticleer Inn (rated by *Oregon* magazine as the best B&B in the state), for instance, innkeepers Jim and Nancy Beaver furnish each guest room with scripts of the plays currently being produced. Conversation around the breakfast table usually focuses on the previous night's performance.

When you write or telephone the festival for information, they will send you literature that describes various packages that include lodging. You can purchase your performance tickets and make reservations for lodging at the same time through Southern Oregon Reservations Service.

While you're in Ashland, visit the Shakespeare Exhibit Center, which displays a history of the festival complete with costumes, props, and set designs. Stroll through lovely 100-acre Lithia Park, with its Japanese garden and nature trails. First-time visitors are often persuaded to try the local Lithia water, which runs from pipes at the edge of the park. Purported to have health-giving properties, it's strong with hydrogen sulfide, tastes awful, and smells like rotten eggs.

The Peter Britt Festivals, held in nearby Jacksonville, are some of the Northwest's most delightful outdoor events. Whether your taste runs to modern, country/folk, or classical music, you'll find it in Jacksonville from the last weekend in June through Labor Day weekend.

On a warm summer evening you walk to the festival grounds on an oak-studded hillside above town. Sitting under the stars you listen to the strains of Chopin, Debussy, or Mendelssohn, jazz or folk music, as a slight breeze wafts through the trees, and lights twinkle in the valley below. Sublime.

On Sunday mornings you can attend a Serendipity Sunday chamber music performance. James DePriest, conductor of the Portland Symphony and summer conductor at the Britt, explains: "You come up on the hill and you bump into things that are pleasant. You have no idea what you're going to hear. That's serendipity." There is no announced program. Members of the chamber music group, dressed informally in jeans and sweatshirts, pick whatever piece they feel like playing.

There is reserved bench seating at the Britt, or you can come and spread your blanket on the hillside. You can rent pillows and seat backs. Many people bring a picnic lunch; several restaurants in Jacksonville sell box lunches, and there are concession stands on the grounds.

But aside from the Peter Britt Festivals, Jacksonville is worth a visit any time of the year. The town itself is a fine old museum piece, preserved from its gold rush heyday in the 1850s and now a National Historic Landmark.

We like it best early in the morning, when low sunlight filters through the oaks and sets ornate cornices, wooden gingerbread, scarred brick walls, and faded signs into bold relief. Except for an occasional logging truck rumbling through town, the streets are nearly deserted. You may encounter a stray dog, a merchant hosing off the sidewalk in front of his store, or a boy delivering newspapers on a bicycle, but otherwise you'll have the place nearly all to yourself and the time and space for some creative photography.

A couple of mule skinners discovered gold on Daisy Creek in 1851 and within a year Jacksonville was thriving. By the latter part of the nineteenth century, this was the county seat and the most important town in southern Oregon. Banks, hotels, brick business blocks, a courthouse, and other substantial structures testified to Jacksonville's prosperity. When the railroad and the main highway went through nearby Medford, Jacksonville began to die on the vine. Fortunately, wreckers never tore down the buildings and there were always enough residents to keep the town from being vandalized.

The town is only a few blocks square, ideal for exploring on foot. (During the summer, you can also board a motorized trolley for a 50-minute narrated tour.) Stroll along California Street and examine the marvelous faded advertisements painted on the old brick buildings. One reads "Wendt's Dairy. Delivered daily at your home" above the picture of a Jersey cow. Another advertises Bull Durham smoking tobacco. The F. A. Stewart Building looks as old as the rest, but part of it was built in 1970 for the filming of *The Great Northfield Minnesota Raid*.

Kennedy's Tin Shop is now the Jacksonville Bakery, selling a variety of goodies from donuts to cream puffs and breads. It opens at 7 A.M. and it's a good place to stop for early morning coffee and pastry. The Beekman Bank is furnished as it was in the 1860s, when more than $31 million in gold crossed its counters. A descriptive sign explains that the bank "never paid any interest or made any loans." Across the street there are window displays of a dentist's office and a saddlery. Around the corner, on Oregon and C streets, the Rogue River Valley Railway depot, built in 1881, houses an office where you can obtain information on Jacksonville and the surrounding area.

But the highlight is the 1883 county courthouse, now the Jacksonville Museum. Exhibits detail the lusty history of the mining town, the discovery of the Oregon Caves, and the local Indian culture, and there are displays of pioneer tools and firearms. One room is devoted to pioneer photographer Peter Britt, for whom the Britt Festivals are named. Upstairs in the former courtroom you'll find exhibits of the D'Autremont brothers, who were tried here in 1927 for the nation's last train robbery. Next door is a delightful children's museum.

Don't miss the fine old houses and churches on the back streets. About 80 buildings are marked and dated with signs. In the Jacksonville cemetery just northwest of town are the graves of many pioneers, some of whom died of smallpox, in Indian attacks or gunfights, or by hanging.

If you have time for some further sightseeing, follow Oregon 238 from Jacksonville along the Applegate River to U.S. 199 just west of Grants Pass. The highway traces a historic route through the Applegate Valley, and back roads lead to many of the old gold mining sites. A short detour south at Ruch leads to the 1917 McKee covered bridge. Turn south on U.S. 199 for about 30 miles to Cave Junction, then take Oregon 46 20 miles to Oregon Caves National Monument.

Tucked away high inside a remote mountain in the Siskiyou Range is a large labyrinth of limestone caverns, the largest west of New Mexico. Take the 1¼-hour guided tour; it's well worth the time. You wind through a maze of passageways and caves festooned with remarkable natural sculptures and highlighted by illumination. The stone formations resemble waterfalls, chandeliers, and clusters of bananas or gems. Wear good walking shoes and take a jacket or sweater; the temperature in the caves is in the mid-40-degree range. Meals and overnight accommodations are available at the handsome old log Oregon Caves Chateau across from the caves' entrance from mid-June through September.

Of the three principal cities of the Rogue River Valley—Ashland, Medford, and Grants Pass—Grants Pass takes the honors as the outdoor recreation capital of this area. Flowing right through the middle of town, the Rogue River is a water route into the roadless forests to the west. The Rogue River Trail leads for 40 miles downstream past several riverside lodges. With several days to spend, you can hike from lodge to lodge along the river. Fishing on the Rogue is legendary in this part of the world. You can hire a local guide to go out for steelhead, salmon, and rainbow trout, or try your luck on your own. The best fishing is from September through May.

Another way to experience the Rogue is on one of the white-water trips that go down the river in rafts, dories, kayaks, or canoes. They last from two to four days, from May through September. You can also sample the river on a shorter half-day or full-day trip from Grants Pass. Visitors with not much time to spend opt for one of the big passenger-carrying jet boats that make two-to-five-hour trips. Though the jet boats are convenient, they are noisy and a real annoyance if you're staying at accommodations on the river in Grants Pass.

Depending on your time and inclinations, you may want to include any of the following on your trip to the Rogue River Valley. Butte Creek Mill in Eagle Point has been grinding grain since 1872. Detour off I-5 near Medford (Exit 30) to visit the old building constructed of hand-hewn beams joined by oak pegs and whipsawn lumber fastened with square nails. Inside you'll see the original water-driven stones, which grind 300 to 400 pounds of wheat, rye, and corn an hour. You can purchase the stone-ground flours at the mill store.

Twenty miles north of Grants Pass at Exit 76 off I-5 stands Wolf Creek Tavern. Built around 1857, the classic revival–style hostelry served as an overnight stage-coach stop for passengers traveling between Sacramento and Portland via the California Stage Company. You can still stay in one of the 16 modest rooms, but ask for a room at the back of the house to avoid the noise from the nearby interstate. The inn's kitchen also serves three hearty meals a day.

Another delightful discovery is the Rogue River Valley Creamery, located on North Front Street in Central Point. It's the only cheese factory west of the Mississippi producing blue cheese. They also make and sell cheddar, raw milk cheddar, jack, colby, and other varieties of cheese.

Area Code: 503

DRIVING DIRECTIONS Interstate 5 connects Portland with Grants Pass (245 miles south), Medford (273 miles), and Ashland (285 miles).

AIR TRANSPORTATION *Horizon Air* and *United Express* serve Medford from Portland. Round-trip fares begin at about $183.

SIGHTSEEING *Oregon Shakespeare Festival,* P.O. Box 158, Ashland 97520, 482-4331 for tickets and information. *Festival Exhibit Center,* 15 South Pioneer Street, Ashland, 482-2111. Daily except Monday 9 A.M. to 5 P.M. Backstage tour daily except Monday at 10 A.M., includes admission to Exhibit Center, $6. *Shakespeare Art Museum,* 460 B Street, Ashland, 482-3865. April to October Wednesday to Monday 10 A.M. to 5 P.M. Adults $2.50, 12–18 $1.50, seniors $2.50. Displays contemporary art that interprets Shakespeare's works. *Actor's Theater of Ashland,* 110 East Main Street, Ashland, 482-3486. Ashland's experimental theater, often called "Off Shakespeare." *Peter Britt Festivals,* P.O. Box 1124, Medford 97501, 773-6077 or (800) 88-BRITT for tickets and information. *Trolley Tours,* Jacksonville, 535-5617. Depart hourly between 9 A.M. and 5 P.M. in summer from Wells Fargo Building at Third and California streets. Adults $2.50, under 12 $1. *Beekman Bank,* Third and California streets, Jacksonville. Daily 1 to 5 P.M., living history program on Saturday and Sunday Memorial Day to Labor Day. Free. *Beekman House,* 352 East California Street, Jacksonville, 899-1845. Memorial Day to Labor Day daily 1 to 5 P.M. Free. Vintage 1875 Victorian home with original furnishings; costumed actors conduct tour. *Children's Museum,* Fifth and D streets, Jacksonville, 899-1847. Memorial Day to Labor Day daily 10 A.M. to 5 P.M., rest of year Tuesday to Sunday 10 A.M. to 5 P.M. Free. Hands-on museum in the

old jail details pioneer life. *Jacksonville Museum*, in old Jackson County Court-
house, on Fifth between C and D streets, 899-1847. Memorial Day to Labor Day
daily 10 A.M. to 5 P.M., rest of year Tuesday to Sunday 10 A.M. to 5 P.M. Free.
Kerbyville Museum, 2 miles north of Cave Junction on U.S. 199, 592-2076. Mid-
May to September daily 10 A.M. to 5 P.M. Donations. Historical museum in 1870s
building includes exhibits of farm and mining machinery, firearms. *Oregon Caves
National Monument*, 20 miles east of Cave Junction on Oregon 46, 592-3400.
Tours at frequent intervals June to September daily 8 A.M. to 7 P.M., rest of year
at 10:30 A.M. and 12:30, 2, and 3:30 P.M. Adults $6.75 6–11, $3.75. *Butte Creek Mill*,
on Oregon 62 in Eagle Point, 826-3531. Monday to Saturday 9 A.M. to 6 P.M. Free.
Harry and David's, 2836 South Pacific Highway, Medford, 776-2277. Daily 8 A.M.
to 6 P.M. Free. Famous fruit mail-order house has factory tours, gift shop, fruit
stand, restaurant. *Woodville Museum*, First and Oak streets, Rogue River, 582-
3088. May to September Tuesday to Sunday 10 A.M. to 4 P.M., October to April
Tuesday to Saturday. Free. Vintage home displays turn-of-the-century clothing,
furniture, glassware, china. *Rogue River jet boat trips* (prices range from $15 to $30
depending on the length of the trip): *Hellgate Excursions*, P.O. Box 982, Grants
Pass 97526, 479-7204, dock and ticket office at Riverside Park; *Rogue Jet Boat
Excursions*, 933 Southeast Seventh Street, Grants Pass 97526, 476-2628, (800)
331-4567 (in OR), (800) 334-4567 (outside OR). *White-water rafting/kayak trips
on the Rogue* (prices range from about $45 for a single-day trip to $400 for a
3-day everything-included trip): *Orange Torpedo Trips*, P.O. Box 1111, Grants
Pass 97526, 479-5061; *River Adventure Float Trips*, 2407 Merlin Road, Grants Pass
97526, 476-6493; *Rogue River Raft Trips*, 8500 Galice Road, Merlin 97532, 476-
3825, (800) 826-1963 (outside OR); *Rogue Wilderness*, 3388 Merlin Road, Grants
Pass 97526, 479-9554.

EVENTS *Pear Blossom Festival*, Medford, 772-5194, second weekend in April.
Parade, band festival, and marathon celebrate spring blossom season in the
orchards. *Jedediah Smith Mountain Man Rendezvous & Buffalo Barbecue*, Grants
Pass, 476-7717, Labor Day weekend. Muzzle loader and black powder matches,
frontier costumes, barbecue.

LODGING *Southern Oregon Reservation Center*, P.O. Box 477, Ashland 97520,
(800) 547-8052 (outside OR), (800) 533-1311 (in OR). Offers 1-call reservations
service for events tickets, lodging, and activities. *Windmill's Ashland Hills Inn*, 2525
Ashland Street, Ashland 97520, 482-8310. South of town with expansive view of
valley, Siskiyous; putting green, tennis courts, bicycles; $$$–$$$$. *Stratford Inn*,
555 Siskiyou Boulevard, Ashland 97520, 488-2151. Walking distance to theaters,
$$$. *Chanticleer Bed & Breakfast Inn*, 120 Gresham Street, Ashland 97520, 482-
1919. One of the top B&Bs in Oregon, lavish breakfast, $$$. *Arden Forest Inn* (bed

and breakfast), 261 Hersey Street, Ashland 97520, 488-1496. 5 guest rooms in remodeled farmhouse and carriage house, $$. *Country Willows* (bed and breakfast), 1313 Clay Street, Ashland 97520, 488-1590. 4 guest rooms in turn-of-the-century country home on 5 acres, $$. *McCall House* (bed and breakfast), 153 Oak Street, Ashland 97520, 482-9296. Elegant Italianate Victorian a block from the theaters, $$$. *Mt. Ashland Inn* (bed and breakfast) 550 Mt. Ashland Road, Ashland 97520, 482-8707. 5 guest rooms in massive loft structure with spectacular views of Cascade and Siskiyou ranges. $$$–$$$$. *Jacksonville Inn,* 175 East California Street, Jacksonville 97530, 899-1900. Rooms in historic inn include full breakfast; there's also a honeymoon cottage; $$$. *Reames House 1868* (bed and breakfast), 540 East California Street, Jacksonville 97530, 899-1868. 4 guest rooms in Victorian home on national register, walking distance to the Britt, $$$. *Oregon Caves Chateau,* P.O. Box 128, Cave Junction 97523, 592-3400. 22 rooms in splendid old timbered lodge, open June through September, $$. *Red Lion Inn,* 200 North Riverside Street, Medford 97501, 779-5811. Upscale motor inn convenient to interstate, $$$–$$$$. *Best Western Medford Inn,* 1015 South Riverside Street, Medford 97501, 773-8266. Good value, 2 blocks off interstate, $–$$. *Doubletree Ranch,* 6000 Abegg Road, Merlin 97532, 476-0120. Complete guest ranch with horseback riding, fishing, trails, on 160 riverfront acres, $$$. *Riverbanks Inn* (bed and breakfast), 8401 Riverbanks Road, Grants Pass 97527, 479-1118. Contemporary home on 12 acres on the Rogue River, $$–$$$. *Wolf Creek Tavern,* Wolf Creek 97497, 866-2474. Spartan rooms in 1850s stagecoach inn, $.

CAMPING *Valley of the Rogue State Park,* 12 miles east of Grants Pass off I-5 on river, 582-1118. 97 full-hookup sites, 55 electric only, $11. *Howard Prairie Lake Resort,* 21 miles northeast of I-5 Exit 14, lakeside campground at 4,500 feet, 482-1979. 268 sites, 60 full hookups, mid-April to October, $8–$10. *KOA-Glenyan,* 3½ miles southeast of I-5 Exit 14, on Oregon 66, 482-4138. 68 sites, 11 with hookups, mid-February to October, $13–$16.50. *Medford Oaks Campark,* 13 miles northeast of Medford on Highway 140, 826-5103. 87 sites, 20 with full hookups, 37 water-electricity, $11.50–$13.50. *Holiday RV Park,* 3 miles south of Medford off I-5 Exit 24, 535-2183. 110 full-hookup sites, $15. *Sunny Valley KOA,* 14 miles north of Grants Pass off I-5 Exit 71, 479-0209. 79 sites, 15 full hookups, 57 electricity-water, $11.50–$15.

DINING *Chateaulin,* 50 East Main Street, Ashland, 482-2264. Dinner daily; small, intimate restaurant near theaters; $$. *Winchester Inn,* 35 South Second Street, Ashland, 488-1115. Dinner Tuesday to Sunday, brunch Sunday; upscale fare in 1880s Victorian inn, outdoor dining; $$. *Bayou Grill,* 139 East Main Street, Ashland, 488-0235. Dinner Tuesday to Sunday, Cajun dining within a half block of the Angus Bowmer Theater, $$. *Thai Pepper,* 84 North Main Street, Ashland,

482-8058. Dinner daily, Thai cuisine, $$. *Ashland Hills Inn* (see "Lodging"), 482-8310. Breakfast, lunch, and dinner daily, Sunday brunch; steak, seafood, traditional menu; $$. *Jacksonville Inn Dinner House,* Jacksonville Inn (see "Lodging"). Lunch and dinner daily; Continental, Northwest preparations in historic inn; $$. *Mon Desir,* 4615 Hamrick Road, Central Point, 664-6661. Dinner daily, brunch Sunday; converted mansion has elegant surroundings, famous for its fine dining since *Life* magazine discovered it years ago; $$–$$$. *The Sandpiper,* 1841 Barnett Road, Medford, 779-0100. Dinner daily, noted for its seafood, $$. *Hungry Woodsman,* 2001 North Pacific Highway, Medford, 772-2050. Lunch Monday to Friday, dinner daily; brawny loggers' atmosphere, steaks, seafood; $$. *Yankee Pot Roast,* 720 Northwest Sixth Street, Grants Pass, 476-0551. Dinner daily; in historic home, pot roast specialty; $$. *R Haus,* 2140 Rogue River Highway, Grants Pass, 476-4287. Dinner daily; long-time favorite for its Italian, beef, seafood menu; $.

FOR MORE INFORMATION Southwestern Oregon Visitors Association, 88 East Stewart Avenue, Medford 97501, 779-4691, (800) 448-4856.

East of the Cascades

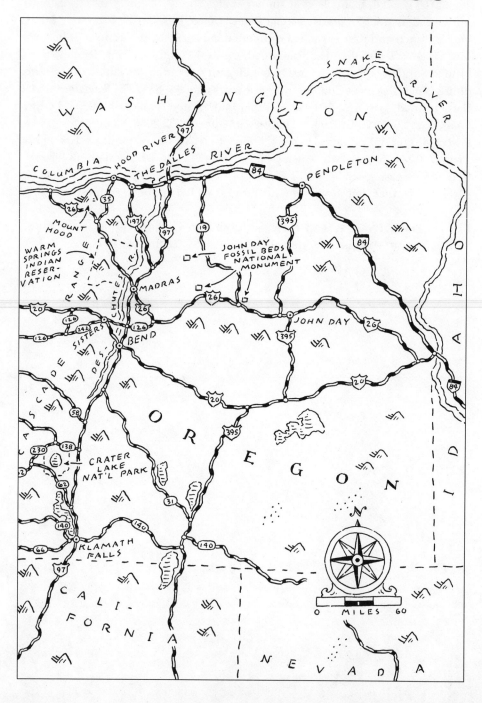

Through the Columbia River Gorge

The forces of nature have left an incredible legacy of scenic riches to the Pacific Northwest—glistening snow-capped peaks, wild seascapes without limit, cool green rain forests, rugged volcanic badlands. But none is more stunningly beautiful than the gorge carved through the Cascade Mountains by Ice Age floodwaters. Protected as a national scenic area just a few years ago, the Columbia River Gorge is a rare combination of awesome scenery, a working river, a major route for rail and highway traffic, and scores of trails, glens, side gorges, waterfalls, and secluded forest hideaways within only an hour's drive east of Portland.

We suggest you make this a leisurely weekend. There aren't many miles to cover, but there are plenty of places to stop and hike a trail, picnic in a shady grove, or sit on a rock and watch the ever-changing river. The best of the scenery and most of the chances for exploring are on the Oregon side of the river. On the other hand, the best long-distance views of the Oregon side are from the Washington side of the river. Schedule your trip so that you drive east on the Oregon bank, cross over at Biggs and return on the Washington side. Hood River has the best choice of accommodations and is also very popular with tourists and board sailers. For something a little bit different, consider staying in Cascade Locks or The Dalles in Oregon or at Goldendale or White Salmon in Washington.

The vistas are magnificent. Basalt cliffs rise sheer from the river. Thready waterfalls pour over the rim and dissolve in the wind before they hit bottom. Evergreen-fringed bluffs shoulder their way down to the river, and on the water, pagoda-towered towboats shove grain-laden barges downstream to Portland.

I-84 on the Oregon side and Washington 14 get you through the gorge in a hurry. But to really savor it, take the old Columbia River Scenic Highway. Completed on the south side in 1915, it was considered an engineering triumph, with its intricate stonework, arched bridges, and lookout points. I-84 has obliterated some of the highway beyond Multnomah Falls, but there are still 24 delightfully meandering miles to enjoy.

To reach it, take Exit 16B, the Crown Point Highway, off I-84 east of Portland. Outside of Troutdale, cross the Sandy River, made famous by the line "Sandy, Willamette and Hood River, too" in Woody Guthrie's "Roll on Columbia."

The narrow road meanders through lush stands of alder, maple, and Douglas fir, past cliffs covered with ferns and clumps of wildflowers. In the spring you can see the sharp green of new growth and smell the sweetness of blossoming things. If you've brought a picnic lunch, you'll find day-use areas in several state parks along the way. Little restaurants such as Tippycanoe and Tad's Chicken and Dumplings are remnants of another day, when this was the main highway along the gorge.

The road narrows and climbs to Vista House at Crown Point, 733 feet above the river. Built in 1918 as a memorial to Oregon's pioneers, the octagon-shaped stone building houses a collection of historical photos and a craft gallery. Views of the gorge are splendid from here. Upriver on the Washington side you'll see landmark Beacon Rock, a sheer 800-foot monolith at river's edge.

Take the time to explore some of the side canyons and marvel at the waterfalls that plunge over the cliffs. Dozens of trails, from less than ½ mile to 21 miles, and elevation gains of zero to as much as 4,900 feet, lace the area. Your best companion is the U.S. Forest Service map called "Forest Trails of the Columbia Gorge." It's available for $1 at the U.S. Forest Service regional office at 319 Southwest Pine Street in Portland, the National Scenic Area Information Center at 902 Wasco Avenue in Hood River, and ranger stations at Troutdale, Mount Hood–Parkdale, and Gresham in Oregon, and Vancouver, Carson, and Trout Lake in Washington.

First of the waterfalls is Latourell, just east of Crown Point, followed by Bridal Veil, Mist, Wahkeena, and Horsetail. An 800-foot trail through narrow Oneonta Gorge is a cool route between green, mossy walls that leads to a waterfall.

Best known is 620-foot Multnomah Falls, actually twin falls, and the highest in the Northwest. Leave your car in the parking lot and walk the paved trail that loops across the face of the falls and crosses over a soaring bridge between the lower and upper levels. The trail becomes steeper toward the end of its 1.2 miles and leads to a platform above the falls with sweeping views of the gorge.

Schedule a meal stop at the wonderful old lodge at the foot of the falls. Built in 1925, the two-story stone structure has a dining room and coffee shop on the upper level, a snack bar and gift shop below.

A few miles to the east, the old highway funnels into the interstate for water-level views of the gorge. Bonneville, first of the hydroelectric dams that have turned the Columbia River above this point from a wild river into a series of big lakes, was built by the Roosevelt administration in the late 1930s. Woody Guthrie was commissioned by the federal government to write a series of songs extolling the virtues of the new hydroelectric projects. The dam site, part of which is included in a 96-acre area designated in the National Register of Historic Places, includes a visitor center, fish ladders, and navigation locks. Pause at the adjacent state fish hatchery to view the giant sturgeon kept in ponds here.

At Cascade Locks, named for the navigation locks built in 1896 to move steamboat traffic past cascades in the river, the Bridge of the Gods crosses into Washington (toll: 50 cents). The locks became obsolete in 1937 when they were covered by water backed up by Bonneville Dam. There's a modest museum of river history at the locks, as well as the Oregon Pony, Oregon's first steam locomotive. Cascade Locks is also the departure point for cruises on the sternwheeler *Columbia Gorge*. Excursions include two-hour daytime trips and sunset dinner cruises on Friday and Saturday nights.

Anyone who has visited the little apple orchard town of Hood River in the past may be astonished at the changes that now meet the eye. Because of the unusual coincidence of downstream currents and strong winds blowing east through the gorge, the waters here have become a major center for board sailing. The streets, populated by young, muscular surfer types, resemble those of a California beach town. Volkswagens and other vintage cars surmounted by surfboards and sails are parked along the side streets, and several sailboard shops advertise their wares in Day-Glo colors.

Seattle Post-Intelligencer columnist John Owen summed it up when he wrote, "A few years ago, [Hood River] was the place where dad's hat blew off and landed in the river. The wind was a nuisance to visitors but was mainly ignored by residents, who seemed to spend their weekends inspecting hubcaps and pickup-truck tires at [a local tire dealer's].

"Today, Hood River is Maui on the Columbia. No, that's incorrect. You can't drive to Maui. Yet on one recent evening in Hood River, cars parked within a block of Chianti's wine and pasta hangout—where boardsailing videos are shown in the bar—bore license plates from Utah, Montana, Colorado, Minnesota, Wyoming, Florida, Texas, California, and British Columbia. And a car from Alberta bore the vanity plate, 'Bordhead.' "

For those who don't partake, just watching the sailboarders is a major activity. Find any spot along the riverbank or down by the marina, and watch these athletes jump the whitecaps with their boards, race at breathtaking speed across the river, then suddenly reverse direction with the agility of acrobats. International competitions are held off Columbia River Gorge Sailpark (Exit 64). Three of the big ones take place in June and July.

There are plenty of accommodations to choose from in Hood River, but the Columbia Gorge Hotel is a bit special. If you're not going to stay there, take the time to visit this old hotel perched on a bluff west of town. Sited on the rimrock in a grove of pines, the place commands sweeping views of the Columbia River and the green hills of Washington. To the south, Mount Hood's 11,235-foot snowy cone dominates the skyline. Cold, clear Phelps Creek meanders through the landscaped grounds to plunge into the gorge, 207 feet below. All in all it's a splendid location for a hotel. Back in 1921, Simon Benson thought so, too.

At that time, engineers had just punched the first modern highway through the Columbia River Gorge. Simon Benson—lumber tycoon and chairman of the commission responsible for the new highway (he's also responsible for the drinking fountains in downtown Portland)—anticipated a boom in tourist traffic and opened a new hotel at Hood River. Promptly christened "the Waldorf of the West," the elegant three-story property—built in the then-popular Neo-Moorish style—boasted 42 rooms "all with bath" and the state's only ballroom east of Portland.

Benson had thought of almost everything. What he neglected to realize was that the same efficient highway bringing motorists from Portland in less than three hours also took them home again the same day. They came for lunch and a look, but not to stay. Although a few luminaries—Rudolph Valentino, Clara Bow, Richard Dix—did stop for the night, too many rooms remained empty. For more than half a century the hotel languished. In 1978 extensive refurbishing began and the hotel has since been restored to its former glory.

If you stay there, try to reserve room 239 or 339; they're right above the falls, whose rushing waters will lull you to sleep if you leave the window open a bit. The hotel is also famous for its lavish breakfasts, something you might want to include in your itinerary.

Another sightseeing highlight of Hood River is the Mount Hood Railroad. Built in 1906 to serve the lumber mills and fruit orchards in the Hood River Valley, the little line is now used exclusively for excursions. Diesel-powered trains depart from the 1911 depot on the east side of town, thread their way south through a narrow valley, reverse direction on a switchback track, then climb steeply to the orchard-studded plateau above town. Excursions run 8½ miles south to Odell or 12½ miles south to Parkdale, depending on the day of the week. The train includes a snack car.

Long before Hood River was known for its windsurfing, it was famous for its apple orchards, which burst into clouds of white blossoms that carpet the slopes south of town every April. If you decide to join your Columbia Gorge trip with a trip around Mount Hood (see "Around Mount Hood"), you'll follow Oregon 35 through these orchards.

Hood River also has a modest historical museum featuring pioneer displays. Anglers may be interested in visiting the Luhr Jensen & Sons plant, which manufactures fishing lures, fishing tackle, and home smokers for meat and fish. Two wineries, Hood River Vineyards and Three Rivers, lie just south of town. Both produce pinot noir, chardonnay, gewürztraminer, and riesling wines and are open for tours and tasting.

Follow I-84 21 miles east to The Dalles, located at a great bend in the Columbia and named by French trappers for the falls located here. As you drive east, notice the abrupt change from the lush greenery around Hood River to the dry, brown hills at The Dalles, a remarkable occurrence in so short a distance. There's a scenic alternate to I-84 that begins at Mosier and follows the high bluffs overlooking the river.

The Dalles Dam, which stretches across the river three miles east of The Dalles, is considered by many to be one of the great travesties of modern progress. Prior to the dam's completion in 1957 and the forming of Celilo Lake, the river tumbled over Celilo Falls just east of here. For scores of generations these waters were the traditional fishing grounds for Indians who came from all over the Northwest to dip-net salmon from spindly platforms built over the river. Indians trekked from as far away as western Montana, trading furs, meat, and other goods to the local Indians for the privilege of fishing at Celilo Falls. The falls were also a major barrier to river navigation and until 1915, when a canal was built, forced travelers, including pioneers on the Oregon Trail, to detour around the falls on trails and later on a 13-mile railroad. Many Oregon museums display photos of the falls and fishing platforms prior to their inundation. Some of the money appropriated to compensate the Indians for the loss of these fishing grounds went to the Warm Springs Tribe, who used it to build the resort at Kah-Nee-Ta (see "Into Indian Country").

Guided tours of the dam include a train ride to the powerhouse, fish ladders, and locks. The Dalles boasts a number of handsome nineteenth-century residences on its side streets as well as the red-brick Saint Peter's Landmark Church, with its 176-foot steeple, 36 stained-glass windows, and Madonna carved from the wood of a ship's keel; Saint Paul's Church, built in 1875; and the original 1858 Wasco County Courthouse. Brochures detailing self-guiding walking tours of the historic portions of the city are available from the Chamber of Commerce. The works of local artists are displayed at the Oregon Trail Art Gallery. Fort Dalles Museum is located in the old post's surgeon's quarters, built in 1856 and the last remaining building from that military fort.

Continue east another 20 miles to Biggs, cross the river to the Washington bank, and follow the signs uphill on U.S. 97 to Maryhill, one of the most unusual attractions in the West. There, perched on a bare brown hill above the Columbia and looking as out of place as a rodeo at Versailles, is an imposing three-story château, one of the finest art museums in the Northwest.

Maryhill didn't start out to be a museum. When Sam Hill, wealthy Seattle lawyer and son-in-law of railroad entrepreneur James Hill, began construction in 1914, he intended the place to be a family home and named it after his wife, Mary. (Hill originally chose the site for a colony of Belgian Quaker immigrants, but they couldn't make a living from the rocky soil and soon moved away.) Hill lost interest in the home and decided instead to turn it into an art museum. The museum was dedicated by Queen Marie of Romania, a friend of Hill's and granddaughter of Queen Victoria, in 1926. Neither Hill nor his wife ever lived here. After Hill's death in 1931, the museum collection was put together by his friend Alma Spreckles, a wealthy art collector. With her husband, Adolph Spreckles, a San Francisco sugar magnate, she had established the California Palace of the Legion of Honor in 1924.

Maryhill's interior is grand. You enter on the high-ceilinged middle level where you'll see Queen Marie's carved wooden throne, a replica of her crown, her silver-and-platinum-gold-lamé court gown, furniture, and other belongings. The museum houses some fabulous collections, including Fabergé eggs and nineteenth-century Eastern Orthodox icons, and there's an unusual clock that belonged to Hill that looks like a forerunner of today's digital watches.

A painting of Czar Nicholas II shows ravages of a looting that occurred when it hung in the Russian embassy in Belgrade, Yugoslavia. The painting was slashed and the Russian ambassador killed. There's a fine collection of sculpture by Auguste Rodin, including a miniature plaster of his most famous work, *The Thinker*. Also displayed are European and American paintings from the nineteenth and early twentieth centuries, a splendid collection of chess sets, weapons, Cypriot pottery, and 1940s French fashions.

If you have the time after leaving Maryhill, detour about three miles east on Washington 14 to Hill's replica of Stonehenge. Northwest author By Fish relates in his book *Go Unbeaten Paths*, "Hill sent a team to England to make plaster casts of the stones which were then duplicated in concrete. Stones in the circular original have fallen down or are missing, but Hill restored his version." The monument was built in memory of Klickitat County men who died in World War I.

Continue down the Washington side of the river on Highway 14 for 35 miles to the twin towns of Bingen and White Salmon. Both have splendid views of the Columbia River and are gateways to the backcountry lakes and streams around Mount Adams to the north. The architecture in both Bingen, a sister city to Bingen, Germany, and White Salmon resembles counterparts in Germany, especially White Salmon's Glockenspiel Tower. Mont Elise Vineyards in Bingen is the oldest family-owned winery in Washington and produces seven wines, the most popular of which is gewürztraminer.

Highway 14 hugs the riverbank for most of the way, plunging through rock tunnels and paralleling the Burlington Northern (formerly Spokane, Portland, and Seattle) railroad. Highlights include hot springs and mineral baths at the old Carson Hotel in Carson, the Skamania County Historical Museum in Stevenson with its collection of 4,000 rosaries, the Washington Shore Visitor Center (Bonneville Dam) at North Bonneville, and Cape Horn Viewpoint with its stunning views east through the gorge. Beacon Rock State Park features the 800-foot-high monolith beside the Columbia River. You can climb to the top on a stairway trail built by local resident Henry Biddle with his own time and money in 1915.

Return to Portland through Camas and Vancouver.

Area Codes: Oregon, 503; Washington, 509 and 206

DRIVING DIRECTIONS Except for detours suggested above, follow I-84 east through the Columbia Gorge to Biggs, cross the river, and return via Washington 14 on the north bank. Round trip is 198 miles.

SIGHTSEEING *Bonneville Dam,* 374-8820. July to Labor Day daily 8 A.M. to 8 P.M. Memorial Day to July 4 8 A.M. to 6 P.M., rest of year 9 A.M. to 5 P.M. Free. Bradford Island Visitor Center has 4 floors of displays, observation deck, underwater fish-viewing room, audiovisual programs. *Cascade Locks Visitor Center,* 374-8619. May to September daily 8 A.M. to 6 P.M., rest of year Monday to Friday 8 A.M. to 5 P.M. Free. *Cascade Locks Museum,* 374-8619, 374-8427. June to September daily noon to 5 P.M. Free. *Sternwheeler* **Columbia Gorge,** 606 Northwest Front Street, Portland 97209, 223-3928, 374-8427. Daily 2-hour excursions departing marina at Cascade Locks at 10 A.M. and 12:30 and 3 P.M., dinner cruise Wednesday through Sunday evenings, mid-June through September. Day excursions adults $9.95, 4–12 $5, under 3 free; dinner cruise $17.95–$31.95, reservations required. The sternwheeler operates out of Portland on the Willamette and Lower Columbia rivers the rest of the year. *Mount Hood Railroad,* 110 Railroad Avenue, Hood River, 386-3556. Early April to June, September, and October, Wednesday to Sunday 10 A.M. and 3 P.M. July through August, Tuesday to Sunday. November to early December, Saturday and Sunday. To Odell, adults $10, seniors $8, 2–11 $6; to Parkdale $17, $15, and $10. *Hood River Historical Museum,* Port Marina Park, Hood River, 386-6772, 386-4274. Mid-April to October Wednesday to Saturday 10 A.M. to 4 P.M., Sunday noon to 4 P.M. Free. *Luhr Jensen & Sons, Inc.,* 400 Portway, Hood River, 386-3811. Tours Tuesday to Thursday 11 A.M. and 1:30 P.M. Free. *Hood River Vineyards,* 4693 Westwood Drive, Hood River, 386-3772. March to December daily 10 A.M. to 5 P.M. *Three Rivers Winery,* 275 Country Club Road, Hood River, 386-5433. Monday to Saturday 11 A.M. to 5 P.M., Sunday 1 to 5 P.M. *The Dalles Dam,* 296-1181. Guided tours Memorial Day to Labor Day daily 10 A.M. to 4:30 P.M., self-guiding tours rest of year. Free. *Fort Dalles Museum,* Fifteenth and Garrison streets, The Dalles, 296-4547. March to October Monday to Friday 10:30 A.M. to 5 P.M., Saturday and Sunday 10 A.M. to 5 P.M.; rest of year Wednesday to Friday noon to 4 P.M., Saturday and Sunday 10 A.M. to 4 P.M. Free. *Maryhill Museum,* 773-3733. Mid-March to mid-November daily 9 A.M. to 5 P.M. Adults $3, seniors $2.50, 6–16 $1.50. *Skamania County Historical Museum,* Vancouver Avenue, Stevenson, 427-5141, 427-9435. Monday to Saturday noon to 5 P.M., Sunday 1 to 6 P.M. Free. *Washington Shore Visitor Center,* Bonneville Dam, 427-4281. July 4 to Labor Day daily 8 A.M. to 8 P.M. Memorial Day to July 4 8 A.M. to 6 P.M., rest of year 9 A.M. to 5 P.M. Free.

E V E N T S *Hood River Blossom Festival,* Hood River, 386-2000, late April. Orchard tours, arts and crafts displays, Mount Hood Railroad begins its season. *Gorge Cities Blow Out,* 667-7778, mid-July. 20-mile downriver sailboard races from Hood River to Cascade Locks.

L O D G I N G *Columbia Gorge Hotel,* 4000 Westcliff Drive, Hood River 97031, 386-5566, (800) 345-1921. Elegant, restored 1920s hotel, $$$$. *Inn at Hood River,* 1108 East Marina Way, Hood River 97031, 386-2200. Excellent location on the Columbia River, $$–$$$. *Lakecliff Estate* (bed and breakfast), 3820 Westcliff Drive, Hood River 97031, 386-7000. Handsome old home in woods with view of river features 5 stone fireplaces and was designed by Albert Doyle, who also designed the Benson Hotel in Portland and the Multnomah Falls Lodge, $$. *State Street Inn* (bed and breakfast), 1005 State Street, Hood River 97031, 386-1899. 4 guest rooms in Hood River residence with view of Mount Adams, $$. *Best Western Tapadera Motor Inn,* 112 West Second Street, The Dalles 97058, 296-9107. Good location convenient to freeway, restaurant, $.

C A M P I N G *Ainsworth State Park,* Bonneville, 695-2261. 45 sites with full hookups on the Columbia River, $11. *Cascade Locks KOA,* Airport Road, Cascade Locks, 374-8668. 100 tree-shaded sites, most with full hookups, $13–$19. *Viento State Park,* 8 miles west of Hood River off I-84, 374-8811. 63 riverfront sites with water and electricity, $7–$11. *Memaloose State Park,* 11 miles west of The Dalles off I-84 (westbound access only). 43 full-hookup sites, 67 tent sites on the river, $9–$11. *Maryhill State Park* (WA), U.S. 97 near Washington 14, 773-5007. 50 full-hookup sites on the Columbia River, $12.

D I N I N G *Multnomah Falls Lodge,* off I-84 at Multnomah Falls, 695-2376. Breakfast, lunch, and dinner daily; handsome old stone lodge makes a good meal and rest stop while touring the gorge; $$. *Columbia River Court Dining Room,* in Columbia Gorge Hotel (see "Lodging"), 386-5566. Breakfast, lunch, and dinner daily; dining room has view of river, noted for lavish breakfasts; $$$. *Stonehedge Inn,* 3405 Cascade Drive, Hood River, 386-3940. Dinner Wednesday to Sunday; vies with the Columbia River Court as the best restaurant in Hood River, tucked away in the woods, contemporary American menu; $$. *Chianti's Restaurant,* 509 Cascade Street, Hood River, 386-5737. Dinner daily; a favorite gathering spot for the young and the young at heart, Italian cuisine; $$. *Jack's Fine Food,* Biggs Junction, I-84 and U.S. 97, 739-2363. Breakfast, lunch, and dinner daily; unpretentious truck stop that's one of our favorites for big breakfasts; $.

FOR MORE INFORMATION Columbia River Gorge National Scenic Area, 902 Wasco Avenue, Hood River 97031, 386-2333. Hood River County Chamber of Commerce, Port Marina Park, Hood River 97031, 386-2000.

Around Mount Hood

Mount Hood is Portland's signature landmark. More than any other topographic feature (except perhaps the Willamette River), the symmetrical white cone on the eastern horizon dominates nearly every view of Portland. And for Portlanders the 11,235-foot peak is a tremendous recreational resource just over an hour's drive away. In winter and spring its slopes offer superb skiing and other winter sports. In summer trails through the national forest around its base invite hikers to get out and exercise close to home; camps are full of tents and RVs, and several mountain lakes produce plenty of trout. In fall the roads and trails around Mount Hood are ablaze with the autumn foliage of vine and big-leaf maples, alders, huckleberries, and other native species.

There's both a quick way and a scenic way to get to Mount Hood. If you're in a hurry to reach the mountain, two-lane U.S. 26 will lead you the 55 miles to Government Camp as fast as traffic will permit. But to combine Mount Hood with a rewarding weekend of sightseeing, we suggest you follow the highways that loop the mountain, heading east through the Columbia Gorge to Hood River (see "Through the Columbia River Gorge"), then around the east flank on Oregon 35 and home on U.S. 26.

Several years ago the tourism promoters of Hood River, in an effort to divert more visitors to their town, published a humorous pamphlet that listed 35 reasons (as in Highway 35) to avoid U.S. 26 when returning from skiing on Mount Hood. The reasons were keyed to points on a map of U.S. 26. Some samples: "#14—500 cars stop to remove chains; #17—Winnebago fails to use slow moving vehicle turnoff; #20—Kelso Women's Bridge Club still driving with chains on—24 mph (sparks flying); #21—Traffic slows to ponder the question, 'What is a Wemme?' " (Wemme is a town on U.S. 26.)

From Hood River, Highway 35 climbs the northeast flank of Mount Hood following Hood River through hundreds of acres of apple and pear orchards that display clouds of blossoms in mid-April. In the summer and fall, produce stands along the highway and in the orchards sell a variety of local fruits and vegetables. As you climb, the snowy slopes of Mount Hood loom ahead; in your rearview mirror you can see 12,276-foot Mount Adams on the other side of the Columbia River. Stop at Panorama Point for superb views of the valley and river below.

If you have time to spare, consider detouring to Lost Lake, 28 miles southwest of Hood River over a paved road via Dee. Blossoming rhododendrons line this road in May, and the huckleberry bushes are loaded with wild fruit in fall. The pristine lake, which frames a reflection of the mountain, provides some fine trout fishing. Boat rentals are available and there's a Forest Service campground (no hookups).

About 24 miles south of Hood River, a side road detours west ten miles to Cloud Cap Inn, a historically important landmark. Now closed to the public, this rustic 1889 inn served for years as the starting point for ascents of Mount Hood. Views of the north side of the mountain are splendid from here. Cooper Spur Ski Area, limited to day use, is one of five ski areas on the mountain. It is located off the same spur road. Mount Hood Meadows, perched on the east side of the mountain just off Highway 35, is the largest ski area on the mountain, offering both alpine and cross-country skiing and some fine runs down Heather Canyon.

Highway 35 crests 4,674-foot Bennett Pass about 37 miles south of Hood River, dips through the forest for about four miles, then crosses 4,157-foot Barlow Pass, summit of the Cascades and junction with the Pacific Crest Trail. The pass is named for Samuel K. Barlow, who constructed the Barlow Road in 1845. The primitive wagon road around Mount Hood to Oregon City served westbound pioneers as an alternative to rafting down the treacherous Columbia River. From Government Camp west, U.S. 26 follows essentially the same route as the Barlow Road. About two miles beyond the pass a short side road leads to the grave of a pioneer woman who perished coming over this road.

The highlight of any trip to Mount Hood is a visit to Timberline Lodge, perched on the south slope just above Government Camp. The magnificent old structure is one of the true architectural monuments of the West. It is, in fact, a masterpiece, born of the Great Depression and the efforts of the Works Progress Administration to stimulate the economy by creating projects for the unemployed. The lodge provided jobs for hundreds of the best stone masons, woodcarvers, wrought-iron workers, weavers, sculptors, painters, and other craftsmen. President Franklin Delano Roosevelt dedicated it on September 28, 1937. The lodge is now on the National Register of Historic Places. A small museum on the lower level details its construction.

During the snow season, the lodge's small cozy rooms, restaurants, and lounges are crowded with skiers and the thump of ski boots echoes through the halls. If you're looking for the solitude this place can offer, go in late spring or fall. Enter the lobby and look up at the huge stone fireplace, big beams, and soaring spaces. The rugged architecture is offset by hundreds of finely crafted details—ornamental ironwork, wood carvings of bears and rams heads in the newel posts, painted murals, woven hangings, mosaics in wood and stone, and dozens of original paintings. The sunsets and sunrises over the Cascades are awesome from Timberline. It seems you can see over the top of the world as you look south to

Mount Jefferson turning pink, purple, and gold. Then, if there's a bit of a nip in the air, you can retreat to the lobby to lounge beside a crackling fire and pet the resident Saint Bernard.

Timberline, Summit, and Ski Bowl are all located in the Government Camp area and offer a variety of terrain and facilities from bunny slopes to challenging runs recommended only for experts. Skiing at the mountain's higher elevations lasts into August. Like Washington's Mount Rainier, Mount Hood is a popular destination for mountain climbers. Several thousand people climb the mountain annually and there are occasional fatalities. Experienced guides lead climbing parties, and you can rent equipment on the mountain. The prime climbing season is from March to mid-July. During the summer months the Magic Mile Chairlift at Timberline operates as a sightseeing lift.

Though Mount Hood really comes into its own in ski season, surrounding Mount Hood National Forest is a popular warm weather destination as well. Paved Forest Service roads lead off U.S. 26 along the crest of the Cascades to Clear Lake, Timothy Lake, and other alpine lakes filled with trout. Their shoresides are dotted with campgrounds. Experienced hikers enjoy the rugged but beautiful Timberline Trail that circles the mountain at the timberline level for 37½ miles. Mount Hood, Salmon Huckleberry, Bull of the Woods, and Badger Creek wilderness areas offer secluded hiking and camping away from logging operations, motorized vehicles, and most other people.

Heading west from Government Camp, U.S. 26 descends quickly through dense conifer forest. The little town of Rhododendron provides a clue to the main feature of this route in May—roadsides lined with the pink blossoms of native rhododendrons.

If you're looking for a resort where you can experience the outdoor recreation of the Mount Hood area, yet return to quality accommodations and dining in the evening, consider the Resort at the Mountain in the town of Welches, 43 miles east of Portland and 12 miles west of Government Camp. Located in a broad, green valley ringed by bulky conifer-clad mountains and straddling the Salmon River, the resort sits at a 1,300-foot elevation. Formerly called Rippling River, it earned its reputation on its golf courses. Three separate nines wind through the trees on 350 acres. This is fly-fishing country, and there are fly shops nearby as well as tennis courts, mountain bikes for rent, and a full range of exercise equipment.

Area Code: 503

DRIVING DIRECTIONS To complete the Mount Hood Loop from Portland, follow I-84 to Hood River, Oregon 35 south to its junction with U.S. 26, then return to Portland on U.S. 26. The complete loop covers 164 miles.

SIGHTSEEING *Cooper Spur Ski Area,* 352-7803. Vertical drop 500 feet, 1 rope tow, 1 T-bar, cross-country, day-use area, night skiing on weekends, overnight at nearby Cooper Spur Inn. This area on the north side of Mount Hood has the gentlest slopes, ideal for beginners, children. *Mount Hood Meadows,* 337-2222. Vertical drop 2,777 feet, 9 chairs, 1 rope tow, instruction, cross-country, rentals, 4 restaurants, night skiing Wednesday to Sunday, mostly intermediate slopes with some advanced. *Ski Bowl,* 272-3522. 1,450-foot vertical drop, 4 chairs, 6 rope tows, cross-country, rentals, ski school, 2 cafeterias, night skiing, wide variety of terrain, open slopes mostly facing north. *Summit Ski Area,* 272-3351. Vertical drop 400 feet, 1 chair, 1 tow, tubing and cross-country, instruction, day lodge, weekends and holidays only, beginner and intermediate slopes. *Timberline Ski Area,* 272-3311. Vertical drop 2,500 feet, 6 chairs, ski school, rentals, cross-country, touring, tobogganing and tubing, night skiing, 31 trails, meal and overnight facilities in lodge.

EVENTS *Winter Games of Oregon,* at Mount Hood ski areas, 224-7158, mid-March. Series of skiing and winter sports competitions.

LODGING *Lost Lake Resort,* Lost Lake Mount Hood National Forest, 386-6366. 8 units in rustic lakeshore resort on slopes of Mount Hood, Memorial Day to Labor Day, fishing, boating, $–$$. *Inn at Cooper Spur,* 10755 Cooper Spur Road, Mount Hood 97041, 352-6692. Rooms in main lodge, cabins, fireplaces, hot tubs, excellent views, ski packages, $$$. *Timberline Lodge,* Timberline Ski Area 97028, 231-5400, (800) 452-1335 (in OR, outside Portland), (800) 547-1406 (in WA, ID, NV, UT, CA). Wide range of room types with either mountain or Cascade views, modern facilities, ski packages, $$$–$$$$. *Falcon's Crest* (bed and breakfast), 87287 Government Camp Loop Highway, Government Camp 97028, 272-3403. 3-story mountain lodge with 5 guest rooms, rate includes breakfast and dinner, $$$. *Huckleberry Inn,* Business Loop Highway 26, Government Camp 97028, 272-3325. 15 rooms in center of winter activity on the mountain, $–$$. *Mount Hood Val-U Inn,* 87450 East Government Camp Loop Road, Government Camp 97028, 272-3205. Modern motel convenient to ski slopes, mountain trails, $$$. *Resort at the Mountain,* 68010 East Fairway Avenue, Welches 97067, 622-3101 or (800) 669-7666. Full-service resort ¾ mile off the highway, $$$–$$$$.

CAMPING *Lost Lake* (national forest), on the shore of Lost Lake, 666-0701. 91 sites with full hookups, mid-May to mid-October, $8. *Trillium Lake* (national forest), on lakeshore south of Mount Hood, 666-0704. 39 sites, no hookups, Memorial Day to Labor Day, $6–$8. *Mount Hood RV Village,* 65000 East Highway 26, Welches, 622-4011. Large, new RV park on river with 420 full-hookup sites, full services, $15–$22.

DINING *Inn at Cooper Spur* (see "Lodging"). Breakfast, lunch, and dinner daily; hearty portions, prime rib, steak; $$$. *Cascade Dining Room,* Timberline Lodge (see "Lodging"). Breakfast, lunch, and dinner daily; menu includes beef, seafood, pasta; $$–$$$. *Barlow Trail Inn,* 69580 U.S. 26, Zigzag, 622-3877. Breakfast, lunch, and dinner daily; comfortable, laid-back log lodge serves ample breakfasts, burgers, steaks; $$. *Salazar's,* 71545 U.S. 26, Rhododendron, 622-3775. Dinner daily; a local favorite, the restaurant is filled with the owner's collections; $$. *Resort at the Mountain* (see "Lodging"). Breakfast, lunch, and dinner daily; upscale dining room overlooks swimming pool; traditional fare of seafood, beef, Northwest specialties; $$$. *Chalet Swiss,* Welches Road and U.S. 26, Welches, 622-3600. Intimate spot off the highway at Welches specializes in Swiss, Continental cuisine including fondue, seafood, raclette; $$–$$$. *The Store,* Highway 26, Wemme, 622-3130. A local treasure and gathering place for backpackers, cyclists, and those who are "getting in touch"; health food, lunches-to-go, home cooking; $–$$.

FOR MORE INFORMATION Mount Hood Recreation Association, P.O. Box 342, Welches 97067, 224-7158.

Into Indian Country

Most people think of the Southwest when they think of Native American culture, but the Pacific Northwest also has plenty of its own to offer, both in terms of historical sightseeing and experiencing contemporary Indian culture. In Washington, the Makah Museum at Neah Bay and the Yakima Nation Cultural Center at Toppenish are standouts. Idaho has the Nez Perce National Historical Park east of Lewiston. But the Central Oregon Indian experience is unique.

Look at a map of Oregon and you'll see a large, nearly featureless area in the north-central part of the state labeled Warm Springs Indian Reservation. Cross it on U.S. 26 and you'll think this must be a set for a classic Saturday matinee Western—flat-topped buttes, sage-and-juniper-studded hillsides, rocky canyons, limitless vistas. You almost expect John Wayne and the cavalry to come riding around the next bend in the road.

Smack-dab in the middle of all this magnificent scenery is Kah-Nee-Ta, Indian owned and operated, and one of the best family resorts in the Northwest. Along with its remarkable setting and 300-plus days of sunshine, it offers a wide variety of activities and accommodations.

The legendary Kit Carson guided that intrepid Western explorer, John C. Fremont, through here on an expedition mapping the Oregon Country in 1843. Their route closely paralleled the present-day reservation road to Simnasho. The expedition passed this way during a chilly November and were delighted to discover the springs that give the tribe and reservation its name. Fremont's journal entry for the twenty-ninth reads: "We emerged from the basin by a narrow pass, upon a considerable branch of Fall River [the Deschutes River, the branch was the Warm Springs River], running to the eastward through a narrow valley. The trail, descending this stream, brought us to a locality of hot springs . . . were formed into deep handsome basins and would have been delightful baths, if the outer air had not been so keen, the thermometer in these being 89 degrees."

The Confederated Tribes of Warm Springs Indian Reservation built the resort around these hot springs at the eastern edge of its 640,000-acre reservation with $4 million it received as compensation from the federal government when the tribe's traditional salmon fishing grounds on the Columbia River at Celilo Falls were submerged behind The Dalles Dam (See "Through the Columbia River Gorge").

There's a family-oriented village and a more elegant lodge about a mile apart. Most of the activity focuses on the village, nestled beside the swift-running Warm Springs River. Here, 145-degree water from the hot springs feeds mineral baths and, after it has been cooled to swimmable temperatures, a huge outdoor pool. There's another pool at the lodge. The complex includes a miniature golf course, snack shops, and gift shops where you can purchase Indian crafts. There are bicycles for rent, and the stables across the road offer guided trail rides into the surrounding hills. The River Room restaurant serves modestly priced meals, including the specialty of the house, Indian fry bread. There's trout fishing in the Warm Springs River and fishing and white-water rafting on the nearby Deschutes River.

One- and two-bedroom cottages adjacent to the pool are called *neeshas;* the two-bedroom units have kitchens. If you really want to get into the reservation spirit, you can camp in one of the full-size tepees. Equipped with fireplace and picnic table, they'll sleep up to ten, but bring an air mattress—the floors are concrete. There's also a large RV park with full hookups.

Perched on a hill a mile down the road is the four-story oak-and-cedar lodge, built in the shape of an arrowhead. There are several tennis courts on the grounds and an 18-hole golf course sprawls along the valley floor. The lodge's Juniper Room is a great place to watch the sunset and the twinkling lights of the village below. Menu specialties include game hen baked in clay. Each Saturday evening from Memorial Day to Labor Day, tribeswomen arrange an Indian-style salmon bake on the lodge grounds followed by a program of traditional Indian dancing.

In the nearby town of Warm Springs, reservation headquarters, you'll find the tribal information center and gift shop as well as other shops selling Indian crafts, especially decorative beadwork, woven baskets, and rawhide leather goods.

Just beyond the southwestern corner of the reservation, the Deschutes, Crooked, and Metolius rivers come together in a steep basaltic canyon to form Lake Billy Chinook behind Round Butte Dam. The lake has an abundance of trout and you can fish from the bank or from a boat; rentals are available. A marina on the Metolius arm of the lake also rents houseboats. Central Oregon's most popular park, Cove Palisades, is located on the southeastern shore.

Madras, about 16 miles east of Warm Springs, is Oregon's rockhounding capital, noted for the abundance of agates and thunder eggs (the state rock) in the surrounding countryside. (The thunder egg formed as a gas bubble in a rhyolite (lava) flow about 60 million years ago. Subsequently, silica filled in the hollow center and solidified to create lovely patterns in the rock. From the outside a thunder egg looks just like any other nearly spherical rock, but once you slice it open with a diamond saw, the interior can be dazzling.) There are several versions of how the town got its curious name—the same as the cotton fabric manufactured in Madras, India. One account has it that around the turn of the century some townspeople were debating in the local general store on what to call their new settlement. Someone noticed ''Madras'' stamped on bolts of cloth on the shelves and suggested it as a name not likely to have been taken by any other town in the Northwest.

If you'd like to try your hand at rockhounding but are inexperienced, there's an easy way to do it. Head for Richardson's Recreational Ranch, about 14 miles northeast of Madras on U.S. 97. At first glance, the 17,000-acre ranch looks like any other western cattle spread with its white-faced Herefords grazing in the grassy valleys, big ranch house, barn, and windmill. But rocks, not cattle, are the main business at Richardson's.

The ranch sits atop one of the finest thunder egg beds in the world, as well as substantial deposits of agate, petrified wood, fossils, and gemstones. About 4,000 acres of ranch are devoted to rockhounding, with 22 active sites now being excavated. One, the Blue Bed, has been producing thunder eggs continuously since 1928.

Rockhounds (called ''pebble puppies'' by the Richardsons) come from all over the world to dig here. The Richardsons make it easy for first-timers. They lend you a pointed geologist's pick, give you a map, and direct you to the best beds. The digging is free; you only pay a small fee for the rocks you take home.

You drive off from the ranch house over rutted dirt roads, through juniper-and-sage-covered hills, and winding around cliffs, buttes, and into canyons. When you reach the beds, you're likely to find a dozen or so other rockhounds, who tend to be a friendly group and will usually offer advice on where to dig and what to look for. When you've collected several likely looking specimens, you drive back to the ranch house, where you can have them cut and polished if you wish.

The cost of this service varies with the size of the rock, but you'll be able to take home several thunder eggs for under $10.

If you'd rather not bother with the digging, the Richardsons will sell you uncut rocks that you can have cut when you get home, or they will cut them here for you. In addition, they offer a wide variety of gemstone-quality rock from all over the world, including obsidian, banded agate, moss agate, jaspers, jasp-agate, Oregon sunset, and rainbow agate. Jewelry and decorative items made from rock are also for sale.

For more information on rockhounding, the Madras Chamber of Commerce offers a free printed guide to the best sites in the area.

Area Code: 503

DRIVING DIRECTIONS From Portland, follow U.S. 26 east across the Cascades for 100 miles to Warm Springs, then 10 miles north on a reservation road to Kah-Nee-Ta.

SIGHTSEEING *Hunter Expeditions,* U.S. 26 in Warm Springs, 593-3113, 389-8370. Specializes in raft trips of varying length down the Deschutes River. *Richardson's Recreational Ranch,* Gateway Route, Box 440, Madras 97741, 475-2680.

EVENTS *Pi-Ume-Sha Pow Wow and Rodeo,* Warm Springs, 553-3243, mid-June. Rodeo, traditional Indian dances, stick games, salmon bake.

LODGING *Kah-Nee-Ta Resort,* P.O. Box K, Warm Springs 97761, 553-1112 or (800) 831-0100, $$$. *Sonny's Motel,* 1539 Southwest Highway 97, Madras 97741, 475-7217. Swimming pool, restaurant, $. *Master Host Motor Inn,* 203 Fourth Street, Madras 97741, 475-6141. Swimming pool, $.

CAMPING *Kah-Nee-Ta Resort* (see "Lodging"). Camping in teepees $50 for up to 5 people, full-hookup RV sites $12–$20. *KOA Madras,* 2435 Southwest Jericho Street, 9 miles south on U.S. 97, 546-3073. 81 hookup sites on 10 rural acres, open mid-April through October, $10.50–$14. *The Cove Palisades State Park,* on Lake Billy Chinook, 15 miles southwest of Madras off U.S. 97, 546-3412. 87 full-hookup sites, 91 with electric, 94 tent; dramatic rock formations, marina, open mid-April through October, $8–$11.

DINING *River Room,* at Kah-Nee-Ta Resort (see "Lodging"). Breakfast, lunch, and dinner daily; modest fare served beside the river, $. *Juniper Room,* at Kah-Nee-Ta Resort (see "Lodging"). Dinner daily; upscale dining room, some game and Indian specialties; $$–$$$. *Grandma Hoffy's,* 590 North Highway 26, Madras, 475-7369. Breakfast, lunch, and dinner daily; family restaurant, steak, salad bar; $–$$.

FOR MORE INFORMATION Madras Chamber of Commerce, 366 Fifth Street, Madras 97741, 475-2350.

The Secrets of John Day

We are aware that not every weekend we recommend will suit everyone's taste. Take the John Day country of eastern Oregon, for example. Some visitors find incredible beauty in its multicolored, rocky landscapes; a primitive appeal in its vast open spaces; and a soul-soothing quality in a territory that has been little changed by man.

Others come away with memories of hot sun, dry dusty earth, a lonely emptiness, and visitor services that are few and far between. People either love it or they hate it, but few are indifferent.

The first time you see the John Day country you may feel you've been there before. It's typical of the settings of countless Hollywood Westerns. Dramatic bluffs conjure up the image of a column of mounted Indians silhouetted there against the sky. You can visualize a wagon train winding its way through the river gorge below.

Fat Herefords graze in pastures beside the highway. Big, old ranch houses nestle beneath cooling groves of cottonwoods. In the small towns, battered pickups line the dusty streets and the saloons are crowded on Saturday nights.

But the main reason to head for this remote area of eastern Oregon is John Day Fossil Beds National Monument. Here, preserved in volcanic and sedimentary rocks, is one of the world's most complete fossil deposits. It traces the evolution of plants and animals from more than 50 million years ago to about 5 million years ago. Thousands of marine fossils, teeth, and bones of extinct animals, and impressions of trees and plants have been found imbedded in the rocks.

The national monument comprises three widely scattered units located between 50 and 110 miles east of Madras adjacent to Oregon 218 and U.S. 26. Before you begin touring, stop at monument headquarters in the town of John Day to look at the fossil exhibits, pick up maps, and get advice on what to see.

The Sheep Rock Unit gets its name from a massive promontory that overlooks the John Day River. Largest of the monument's three units, it flanks the river for about seven miles along Oregon 19. Historic buildings of Cant Ranch (now the monument's primary information center) provide a glimpse of rural Oregon life in the late nineteenth century as well as some fine displays of fossils. Self-guiding trails lead to Blue Basin; U.S. 26 and the John Day River take your through spectacular Picture Gorge, where alternating layers of basalt and ash make the cliffs look like a layer cake.

The natural earth colors—from green, bronze, yellow, and ocher to rusty red, white, and blue-gray— in this country are startling at first, then become increasingly lovely as your eye picks out the shapes and patterns in the deposits. The best times to view them are just after dawn and just before sunset. And, if you're lucky enough to be here during a summer thunderstorm, you'll find the vivid colors almost eerie.

Try to visit the Painted Hills Unit in early morning or late afternoon, when low light enhances the shades of red, pink, buff, gold, bronze, and black displayed in bands of mineral-bearing clays along the flanks of the hills. The unit is located four miles west of Mitchell on U.S. 26, then six miles north along Bridge Creek. If you spend some time here, you'll discover that the colors are not constant but change with the changing light. Trails lead to the unusual formations at Painted Cove.

Dramatic palisades that rise abruptly from a narrow canyon mark the Clarno Unit on Highway 218 about 20 miles west of Fossil. From the Clarno beds, paleontologists have unearthed the remains of crocodiles, rhinoceroses, miniature horses, and several animals that have no modern descendants. Two trails lead past many plant fossils preserved in the mudstone. Picnic tables scattered through the junipers make this a good choice for a midday meal stop.

As you drive the highways and byways of John Day country, you'll notice a frozen-in-time quality to the place. Its silent landscapes seem an appropriate final resting place for the life that flourished here millions of years ago.

If you enjoy exploring small towns, you'll be delighted when you discover Fossil. The 1901 red-brick Wheeler County Courthouse presides among the shade trees at one end of town. Its turret and fish-scale shingles make it a curiosity well worth photographing. Don't miss the circuit court (second floor, rear) and its old-fashioned jury room with potbellied stove. The two-story brick IOOF (International Order of Odd Fellows) Building houses the Fossil Museum. Asher Car Museum, across the street, preserves a dozen antique automobiles, among them a 1929 Olds Sports Sedan and a 1926 Model T Roadster. Both museums have irregular hours, but if you ask, there's usually someone around to let you in to see the exhibits. Browse the shelves in "The Merc," a local general store, to the accompaniment of country-western music and receive your change from an old chrome-plated hand crank cash register.

John Day is an authentic cattle town, and if you visit in May, you may see herds of cattle being driven through the streets on the way to summer pasture. Restaurants feature menus emblazoned with local cattle brands, and the only songs on the jukeboxes are country-western.

This town took its curious name from the John Day River, which in turn was named for a Virginian who was a member of the Astor-Hunt overland party of 1811–1812. Day and Ramsay Crooks, another member of the expedition, became separated from the main party in the Snake River country, wandered through the Blue Mountains in winter, and were befriended by Walla Walla Indians in spring. Continuing westward, they met hostile Indians in the vicinity of the John Day River who robbed them, even of their clothes, and forced the two naked men to wander through the wilderness until they eventually met up with and were rescued by another party of explorers. One speculates on why the geographers didn't choose Ramsay Crooks's name for the river, town, dam, or various other geographic features here. John Day seems to have acquired a prominence out of all proportion to his role in history.

The Kam Wah Chung & Co. Museum, in John Day, is unique among museums. As you enter the dim confines of the old building by the river, you step into the exotic environment of a Chinese home/store/clubhouse of the gold mining era. Two young Chinese immigrants, Ing Hay and Lung On, came to John Day in 1887, took up residence in the 1860s buildings, and lived here until the 1940s. According to historians, Lung On was a gambler and a ladies' man, a shrewd businessman who obtained the first liquor license near the gold fields of the Blue Mountains. Ing Hay was a healer whose ability to diagnose an illness by feeling a person's pulse attracted patients from a wide area. The two served the needs of one of the largest Chinese communities between San Francisco and Seattle in the late nineteenth century. Canned goods, sleeping quarters, medicinal herbs, clothing, and religious shrines are just as the two men left them in the windowless building, whose walls have been blackened by years of smoke. Tobacco, incense, or opium? Who can say?

Nearby Canyon City boomed with a gold rush in the 1860s, with millions of dollars in gold taken from Canyon Creek and from later hydraulic excavations of the hillsides. As with many boom-and-bust mining towns in the West, this one swelled to more than 10,000 residents during its heyday. Some of the town's original buildings still stand above Canyon Creek. The Grant County Historical Museum preserves many relics and photographs of the era. Joaquin Miller, the frontier poet, lived for a time with his family in the cabin that is now next to the museum.

If you have a hankerin' for some anglin', try nearby Strawberry Mountain Wilderness, where you'll find several high-country lakes stocked with trout and miles of secluded hiking trails. In late spring, the North Fork of the John Day River makes a challenging white-water raft trip. Rapid Transit Outfitters in Canyon City will take you on one-, two-, or three-day expeditions.

Area Code: 503

DRIVING DIRECTIONS The most direct route to John Day from Portland is to follow U.S. 26 east around the southern shoulder of Mount Hood, southeast across the Warm Springs Indian Reservation, then east from Prineville. The mileage is longer, but you could save time by heading east on I-84 to Biggs, then taking U.S. 97, Oregon 206 and 19, then U.S. 26 into John Day. In any case, the minimum mileage from Portland is about 264.

SIGHTSEEING *Kam Wah Chung & Co. Museum,* adjacent to the city park on the river in John Day, 575-0547. May to October Monday to Thursday 8 A.M. to 12 noon and 1 to 5 P.M. and Saturday and Sunday 1 to 5 P.M. Adults $1.50, 1–8 50 cents. *Grant County Historical Museum,* on U.S. 395 in Canyon City, 575-0362. June to September Monday to Saturday 9:30 A.M. to 4:30 P.M. Adults $2, seniors and teenagers $1, 6–12 50 cents.

EVENTS *Grant County Fair and Rodeo,* John Day, 575-0547, late August. The state's oldest continuous county fair features traditional rodeo cowboy events, carnival, agricultural exhibits.

LODGING *Best Western Inn,* 315 West Main Street, John Day 97845, 575-1700. Modern motel, indoor pool, $. *Dreamers Lodge,* 144 North Canyon Boulevard, John Day 97845, 575-0526. Conventional motel, in town, $. *The Sunset Inn,* 390 West Main Street, John Day 97845, 575-1462. Indoor pool, restaurant, $.

CAMPING *Clyde Holliday State Wayside Area,* 7 miles west of John Day on U.S. 26, 575-2773. 30 sites with water-electricity, open mid-April to October, $9. *Shelton State Park,* 10 miles southeast of Fossil on Highway 19, 869-2365. 36 sites, no hookups, $8. *Depot Park,* Main Street, Prairie City, 820-3605, 25 sites, 15 full hookups, May to October, $8.

DINING *The Sunset Inn* (see "Lodging"). Breakfast, lunch, and dinner daily; steak, salad bar; $. *The Grubsteak,* 149 East Main Street, John Day, 575-1970. Lunch Monday to Friday, dinner Monday to Saturday; specialty is rib-eye steak; $. *Ferdinand's,* 128 Front Street, Prairie City, 820-9359. Lunch and dinner Tuesday to Saturday; Old West–style restaurant in former 19th-century butchershop features 2 ornate bars, locally famous burgers; $.

FOR MORE INFORMATION John Day Fossil Beds National Monument, 420 West Main Street, John Day 97845, 575-0721. Grant County Chamber of Commerce, 281 West Main Street, John Day 97845, 575-0547.

The Sublime Meadows of the Metolius

Most people who know about Metolius Meadows in central Oregon are reluctant to tell you. Or, if they do, you're not likely to believe them.

The Metolius is one of those rare pockets of crystal water, tall trees, and lush meadows that remain largely undiscovered by the travelers who speed by just a few miles away on U.S. 20. It's a gentle place of just a few square miles, studded with 600-year-old Ponderosas and carpeted with knee-high grass. Against a backdrop of the snow-capped Cascade spires of Mount Jefferson, Three-Fingered Jack, and Mount Washington, the Metolius River springs icy and clear from a bubbling hole and meanders through forest and meadow to the Lake Billy Chinook reservoir at its rendezvous with the Deschutes.

This is premier fly-fishing country, and 11 miles of the river is devoted to the catch-and-release technique. There are rainbow, Dolly Varden, and even a few brown and brook trout.

The heart of Metolius Meadows is Camp Sherman, settled by dry land farmers from Sherman County who first came to this cool, green retreat to escape the hot summers of eastern Oregon in the 1920s. They named Camp Sherman after their home county. The town is located in a wide spot beside the river with a handful of summer homes, rustic resorts, a general store and gas station, and a café. There isn't much to do except relax, perhaps fish or hike or ride horseback, ski in the winter, and drink in the scenery, magnificent year-round. And that's exactly why those who know it come here.

The newly rebuilt café at Metolius River Resort is the gathering place. Locals and vacationers stroll in for breakfast to exchange gossip and find out where the fish are biting. Even though the Metolius River can be fished year-round and lodgings are open in the winter, many visitors perceive that facilities in the area shut down when the lowland lake fishing season (the third week in April to the middle of October) is over.

No doubt about it, the fishing here is challenging. Because the temperature of the spring-fed river never gets above 48 degrees or so and the water is crystal clear, the native trout is wily and difficult to catch. Hatchery-raised trout are planted each weekend from mid-April through Labor Day. The locals call the Metolius "a banker's river" because the best times to fish are from mid-morning to late afternoon. The Camp Sherman Store and Fly Shop prints a guide to the insect hatches on the river, sells flies and tackle, and will offer advice on where to fish and the best flies to use.

For visitors who don't like to fish, there are dozens of miles of trails lacing the area. One favorite hike takes you upstream a couple of miles to the source of the Metolius. There are theories that the river is snowmelt from the Cascades that travels underground for miles through lava tubes to emerge here. But no one knows for sure. Along the hiking trails, you're likely to see deer grazing in the meadows, eagles or ospreys soaring overhead, and raucous-voiced great blue herons feeding on trout. Mink, otter, beaver, and raccoon are abundant, as are the ubiquitous chipmunks and squirrels. Horses are for rent at stables that also offer guided trail rides. You can join an all-day wilderness ride or overnight pack trips. Boaters will find water sports, a marina, and a resort at nearby Blue Lake.

Just down the road from Camp Sherman, about 15 minutes away, is Black Butte Ranch, one of central Oregon's best resorts. The 1,800-acre residential property rents bedrooms, condominiums, and private homes and is an excellent choice if you're a golfer. Two 18-hole courses have some of the most spectacular views in the Northwest. Flanked by pines, green-carpeted fairways face seven snow-capped mountains—the Three Sisters, Broken Top, Three-Fingered Jack, Mount Washington, and Mount Jefferson—plus Black Butte, a 500-foot-high cinder cone.

One of the best ways to take in the view is from the seat of a bicycle. Eighteen miles of level paths wind through the ranch. If you don't bring your own bike, you can rent one here. If tennis is your game, you can choose from 19 plexi-paved courts. They're free to guests, but you should reserve one in advance. Black Butte Stables offers hourly, half-day, and all-day horseback rides, plus breakfast and steak dinner rides. Lodge Lake, on the ranch grounds, is available to guests for fishing with barbless hooks and flies.

Highway 20 leads east eight miles from Black Butte Ranch to the Western-theme town of Sisters. In recent years, business owners have remodeled their buildings in 1880s style, with false fronts, gingerbread architecture, and board-walks. You could easily spend a couple of hours browsing through the art galleries, antiques stores, gift shops, and boutiques. Stop for an ice-cream cone at the Palace, a combination art gallery and old-fashioned soda fountain, located at the corner of Cascade and Elm streets.

Area Code: 503

DRIVING DIRECTIONS From Portland it's 130 miles to the junction of the Camp Sherman road via I-5 to Salem, Oregon 22, and U.S. 20 over Santiam Pass. At the signs on Highway 20, turn left (north) 4 miles to Camp Sherman.

LODGING *Metolius River Lodges,* P.O. Box 110, Camp Sherman 97730, 595-6290. Cozy, 12-unit lodge on the river, kitchens, fireplaces, $$–$$$. *House on the Metolius,* P.O. Box 601, Camp Sherman 97730, 595-6620. Cabins with fireplaces, kitchens, set on 200 forested acres, $$$. *Lake Creek Lodge,* Star Route, Sisters 97759, 595-6331. Venerable fishing retreat with cabins, lodge rooms, breakfast and dinner available to guests, private trout pond for children, $$$. *Blue Lake*

Resort, Star Route, Box 13900, Sisters 97759, 595-6671. Housekeeping cabins on prime fishing and water recreation lake, boat rentals, horseback riding, $$. *Black Butte Ranch,* P.O. Box 8000, Black Butte Ranch 97759, 595-6211 or (800) 452-7455. Complete resort featuring golf, tennis, horseback riding, $$–$$$$. *Best Western Ponderosa Lodge,* 505 West Highway 20, Sisters 97759, 549-1234. Large, well-maintained motel, swimming pool, $$.

CAMPING *Deschutes National Forest,* 549-2111. Operates 6 campgrounds, all within 9 miles of Camp Sherman, with a total of 120 sites without hookups, from May to mid-October. *Blue Lake Resort* (see "Lodging"). 38 sites with hookups, $8–$14. *Circle 5 Trailerpark & Campground,* ½ mile east of Sisters on U.S. 20, 549-3861. 33 tree-shaded sites with hookups, $15. *KOA-Sisters,* 4 miles southeast of Sisters on U.S. 20, 549-3021. 77 sites, 18 full hookups, $15.75.

DINING *Black Butte Ranch* (see "Lodging"). Breakfast, lunch, and dinner daily; upscale dining room overlooks lake, meadow, and mountains; $$–$$$. *Hotel Sisters and Bronco Billy's Saloon,* 101 Cascade Street, Sisters, 549-RIBS. Breakfast, lunch, and dinner daily; hearty Western meals, plus Mexican dishes, highlight this Western-theme restaurant; $$. *The Gallery,* 230 West Cascade Street, Sisters, 549-2631. Breakfast, lunch, and dinner daily; simple food, large portions, good choice for breakfast; $.

FOR MORE INFORMATION Metolius Recreation Association, P.O. Box 64, Camp Sherman 97730, 595-6117. Sisters Chamber of Commerce, 340 Southwest Cascade Street, Sisters 97759, 549-0251.

Bend: Oregon's Sun Country

When the long, gray days west of the Cascades begin to seem interminable to Northwesterners, most start thinking about heading for sun country. For both Oregonians and Washingtonians, that often means the two-thirds of their states that lie east of the Cascades. And, of the dozens of attractive sun country destinations in both states, none has as much to offer as central Oregon around the city of Bend.

Boasting more than 300 days of sunshine a year, the Bend area has spawned several excellent resorts. This is horse country, but it also has some of the best river rafting, fly-fishing, golf and tennis, and bicycling in the Northwest. A year-round destination, it also claims the best ski area in the American Northwest, second only to Sun Valley.

The landscapes of central Oregon are a sharp contrast to the lush evergreen country west of the Cascades. Juniper-and-sagebrush-studded high desert covers most of the area. South of Bend, the view of vast lava fields, cinder cones, and other volcanic matter stretches away in all directions. All along the western horizon the jagged snow-capped peaks of the Three Sisters and other Cascade mountains punctuate the skyline. Northwest and northeast of Bend, rivers have cut dramatic gorges through sedimentary rock. Wherever there is water, either streams or pumped irrigation water, hay and alfalfa ranches brighten the landscape with patches of green. As elsewhere in the Northwest, the area is growing rapidly, and many of those moving here are building or purchasing expensive rural retreats. Increasingly, you'll pass pastures of sleek riding horses and pet llamas on property owned by wealthy hobby ranchers.

If you're planning a weekend in central Oregon, you'll want to choose accommodations first. Sunriver, 15 miles south of Bend, is the largest and most complete resort in the area, with 36 holes of golf, 31 tennis courts, racquetball courts, swimming pools, rental bicycles, a nature center, several restaurants, and more. Smaller, but with excellent facilities, is Inn of the Seventh Mountain, on the Cascade Lakes Highway west of Bend. One of our favorites is Rock Springs Guest Ranch, about six miles northwest of Bend off U.S. 20. If you're planning a weekend of skiing at Mount Bachelor, you should be aware there are no overnight facilities at the area; most people stay in town or at one of the resorts and drive or catch a shuttle bus to the slopes. Also, Bend is suffering growth pains, especially traffic congestion. If you select a motel in town, be forewarned that traffic can be a hassle.

Bicyclists head for central Oregon for the area's outstanding classic road tours. One of the favorite spring tours includes Smith Rock State Park, about 23 miles north of Bend, where the Crooked River cuts around massive columns of reddish rock. This is also a favorite destination for rock climbers, who come to scale its nearly vertical faces. Any warm-weather weekend you can drive out to the park and watch these intrepid climbers clinging like human flies to the rock.

The Deschutes, which rivals the Rogue and the Umpqua as Oregon's top recreational river, flows northward through the heart of this country, providing outstanding waters for rafting, kayaking, and fishing. Upstream from Bend, the river offers a variety of rafting ranging from slack water up to class IV rapids and one class VI (suicidal) 15-foot drop at Dillon Falls. One of the side benefits of rafting the Deschutes in the height of the season (May through July) is that the weather is usually hot and dry in this semidesert region. If you get drenched with waves and spray, you'll soon dry off.

The Deschutes below Bend is open year-round for rainbow and brown trout fishing. The Crooked River is another favorite, but somewhat difficult to reach. Among fly fishermen, the lower Deschutes is legendary. It lies a couple of hours north of Bend, but most visitors hire a fishing guide, the majority of whom operate out of Bend or Sisters. A professional guide will take care of the necessary permits, provide a drift boat, and find the best spots to wet your line.

One local guide, who bills himself as "the Patient Angler," says, "It's not an easy river to fish. There's a lot of line technique you have to know, or will know before the day is over. The water is fast. You can't fish from a floating device, so you have to wade the river. It's a very rewarding river for the fish you catch, but it's also a very challenging river."

Mount Bachelor, Oregon's largest ski resort, is a popular destination from anywhere in the Northwest for several reasons: it's well connected by air and rail from both Portland and Seattle (as well as San Francisco); it's oriented toward family skiing, having a large proportion of intermediate runs, a ski school, and day-care facilities for children; and it's reasonably priced, with most resorts and major motels offering discounted packages that include lift tickets and accommodations. The season usually begins in mid-November and often lasts past July because of the 9,000-foot summit of Mount Bachelor. With an annual snow pack averaging 16 feet and more than 6,000 acres of skiable terrain, including an extensive network of cross-country trails, Mount Bachelor remains relatively uncrowded on all but holiday weekends. The base of the mountain is about 22 miles west of Bend over well-plowed roads. There's also plenty of public transportation available.

You may want to include some sightseeing in a central Oregon weekend otherwise packed with activity. Tops on the list of sightseeing drives is Cascade Lakes Highway, which makes a spectacular hundred-mile loop from Bend west and south along the eastern slopes of the Cascades. Along the way you pass a chain of lovely translucent lakes with the massive mountains in the Three Sisters Wilderness Area as a backdrop. The highway leads past Mount Bachelor, where, during the summer months, the summit chair lift is in operation to carry sightseers to the top of the 9,060-foot mountain for sweeping views of the tops of the Cascade peaks. At Crane Prairie Reservoir, there's a short nature trail that leads to a nesting area where you may observe osprey.

The area south of Bend, known as Lava Land for its extensive volcanic landscapes, makes for a fascinating day of sightseeing. Head south on U.S. 97 for six miles. First stop is the High Desert Museum, one of the finest nature centers in the West. Set back from the highway in a grove of pines, it looks deceptively small. Actually, it covers 150 acres, including 20 acres of outdoor trails. The main building contains exhibits describing the high-desert environment, Indian exhibits including a full-sized wickiup, seasonal calendars, and hands-on displays.

The real treasures are found along a nature trail that loops through the woods. There's a birds-of-prey enclosure with owls, hawks, and eagles in residence; exhibits pertaining to forest ecology; and a delightful river otter pond with underwater viewing windows. If you ask, one of the attendants may take one of the museum's porcupines out of its den so you or your children can pet the soft underside. The museum has an outstanding series of workshops, programs, and lectures throughout the summer geared to both adults and children.

Continue south on U.S. 97 to Lava Lands Visitor Center, about ten miles south of Bend. It sits at the base of 500-foot-high Lava Butte, a cinder cone that dates from volcanic eruptions about 6,000 years ago. Inside the visitor center are displays and audiovisual programs detailing the eruptions, lava flows, and geologic phenomena of the area. You can drive to the top of the adjacent cinder cone for sweeping views of the Cascades and some of the 400 other cinder cones that dot the area. There are also three interpretive trails branching out from the visitor center.

Depending on how much time you have, there are several other volcanic points of interest worth visiting. At Lava Cast Forest you'll see a fine collection of tree molds formed when flowing molten lava surrounded living trees. Numerous lava and ice caves, some of them illuminated, are scattered through the area. A four-mile drive past the center on a cinder road plus one mile on an easy trail will bring you to Benham Falls, a crashing series of rapids on the Deschutes River. Ask for detailed directions to all of these points at the visitor center.

At Lava River Caves State Park, you can rent a lantern and follow a paved path through a half-mile-long lava tube. On a spur road off U.S. 97, Newberry Crater National Volcanic Monument, a giant volcano some 25 miles in diameter, was 9,000 feet high before it collapsed about 10,000 years ago. It contains two lakes, waterfalls, massive obsidian flows, and an interpretive trail.

A couple of close-in viewpoints are worth a quick trip from Bend. Drive to the top of Pilot Butte via Greenwood Avenue on the east side of Bend for fine views of the Cascade peaks all the way north to Mount Hood. Fourteen miles west via Franklin and Galveston avenues, lovely Tumalo Falls plunges 97 feet into a forest-ringed pool.

Area Code: 503

DRIVING DIRECTIONS Bend lies 160 miles southeast of Portland via I-5 to Salem, Oregon 22, and U.S. 20.

AIR TRANSPORTATION *Horizon Air* and *United Express* serve the Redmond airport (16 miles northwest of Bend, an airport shuttle connects with major motels and resorts) from Portland. Round-trip fares begin at about $165. Six rental car firms are located in Bend.

RAIL TRANSPORTATION *Amtrak's Coast Starlight,* which joins Seattle and Portland with San Francisco and Los Angeles, stops at Chemult, 60 miles south of Bend. You can arrange with TransCentral, 382-0800, to be picked up at Chemult.

SIGHTSEEING *Mount Bachelor,* 22 miles west of Bend, 382-2442, ski report 382-7888, package reservations (800) 547-6858. The area has a vertical drop of 3,100 feet and is served by 10 chair lifts and 2 tows and offers cross-country trails, ski touring, rentals, ski school, and day lodge. *High Desert Museum,* 59800 South Highway 97, 382-4754. Daily 9 A.M. to 5 P.M. Adults $4.50, seniors $4, 6–12 $2.50. *Lava Lands Visitor Center,* 58201 South Highway 97, 593-2421. May to September daily 9 A.M. to 5 P.M. Free. *Deschutes Historical Center,* 129 Northwest Idaho Street, Bend, 389-1813. Wednesday to Saturday 1 to 4 P.M. Historical displays including Indian artifacts, pioneer schoolroom, timber industry history. *Rimrock Scenic Rail Tours,* 447-4838. Operates 2½-hour train trips from Ochoco Creek Park in Prineville along the scenic Crooked River. Excursions depart Saturday and Sunday at 1 P.M. from the first weekend in July through September. There's also a Saturday evening dinner train departing at 7 P.M. Fares are $15 for adults, $7.50 for children 5–12; dinner train $45. *River Rafting Operators: Hunter Expeditions,* 389-8370; *Inn of the Seventh Mountain,* 382-8711, ext. 595; *Rapid River Rafters,* (800) 962-3327; *Sun Country Tours,* 593-2161. *Guided Fishing Trips: The Fly Box,* 388-3330; *Four Winds Fishing Adventures,* 593-8950; *High Desert Drifter,* 389-0607; *Rapid River Outfitters,* (800) 962-3327. *Smith Rock Climbing School & Guide Service,* 548-1888. Teaches and guides on rock climbing trips. *Oregon Cycling Adventures,* 388-0064, and *High Cascade Descent,* 389-0562, offer guided single-day and multiday bicycling tours of the area.

EVENTS *Cascade Festival of Music,* Drake Park Pavilion, Bend, 382-8381, late June. A week of musical performances from Bach to jazz. *Sunriver Music Festival,* in 450-seat Great Hall, Sunriver, 593-1221, mid-August. Features 5 major classical music performances over the 12-day event.

LODGING *Sunriver Lodge and Resort,* P.O. Box 3609, Sunriver 97707, 593-1221 or (800) 547-3922. The area's premier full-service resort, $$$–$$$$. *Inn of the Seventh Mountain,* P.O. Box 1207, Bend 97709; 382-8711 or (800) 452-6810. Tennis, miniature golf, putting green, stables, rental bicycles, nature program, fireplaces, $$$. *The Riverhouse Motor Inn,* 3075 North Highway 97, Bend 97701, 389-3111 or (800) 547-3928. Best of the in-town accommodations, adjacent to the Deschutes River, restaurant, $$. *Rock Springs Guest Ranch,* 64201 Tyler Road, Bend 97701, 382-1957. Comfortable cabins with kitchens, fireplaces, riding, tennis, fishing, children's programs, minimum 3-day stay in summer, modified American plan, $$$. *Deschutes River Ranch,* 20210 Swalley Road, Bend 97701, 382-7240. Overlooking the Deschutes River on 410 acres, trail rides, fishing, $$$.

Mount Bachelor Village, 19717 Mount Bachelor Drive, Bend 97702, (800) 547-5204 (outside OR), (800) 452-9846 (in OR), 389-5900. Good choice for skiers; fireplaces, kitchens; $$$. *Elk Lake Resort,* P.O. Box 789, Bend 97709, radio phone YP7 3954. Rustic resort with magnificent setting on lake off Cascade Lake Highway, Memorial Day to mid-October, $. *Cultus Lake Resort,* P.O. Box 262, Bend 97709, 389-3230. About 24 cabins on large fishing lake, restaurant, boat rentals, May to October, $$. *Farewell Bend Bed & Breakfast,* 29 Northwest Greely Street, Bend 97701, 382-4374. 3 guest rooms in 1920s home, no smoking, no children under 12, $$. *Mountain View Lodge at Bend,* P.O. Box 7409, Bend 97701, 388-3855. 7 guest rooms in large Western-style lodge, recreation room, outdoor spa, $$–$$$$.

CAMPING *LaPine State Park,* 27 miles southwest of Bend off U.S. 97 on Deschutes River. 95 full hookups, 50 with electric, mid-April to October, $9–$11. *Crane Prairie Resort,* Crane Prairie Lake west of LaPine, 385-2173. 31 full hookups on lake, boat rentals, late April to October, $10. *Prineville Reservoir State Park,* 17 miles southeast of Prineville, 447-4363. 22 full hookups, 48 tent sites, $9–$11. *Tumalo State Park,* 5 miles northwest of Bend off U.S. 20 on Deschutes River, 388-6055. 20 full hookups, 68 tent sites, bicycle camping, $8–$11. *Bend KOA,* 63615 Highway 97 North, 382-7728. 117 sites, 42 full hookups, 75 water-electricity, $15–$17. *Crown Villa RV Park,* 60801 Brosterhous Road, Bend, 388-1131. 106 full-hookup sites, $18.

DINING *The Meadows,* Sunriver Lodge and Resort (see "Lodging"). Breakfast, lunch, and dinner daily; overlooking golf course, has no competition for the finest dining in the area; $$$. *Pine Tavern Restaurant,* 967 Northwest Brooks Street, Bend, 382-5581. Lunch Monday to Saturday, dinner daily, brunch Sunday; historic favorite for more than 70 years, overlooking Mirror Pond, prime rib, lamb, ribs; $$. *Players Grille,* 61 Northwest Oregon Avenue, Bend, 382-5859. Lunch Monday to Friday, dinner Monday to Saturday; has won awards for Bend's best restaurant, California cuisine; $$. *Pescatore!,* 119 Northwest Minnesota Avenue, Bend, 389-6276. Lunch Monday to Friday, dinner daily; northern Italian and continental cuisine, seafood a specialty; $$. *Deschutes Brewery & Public House,* 1044 Bond Street, Bend, 382-9242. Lunch and dinner daily; brewpub serving ales brewed here, plus light food; $$. *Giuseppe's Ristorante,* 932 Northwest Bond Street, Bend, 389-8899. Dinner daily, northern Italian cuisine, $$. *McKenzie's Ore House,* 1033 Bond Street, Bend, 388-3891. Dinner daily; good choice for steaks, entertainment, dancing; $$. *Mexicali Rose,* 301 Northeast Franklin Street, Bend, 389-0149. Dinner daily, voted one of Oregon's best Mexican restaurants, $$. *Tumalo Feed Company,* 64619 Highway 20 West, 6 miles north of Bend, 382-2202.

Family-style dinner daily, Sunday ranch breakfast; comfortable as an old shoe, turn-of-the-century ranch decor, good family choice; $$. *Yoko's Japanese Restaurant,* 1028 Northwest Bond Street, Bend, 382-2999. Lunch Monday to Friday, dinner Monday to Saturday; central Oregon's only Japanese restaurant, sushi bar; $$.

FOR MORE INFORMATION Central Oregon Recreation Association/ Reservation Center, P.O. Box 230, Bend 97709, (800) 547-6858 (outside OR), 382-8334. Provides visitor information and makes lodging referrals to all area accommodations, including air packages. Bend Chamber of Commerce, 63085 North Highway 97, Bend 97701, 382-3221.

Exploring the Palouse

The landscapes are reminiscent of paintings by Andrew Wyeth—vast rolling wheat fields stretching to the horizon, neat red-and-white barns, stands of cottonwoods tracing the courses of streams. This is the Palouse, named for the Palouse Indians who once inhabited the northeastern corner of Oregon, and the land where Oregon, Washington, and Idaho now come together. It's a vaguely defined area, measuring roughly 85 by 100 miles, that straddles the border between Washington and Idaho. It's also the richest wheat land in the country (in good years yielding more than 50 bushels per acre) and second in the world only to the Ukraine.

Go in the spring when the rolling hills are covered with the intense velvety green of growing wheat. By April wildflowers are brightening the roadsides. Summer is hot and harvest begins in early July, moving slowly northward through early August, when you can see phalanxes of giant side-hill combines crawling in formation over the slopes and heavily laden grain trucks on their way to the elevators in town. (The side-hill combine is a curiosity unique to the Palouse. It's a motorized harvester with a tilting cutting head to conform to the hills, and was developed and is used only here.) In September and October, the harvest is over and the summer heat has passed, the elevators are bulging, and giant tractors with tires taller than a man move over the fields turning under stubble or planting winter wheat.

The vistas of farm and field are splendid, but the real treasures of the Palouse can be found in its towns, some of which are so tiny they don't even appear on maps. Dominated by grain elevators and dealers' lots crammed with massive International Harvesters and John Deeres, the towns remind you of the fictional Anarene, Texas, in the movie *The Last Picture Show.* Except for late-model cars, they seem frozen in the Twenties or Thirties. Empty stores, a boarded-up theater, and a decaying brick hotel testify not to poverty but to a prosperous mobile society that now does its business in the large market towns.

Exploring the Palouse is a delight. Nearly empty two-lane roads let you set your own leisurely pace, and if you poke about the towns, you'll usually turn up someone who sells antiques and collectibles. A lunch in one of the local cafés may be the best home-cooked food you've tasted in years.

There's no set way to see this country; just follow your instincts, backtracking here and there. Accommodations in country towns are almost nonexistent; it's best to establish headquarters in one of the larger towns—Pullman or Clarkston (in Washington) or Lewiston or Moscow (in Idaho)—and make excursions from there. The distance involved (345 miles from Portland to Lewiston, for example) makes this a stretch for a conventional weekend, so consider making it a three- or four-day trip.

One rewarding route leads north from Pullman (named after the sleeping-car tycoon) on Washington 27. About six miles from town, off Albion Road, Three Forks Pioneer Village Museum displays several nineteenth-century small-town buildings as well as an excellent collection of early farm and logging equipment. Lining the Old West street front are a log cabin, Chinese laundry, barbershop, doctor's office, and the Wawawai General Store, all filled with antiques of the period.

If you have your camera, all of these towns offer great subject matter, particularly photogenic in the early morning or late afternoon light. You will come upon handsome old brick business blocks and the 1897 R. C. McCroskey House in Garfield, a general store decorated with pre–World War II posters in Elberton, an abandoned schoolhouse atop a hill at Belmont, and a steam locomotive and ramshackle depot at Potlatch. In several towns there are dusty stores where you can buy tintypes, old colored-glass bottles, stove-top irons, and glass electric insulators, among other collectibles.

Two peaks in the area—Kamiak Butte (3,360 feet) and Steptoe Butte (3,612 feet)—offer sweeping views of the Palouse, and have both picnic facilities and hiking trails. On your return to Pullman via U.S. 195, stop at Rosalia to see the 20-foot street clock, the turreted Howard House, and the Harthill Clock Museum.

Pullman and Moscow (locally pronounced "MOS-coh") are worth at least a half day of your time. Located just eight miles apart, these towns are home to Washington State University and the University of Idaho (bumper stickers read "Wear Wool—Eat Lamb"). Washington State University offers free campus tours each weekday, (1 P.M., French Administration Building, Room 442), and on your own you may want to visit the natural history, art, entomological, and anthropological museums; the observatory; and the planetarium. Ferdinand's Dairy Bar is the retail outlet for WSU's dairy operations; try homemade ice cream, Cougar Gold and cheddar cheeses, a rich milk shake, or an old-fashioned ice-cream soda. The dairy itself invites visitors to watch milking daily from noon to 3 P.M. And while you're in town, stop at the Flat House, at 142 Grand Avenue, which sells everything from cowbells and horse collars to crystal doorknobs and antique bottles.

Between Pullman and Moscow, you'll come across the Appaloosa Museum. This modest museum contains a number of excellent Nez Perce Indian artifacts from the time of Chief Joseph in the 1870s. The museum is named after the breed of horse developed by the Nez Perce, and whose name in turn derives from "a Palouse horse." More than 250,000 of the distinctively spotted horses are registered at the Appaloosa Horse Club, which is located here as well.

The University of Idaho campus boasts the first domed stadium built west of the Mississippi, a small art museum, and displays of gemstones in the College of Mines. While you're in Moscow (once officially named "Hog Heaven"), you might also pay a visit to the Latah County Museum Society in the ornate 1883 McConnell Mansion. It's less than an hour's drive from Pullman to Lewiston, but don't zip through little Uniontown on the way or you'll miss Saint Boniface Catholic Church on one of the side streets. Built in 1905, the structure is a marvel of handsome twin wooden towers and splendid stained-glass windows. Just above Lewiston, you reach the top of infamous Lewiston Grade, a nightmare to travelers of generations past. Highway U.S. 195 bypasses it, but you can make the 64-loop, 2,750-foot descent on the old road if you wish. Stop at the summit for panoramic views of Washington, Oregon, Idaho, and, far below, the confluence of the Snake and Clearwater rivers.

Depending on how much time you have, detour to see part or all of Nez Perce National Historic Park, which begins just up the Clearwater from Lewiston. This park commemorates the tragic flight of Chief Joseph and his Nez Perce tribe from the U.S. Army, the settlements of early missionaries, and a portion of the route taken by the Lewis and Clark expedition. The park is unusual in that it consists of 24 different sites scattered over more than 300 miles.

Begin at the visitor center on U.S. 95 at Spalding, about eight miles east of Lewiston, where you can pick up a map and directions to the various sites. The visitor center offers displays and audiovisual programs relating to the Nez Perce and the history of the region; in summer Nez Perce demonstrate basketry, weaving, and other Indian skills. About a mile down the road is the site of the Spalding mission and an old cemetery with the graves of missionaries and Indians, including the grave of Josiah Red Wolf, last survivor of the Nez Perce War.

If you don't have the time or the desire to visit all the park sites, concentrate on those along U.S. 95: Saint Joseph's Mission (1874); the old military buildings at Fort Lapwai; and the White Bird Battlefield, where the vastly outnumbered Nez Perce won a stunning victory over the U.S. Army.

Another good route for savoring the Palouse is U.S. 12 heading west from Lewiston and Clarkston. Lewis and Clark used this same route when returning from their expedition to the Pacific coast in 1806. Your first stop is Pomeroy, where huge grain elevators dominate the main street. There are some handsome old homes on back streets, a 1901-vintage courthouse topped by a clock tower, and a statue of Justice and the small pioneer Garfield County Museum. At Delaney, detour to Palouse Falls. Here you can look over the rim and watch the Palouse River as it thunders 198 feet into a canyon, creating a pattern of rainbows in the mist. Back on U.S. 12, stop at Dayton to visit the Victorian Depot, a national historic site that now serves as a museum. Nine miles beyond in Waitsburg is the best-preserved Victorian house in the Palouse—the Bruce Memorial Museum. Here, you've reached the western edge of the Palouse. If you want to break your return journey to Portland with an overnight stop, try Walla Walla, just 21 miles farther down U.S. 12. It has the best selection of motels in the area.

Area Codes: Washington 509, Idaho 208

DRIVING DIRECTIONS From Portland take I-84 east to Pendleton, then Oregon 11 north to Walla Walla and U.S. 12 into Lewiston. It's 345 miles via this route, another 25 miles north via U.S. 95 to Pullman.

AIR TRANSPORTATION *Horizon Air* and *United Express* serve Lewiston and Pullman from Portland. The round-trip fare begins at about $195.

SIGHTSEEING *Perkins House,* 623 North Perkins Street, Colfax, 397-2555. Thursday and Sunday 1 to 5 P.M. Donation. Vintage home of one of the founders of Colfax, furnished. *Newspaper and Printing Museum,* 108-110 East Main Street, Palouse, 334-2019. Thursday and Saturday 1 to 5 P.M. Free. Pioneer small-town newspaper with vintage equipment. *Three Forks Pioneer Village Museum,* Highway 27 north from Pullman, left to Albion for 2 miles, then right on Anderson Road for 2.8 miles, 332-3889. April to September by appointment, "by chance" Sundays 1 to 6 P.M. $2. *Washington State University:* French Administration Building, Room 442, 335-4527. Tours Monday to Friday at 1 P.M. Anthropology Museum in College Hall, 335-3441. Indian basketry, Pacific Rim exhibits; Monday to Friday 10 A.M. to 4 P.M. Jacklin Collection of petrified wood, dinosaur bones, and fluorescent minerals, Johnson Hall, 335-7014; Monday to Friday 7:30 A.M. to 4 P.M.

James Entomological Museum, Johnson Hall, 1 million insect specimens; Monday to Friday 7:30 P.M. to 4 P.M., 335-5504. Mycological Herbarium, Johnson Hall, 355-9541. Fungi and mushroom collection; Monday to Friday 7:30 A.M. to 4 P.M. Ownbey Herbarium, Heald Hall, 335-3250. Fern and moss specimens; Monday to Friday 7:30 A.M. to 4 P.M. Museum of Art, Fine Art Center, 335-1910. Changing exhibits; daily 9 A.M. to 5 P.M. September to April. Ferdinand's Dairy Bar, Food Science and Human Nutrition Building, 335-4014. Monday to Friday 9:30 A.M. to 4:30 P.M. WSU Dairy, Country Club Road, 335-1338. Milking daily 12:30 to 3 P.M. *Appaloosa Museum,* Pullman-Moscow Highway, 882-5578. Monday to Friday 8 A.M. to 5 P.M. Free. *Latah County Historical Museum,* McConnell Mansion, 110 South Adams Street, Moscow, 882-1004. Wednesday to Sunday 1 to 4 P.M. Donation. Idaho memorabilia displayed in former governor's Victorian home. *Nez Perce National Historic Park,* Spalding, 843-2261. June to Labor Day daily 8 A.M. to 6 P.M., rest of year 8 A.M. to 4:30 P.M. Free. *Luna House Museum,* Third and C streets, Lewiston, 743-2535. Tuesday to Saturday 9 A.M. to 5 P.M. Free. Indian and pioneer exhibits. *Alpowai Interpretive Center,* Chief Timothy State Park, Highway 12, 8 miles west of Clarkston, 758-9500. June to Labor Day Wednesday to Sunday 1 to 5 P.M. Free. Details Lewis and Clark expedition, Indian and geological history of area. *Dayton Historical Depot,* Dayton, 382-4825. Tuesday to Saturday 1 to 4 P.M. $1. Oldest railroad depot in the state. *Bruce Memorial Museum,* 318 Main Street, Waitsburg, 337-6582. Call for appointment. Free. Restored turn-of-the-century home.

EVENTS *International Jet Boat Races,* Lewiston, 743-6276, week in mid-June. This leg of 3-part state jet boat races features competition through Hells Canyon. *Lewiston Roundup,* Lewiston, 743-5531, weekend after Labor Day. Major regional rodeo.

LODGING *Quality Inn Paradise Creek Motor Inn,* Southeast 1050 Johnson Avenue, Pullman, WA 99163, 332-0500. Located along small creek away from traffic, near WSU campus, $$–$$$. *Nendel's,* Southeast 915 Main Street, Pullman, WA 99163, 332-2646, (800) 547-0106. Convenient to WSU campus, $–$$. *Best Western University Inn,* 1516 Pullman Road, Moscow, ID 83843, 882-0550. Large modern facility with indoor pool, game room, putting green, $$. *Mark IV Motor Inn,* 414 North Main Street, Moscow, ID 83843, 882-7557. 86-unit 2-story motel with indoor pool, good restaurant, $. *Best Western Rivertree Inn,* 1257 Bridge Street, Clarkston, WA 99403, 758-9551. Smaller motel with loft units, $–$$. *Quality Inn Clarkston,* 700 Port Drive, Clarkston, WA 99403, 758-9500. On the river, 9-hole golf course, $–$$. *Pony Soldier Motor Inn,* 1716 Main Street, Lewiston, ID 83501, 743-9526. Conveniently located on U.S. 12 Business Route, $$. *Ramada*

Inn, 621 Twenty-first Street, Lewiston, ID 83501, 799-1000. Largest motel in Lewiston, pool, restaurant, $$. *Sacajawea Motor Inn,* 1824 Main Street, Lewiston, ID 83501, 746-1393. Good value for budget travelers, pool, restaurant, $. *Carriage House,* 611 Fifth Street, Lewiston, ID 83501, 746-4506. 2 private suites, full breakfast, airport pickups, $$.

CAMPING *Lewis and Clark State Trail State Park,* Highway 12, 4 miles east of Waitsburg, 642-3078. 30 sites in lovely wooded location on the Touchet River, $8. *Lyons Ferry State Park,* 8 miles northwest of Starbuck on Highway 261. 50 sites at confluence of Snake and Palouse rivers, $8. *Central Ferry State Park,* 22 miles west and north of Pomeroy on Highway 127, 549-3551. 60 sites with hookups, on Snake River, $8–$12. *Chief Timothy State Park,* 8 miles west of Clarkston on Highway 12, 758-9580. 66 sites with hookups, on Snake River, $8–$12. *Hells Gate State Park,* 4 miles south of Lewiston on Snake River, 743-2363. 93 sites with electricity and water, $4–$9.

DINING *The Seasons,* 215 Southeast Paradise Street, Pullman, 334-1410. Dinner Tuesday to Sunday; in an old house perched above the street; changing menu features seafood, chicken, homemade bread; $$. *Swilly's,* 200 Northeast Kamiaken Street, Pullman, 334-3395. Lunch and dinner Monday to Saturday; located in town's old railroad depot, specializes in fresh local ingredients, deli menu; $–$$. *Hilltop Restaurant and Cliff Room,* Colfax Highway atop the hill north of Pullman, 334-2555. Lunch and dinner daily, brunch Sunday; steakhouse with a view, menu includes seafood; $$. *Biscuitroot Park,* 415 South Main Street, Moscow, 882-3560. Lunch and dinner daily, excellent menu ranging from Mexican burlata to New Orleans jambalaya, $$. *Henry's,* 200 Bridge Street, Clarkston, 758-9613. Breakfast, lunch, and dinner Monday to Saturday; steaks, seafood; $$. *Helm Restaurant,* Sacajawea Motor Inn (see "Lodging"), Lewiston, 746-9661. Breakfast, lunch, and dinner daily; steaks, seafood; $–$$. *Country Cookery,* 1516 Main Street, Lewiston, 743-4552. Breakfast, lunch, and dinner daily; pancakes, chicken, steak, good choice for children; $. *Jonathan's,* 301 D Street, Lewiston, 746-3438. Lunch and dinner Monday to Saturday, dinner Sunday; in historic district; sophisticated setting and imaginative menu of beef, seafood, Cajun, and Mexican; $$. *Patit Creek Restaurant,* 725 East Dayton Avenue, Dayton, 382-2625. Lunch Tuesday to Friday, dinner Tuesday to Saturday; best restaurant in the Palouse, serving local ingredients superbly prepared; $$.

FOR MORE INFORMATION Pullman Chamber of Commerce, North 415 Grand Street, Pullman, WA 99163, 334-3565. Lewiston Chamber of Commerce, 2207 East Main Street, Lewiston, ID 83501, 743-3531.

Delivering the Mail in Hells Canyon

This final section concerns a two-day, mid-week trip rather than a weekend, but we think it's one of the finest trips in the Northwest. We've been taking it for more years than we like to count, and each time we go it just seems to get better.

Over in the southeastern corner of the Palouse, where Washington, Oregon, and Idaho come together, the Snake River slices the deepest gorge in North America—Hells Canyon. For nearly 100 miles as it flows out of Idaho, forming the border with Oregon and meeting the Clearwater at Lewiston, the Snake boils and foams through some of the ruggedest canyonlands imaginable. This area is roadless for the most part, yet a handful of hardy farmers and ranchers eke out a living all but isolated from the rest of the world. Their weekly link with civilization is the Snake River mailboat from Lewiston.

When we first started making this trip crusty riverman Dick Rivers, who once owned and ran the four-jet-boat fleet of Rivers Navigation Co., piloted the mailboat. A trip with Rivers was a running dialogue of tall tales, bits of geologic lore, observations on wildlife, and caustic comments on everything from "long-haired hippies" to the engineers who were proposing to dam "his" Snake.

Rivers retired several years ago, and Wally and Myrna Beamer now run the mailboat as well as other river excursions. The Beamers are real river folk, with a hearty manner and a warm friendliness as big as the country they traverse.

The mailboat makes a 186-mile round trip in two days, departing Lewiston early on Wednesday mornings and returning Thursday afternoons, with an overnight at Copper Creek Ranch. Other boats make the trip through Hells Canyon on other days of the week, including weekends. You can even raft down through Hells Canyon if you wish. But none of these other craft carry the mail, and delivering the mail is an essential part of the experience. You can avoid the long drive to Lewiston from Portland or Seattle by flying with one of the regional air carriers.

The best times to go are March through May and September through early November. Summer heat in the canyon climbs well above the century mark and can make the trip an ordeal. We've always had the desire to make the trip just before Christmas, when the mailboat is delivering presents to the canyon's isolated residents.

Every Wednesday morning, the *Myrna Bea* leaves the dock at Lewiston with Captain Wally Beamer at the helm. Nineteenth-century French *voyageurs* appropriately described this stretch of the Snake as *la maudite rivière enragée*—the accursed mad river. Traditional boats can't negotiate its turbulent and shallow waters; protruding rudders and propellers snag on barely submerged rocks. Specially designed aluminum jet boats like the *Myrna Bea* have intakes below the waterline that scoop up the water, and powerful hydraulic pumps that hurl it aft for propulsion. Steering is accomplished by changing the direction of the water-exhaust nozzles.

The Beamers are a working team. As captain, Wally knows every one of the 85 rapids, creeks (locally pronounced "cricks"), and side canyons by name. You quickly give him a large measure of respect as you watch him maneuver his craft through boiling rapids or pick a course with the delicacy of a ballet dancer through a jumble of huge rocks that are seemingly impassable. Passengers often applaud when he takes the *Myrna Bea* downstream through rapids that suddenly drop the boat 20 feet or more. Myrna takes care of the business side of things and, most important, is responsible for the meals at Copper Creek Ranch. "I can't cook," says Wally, "and she can't drive a boat."

From Lewiston's Hellsgate Marina, the *Myrna Bea* makes her way upriver past rugged hills, green and covered with wildflowers in the spring, burned brown and dusty in the summer. First stop is Heller Bar on the Washington side of the river for morning coffee and pastry. By mid-morning Buffalo Eddy, the confluence of the Grande Ronde River and the last road have dropped astern and the canyon walls begin to press in on both sides. You pass the turbulent mouth of the Salmon River ("the river of no return") and plunge through a slot a mere two dozen yards wide flanked by sheer rock walls rising hundreds of feet above. Here and there a small ranch clings to a fertile bench where the canyon walls widen out temporarily.

The area is rich in wildlife. It's a good idea to take a pair of binoculars, a camera equipped with a telephoto lens, and your favorite field guides to birds, plants, and minerals. You're apt to see cliff swallows darting into holes in the canyon walls, elk or bighorn sheep standing in the high meadows, a shy coyote scurrying up a hillside, or deer drinking at the water's edge. Golden eagles have their aeries in the crags overhead, and if you search carefully with binoculars you're likely to spot one.

The canyon is also historically rich. Beamer will point out a series of well-preserved Indian petroglyphs carved on the dark basalt rock, a Nez Perce Indian foot trail, and the place where Chief Joseph led his people across the river in the spring of 1877, pursued by the army.

The mail run is a slice of Americana. The Beamers do more than carry the mail; they pick up prescriptions and boots for repair, and carry groceries and "lots of dog food." Garden Creek, Purcell, Van Pool, and Wilson ranches all receive their mail and newspapers in riverside boxes. The Beamers also bring the latest gossip from downriver to people who may not see another human all week.

At most mail stops, a rancher or his wife, sometimes with a youngster in tow, will come down to chat. They drag the conversation out to the last possible moment, reluctant to say good-bye for another week.

Around noon, Beamer heads the boat into China Beach, on the south side, for a lunch stop. Passengers spread out on the sand and open sack lunches. By mid-afternoon, some nine hours and 70 miles from Lewiston, the boat arrives at Copper Creek Ranch, a cluster of trim white cabins nestled against the side of the canyon. There are 18 rooms in all. Some guests share a bath; for others, there are two separate large bathhouses with showers, sinks, and toilets. House-keeping is immaculate. Sometimes Wally Beamer will take guests out on the river to try their hand at catching the giant sturgeon that live in these waters. Other-wise, guests just relax at the ranch. It's a great place to unwind.

And then it's time for Myrna's magic—dinner. Raised on a ranch in Montana, she grew up cooking for large groups of people. The menu varies, but typically might include barbecued steak, smoked chicken, halibut, rice, corn on the cob, asparagus, homemade rolls, vegetable salad, fruit salad, and peach pie. No one goes hungry, and if you're on a diet, better leave it at home.

After the sound of roaring motors all day, the silence is deafening. Guests sit on the big lodge deck and watch the shadows descend on the canyon as the sun drops behind the mountains. Across the river, deer will be coming down for their evening drink. The clear night skies, free of urban pollution, are incredi-ble. Stars cover the sky from canyon rim to canyon rim, and the occasional meteorite or shooting star brings collective "ahs" from the guests.

Next morning, after a belt-bursting breakfast, everyone reboards the boat for the last 23 miles upriver to the deepest part of Hells Canyon and the end of navigation. Here, the canyon measures almost 8,000 feet deep. Beamer usually schedules a stop on this part of the trip at Kirkwood Historic Ranch on a grassy bench above the river.

On the return trip, after a stop at Copper Creek Ranch for lunch, the *Myrna Bea* races downriver at a heart-stopping 35 miles an hour, bucking like a bronco, whipping through rapids and drenching everyone imprudent enough to remain on the open afterdeck with spray. What took nine hours going up takes just over three coming back. By mid-afternoon the boat is docked back in Lewiston with plenty of time for everyone to catch a flight or make the long drive home.

Area Codes: Washington 509, Idaho 208

DRIVING DIRECTIONS (See "Exploring the Palouse")

AIR TRANSPORTATION (See "Exploring the Palouse")

SIGHTSEEING *Beamer's Landing,* P.O. Box 1223, Lewiston, ID 83501, 743-4800, (800) 522-6966 or 758-4800 in Washington. Beamer's operates the 2-day Snake River mailboat on Wednesdays, other overnight excursions on other days, $195; single-day excursion is $80. Other jet boat operators on the Snake River include: *Cougar Country Lodge,* P.O. Box 448, Asotin, WA 99402, (509) 758-1441; *Snake Dancer Excursions,* 614 Lapwai Road, Lewiston, ID 83501, 743-0890, (800) 234-1941; *Hells Canyon Adventures,* P.O. Box 159, Oxbow, OR 97840, (800) 422-3568; *S & S Outfitters,* 912 Burrell Street Lewiston, ID 83501, 746-3569; *Snake River Adventures,* 717 Third Street, Lewiston, ID 83501, 746-6276, (800) 262-8874; *Snake River Outfitters,* P.O. Box F, Lewiston, ID 83501, 743-6276.

LODGING, CAMPING, DINING, FOR MORE INFORMATION
(See ''Exploring the Palouse'')

General Index

Category Index

Rocky Reach Dam, 92, 94
Roslyn Museum, 103, 105
Royal British Columbia Museum, 121, 124
Royal London Wax Museum, 124
San Juan Historical Museum, 55
Science World, 135, 137
Seaside Aquarium, 205, 208
Seattle Aquarium, 161, 166
Seattle Art Museum, 164, 166
Seattle Center, 165–166
Seattle Children's Museum, 166
Shafer Museum, 97, 100
Shakespeare Art Museum, 236
Shakespeare Exhibit Center, 233, 236
Sheraton Seattle Hotel, 164
Siuslaw Pioneer Museum and Gallery of
     Local Arts, 224
Skagit County Historical Museum, 39–40
Skamania County Historical Museum,
     246–247
Snoqualmie Valley Historical Museum, 60
South Slough National Estuarine Reserve,
     228, 230
Steilacoom Historical Museum, 21
Suquamish Museum, 7, 9
Tacoma Art Museum, 20
Three Forks Pioneer Village Museum,
     270, 272
Undersea Gardens, 213
University of Idaho, 271, 273
University of Oregon, 194, 196
University of Washington, 170–171, 174
Uppertown Firefighters Museum, 146,
     148
Valley Museum of Northwest Art, 39
Vancouver Aquarium, 136
Vancouver Art Gallery, 134
Vancouver Art Museum, 135–136
Vancouver Museum, 135–136
Victorian Depot, 272
Washington State Historical Society Mu-
     seum, 19–21
Washington State University, 270, 272–
     273
Wax Works, 213
Western Washington University, 45
Westport Aquarium, 36
Whale Museum, 52, 54
Whatcom Museum of History and Art, 45
Willamette Science and Technology Cen-
     ter, 194, 196
Willis Carey Historical Museum, 90–91
Wing Luke Asian Museum, 166

Woodville Museum, 237
World Forestry Center, 76
Yakima Indian Nation Cultural Center,
     109–111
Yakima Valley Museum, 108, 111
Yaquina Bay Lighthouse, 212–213

Shopping and Antique Collecting
Bandon, Oreg., 227
Canby, Oreg., 178
Cannon Beach, Oreg., 207
Eugene, Oreg., 193–194
Fall City, Wash., 58, 60
Gilman Village, Issaquah, Wash., 57
Independence, Oreg., 189
La Conner, Wash., 39–40
Lafayette, Oreg., 184–185
Leavenworth, Wash., 87
Mount Vernon, Wash., 40
Pike Place Market, Seattle, Wash., 161,
     166
Portland, Oreg., 74–75, 77, 79–80
Port Orchard, Wash., 11
Port Townsend, Wash., 23
Poulsbo, Wash., 8
Seaside, Oreg., 205–206
Seattle, Wash., 161, 163–164, 171
Sisters, Oreg., 262
Snohomish, Wash., 85
Steilacoom, Wash., 20–21
Vancouver, B.C., 134–135
Vancouver Island, B.C., 127
Van Zandt, Wash., 43–44
Vashon, Wash., 16–17
Victoria, B.C., 122
Yakima, Wash., 108

Special Events
Alpine Days, 61
Apple Blossom Festival, 90
Apple Squeeze, 21
Arlene Schnitzer Concert Hall, 82–83
Armed Forces Day Parade, 13
Art à la Carte, 21
Artquake, 77
Arts and Crafts Festival, 5
Bite!!!, The, 78
Bite of Seattle, 165, 167
Blessing of the Fleet, 36
Bumbershoot, 165, 167
Cascade Festival of Music, 267
Central Washington State Fair, 112
Centrum Foundation, 25